# Lines In The Sand

# SYDNEY INSTITUTE OF CRIMINOLOGY SERIES NO 28

Series Editors: Professor Chris Cunneen, University of New South Wales
Professor Mark Findlay, University of Sydney
Associate Professor Gail Mason, University of Sydney
Professor Julie Stubbs, University of Sydney
Professor Pat O'Malley, University of Sydney

## Titles in the Series

*Criminal Discovery* Moisidis, C (2008)

*Conflict of Interest in Policing* Davids, C (2008)

*Recapturing Freedom* Goulding, D (2007)

*Imprisoning Resistance* Carlton, B (2007)

*Interrogating Images* Dixon, D (2007)

*Reshaping Juvenile Justice* Chan, J (ed) (2005)

*Refugees and State Crime* Pickering, S (2005)

*Aboriginal childhood separations and guardianship law* Buti, A (2004)

*Global Issues, Women and Justice* Pickering, S & Lambert, C (eds) (2004)

*Bin Laden in the Suburbs* Poynting, S; Noble, G; Tabar, P & Collins, J (2004)

*A History of Criminal Law in New South Wales* Woods, G (2002)

*Regulating Racism* McNamara, L (2002)

*When Police Unionise* Finnane, M (2002)

*Indigenous Human Rights* Garkawe, S; Kelly, L & Fisher, W (eds) (2001)

*Developing Cultural Criminology* Banks, C (ed) (2000)

*Defining Madness* Shea, P (1999)

*A Culture of Corruption* Dixon, D (ed) (1999)

*Reform in Policing* Bolen, J (1997)

*Anatomy of a French Murder Case* McKillop, B (1997)

*Gender, 'Race' and International Relations* Cunneen, C & Stubbs, J (1997)

*Fault in Homicide* Yeo, S (1997)

*Women, Male Violence and the Law* Stubbs, J (ed) (1994)

*The Prison and the Home* Aungles, A (1994)

*Cricket and the Law* Fraser, D (1993)

*Psychiatry in Court* Shea, P (1996)

*Doing Less Time Penal reform in crisis* Chan, J (1992)

*Aboriginal Perspectives on Criminal Justice* Cunneen, C (1992)

# Lines In The Sand

# The Cronulla Riots, Multiculturalism and National Belonging

## Gregory Noble

Sydney 2009
The Institute of Criminology Series 28

**Published by**
> Institute of Criminology Press
> Sydney Institute of Criminology
> University of Sydney Law School
> Sydney NSW 2006
> www.criminology.law.usyd.edu.au

**Distributed by**
> The Federation Press
> PO Box 45 Annandale 2038
> www.federationpress.com.au

**National Library of Australia Cataloguing-in-Publication entry**

Title:       Lines in the sand : the Cronulla riots, multiculturalism
             and national belonging / editor Gregory Noble.

ISBN:        9780975196786 (pbk.)

Notes:       Includes index.
             Bibliography.

Subjects:    Riots--New South Wales--Cronulla.
             Social conflict--New South Wales--Cronulla.
             Race relations--Australia.
             Multiculturalism--Australia.

Other Authors/Contributors:    Noble, Gregory.

Dewey Number:   303.62309944

Cover design and picture research by Judith Love
Typeset by The Institute of Criminology
Printed by University Publishing Service
       Cover image: Photography by Simon O'Dwyer, Fairfax Photos

# Table of Contents

# Acknowledgements

Many of these papers came out of the 'Everyday Multiculturalism' conference, organised by Amanda Wise and Selvaraj Velayutham at the Centre for Research on Social Inclusion at Macquarie University, 28-29 September, 2006, and supported by the Cultural Research Network. This event was an inspiring occasion which helped many of us to think about the issues which frame this work.

The publication of this book has been made possible through generous support from a number of organisations and individuals: the College of Arts, University of Western Sydney; Hass Dellal and the Australian Multicultural Foundation; Ali Roude and Rissalah College; and Imad Kaoutarani. I heartily thank these organisations and individuals for making this collection of essays possible.

I'd also like to thank the team from the Institute of Criminology – Kristin Moore, Dawn Koester, Mark Findlay, Murray Lee, Gail Mason and Julie Stubbs – with an especial thanks to Kristin for her indefatigable labour and her tireless attention to detail, and Judith Love for the cover design and picture research.

I would lastly like to thank my co-authors not only for their contributions, but their patience and collegial support.

I hope this work will make a critical but productive contribution to the ongoing debates about cultural diversity, social policy and Australian multiculturalism.

Greg Noble

# Contributors

**Jock Collins** is Professor in the School of Economics and Finance and Co-Director of the Cosmopolitan Civil Societies Research Centre, University of Technology, Sydney.

**Chris Cunneen** is Professor of Criminology at the Cairns Institute, James Cook University, and a Conjoint Professor in the Faculty of Law at the University of New South Wales.

**Kevin Dunn** is Professor in Human Geography and Urban Studies in the School of Social Sciences, University of Western Sydney.

**Clif Evers** is Postdoctoral Research Fellow in the Journalism and Media Research Centre, University of New South Wales.

**Ghassan Hage** is Future Generation Professor of Anthropology and Social Theory, University of Melbourne.

**Andrew Jakubowicz** is Professor of Sociology and Co-Director of the Cosmopolitan Civil Societies Research Centre, University of Technology, Sydney.

**Andrew Lattas** is Associate Professor in the Department of Social Anthropology, University of Bergen.

**Judy Lattas** is Director of the Interdisciplinary Women's Studies, Gender and Sexuality Program in the Department of Sociology, Macquarie University.

**Geoffrey Brahm Levey** is a Senior Lecturer in Politics at the University of New South Wales.

**Dirk Moses** is Associate Professor in the Department of History, University of Sydney.

**Greg Noble** is Associate Professor in the Centre for Cultural Research and the School of Humanities and Languages, University of Western Sydney.

**Scott Poynting** is Professor in Sociology at Manchester Metropolitan University.

**Wendy Shaw** is Senior Lecturer in the School of Biological, Earth and Environmental Sciences, University of New South Wales.

**Paul Tabar** is the Director of the Institute for Migration Studies and Associate Professor of Sociology/Anthropology at the Lebanese American University, Beirut.

**Affrica Taylor** is Senior Lecturer in Sociology and Cultural Studies in the Faculty of Education at the University of Canberra.

**Amanda Wise** is Senior Research Fellow in the Centre for Social Inclusion, Macquarie University.

# List of Illustrations

# List of Tables

# 'Where the bloody hell are we?' Multicultural manners in a world of hyperdiversity

## Greg Noble

On the infamous afternoon of Sunday 11th December, 2005, on Sydney's Cronulla beach, a crowd of approximately 5000 – mostly White, English-speaking background youths – went on a rampage around the vicinity of the beach, shops and railway station, attacking anyone of 'Middle Eastern Appearance'.[1] The day began peacefully enough, as a response to what many saw as the unacceptable behaviour of some Middle Eastern men.[2] An incident the previous weekend had been, it was claimed, the last straw. Several off-duty lifesavers and a group of Lebanese men had come into conflict over the use of space on the beach, resulting in a fight in which the lifesavers were injured. As the *Hazzard Report* – the review of the policing response to the riots overseen by Norm Hazzard, the then Assistant Commissioner for Counter Terrorism and Public Order Management – suggested, such incidents are not uncommon on beaches amongst young men, even when cultural difference is not involved (Strike Force Neil, 2006: 6). Yet rarely do they lead to large-scale protest or ethnically-defined violence.

Two things happened during the week to transform a nasty but incidental event. On the one hand, mainstream media – in particular talk-back radio and tabloid newspapers – took up the incident, drawing in local, state and federal politicians and other 'moral entrepreneurs' which amplified the sense of panic (Cohen, 1980) and made it into a national debate about crime, ethnicity, violence, multiculturalism and the 'threat to the Australian way of life'. On the other, the 'new media' of text messaging became central to connecting local discontent to wider groups through a campaign of scare-mongering, partly driven by right-wing groups.[3] These messages, calling on 'Aussies' to participate in a 'Leb and wog bashing day', were aired on the 'old media', increasing their reach and the scale of the problem. The *Hazzard Report* concluded that, given the unremarkable nature of the original skirmish, it was the role of the media, and especially the exaggerated and distorted reportage promoted by some radio and newspaper commentators, that resulted in the scale of the riots (Strike Force Neil, 2006: 8).

By the end of the day the protest had turned into an ugly, violent and drunken mob, many of whom had adorned themselves in the Australian flag and other symbols of nationalism. Over a dozen were injured, and another dozen were arrested by a police force unable to quell the violence.[4] Images of this violence dominated the media (flying across Australia and the world) and, over the next few nights, groups of young men of 'Middle Eastern appearance', largely from the south-western suburbs of Sydney, conducted revenge attacks in convoys of cars. These were also organised through text messaging and were perpetrated on people, cars and shops who were seen to represent the 'Australian' mob.

The consequences, both short and long term, are still being worked out. Over the summer, there was an intimidating police presence around Sydney's beaches, transforming spaces of leisure into sites of surveillance. Cronulla was almost emptied, much to the misfortune of local businesses in a beach-based economy. A year after the riots, many, especially those of Lebanese and Muslim background, continued to avoid the beach (Murphy, 2006:11).

Many Australians, used to seeing images of ethnic violence in other parts of the world, were shell-shocked, and in the following weeks public and private debates canvassed the causes of the conflict – youth, drunkenness, masculinity, mobile phones, disadvantage, alienation and, of course, perceived cultural conflict. In contrast to the *Hazzard Report's* criticism of the media, a poll of 45,000 readers conducted by the *Sydney Morning Herald* (2005b), listed the main sources of blame as racism (26%), stupidity (24%), poor parenting/schooling (19%), tribalism (18%), xenophobia (8%) and alcohol (6%). A common theme has been the failure of multiculturalism. As we shall see in this book, these events represent lines of fracture that test the limits of multiculturalism and nationalism in Australia.

What emerged in these debates was an inability to agree about the very nature of 'the problem': was it Australian racism or Middle Eastern cultural intolerance, was it a local or a national issue, was it Muslim misogyny or all 'boys behaving badly'? As events unfolded, two different narratives – of White racism and troublesome 'Lebs' – shaped the 'facts' presented. The involvement of surf lifesavers – an Australian icon famous for protecting citizens – added significance, especially since they were seen to be 'protecting' young 'Australian' women. In this regard the 'facts' were being made to fit a narrative of national belonging.

As the *Hazzard Report* pointed out, it was commonly assumed that the Cronulla event was a 'race riot' comparable to riots in Los Angeles, England and France. Yet these comparisons, borrowing heavily from pre-fab narratives of cultural conflict, misread the specificity of the events at Cronulla. They shifted the emphasis onto a generic picture of racism or of 'alienation' (however sympathetically) amongst Lebanese or Muslim youth (Stewart and Hodge, 2005:11). Ironically, such analyses share this emphasis with those conservative critics who continue to frame the problem in terms of the racism, sexism, aggression and criminality of Lebanese boys: 'the abuse and intimidation from a disconnected, racist, violent, moronic and sexually dangerous subculture' (Sheehan, 2006a:31). This dredged up stereotypes of the 'Arab Other' which mesh, as Poynting et al. (2004) argue, discrete events (terrorism, gangs and rape) into a single entity that rests on assumptions about the sexuality and violence of those from the Middle East. The *Hazzard Report* concluded in fact, that: 'Crime trends and police interaction ... did not identify any significant trend for involvement by people of Middle Eastern background in local incidents. Research also indicated that the majority of crime in the local area command is committed by people who live in the Sutherland Shire' (Strike Force Neil, 2006: 6).

Yet the claims that the riots revealed the 'racist underbelly' of Australian society are no less enlightening, because they reduce complex phenomena to single frames of analysis. This is not to side with those politicians who refused to see racism, insisting that 'Australia's not racist' (Brown, 2006:7). Nor is it to side with conservatives who argued that the 'racism' came from the Lebanese, and that events at Cronulla represented a 'protest *against* racism' (Sheehan, 2006b:362). Nor is it to agree with those who insisted that it was not a question of racism but 'intercommunal violence', in which each side shares blame (Burchell, 2006: 12). This naïve story entails an equivalence of guilt which ignores the asymmetrical nature of power relations underlying experiences of conflict (Perera, 2006).

What is extraordinary about these riots is that, unlike the events in the US, the UK and France, in which the suffering of marginalised groups burst forth as a rage against ethnic ghettoisation and inequality, the 'protest' at Cronulla came from a relatively privileged group: White, English-speaking background Australians who by and large lead a comfortable existence. Further, their protest was against the behaviour of minority groups as a 'pattern of incivility' (Greenlees, 2006) which disturbed the civil order and contravened the everyday culture of 'ordinary' Australians. Indeed, while there was talk about violence, gangs and the harassment of 'Australian' girls, the overarching theme was that the 'Lebanese troublemakers' were simply rude young men who had no respect for others and were guilty of 'anti-social' behaviour. The significance of this outburst against bad manners – with national, social and cultural dimensions – requires explanation.

## Talking with strangers

In 2006, a month after the riots, Tourism Australia released an AUD$180m international campaign promoting Australia as a tourist destination. This campaign, with the tag 'So Where the bloody hell are you?' (*Age*, 2006), conveyed an image of hospitality through a down-to-earth informality seen to be typical of the Australian character. The sequence of images in the main advertisement was about getting the place ready for 'you', serving 'you', but was framed by the feigned abruptness of the question, a marker, in the Australian vernacular, of boisterous intimacy. It included the image of Lara Bingle – a Cronulla girl – emerging from the surf saying she had saved us a spot on the beach (which is empty – like most of the scenes in the ad, Australia is unpeopled, implying there is plenty of room for others!). However, the advertisements were criticised overseas for using 'colourful' language and indicating not friendliness but rudeness. The ads offended some sensibilities, especially in the UK (*Mail and Guardian*, 2006). In Australia this was met with glee, since there is some pleasure in offending the English and demonstrating an irreverence that confirms a populist self-image (Farr, 2006:3).

However, it also caused local consternation, especially amongst politicians. Queensland Premier Peter Beattie and Federal Parliamentarian Alan Cadman voiced the concern that the profanities were a 'dreadful gaffe'. "People usually can say those things to somebody they know well", Cadman said, "I don't think they would use it to a stranger and, in this instance, we're talking to strangers of a different culture who I think may be offended". Scott Morrison, Managing Director of Tourism Australia, admitted that Asian countries would get 'expletive-deleted' versions: "We're being a bit cautious up in Singapore" (*Mail and Guardian*, 2006).

There are two points in this kerfuffle. On the one hand, Australians were presented as an easy-going people, echoing our perception that we are a hospitable nation, whose 'rudeness' is at once evidence of having few airs and graces and a sign of our easy-welcoming nature and egalitarianism. On the other hand, the response showed how sensitive to cultural differences Australians can be, especially when dollars count. Both exemplify, in different ways, a tolerance towards 'strangers' that is often touted as the hallmark of Australian society, an 'unmannered manners' that is accepting of all.

'Strangers', Bauman (1995) argues, are people who pose a threat because they are 'undecideables', who don't fit into our cognitive and moral maps of the world. In the tourist campaign, however, strangers are not a problem, but rather people who need to be made to feel at home, to be made familiar to us, and whose folkways are to be respected and accommodated, especially if they have money in their pockets. In contrast, a theme that emerged in the weeks before and after the riots was a concern over the appalling behaviour of (some) Australians, demonstrating, it was claimed, a lack of respect and a decline in standards of public behaviour. To unpack the significance of the riots we need to think not just about the big questions of racism and cultural conflict, but about how the concern with issues of conduct in public places provides an entrée into understanding these incidents in terms of anxieties around shared values. The criticism of bad behaviour was levelled first at young men of Arabic and Muslim background who were seen as 'outsiders' – visitors to the beach – and the cause of the initial incident. It was levelled then at the largely White protesters who engaged in violent and racist behaviour in the riots. Finally, it was directed at those young Arabic and Muslim men who conducted revenge attacks over the following nights.

A *Sydney Morning Herald* article on the 'cultural divide' following the initial brawl, published the day before the riot, was headed, 'A lesson in beach etiquette, Shire-style' (McMahon, 2005:3). It quoted one local saying their reaction to the 'aggressive invasion' of youths of Middle Eastern background was 'not about race, just manners. They have no respect for anyone'. It featured a picture of Shaun, standing above the beach wearing a blue singlet emblazoned with an Australian flag, board shorts and sunglasses, holding a bottle of beer. He stands 'on guard' at an entrance to the beach. Shaun 'dislikes visitors he says are rude'. 'They look down on our women', he said, 'They don't really assimilate to our way of life'.

The public conduct of Middle Eastern youth was a key talking point on radio leading up to the riots. Alan Jones famously referred to these youth as 'Middle Eastern grubs' and scum (Mediawatch, 2006) – terms which denote someone of low moral standards rather than a criminal. There was media reportage of long-standing complaints about Lebanese men harassing women, spitting, littering and engaging in boisterous behaviour that ruined the beach for others. This claim was repeated in blogs and media web sites. Arabic men were said to have 'cocky, arrogant attitudes' and 'be loud, rude and obnoxious'; it was claimed they 'disrespect the peace of others' and are guilty of 'harassment of innocent bystanders', 'intimidation by numbers', making 'lewd comments to females' and 'foul language' (*Sydney Morning Herald*, 2005a).

Even after the focus shifted to the revenge attacks (Brown et al, 2005:1), there was still concern with daily incidents of anti-social behaviour. Mark Lopez, the author of a history of multiculturalism, said locals in the Shire (as Sutherland Shire is commonly known) had put up with 'a lot of shit' from Muslim youths over the years (Kerin and Leys, 2005:4). Bloggers continued to opine that Lebs 'have no manners or concern for people' ('interbreeding', 2005). Young locals interviewed as part of the ABC's *4 Corners* program (Jackson, 2006) reiterated this claim. One man insisted that 'The way they're brought up and the way we're brought up...just the morals our parents teach us and the morals their parents teach is completely different ... it's got to do a lot with respect for women'.[5]

Just as with the concern with 'queue-jumpers' during the boat people crises, and ongoing discussions of the 'uncivilised' behaviour of young Arabic or Muslim men, there seems a wider concern with the absence of shared values – not just around 'Australian-ness' but around fundamental social behaviour; a 'problem' which underlies social disharmony. NSW Police Commissioner Moroney blamed anti-social behaviour such as the riots on a 'lack of manners' and 'the absence of common courtesies' among the young, and he said migrants needed to demonstrate 'the common courtesy of embracing our culture,... the norms of this community' (McIlveen, 2006: 3). Claims about shared values – including respect – recurred in the debates around 'Australian values' throughout 2006.

Criticisms around manners were also directed at the protesters, but the burden of guilt was seen to lie with the young men of Lebanese background. As the debate around 'Australian values' escalated Prime Minister Howard complained that Australians needed to improve their manners and be more polite, criticising bad parenting and TV. He was careful about *who* he blamed, but many saw him as referring to some migrant groups, and later spoke of the failure of some Muslims to integrate. NSW Premier Iemma added that 'the poor state of manners and respect had led to events such as ... [the] Cronulla race riot' (*Sydney Morning Herald* 2006).

Amidst the reportage of large-scale protests, violence, racism and harassment, this seems like a big claim. As this book will explore, there are lots of issues which need to be considered to help understand the conflict. These include questions around masculinity, local cultures and economies, and national belonging in a culturally diverse society. The 'excessive' nature of masculinity – the consumption of alcohol, displays of machismo, 'possession' of territory and women in local environments – is found across cultures, of course, but becomes a source of conflict often *in the name of culture.*

Alongside this, the intersection of local beach cultures, transport hubs and patterns of leisure in an urban economy shape the locations of such conflicts. Research that emerged after the riots suggested that Manly, another beach suburb, is the site of the most frequent incidents of violence, primarily amongst young men and centred on pub culture (Pearlman, 2006). Three years later Manly and Coogee still sit on top of the list of violent pubs (Moore and Walters, 2009). This research points to the mix of unemployment and alcoholism in fuelling violence, which is more commonly found in country towns than Sydney's suburbs. But we might speculate that there are a number of key social and economic processes at stake which make certain beaches places of youth conflict. Cronulla, like Manly, Coogee and Bondi, is a centre for the convergence of youth cultures across Sydney. On the one hand, as Clif Evers makes clear in this volume, there are local tribalisms which have a history of tension. On the other, Cronulla is also a place where people from areas further afield congregate – Cronulla is a traditional weekend destination for those from south-western Sydney because it is at the end of the train line and because it is one of the closest beaches for that part of Sydney. As Amanda Wise shows in her chapter, this means that again there is a history of conflict between locals and 'Bankies' – people seen to be from the area around Bankstown – long before this area was seen as 'Lebanese'. Moreover, Cronulla has become part of a local café and club scene, and hence a magnet for young people from overseas. Local groups mix with a range of near and far 'outsiders' (defined by suburb, region, cultural background or citizenship), day trippers and backpackers, creating tensions within a transient and changing tourist economy.

These particular processes also occurred within a wider process of economic change. Since the mid-1990s, the Shire had

8

been the centre of a particularly heated debate about urban growth and 'overdevelopment', leading to the unseating of members of parliament (Walshe, 1999). By 2002, the complaint of 'overpopulation' and 'too many migrants' had been thrown into the existing mix of poor planning and overdevelopment, and discussed heatedly in state parliament (Collier, 2002).

This mix of social and economic factors adds a greater complexity to the picture of the riots beyond a simple invocation of 'ethnic tension'. Yet these specific flows of people and ensuing tensions have occurred in one of the most culturally homogenous areas of Sydney, as Jock Collins demonstrates in his chapter. Perceptions of 'outsiders' – especially in the wider context of debates about immigration and national identity, social cohesion and cultural difference, social change and 'problem youth' – take on an increasingly 'racialised' dimension, in which broader social phenomenon are seen in ethnic or racial terms (Poynting et al., 2004). Amidst these pressing issues, then, why are manners of such concern?

## Multicultural Manners, or how to live with strangers

Multiculturalism, in so far as it offers an ethos of tolerance and respect, has long been about articulating a kind of etiquette for dealing with people from different cultures: a 'set of rules, of good manners and considerateness, that has helped us get along' (Poynting, 2006). The current multicultural policy statement, released by the previous Howard federal government, famous for its conservative emphasis on 'Australian values', emphasises that the 'freedom of all Australians to express and share their cultural values is dependent on their abiding by mutual civic obligations'. Framed by 'an overriding loyalty to Australia', citizens are nevertheless expected to exhibit 'acceptance and understanding' and 'fairness', a respect for others' culture and beliefs that enables diversity to flourish (Commonwealth of Australia, 2003). The kinds of cultural awareness training that have been around for several decades since the inception of multicultural policies were often about identifying the differences of strangers so one could react appropriately and politely in public and on private occasions. Interestingly, there has been a resurgence in books on etiquette in recent years and often these involve strategies for the avoidance of cultural misunderstanding. *Multicultural Manners* (Dresser, 2005) is one such book from the United States, found in my local bookstore in Sydney just after the riots, which is focused entirely on such anxieties.

The aim of *Multicultural Manners* is to demystify behaviours of different cultures to produce the sensitivity necessary to avoid cross-cultural blunders. The book details what it sees as culturally-specific body language, child rearing, dress, classroom behaviour, religious practices and gender norms. It includes a guide to the world's cultures and their customs, and includes handy hints (such as Albanians nod to say no and shake their head to say yes, and advice that we should avoid body contact between males and females when dealing with Muslims, Jews and Koreans). It provides strictures regarding body movements when bowing to Japanese people: hands should slide down towards the knee or remain at side, the back and neck should be held rigid, with eyes downcast. The person in inferior position always bows longer and lower. It also advises that it is wise 'to avoid stereotypes and generalisations and making assumptions', then stereotypes, generalises and makes assumptions. It is easy to caricature such a book, but it does, especially in the wake of 9/11, urge us not to assume someone who looks different is not a citizen.

The promotion of multicultural manners and the castigation of bad beach manners represent a cultural fetishism – indeed codification – of categories of culture, whether valued positively or negatively. Yet there is a difference here. The identification of bad manners aims to shame perpetrators; perpetrators who are typically people of marginalised cultural backgrounds. This is a process that serves relations of inequality. The preoccupation with bad manners imposes a singular moral universe that reflects the dominant culture. This was realised in the booklet which emerged after the riots and the ensuing 'Australian values' debate which explains 'Aussie' manners to migrants in the hope they will respect and assimilate to them. It tells migrants '[w]hen to say please and thank you, what to say if you accidentally bumped into someone in the street', and warns against spitting, recommends blowing your nose into a handkerchief and endorses punctuality. In a way that marked specific groups as potential perpetrators of bad manners, it pointed out that it was forbidden to slaughter animals in the backyard (Burke, 2006:9).

The promotion of multicultural manners, however, attempts to show 'how to get along with others who are culturally different'. As Patsy Rowe (2000) says, in her *Manners for the Millennium*, manners are 'the oil that lubricates our daily lives and greases the wheels of our social interaction with others'. The kinds of stereotyping here, no matter how problematic, are intended to avoid offending someone and demystification is undertaken in a spirit of engagement. The discourse of multicultural manners recognises values are culture-specific and acquired (not universal) and sometimes problematic and hopes instead to encourage mutual understanding between cultures, however flawed its understanding may be. As Geoff Gallop (2007:36), past premier of Western Australia said in his discussion of the difficulties of multiculturalism: 'A good society will draw a line in the sand when cultural or religious practices undermine civility and infringe rights. However, knowing where to draw that line is not easy'.

## Many lines in many sands

The concern about displaying bad manners *to* strangers, and our preoccupation with the bad manners *of* strangers, is paralleled by a deeper anxiety about the manners of all Australians. Indeed, at the time of the riots it wasn't just the Lebanese who were seen to behave badly, but also those who 'protested' against that behaviour and committed acts of harassment and violence. This fits into a longer debate about the absence of standards of behaviour in Australia as a whole (Gregory, 2007:3). Columnists like Miranda Devine (2002:15) have lamented the 'decline of civility', citing road rage, queue rage and air rage. Her belief that there is a 'widespread confusion about social rules' involves an implicit concern with the consequences of migration and multiculturalism (she is writing in the wake of debates around gang rape and ethnic crime, themes she frequently discusses), but her piece suggests a deeper set of issues around social incivility and moral order in contemporary societies, in which cultural diversity is only one source of anxiety.

Tabloid television has been in the forefront of documenting how Australia is becoming a ruder and less caring society; *Today Tonight* (Robson, 2006) listed the ten rudest things people do – including inconsiderate use of mobiles, spitting, swearing, jumping queues, stealing a parking place – and deplored the 'downward trend' that saw manners 'flying out the window'. As their expert, Patsy Rowe, pointed out, manners are not just about polite society, they are 'the glue that holds things together'. Here, the problem is seen not to be the presence of impolite foreigners, but a consequence of 'modern life', the ways in which we live in cities, jammed against each other, working longer hours in confined spaces with increasingly technologically mediated communication (Bounds, 2006:22). When a blog was posted on the *Herald* web site talking about research comparing rudeness in Sydney to cities around the world, there were 308 responses (Woodburn, 2006). Manners matter.

Manners are like drawing lines in the sand – they define what is appropriate and what is not – but lines are drawn in many different places, and they don't necessarily stay in one place. Moreover, there is a paradox in the ways etiquette operates: such lines are at once mechanisms for producing civil order ('good fences make good neighbours') and for excluding people. As Zerubavel (1991) has elegantly shown, lines are crucial to human thought and practice – they are useful tools of differentiation which function to enable perception – we can only see something when it is made distinct from its surroundings and from other, comparable entities. This process of classification applies to everything – objects, time, space, animals as well as humans – and becomes felt as 'natural'. It mlakes it possible to experience ourselves as humans with agency. But these very social processes of classification also shape who is 'inside' and who is 'outside', who we identify with, and who we identify against, who we trust and who we fear, who is 'pure' and who is 'filth'. They are not just perceptual but social, cultural and political. In the case of Cronulla, they have a normative function which divides beach and shops, suburb from suburb, nation from nation, males and females, Anglos and wogs (Johns, 2008). Importantly, these lines are often felt as *moral* divisions. It is not surprising, then, that so much of the language involved metaphors of dirt. A poster displayed in the Sutherland Shire entitled, 'Clean up Australia Day', referred to young men of Middle Eastern appearance as 'the filth that crawls off the trains and pollutes our beaches', declaring it is 'time to "take out the trash" and clean up our beaches' (Strike Force Neil, 2006: 35).

Moreover, lines *in the sand* are also challenges and provocations – particularly to masculine honour and national pride. You can see this in the pose Shaun strikes in the 'etiquette' article cited above: he is 'on guard' ready to block unwelcome visitors; a line that has to be forced to be crossed (McMahon, 2005:3). There is a tension, then, between the way in which manners are a form of social lubricant which works productively to give people a sense of social order and enable cohabitation, and the way manners are used to police marginalised groups, moral deviance and social inequality.

The history of manners – particularly Elias' classic *Civilising Process* (1994) – shows that we become preoccupied with etiquette during periods of social change, because such change produces strains on community life and requires formalised codes of conduct to return some sense of order. We live our lives via moral codes which guide us through and help us avoid conflicts. If the social world or the moral codes change, we panic. Elias argues that the concept of civility emerged as medieval society and church were in the process of breaking down. He describes a context of social restructuring, disintegration and reintegration, and a process of social formation drawing together diverse nationalities and languages. The rituals of living together were in flux, but codified manners served to manage the differentiation of the social fabric alongside the centralisation of the state and the negotiation of class relations.

We don't need a sense of world-historical restructuring to explain how manners play their part in social change. Garfinkel's (1984) work in the twentieth century showed how social order is experienced as moral order. This is not the same as the popular idea that commonplace incivility is evidence of social fragmentation (Phillips and Smith, 2003). Garfinkel argued that to make daily life possible, we need certain types of cultural understandings to become shared and implicit – rules about interpersonal, social and economic exchange become rule-like because social life becomes chaotic if they are not observed, therefore they must be internalised as the 'right' thing to do, as his example of the queue demonstrates. For Garfinkel these rules were primarily a pragmatic feature of social life, it was about 'getting things done'. For Elias it involved bigger questions of social power. I don't want to draw a distinction between these two levels, but rather to recognise that in the conduct of daily life, they hold together.

To return to the discussion about Cronulla, the concerns with forms of social conduct that allow people to get along in local spaces also involve larger questions of racialised perceptions of order. We see in the events in Cronulla and in the discussion in the following days and weeks the bringing together of two discourses which relate to manners. One is about the loss of social order, a theme which has recurred many times, often with increasing anxiety, and which captures broad concerns about the dissolution of social bonds, the erosion of community in the face of globalisation and economic rationalism in government policy and in the neo-liberal marketplace. The second, informed by preoccupations with the so-called 'clash of civilisations', casts the loss of order in terms of the impact of migration, multiculturalism and cultural conflict.

We could argue here that what Taylor (2004) calls 'the social imaginary' or the ways we perceive the ordering of social relationships – which shapes the ways we act – is in fact in articulation with what we might call the *ethnic* imaginary – the ways we perceive the nature of 'ethnic' groups and differences in cultural values and practices, at home and abroad. As Taylor suggests, the social imaginary is founded on a principle of *moral* order, fashioned around assumptions of mutual benefit and the ethical behaviours of individuals to realise our shared interests. Taylor sees this order as shaped by three forms of 'social self-understanding': the economy, the public sphere and democracy. However, we shouldn't assume the coherence of these forms: it may be that these things are distinct imaginaries in their own right, structured as they are around different concerns and different conceptualisations of relations. If, as is true at present, many in the West attempt to hold together neo-liberal beliefs about the functioning of the economy *and* principles of social justice and community, then we may need to think of the economic imaginary and the social imaginary as competing orientations to moral order.

These imaginaries, since they are different forms of ordering, may be in conflict, especially given the broader disjunctures of globalised capitalism (Appadurai, 1990). At times, however, these imaginaries complement each other in more or less adequate ways. In moments when cultural pathologies form particular social functions – in explaining conflict or deviance, for example – then it may be that the social and cultural imaginaries align remarkably well for the dominant. The emergence of the 'Arab Other' as the 'folk devil' of our times (Poynting et al., 2004) suggests one such moment when *cultural* explanations for *social* ills are especially powerful. This helps explain how processes of racialisation, or ethnicisation, connect cultural categories, social order, political threat and moral discourses.

The changing, globalised nature of the world with its vast movements of people, things, values and information, massive shifts in patterns of work and leisure, and the challenges these pose to local populations and their perceptions of 'community' – lies behind the racialisation of social problems. This is not to ignore the materiality of tensions between different systems of values and practices shaped by cultural heritage – but to recognise how, in a moment like the riots, many of these wider social, economic and political forces are seen as *cultural* differences. It's easier to direct blame at one group than address complex problems which we can't easily comprehend. If our daily lives are punctuated by cultural differences which we don't understand, then the confluence of moral order and an ethnic imaginary becomes compelling. In this regard we expect too much of multiculturalism: we expect it to manage the consequences of economic and social change, as we have seen above, simply because these are refracted through a cultural lens. If Cronulla demonstrates to many the 'failure' of multiculturalism, it is not because multicultural policies cannot help to manage cultural diversity but because we have come to invest too much in the promise of multiculturalism – it cannot be made accountable for larger economic and political challenges. It is this burdening of a specific set of policies and programs with the ideal of social cohesion that tests the very limits of multiculturalism.

Australia is fast becoming a society of what Vertovec (2006) calls 'super-diversity', a complexity which surpasses any diversity previously experienced. Super-diversity is distinguished by the dynamic interplay of variables among an increasing number of new and small groups of multiple origins, transnationally connected and socio-economically differentiated. Perhaps *hyper*diversity is a better way of characterising these circumstances because it captures the proliferation of differences and the anxieties attendant upon this process.[6] This state of hyperdiversity is marked not just by a multitude of differences, but by a layering of difference (where nation, ethnicity, faith and language overlap), a diversification of diversity (where class, region, age, gender, generation and settlement patterns entail different experiences of difference), differential forms of exclusion and inclusion (integration into labour markets but denial of access to other areas of life) and a blending of differences through intermarriage, so that some Australians may claim three or more heritages (Ang et al., 2004). This increasing differentiation of difference makes the rigid categories of ethnic identity fostered under multiculturalism untenable, and produces anxiety by breaking the rules governing how we identify and deal with differences.

Yet there is a major 'difference' multiculturalism has always struggled with: because multicultural policies have long been associated with the management of the diversity that arises from migration, it has been identified with the interests of ethnic minorities. As critics from the left as well as the right have pointed out, Anglo-Australians don't recognise themselves in the new narrative of multicultural Australia (Blainey, 1984; Ang, 2001: 98-99). Indeed, there is an increasing sense of exclusion and loss amongst White Australia as the older story of national community and identity is challenged and transformed by this multicultural imaginary (Hage, 1998: 180). This ambivalence about the place of White Australia (and, we should add indigenous Australia) amidst the cultural diversity shaped by recent migration posits another 'limit' for multiculturalism.

The significance of this 'difference' is also why Hage (1998) argues for the need to see racism as a practice through which some social actors attempt to 'manage' the national space, rather than just an act of power or immoral behaviour; a form of belonging which embodies a sense of one's right to shape the nation. But because the nation is what he calls a 'homely imaginary', this right to manage the national space aligns strongly with what I have described above as the management of moral conduct. This helps explain why such a minor, local skirmish can so quickly become an incident on a national scale, and why 'manners' has wider ramifications than interpersonal relations.

## Conclusion

A preoccupation with manners is resurgent because we live in a time of insecurity and uncertainty. In complex societies where we know few of those around us, behavioural cues become salient as principles of social organisation, especially in the ways in which we manage interactions in public spaces (Smith, 1981). In the midst of proliferating differences, many will respond by reasserting a moral and social singularity, as was the case with the protesters – and the revenge attackers – at Cronulla. Such a reassertion offers some coordinates of difference and behaviour, some lines in the sand: schemas of intelligibility of cause and effect, right and wrong, which return order to the complexity of the world. The assertion of the need for a clear set of Australian values offers a similar kind of existential security (Noble, 2002): as Albrechtsen (2006:14) argued, against 'multicultural moral relativism', 'with confident, traditional values comes strength'.

Albrechtsen's comment reminds us that the debate around multiculturalism and 'Australian values' that was reignited by Cronulla is, at its heart, a debate about forms of national belonging. These forms of belonging entail the mixing of national and moral sentiments: a call to decency which casts respectability and responsibility as fundamentally individual moral qualities and which, as Brett argues, has 'wide commonsense appeal' because it accords with Australians' 'egalitarian manners, in which we treat people on their merits' (2005:12). Yet this nationalist call to decency is inflected with class, gender and ethnicity: an array of 'lines in the sand'. This book uses the lens of the Cronulla riots to reflect on cultural diversity, social order and national belonging in contemporary Australia, aiming to draw out the ramifications of these processes by shedding light on this singular but significant event. It offers a critical account of what happened in Cronulla and where it sits in the wider context of Australian society and the world, presenting competing perspectives on why the riots occurred and their implications for multiculturalism and social policy.

## References

*Age* (2006) 'Tourism body pleased campaign reaction', *Age* 26 February, accessed 9 June 2009,
http://www.theage.com.au/news/National/Tourism-body-pleased-campaign-reaction/2006/02/26/1140888739403.html

Albrechtsen, J. (2006) 'With confident, traditional values comes strength', *Australian* 21 June: 14.

Ang, I. (2001) *On Not Speaking Chinese* Routledge, London.

Ang, I., Brand, J., Noble, G. and Sternberg, J. (2006) *Connecting Diversity: the Paradoxes of Australian Multiculturalism* Special Broadcasting Service Corporation, Artarmon.

Appadurai, A. (1990) 'Disjuncture and Difference in the Global Cultural Economy', in M. Featherstone (ed.) *Global Culture* Sage, London: 295-310.

Bauman, Z. (1995) 'Making and Unmaking of Strangers', *Thesis Eleven* 43: 1-16.

Blainey, G. (1984) *All for Australia* Methuen Haynes, Sydney.

Bounds, J. (2006) 'How do you do?', *Sunday Telegraph Sunday Magazine* 12 April: 21-2.

Brett, J. (2005) 'Relaxed and Comfortable: The Liberal Party's Australia', *Quarterly Essay* 19: 1-79.

Brown, M. (2006) 'Australia's not racist' *Sydney Morning Herald* 27 January: 7.

Brown, M., Kennedy, L., Wormald, J. and Wainwright, R. (2005) 'Armed gangs on the rampage', *Sydney Morning Herald* 13 December: 1.

Burchell, D. (2006) 'Both Sides of Political Divide Stoop to Playing the Race Card', *Australian* 27 January: 12.

Burke, N. (2006) 'BYO Aussie manners', *Daily Telegraph* 21 September: 9.

Cohen, S. (1980) *Folk Devils and Moral Panics* (2nd Ed) St. Martin's Press, New York.

Collier, B. (2002) 'Sutherland Shire Overdevelopment and Population' Hansard – NSW Legislative Assembly, 20 November, accessed 9 June 2009, http://www.parliament.nsw.gov.au/prod/parlment/hansart.nsf/V3Key/LA20021120032

Commonwealth of Australia (2003) *Multicultural Australia: United In Diversity*, accessed 9 June 2009, http://www.immi.gov.au/media/publications/settle/_pdf/united_diversity.pdf

Devine, M. (2002) 'Time we made good manners all the rage', *The Sun-Herald* 6 October: 15.

Dresser, N. (2005) *Multicultural Manners* John Wiley and Sons, New Jersey.

Elias, N. (1994) *Civilising Process* E. Jephcott (trans.), Blackwell, Oxford.

Ehrlich, P. and Wilson, E. (1991) 'Biodiversity studies: science and policy', *Science* 253.n5021: 758(5).

Farr, M. (2006) 'Bloody Poms lose sense of humour in the fog', *Daily Telegraph* 10 March: 3.

Gallop, G. (2007) 'Freedom based on tolerance' *Australian* 4 April: 36.

Garfinkel, H. (1984) *Studies in Ethnomethodology* Blackwell, Oxford.

Greenlees, D. (2006) 'In a tide of diversity, Australia faces racism', *International Herald Tribune* 15 February, accessed 9 June 2009, http://www.iht.com/articles/2006/02/15/news/race.php

Gregory, J. (2007) 'Class to mind its manners', *Courier Mail* April 30: 3.

Hage, G. (1998) *White Nation* Pluto Press, Sydney.

Interbreeding (2006) 'My take on Cronulla', 14 December, accessed 9 June 2006, http://interbreeding.blogspot.com/2005/12/my-take-on-cronulla.html

Jacobsen, G. and Clennell, A. (2006) 'Few jailed for their roles in the attacks', *Sydney Morning Herald* 9-10 December: 11.

Jackson, L. (2006) 'Riot and Revenge', *Four Corners*, Australian Broadcasting Commission, March 13, accessed 9 June 2009, http://www.abc.net.au/4corners/content/2006/s1588360.htm

Johns, A. (2008) 'White Tribe: Echoes of the Anzac Myth', *Continuum* 22, 1: 3-16.

Kerin, J. and Leys, N. (2005) 'We're not a bunch of racists, PM says', *Australian*, 13 December: 4.

McIlveen, L. (2006) 'Ken wants to leave law in order', *Daily Telegraph* 25 September: 3.

McMahon, N. (2005) 'A lesson in beach etiquette, Shire-style', *Sydney Morning Herald* 10-11 December: 3.

Mail and Guardian (2006) 'Bugger: Australia's tourism ad banned in Britain', 9 March, accessed 9 June 2009,

http://www.mg.co.za/articlepage.aspx?area=/breaking_news/other_news/&articleid=266203

Mediawatch (2006) 'Jones and Cronulla', ABC TV, February 20.

Moore, M. and Walters, C. (2009) 'Revealed: the violent truth about our pubs' *Sydney Morning Herald* February 21, accessed 9 June 2009, http://www.smh.com.au/national/revealed-the-violent-truth-about-our-pubs-20090220-8doa.html

Murphy, D. (2006) 'Calm after the storm', *Sydney Morning Herald* 9-10 December: 11.

Noble, G. (2002) 'Comfortable and Relaxed: furnishing the home and nation', *Continuum* 16, 1: 53-66.

Pearlman, J. (2006) 'Cocktail of joblessness and drink fuels pub violence' *Sydney Morning Herald* 30 January: 5.

Perera, S, (2006) 'Race Terror, Sydney, December 2005', *Borderlands* 5, 1, http://www.borderlandsejournal.adelaide.edu.au/vol5no1_2006/perera_raceterror.htm

Phillips, T. and Smith, P. (2003), 'Everyday Incivility: Towards a Benchmark', *Sociological Review* 51, 1: 85-108.

Poynting, S., Noble, G. and Tabar, P. (2003) 'Protest Masculinity and Lebanese Youth in Western Sydney', in M. Donaldson and S. Tomsen (eds.) *Male Trouble* Pluto Press, Sydney: 132-155.

Poynting, S., Noble, G., Tabar, P. and Collins, J. (2004) *Bin Laden in the Suburbs* Sydney Institute of Criminology, Sydney.

Poynting, S. (2006) 'Racial violence: who's responsible?' *Green Left Weekly*, 673, 28 June, accessed 9 June 2009, http://www.greenleft.org.au/2006/673/6385

Robson, N. (2006) 'Bad Manners', *Today Tonight* Channel 7, 2 October.

Rowe, P. (2000) *Manners for the Millennium* New Holland Publishers, Chatswood.

Sheehan, P. (2006a) 'Trouble in the Premier's patch', *Sydney Morning Herald* 14-15 January: 31.

Sheehan, P. (2006b) *Girls Like You* Macmillan, Sydney.

Smith, S. (1981) 'Crime in the Inner City', in Jackson, P. & Smith, S. (eds) *Social Interaction and Ethnic Segregation* Academic Press, London.

Stewart, C. and Hodge, A. (2005) 'Isolated and angry', *Australian* 14 December: 11.

Taylor, C. (2004) *Modern Social Imaginaries* Duke University Press, Durham, NC.

Strike Force Neil (2006) Cronulla Riots: Review of the Police Response, Vol. 1. Sydney: NSW Police.

*Sydney Morning Herald* (2005a) 'Your say', 8 December, accessed 9 June 2009, http://blogs.smh.com.au/newsblog/archives/your_say/002978.html

*Sydney Morning Herald* (2005b) 'Racism in Australia' (poll conducted December 12), 21 December, accessed 9 June 2009, http://www.smh.com.au/polls/national/form.html

*Sydney Morning* Herald (2006) 'PM to public: improve your manners', *Sydney Morning Herald* 31 January, accessed 9 June 2009, http://www.smh.com.au/news/national/pm-to-public-improve-your-manners/2006/01/31/1138590476814.html

Vertovec, S. (2006) *The Emergence of Super-Diversity in Britain* Working Paper No. 25, Centre of Migration, Policy and Society, University of Oxford.

Walshe, B. (1999) 'Overdevelopment?!', Bob's Corner, Sutherland Shire Environment Centre Web site, accessed 9 June 2009, http://www.ssec.org.au/resources/bobs_corner/1999_may.htm

Woodburn, R. (2006) 'Streets of shame', *Sydney Morning Herald Blogs: Travel* 17 July, accessed 9 June 2009,

http://blogs.smh.com.au/travel/archives/2006/07/streets_of_sham_1.html

Zerubavel, E. (1991) The Fine Line: Making Distinctions in Everyday Life The Free Press, New York.

# Notes

[1] I will use 'Middle Eastern appearance', Lebanese, Arab and Muslim interchangeably through this introduction – not because they are the same, but because, as is made clear in Poynting et al. (2004), they have merged in the social imaginary into a single, fictitious folk devil, the 'Arab Other'.

[2] Indeed, some residents came to the beach because they had been told it would be a peace rally, aimed at healing tensions.

[3] The *Hazzard Report* claims there were 270,000 individual text messages sent during the riots (Strike Force Neil, 2006: 8).

[4] A year after the riots and revenge attacks, 104 people had been charged but only 7 jailed, while 19 cases were still to be heard (Jacobsen and Clennell, 2006:11)

[5] There is some irony here because Arab and Muslim youths have complained for years that they get no respect from Anglo-Australians (Poynting et al., 2003).

[6] The concept of hyperdiversity is of course borrowed from the biological sciences in which it depicts the exuberant diversity and rapid differentiation of some species. See Ehrlich and Wilson (1991).

# Lines in the Sand

## Part one

# Making sense of the riots: Contexts and perspective

As chapter one suggested, the Cronulla riots drew immediate comparisons with events in North America and Europe. Yet these comparisons were unhelpful because they ignored the specificity of the events at Cronulla. The comparisons made by journalists (and it was usually journalists looking for an international benchmark) assumed that there was a similar story of alienated migrant youth.

There *is* a story about alienated migrant youth to be told, of course, but that story doesn't explain the eruption of events on Cronulla beach. In fact, emphasising the disaffection of disadvantaged groups shifts the responsibility of the violence onto – in this case – the victims of the riots. This doesn't mean socio-economic issues aren't relevant – they are. Nor does acknowledging disaffection absolve those of Middle Eastern background who were involved in the initial brawl or in the revenge attacks – the point here is that *their* disaffection does not explain the riots. To begin to understand the riots requires that we place them in their domestic and global contexts.

The remarkable thing about the Cronulla riots is that they were a protest largely by White, middle class Australians (and mostly young males) *against* those who have been characterised as alienated migrant youth. In terms of some of the key coordinates of social power and privilege comparisons – class, ethnicity and gender – the protesters were by and large relatively advantaged Australians, demonstrating against people who could be considered some of the most marginalised groups in Australian society. They weren't from amongst the most wealthy, of course, but nor were they the battlers from, for example, Sydney's outer west. In this way the Cronulla events were not only different from the overseas events often cited in media reports – the riots in Paris, Bradford or Los Angeles – they were also different from the riots involving indigenous Australians in Redfern in February 2004 (Cunneen, 2007) and the disadvantaged community of Macquarie Fields in February 2005 (Lee, 2007).

Nor does the narrative of alienated youth exhaust what can be said about the nature of multiculturalism in contemporary Australia. The dynamics of cultural diversity are a much more complicated set of economic, political, social and cultural processes than that captured by simplistic arguments about the failure of multicultural policies. Indeed, one of the peculiar features of the riots is that they involve primarily young people, who often are seen to be the most tolerant of cultural difference in Australia. The unreliability of simplistic claims – about cultural diversity and about young people – suggests we need to examine the Cronulla riots much more closely and carefully.

As Jock Collins suggests, to make sense of Cronulla involves locating it in its international, national and local contexts and understanding the peculiar nature of Sydney as one of the great immigrant cities in the world. Sydney (and Australia) prides itself on successfully accommodating large numbers of migrants from a vast array of nations, cultures and faiths and drawing on those resources to transform itself into a thriving, cosmopolitan society. This cosmopolitanism, however, has in recent years been dramatically challenged by domestic and global events. Collins describes a series of episodes – ongoing panics around ethnic gangs, asylum seekers and terrorist attacks in New York (2001) and Bali (2002) – which were used by the Federal Government to foster a climate of fear which manifested itself in a wave of attacks on people of Muslim and Arab background, particularly in Sydney, which has the largest populations of migrants from these backgrounds.

Cronulla, however, is one of the least culturally diverse areas of Sydney. Scott Poynting explores the specific contexts of the riots even further, by considering the peculiarities of Cronulla as a locale shaped by its geography and the culture within the Sutherland Shire. It is located on a peninsula, at the end of a rail line, and has retained a largely monocultural population. While residents see this as providing a very strong sense of local community and indentify proudly as living in 'the Shire', it can be seen to also produce a particularly insular viewpoint which lends itself to populist critiques of multiculturalism. Poynting juxtaposes this local context with the tendency in the conservative elements of the media and government to lay the blame for cultural disharmony at the feet of multiculturalism per se, exploiting the Cronulla riots for their own ideological agendas.

Wendy Shaw gives a very personal account of the local context Poynting outlines, recounting aspects of her own life growing up in

Cronulla. Shaw is a human geographer who specialises in the study of urban areas, particularly in relation to questions of race and her perspectives on Cronulla are far more than personal memories. She captures the peculiar dynamics of change (economic as well as social and cultural) in a suburb such as Cronulla, in which recent housing developments seek to evoke the ambience of her childhood in a beach-based culture. This nostalgia parallels the account of her own childhood memories, but it also captures something of the local mindset and its desire for an Australia of a distant past. As monocultural as Cronulla still is, it doesn't quite have the 'comfortable homogeneity' that she remembers from the 1960s. She recalls intolerance towards differences, a very strong local youth culture and a history of (male) tribal battles over territory, features that became significant in the riots. She also details the strong sense of freedom which pervaded local life, which must surely have been directly threatened by a climate of insecurity in the 5-6 years preceding the riots.

These three chapters, moving between the international and the local, the personal and the social, provide a very strong basis for unpacking the dynamics and consequences of the riots.

## References

Lee, M. (2007) 'The blame game: Struggles over the representation of the "Macquarie Fields riots"' in S. Poynting and G. Morgan (eds.) *Outrageous! Moral Panics in Australia* ACYS Publishing, Hobart: 53-66.

Cunneen, C. (2007) 'Riot, resistance and moral panic: Demonising the colonial other' in S. Poynting and G. Morgan (eds.) *Outrageous! Moral Panics in Australia* ACYS Publishing, Hobart: 20-29.

## Chapter two

# Sydney's Cronulla riots: the context and implications

## Jock Collins

The events of Sunday 11th December, 2005, on Sydney's Cronulla Beach, sent a tremor through Australian community relations. Images of thousands of drunk White males, many of whom waved or wore the Australian flag, chasing and bashing isolated men and women of 'Middle Eastern appearance' were compelling viewing for media audiences in Sydney, the rest of Australia, and internationally. In the following days, carloads of males of 'Middle Eastern appearance' sought revenge in a smash, bash and flee raid on the suburbs surrounding Cronulla. Used to seeing ethnic diversity associated with conflict in other countries but not Australia, the international media put the spotlight on the riots, revealing an ugly side of life in Australia. For months, an unprecedented police presence dominated Sydney's beaches preventing further conflict (unlike the events in Paris the previous month when Arab youth rioted for weeks), but the scars of the Cronulla riots cut deep into a national psyche in which access to the beach is central to the imagination, if not the lives of most Australians.

The significance of these events should not be underestimated. Sydney is Australia's largest and most culturally diverse city (Collins and Castillo, 1998) and has proudly promoted its harmonious, cosmopolitan character and the social, economic and political advantages that accrue to a global city. At the 2001 census, 58 per cent of Sydneysiders were first or second-generation immigrants, with some 180 birthplaces recorded for the resident population (Burnley, 2001). The riots not only worried Sydneysiders who had hitherto had little experience of inter-ethnic conflict, but they seemed to dissipate the international image of Sydney's cohesive diversity which had reached its height during the 2000 Olympic Games.

Despite the shocking images, the riots were significant because they were an aberration. One of the amazing aspects of Australian history of the past six decades is that such a large and diverse immigration program, which has never been particularly popular with the Australian people (Goot, 1988) and which did not deliver on the promise of its architect, Arthur Calwell, that nine out of ten immigrants would be British (Collins, 1991: 22), could in most instances deliver social cohesion to Australian cities. The history of Australian immigration (Collins, 1991: 201-11) has been characterised by long periods of cohesion rather than by violence and conflict. The Cronulla riots were a brutal reminder that no society, whatever the degree or history of ethnic diversity, is always cohesive.

For right-wing critics of multiculturalism, the riots were (finally) the fulfilment of their prophesies that large-scale immigration of non-British minorities would inevitably lead to conflict in the suburbs of Australian cities (Blainey, 1984; Rimmer, 1991; One Nation, 1998; Sheehan, 1998, 2006). They argued that multiculturalism gave immigrant minorities too much power and privilege. For multiculturalism's left-wing critics (Hage, 1998), who highlight the persistence of discrimination and the marginalisation of immigrant minorities, the riots could be read in a different way – as a vindication of the view that multiculturalism was always about maintaining White power and privilege. In this view, the main game of multiculturalism was to provide concessions to minorities in terms of linguistic, religious and culinary diversity while keeping them out of the citadels of real power.

How then to interpret and respond to the Cronulla riots? What do these events tell us about community relations in Sydney after 9/11? What do they say about law and order, ethnic criminal gangs and youth gangs? And what do they say about Australian multiculturalism and racism? This chapter argues that in order to understand why the riots occurred, it is necessary to situate these events in a broader context, probing the international, national and local events that were a backdrop to the riots.

## The National and International Context

In the 2001 Australian national election, the issue of unauthorised 'boat people' seeking refuge in Australia was a decisive factor in the re-election of Prime Minister John Howard and his conservative coalition government (Markus, 2001). In the months before the election, the Howard government ordered the navy to intercept the Norwegian merchant vessel, the *MS Tampa*, which had the temerity to respond to emergency calls to take on board 433 asylum-seekers whose vessel had experienced difficulties and ran low of food and water, leaving its passengers, including children, at risk. These 'boat people' were fleeing tyrannies such as the Taliban in Afghanistan and Saddam Hussein's regime in Iraq. The *MS Tampa* was not the first boat carrying asylum seekers to the Australian shores in recent years – hundreds had arrived during Howard's term as Prime Minister – but it was the first to be turned away. It was not coincidental that this occurred in the weeks leading to the 2001 election, with the Prime Minister using the 'children overboard' photo – which the Defence Minister, Peter Reith, argued showed boat people throwing their children into the ocean - to illustrate how 'un-Australian' and undeserving these refugees were. It later emerged that this image was one of a series recording sailors rescuing children and adults who had jumped off the sinking ship, that the 'children overboard' events did not happen, and that the Howard government knew these facts while continuing to represent the asylum seekers as barbarians (Marr and Wilkinson, 2003).

These asylum seekers, and those on the boats that followed, were not allowed to land on Australian shores as the Howard government, claiming to seek a 'Pacific solution', directed them to neighbouring countries such as Nauru and New Zealand. The 'boat people' issue demonstrated willingness on the part of the government to exploit public concerns about immigration in general, and Middle Eastern immigration in particular, to their political advantage (Marr and Wilkinson, 2003). In this way the Howard government sent out 'dog whistle' messages to Australian voters that they should be concerned about Middle Eastern immigrants who throw their children into the sea to manipulate the

Australian government, thereby demonstrating an absence of 'Australian' values (Poynting et al, 2004).

Shortly after the Tampa incident, the terrorist attacks on the World Trade Centre in New York on September 11, 2001 produced shock-waves that are still impacting on global and national politics. The horrific images of the planes crashing into the smoking towers, the falling bodies, collapsing buildings, the chaos and confusion, the casualties, the anger, the mourning and the aftermath still linger in our minds. The identification of the terrorists as Muslim Arabs who were part of Osama Bin Laden's Al Qaeda terrorist organisation had significant ramifications here. Australian troops participated in the invasions of Afghanistan and Iraq, national security, intelligence and border control were tightened, including legislation to excise Christmas Island, Cocos Island, Ashmore Reef and thousands of small islands from Australia's migration zone, preventing 'boat people' who might land there from claiming asylum. On October 12 2002, terrorists bombed the Safari Club, in Kuta Beach, Bali, a popular holiday destination for Australians. As the news unfolded, it became apparent that many Australians were among the dead and injured, the threat of terrorism was now perceived as more frightening and immediate because this was on Australia's doorstep. The suspicion of the involvement of Islamist terrorists was soon confirmed and since then attacks in Spain, London and again in Bali have increasingly associated people of 'Middle Eastern appearance' with terrorism, an extreme form of criminal behaviour.

These events all affected community relations in Australia, in the immediate aftermath of September 11 and the bombing in Bali many Arab and Muslim Australians and other religious minorities were subjected to hostility, abuse and violence. A Human Rights and Equal Opportunity Commission (HREOC) study, the Ismae-Listen project conducted national consultations on eliminating prejudice against Arab and Muslim Australians and surveyed 1423 Arab and Muslim Australians. The study reported that as a result of these events the majority of Muslims consulted had experienced escalating prejudice against their race or religion. Reported experiences ranged from offensive remarks to physical violence (HREOC, 2004: 2). The Ismae-Listen project reported that The

Australian Arabic Council recorded a twenty-fold rise in reports of discrimination and vilification in the month after 11 September 2001 (HREOC, 2004: 43), while The Muslim Women's Association of South Australia recorded a 'significant number of reported incidents, specifically of discrimination and harassment against Muslims', most involving offensive verbal abuse of women (HREOC, 2004: 43). The Al Zahra Muslim Women's Association in Sydney also reported a 'phenomenal' increase in discrimination and vilification (HREOC, 2004: 43).

A clearer picture of the impact of these events on Sydney's Muslim, Arabic and Middle Eastern population emerged from data collected from a hotline between September 12, 2001 and November 11, 2001 by the Community Relations Commission for a Multicultural NSW, during which time 248 incidents were logged. There were seven categories of attack: physical assault; verbal assault; sexual assault; threat; racial discrimination or harassment, damage to property; and media attack. Half of all victims were female, seven out of ten were adults. Not surprisingly, the largest language groups to use the hotline were Arabic – 52.4% of calls. 47.2% of all incidents occurred in public spaces. (UTS Shopfront, 2005).

## The Sydney Context

The riots put the spotlight on two segments of Sydney's population – the White, Anglo-Celtic majority and a Middle Eastern minority – and two parts of the city: the Sutherland Shire Local Government Area (LGA) in Sydney's southern suburbs where Cronulla Beach is located (known as 'the Shire'), and the Canterbury and Bankstown LGAs, located in south-western Sydney, where most of the city's Lebanese and Middle Eastern immigrants live.

Sydney is the home to the vast majority of Australia's Lebanese community: 107,405 or 72.2 % of the Lebanese Diaspora in Australia live in Sydney (Collins, 2005:190-191). Australia's Lebanese immigrants arrived in two main migrations, one Maronite Christian and a later, mostly Muslim intake. By 1954 there were 3,861 Lebanese people living in Australia. From the late 1970s,

Lebanese Sunni Muslims began to immigrate to Sydney, establishing a small community in the suburb of Lakemba in south-western Sydney. Today the landscape of Lakemba is dominated by the huge Imam Ali Mosque, which was built in 1976. Lebanese Shi'ite Muslims also arrived in Sydney from the end of the 1970s (Collins and Castillo, 1998: 411-24).

One of the features of Lebanese migration to Australia is their residential concentration within the western and south-western suburbs of Sydney, where most minorities in Sydney live. Media portrayals of Lebanese crime have put the spotlight on suburbs such as Bankstown, Punchbowl and Lakemba as 'no-go' enclaves (Collins et al., 2002). In fact, Sydney's immigrant settlement is so diverse that its multicultural suburbs are settled by a diverse range of ethnicities, with no ghettos of the kind seen in the USA or UK (Jupp et al., 1991). The latest 2006 census data shows that the Shire has the greatest White concentration in Sydney. Table 1 compares 2006 census data on birthplace, ancestry, language and religion of the population of three LGAs: the Shire, Bankstown and Canterbury. Nearly eight out of ten (78.1%) of people living in the Shire in 2006 were born in Australia, with 73.1% of the Shire's population claiming Anglo-Celtic ancestry. This compares with the profile of Bankstown (56.7% born in Australia but only 38.6% of Anglo-Celtic ancestry) and Canterbury (44.5% born in Australia but only 24.8% of Anglo-Celtic ancestry). Only 14.4% of the Shire's population spoke a language other than English (compared to 56.5% in Bankstown and 69.9% in Canterbury) while less than 1% of the Shire's population were Muslim compared with 15.2% in Bankstown and 13.7% in Canterbury. In 2006 14% of Bankstown's population and 10.5% Canterbury's population were of Middle Eastern Ancestry, compared to only 0.8% of the Shire's population. This data highlights the relative 'Whiteness' of the Shire compared to the cosmopolitan (including Muslim, Middle Eastern and Lebanese and many other immigrant minority groups) character of the Bankstown and Canterbury LGAs. This cultural geography of space in Sydney is critical to an accurate reading of the events of the Cronulla Beach riots.

# Table 1: Profile of Sutherland Shire, Bankstown and Canterbury Local Government Areas

| Birthplace | Sutherland Shire | Bankstown | Canterbury |
|---|---|---|---|
| Australia | 78.1% | 56.7% | 44.5% |
| Overseas | 21.9% | 43.3% | 55.5% |
| Middle East | 0.5% | 8.7% | 7.0% |
| Lebanon | 0.3% | 7.1% | 5.5% |
| **Ancestry** | | | |
| Anglo-Celtic* | 73.1% | 38.6% | 24.8% |
| Middle-Eastern** | 0.8% | 14.0% | 10.5% |
| **Language spoken at home** | | | |
| Speaks English only | 85.6% | 43.5% | 30.1% |
| Speaks another language | 14.4% | 56.5% | 69.9% |
| Speaks Arabic | 1.0% | 19.3% | 14.4% |
| **Religion** | | | |
| Christianity | 76.1% | 61.0% | 57.9% |
| Islam | 0.7% | 15.2% | 13.7% |

(Australian Bureau of Statistics, 2006)

*Summation of Ancestry responses 'Australian', 'English', 'Scottish' and 'Irish'

**Summation of Ancestry responses 'Lebanese' and 'Turkish'

A socio-economic profile of Sydney's Lebanese community shows that they are over-represented as small-business owners and among the unemployed. At the 2006 census the rate of entrepreneurship of first-generation Lebanese immigrant males in Sydney was nearly double that of the Sydney male average. Persistently high unemployment has also been suffered by Lebanese immigrants, particularly those of the Muslim faith. While the unemployment rate for the Australian-born was 7% in 1996, the unemployment rate of Arabic-speaking Christians in Sydney was 21.1% and for Arabic-speaking Muslims 31.1% (Collins, 2005: 201).

Lebanese-born people in the Australian labour market are also over-represented at the bottom end of the occupational spectrum ('labourers and related', **intermediate production and transport workers** occupations) and under-represented in the 'top end' occupations such as 'managers and administrators'. However, there is evidence of inter-generational improvement in the labour market profile of Sydney's Lebanese community. For second-generation Lebanese men and women, the rate of professional employment is about 50 % higher than their parents.

While many of those 'White Australians' who participated in the riot were not Shire residents, the character of the Shire's population is an important backdrop to understanding the question 'why Cronulla?'. The beach is the jewel of the Shire, a central part of the White identity of the area and a central location of recreational and social life for locals, particularly for young males, but also for families. Beach culture is a central part of the imaginary and actual life of Sydneysiders, not just those who are lucky enough to live in the beach-side suburbs. For half a century people from the mainly working class western and south-western suburbs of Sydney, particularly those without cars, had three choices if they wanted to visit the beach: catch the train and ferry to Manly beach on the north side of the Sydney Harbour, catch the train and bus to Bondi beach, the first beach on the south side, or catch the train to Cronulla beach, the only Sydney beach directly accessible by train.

Many White and immigrant 'westies' therefore traditionally went to Cronulla. When groups such as the Lebanese arrived in Sydney, they also took this ritual journey, often in extended family groups. As the children grew up, they continued this practice as they bought cars and travelled to Cronulla with their peers or young families. Cronulla locals never enjoyed this influx of 'westies', remaining resentful of the 'invasion' of their beach and fights between young males were common on the beach and in the streets. However, in the context of national and international events, the scene was set for something more serious to occur between White locals and the immigrant minorities living in Western Sydney. But one more element was central to the outbreak of the riots: the moral panic in Sydney about 'Middle Eastern crime'.

## Sydney's Middle Eastern Crime Context

In many ways the events of Cronulla beach in the summer of 2005 fed on years of media and political rhetoric about Middle Eastern crime and youth gangs in Sydney. Since the late 1990s a moral panic about 'ethnic crime' and 'youth gangs' has preoccupied the Sydney media and dominated NSW politics. A series of gang rapes in Sydney in 2000, for which a number of young Lebanese-Australian youth were convicted and sentenced severely, were portrayed by the media as 'race rapes', further intensifying the panic about Lebanese and Middle Eastern youth (Poynting et al., 2004). These media discourses on Lebanese and Middle Eastern crime led to an escalation of the fear of crime in Sydney at the very time that crime statistics in most areas are falling (Collins et al., 2002). Tim Priest (2004: 9), a former NSW Police Officer, typified the sensationalist approach: 'the rise of Middle Eastern organised crime in Sydney will have an impact on society unlike anything we have seen'.

Middle Eastern males were tagged as criminal and un-Australian by the media brush of *ethnic crime*. The problems of youth crime were racialised, with reports linking key events to a criminal Lebanese culture. In cosmopolitan societies like Australia it is true that many immigrants will be involved in crime, the critical question is whether some cultures are predisposed to criminal activity, a view that is presupposed by much media reportage about ethnic crime in Sydney, reportage which has generally equated *immigrant* or *ethnic* with *criminal*. In the public discourse on 'ethnic crime' in Sydney the accused – mostly second-generation immigrants – have been robbed of their nationality. In most media reportage, they are 'Lebanese' or 'Middle Eastern' and rarely, if ever, 'Australian'.

35

These events have formed the basis of cycles of moral panic (Cohen, 1973:9) which have centred around people of Arabic-speaking background and especially, but not exclusively, those of Muslim faith. Such panics have occurred in the past, often in relation to the (alleged) criminality of Chinese, Italian, Greek and other groups (Francis, 1981; Hazlehurst, 1987), though there has been an intensification of these waves since the late 1990s. They have been whipped up by the tabloid press, talk-back radio and opportunist politicians, with a subsequent increase in racial attacks in public places. In the context of the national and international events, Australia saw the construction of 'the Arab Other', as pathologically evil, inhuman, violent and criminal (Poynting et al., 2004). Such a construction was blind to the subtleties of differences between geography, region, religion and culture, lumping together people from diverse ancestries and histories into a homogeneous category of those of Arabic or Middle Eastern or Muslim background, in a totalising media discourse.

As a result of these associations, whole communities shared the burden of blame for crime and terrorism, for disrupting social cohesion and triggering the fear of the Anglo-Celtic mainstream. In assembling this 'Arab Other', the key ideological feature is the systematic 'dehumanising' of those involved, whether they be criminals, terrorists or refugees.

This approach robbed these immigrants of their Australian identity and shifted the focus on immigrant youth away from their victimhood and marginalisation – to being the perpetrators of crime and thus to be feared, scorned and excluded. This in turn diverted attention and funding away from important policy responses to crime; in this discourse, the criminality of individuals became the criminality of cultures. Following this logic, the policy response to such crime was not to be found in the socio-economic realm of policies designed to improve social inclusion of immigrant minorities (jobs, education or better living standards) nor in the realm of policing reform (to provide a more multicultural police force and tackle police racism). Rather the solution was to stop the further immigration of these (dysfunctional) immigrant minorities and to argue for the deportation of 'Middle Eastern' criminals, no matter whether they were Australian citizens or Australian-born. This was accompanied by calls for Imams to control *their* people:, the implication being that Australian society would not take responsibility for these criminals as it did for others, 'Middle Eastern' criminals were not 'our' problem, but 'theirs'. In this way the media construction of immigrant criminality supported negative, prejudicial stereotypes about immigrant communities, which, in turn threatened immigrants' safety. As Bowling and Phillips (2002:14) argued in relation to Britain: 'racist violence has a significant impact on minority communities, leaving them insecure and avoiding many public places for fear of attack'.

The HREOC consultation with Australia's Arab and Muslim communities reported that 47% of respondents felt they had been vilified by the media, complaining of stereotyping and the use of ethnic or religious labels in crime-reporting (HREOC, 2004: 64). Similarly, the Anti-Discrimination Board of NSW (2003) reviewed media coverage of race relations including refugee issues in the wake of the Tampa incident; and other issues affecting Muslim communities. The report concluded that 'It serves governments well when media coverage of crime is racialised, because attention is diverted from the inadequacies of government policies and programs in addressing the underlying causes of criminal behaviour' (Anti-Discrimination Board of NSW (2003:59). While there is evidence of political opportunism in relation to the immigrant or ethnic crime issue in New South Wales state politics since 1998 (Collins et al., 2000 37-54; Poynting et al., 2004: 11-51), it is also evident that this is not a new phenomenon. Writing a decade earlier, Duncan Chappell, the Director of the Australian Institute of Criminology, commented in the foreword to a study on crime prevention and migrant communities :

'In the past a rather gloomy picture of close-knit migrant communities, particularly in urban or industrial areas, has been painted. Biased media reporting and prejudice in wider society has depicted minority group enclaves as suffering from crime, disorder and inter-cultural conflict' (Hazlehurst, 1990: v).

Central to the media coverage of Middle Eastern or Lebanese crime in Sydney over the last decade is the concern about ethnic criminal gangs, particularly youth gangs. It is useful therefore to look at the reportage of 'gang' behaviour related to the Cronulla riots, and to compare and contrast this to that of other similar violent events - 'riots', involving groups of mainly young men in Sydney in recent years. It is also important to look at the evidence for ethnic youth gangs in Sydney, Middle Eastern or otherwise.

Sydney has had a number of events characterised as 'riots' by the media and politicians. One incident occurred in 2004 in inner-city Redfern near 'The Block', a traditional centre for Aboriginal settlement in Sydney, following the death by impalement of a young Koori boy after an alleged police chase. In the days that followed Aboriginal youth and elders clashed violently with police. Another riot occurred in the poor but largely White outer south-western suburb of Macquarie Fields in early March 2005 when youths went on a rampage for days burning cars and confronting police. In neither case were groups of youths constructed as gangs.

In the Cronulla riots, thousands of mainly White, young males gathered in response to calls to 'take back our beaches'. There was detailed footage of the mob violence directed against Middle Eastern Australian but no-one referred to '(White) youth gangs' in the reportage of the events or the subsequent mulling over of causes and effects. It was possible in this instance, as in the Macquarie Fields and Redfern riots, to focus on youth, masculinity, alcohol and violence and to see the individuals outside of gang structures, discipline and (violent) culture. But when it came to reporting the retaliation by 'Middle Eastern' men the following night it was clear that 'ethnic gangs' were back in town.

What is obvious is the social construction of ethnicity and of gangs that emerges from these events. 'Ethnic' means 'problem' and 'gang' means 'ethnic', a spurious linking of common cultural heritage and the experiences of immigration. When young males who are clearly not from just one ethnic minority are involved, the gangs disappear from the discourse. The conclusion is that we panic in a disproportionate way about ethnic gangs, mistaking the phenomenon of immigrant youth hanging out in public spaces as evidence of a plethora of ethnic youth gangs.

There is some research to support this conclusion. A survey of 445 youths who mainly lived in the south western suburbs of Sydney, with 80% of respondents from a non-English speaking background, found that only one in ten of the youth respondents who stated that they hang around in public spaces in Sydney's suburbs defined their friendship group as a gang (Collins et al., 2002:59), suggesting an exaggeration in the public mind about the number of ethnic youth gangs. This does not deny that there are criminal and youth gangs which have ethnicity as the common denominator, but it does suggest that many of the youth gathered together in public spaces such as shopping malls are not members of gangs. This stands in sharp contradistinction to the moral panic about ethnic criminal gangs that has dominated Sydney media for a decade.

## Cronulla, racism and Australian multiculturalism

How do we interpret the events of the Cronulla riots in terms of Australian social cohesion and racism? Some see the events of Cronulla as proof that Australia's immigration and settlement policies are not working. To some extent this is a cruel irony, since multiculturalism which was the philosophy and practice relating to immigrant settlement in Australia since the mid-1970s (Collins, 1991; Castles et al., 1988), has been systematically dismantled since the early 1990s (Collins, 1995) - most intensely following the election of the Howard government in 1996. In 2007 the Government changed the Department of Immigration and Multicultural Affairs to the Department of Immigration and Citizenship. Following the election of the Rudd Labor Government in late 2007, the future of multiculturalism as a policy framework for immigrant settlement in Australia is still unclear.

It could be argued that the events at Cronulla require more multiculturalism, not less, the roots of much of the disquiet among Middle Eastern youth in Australia lie in the realm of socio-economic disadvantage, although cultural disaffection is also part of the picture, particularly given the moral panic about the Middle Eastern 'Other', masculinity also figures highly. Strategies related to education, employment, local facilities, policing and media are more likely to yield positive results than incessantly chanting the dysfunctionality of some immigrant communities. For decades the guts of multiculturalism has lain in policies and programs to help new immigrants at school, in the community and at work. Their intention has been social justice for all, irrespective of language, cultural or religious background. Today we see the need for a revitalisation of Australian multiculturalism, not an abandonment of it in the face of a racialised discourse about immigrant crime.

Of course not all can be laid at the feet of socio-economic disadvantage and the issue of racism has come into the spotlight following Cronulla. The racialisation of immigrant minorities in Australia is as old as the history of immigration, but racialised immigrant minorities are today unlikely to lie down, roll over and take it, especially if they were born in Australia. As Ghassan Hage (2008) has argued, these youth are too assimilated to not demand their rights and fight for what should be theirs. To his credit, NSW Premier Iemma criticised the racism of the White crowds, and labelled their behaviour as un-Australian. Clearly there is racism among, but not exclusive to, Whites in Australian society; and racism has also emerged from within Middle Eastern communities, as well as from and between many other minorities. This serves to highlight the fact that anti-racism must be a central plank of Australian multiculturalism and policy, and that innovative programs to renew Australian multiculturalism in spirit and practice are required.

Other commentators have seen in the events of Cronulla a fulfilment of Blainey's (1984) prophesy that there will be blood in the streets of the suburbs with a large immigrant settlement. According to this argument, taking in non-British immigrants is an historical mistake, a recipe for social conflict. However, the fact that the events of Cronulla are so unique is itself strong evidence for the counterview that, despite all odds, Australia's ethnic diversity has largely occurred without conflict. Social cohesion has been the main trend in cosmopolitan Sydney in the past sixty years of increasingly diverse immigration. People from all corners of the globe live in Sydney and at any moment some of the places from where Sydney's immigrants came will be in conflict, yet rarely does this international conflict overflow into the streets.

It was popular to read into the Los Angeles riots in 1992 the lesson that ethnic diversity will inevitably bring conflict. But the lesson is in fact that unless everything is done to ensure that new immigrants have as much opportunity at work and in society as non-immigrants ethnic diversity will probably lead to conflict. The USA does not have the Australian tradition of multicultural programs to assist immigrants to settle and become economically secure. In this sense Australian multiculturalism is the safety net that has helped steer our culturally diverse society towards social cohesion and away from social conflict between ethnic groups. After the Cronulla riots we need more multiculturalism, not less.

## References

Anti-Discrimination Board of New South Wales (2003) *Race for the Headlines: racism and media discourse* Anti-Discrimination Board of New South Wales, Sydney.

Australian Bureau of Statistics. (2006), accessed 9 June 2009, http://abs.gov.au/websitedbs/d3310114.nsf/Home/census

Blainey, G. (1984) *All For Australia*, Methuen, North Ryde.

Bowling, B. and Phillips, C. (2002) *Racism, Crime and Justice* Longman Press; Harrow.

Burnley, I. (2001) *The Impact of Immigration on Australia: A Demographic Approach* Oxford University Press, South Melbourne.

Castles, S., Kalantzis, M., Cope, B. and Morrissey, M. (1988) *Mistaken Identity – Multiculturalism and the Demise of Nationalism in Australia* Pluto Press, Sydney.

Cohen, S. (1973) Folk Devils and Moral Panics: The Creation of the Mods and Rockers  St. Martin's Press, New York.

Collins, J. (1991) Migrant Hands in a Distant Land: Australia's Post-war Immigration 2nd Edn, Pluto Press, Sydney.

Collins, J. (1995) 'Immigration and the Keating Government', in Hogan, M. and Dempsey, K. (eds.) *Equity and Citizenship Under Keating* Public Affairs Research Centre, University of Sydney: 88-116.

Collins J. (2005) 'From Beirut to Bankstown: The Lebanese Diaspora in Multicultural Australia', in Tabar, P. (ed.) *Lebanese Diaspora: History, Racism and Belonging* Lebanese American University, Beirut: 187-211.

Collins, J., and Castillo, A. (1998) *Cosmopolitan Sydney: Exploring the world in one city* Pluto Press, Sydney.

Collins, J., and Poynting, S. (eds.) (2000) The Other Sydney: Communities, Identities and Inequalities in Western Sydney Common Ground, Melbourne.

Collins, J., Noble, G., Poynting, S. and Tabar, P. (2000) *Kebabs, Kids, Cops and Crime: Youth Ethnicity and Crime* Pluto Press, Sydney.

Collins, J., Noble, G., Poynting, S. and Tabar, P. (2002) *Gangs, Crime and Community Safety: Perceptions and Experiences in Multicultural Australia* UTS Centre for Transforming Culture and UTS School of Finance and Economics, Broadway.

Francis, R. (1981) *Migrant Crime in Australia* University of Queensland Press, St. Lucia.

Goot, M. (1988) 'Immigrants and Immigration: Evidence and Arguments from the Polls 1943-87',

in CAAIP, Commitment to Australia: Consultants' Report, AGPS, Canberra.

Hage, G. (1998) White Nation: Fantasies of White supremacy in a multicultural society Pluto Press, Sydney.

Hage, G. (2008) 'Explosive Selves: On Second Generation Experiences of Racism', *Youth Identity and Migration: Culture, Values and Social Connectedness* Symposium, Deakin University, 21 February.

Hazlehurst, K. (1987) *Migration, Ethnicity and Crime in Australian Society* Australian Institute of Criminology, Canberra.

Hazlehurst, K. (1990) *Crime Prevention and Migrant Communities* Australian Institute of Criminology, Canberra.

Human Rights and Equal Opportunity Commission (2004) *Isma̱ɛ-Listen : National consultations on eliminating prejudice against Arab and Muslim Australians,* Human Rights and Equal Opportunity Commission, Sydney.

Jupp, J., Mcrobbie, A. and York, B. (1991) *Metropolitan ghettoes and ethnic concentration, Working Papers on Multiculturalism No. 1* (2 vols) Office of Multicultural Affairs and the University of Wollongong, Wollongong.

Markus, A. (2001) *Race: John Howard and the remaking of Australia* Allen and Unwin, Crows Nest.

Marr, D. and Wilkinson, M. (2003) *Dark Victory* Allen and Unwin, Sydney.

One Nation (1998) *Pauline Hanson's One Nation Policy Document Immigration Population and Social Cohesion* 27 August, accessed 9 June 2009, http://www.gwb.com.au/onenation/policy/immig.html

Poynting, S., Noble, G., Tabar, P. and Collins, J. (2004) *Bin Laden in the suburbs: Criminalising the Arab Other* Sydney Institute of Criminology, Sydney.

Priest, T. (2004) 'The Rise of Middle Eastern Crime in Australia', *Quadrant* January-February: 9-16.

Rimmer, S. (1991) *The Costs of Multiculturalism* Flinders Press, Bedford Park.

Sheehan, P. (1998) Among the Barbarians: The Dividing of Australia Random House, Sydney.

Sheehan, P. (2006) *Girls Like You* Macmillan, Sydney.

UTS Shopfront (2005) Building Bridges: Community relations in NSW after September 11, 2001 University of Technology, Sydney.

# Chapter three

# Scouring the shire

## Scott Poynting

### 'Ethnic cleansing' at Cronulla

On the sweltering Sunday afternoon of 11th December, 2005 at Cronulla beach, an alcohol-fuelled throng, widely estimated as five thousand strong, violently attacked beachgoers and passers-by identified as being of 'Middle Eastern appearance' (King and Box, 2005: 1; Murphy, 2005: 4). Intervening police and paramedics tending the injured, were also attacked, with fists, feet and bottles; they attested that it was sheer luck that no-one was killed in what Moses (2006) identifies as a 'pogrom'. A young Arab-background man was beaten and had bottles smashed across his back, another youth was found by police, bashed and lying in a puddle of blood, residents looked on while a group of men jumped on another victim's head (Overington and Warne-Smith, 2005: 20). By the Sunday night, at least thirteen people were reported injured and twelve had been arrested (Kennedy et al., 2005: 1). The *Sydney Morning Herald*, perhaps with more hyperbole than history, called it 'possibly Australia's biggest racist protest since vigilante miners killed two Chinese at Lambing Flat in 1860' (Murphy, 2005: 4).

A protest regarding an earlier incident was how the day's events had started out. A fight had occurred on the beach the previous Sunday between three off-duty surf lifesavers and a group of Lebanese-background young men, involving taunts and eventually a physical exchange (Michaels, 2006). This is how the *'Hazzard Report'* – the review of the policing response to the riots overseen by Norm Hazzard, the then Assistant Commissioner for Counter Terrorism and Public Order Management – described this initial incident:

> About 3 pm three Caucasian members of the North Cronulla Surf

Life Saving Club ... had just completed duty on North Cronulla Beach and were walking in the direction of the club house ... It would appear that as the three members of the surf club passed the group of Middle Eastern men, the members of each group were staring at each other. A verbal exchange took place in which a member from each group accused the other of staring at him. At this time one of the Middle Eastern men said to [one of the lifesavers] in response to the staring accusation, 'I'm allowed to, now f"*k off and leave our beach'. [The lifesaver] said during this verbal exchange, 'I come down here out of my own spare time to save you dumb c**ts from drowning, now piss off you scum'. As this verbal confrontation took place the Middle Eastern group formed a half-circle around the Caucasian males. There was an attempt by one of the Middle Eastern men to calm the situation and it appeared that he had been successful and the confrontation was over. However, at this time the Middle Eastern male who was involved in the initial verbal altercation swung a punch at [one of the lifesavers] which missed. Some pushing then occurred between both groups which escalated to a fight. (Strike Force Neil, 2006: 26)

Another, on-duty lifesaver saw the incident and ran to assist. The alleged main offender from the Lebanese group fled, and the victims had to be treated for bruising and other injuries. Conflict over territory is not unusual in male youth cultures, but the popular media, notably tabloid newspapers and talk-back radio, spent the following week exaggerating the numbers involved, the brutality of the attack, the extent of injuries, and the frequency of such events, and racialising all of these as aspects of the inherent criminality and deviant masculinity of Lebanese-Australian young men. The process spiralled into a classic moral panic, and numerous moral entrepreneurs called for a crackdown on 'Middle Eastern' thugs.

The right-wing Labor New South Wales (NSW) government rehearsed its well-worn response to tabloid crime-fear campaigns, with get-tough gestures in the 'law and order auction'. Premier Morris Iemma announced a ludicrous 25-year maximum jail sentence for assaults on lifesavers. Over the following week, the now infamous 'demonstration' was organised for the subsequent weekend, to 'reclaim' Cronulla beach from the incivility and lawlessness of the 'Middle Eastern Other'. Commercial radio 2UE's talk-back announcer Steve Price called it 'a community show of force'; the *Daily Telegraph* announced 'the battle of the beach'. The Assistant Commissioner of Police, recalling how he spent his youth surfing at Cronulla, pledged to defend the Australian way of life at the beach, and explained that:

> 'The Australian way is about coming to the beach with your towel and sunscreen, and maybe a book, and lying back and relaxing. … It is not about congregating and swarming in groups for any sort of anti-social behaviour' (Gee and McIlveen, 2005: 1).

A campaign of mobile phone text messages was mounted over that week, targeting residents of the surrounding Sutherland Shire, and inciting racial violence for the coming weekend. There is suggestion that extreme right-wing White supremacist groups were active in distributing these texts; certainly members of these groups were conspicuous in inciting violence from the 5,000-strong mob during the affray (Hannan and Baker, 2005; Huxley, 2005; King, 2005, *Sydney Morning Herald,* 2005). The *Telegraph* dutifully reprinted one such message in its pages, taking it to the readership of the largest circulation newspaper in NSW: 'This Sunday every Aussie in the Shire get down to North Cronulla to help support Leb and wog bashing day. … Bring your mates and let's show them that this is our beach and they are never welcome. … let's kill these boys'. The broadsheet *Sydney Morning Herald,* while showing disapproval, saw fit to publish this message the very day before the riots, including its exhortation, 'Let's show them that this is our beach … Let's claim back our shire'. Right-wing talk-back radio personality, Alan Jones, had read out the same text message on 2GB during the highest-rating commercial breakfast program: 'Come to Cronulla this weekend to take revenge…,' and he responded with approbation to racist vigilantism from talk-back callers. In fact, when the campaign to 'reclaim' Cronulla beach was in full cry that week, Jones attempted to reclaim the kudos, boasting, 'I'm the person that's led this charge' (Marr, 2005).

Many came to the 'demonstration' prepared for confrontation; one young man wore a t-shirt inscribed 'ethnic cleansing unit'. Exaggeration aside, there was no doubt that many of the self-defined 'Aussie' protagonists wanted to clear 'their' iconic space, the beach, of the intruding Other, variously described as 'Lebs', 'wogs', and Muslims. One local 'hero', 42-year-old ex-rugby league player Glen Steele, shouted to the crowd to 'Get Lebs off the beach' and 'No Lebs in Sutherland Shire'. The mob chanted, 'F--- off Lebs' and 'F--- off, wogs' (Overington and Warne-Smith, 2005: 20; *Daily Telegraph,* 2005: 5). One victim recounted to a *Herald* reporter that the violence had broken out when a 'Lebanese' young man and his girlfriend were walking along the beachfront, and 'two girls turned around and screamed, "Lebanese get off our f---ing beaches"'; then 'the whole street turned on us', according to Mustafa, a bloodied and bruised 19-year-old victim (Brown, 2005: 7). One 16-year-old Cronulla girl told a *Daily Telegraph* journalist, 'I hate the Lebs. Today I punched one fat girl in the face'. We just want them off our beaches' (Carswell, 2005: 21).

For such participants, if we accept their own words, the mode of delivery of the message, and the method of removal of the offending 'outsiders', was always intended to be violent. For 18-year-old Daniel, 'My main point in being here is to bash as many Lebs as I can'. He claimed to have travelled to Cronulla at 7am from Bangor in the western bushland of Sutherland Shire, and to have 'snotted the first Leb of the day' (Carswell, 2005: 21). Muslims were also targeted: Marcus, a 28-year-old builder from Penrith in western Sydney, according to the *Herald,* wore a singlet with the words, 'Mahommid was a camel f---ing faggot', and raised his arms triumphantly, shouting 'F--- off Leb', as a young woman pursued by a frenzied mob of a thousand had her hijab torn from her head by a bare chested young man in board shorts, in the cause of that Australian value, respect for women (Murphy, 2005: 4).

Two Bangladeshi students, unlikely bearers of 'Middle Eastern appearance' but probably suspected of being Muslims, were chased up the street by the violent melee, and managed to escape in their car, though it was attacked and pelted with bottles. 'Where's those Muslims? I'm going to kill them?', shouted a man hefting a carton of beer on his shoulder while running towards the railway station, where, the rumour had circulated, a trainload of 'Lebs' was to arrive. Two young men of 'Middle Eastern appearance', on their way for a swim, were mobbed on one invaded train carriage, and savagely bashed (Overington and Warne-Smith, 2005: 20; Greenhill, 2005:

28; Jones, 2005: 4). A Cronulla local, a 19-year-old young woman, said, 'We are here to support the Shire and get these Lebs off our beaches. This is God's country, and it's time they left' (Carswell, 2005: 21).

## The denizens of 'God's country'

'God's country' is indeed what the locals call Cronulla and the surrounding Sutherland Shire and not all of them in jest. One Cronulla businessman told ABC television in all seriousness in January 2006 that there should be road spikes deployed electronically on the three roads to and from Cronulla to trap lawless outsiders (*7:30 Report*, 2006); he was proposing to levy locals $10 per week each to fund a vigilante squad networked by mobile phones. This insular, possessive and exclusionary attitude did not first arise in 2006. Gabrielle Carey (2005:25), who co-authored a fictionalised account of the Cronulla youth surfing culture in *Puberty Blues* (Lette and Carey, 1979) recently recalled these attributes from her local experience there about three decades ago. In 1989, local surf club informants gave the following 'tip' to the *Sydney Morning Herald* beach guide, indicating incidentally their view of outsiders, 'kids railing in from west and south western suburbs', as the source of tension on the beach: 'Steer clear of the aggro between different ethnic groups because the pushing and shoving sometimes turns ugly' (Monaghan and Rutherford, 1989: 20). In February 2004, a letter-writer to the *Sunday Telegraph*, from a Cronulla address, challenged one of the paper's reporters

> ... to visit one of our beachside parks in the Sutherland Shire (preferably Gunnamatta, Shelly or Cronulla Park) on a Sunday afternoon, when she will find that 90 per cent of the visitors are of Middle Eastern origin: then drop by again at dusk to inspect the remains left by the 'westies' and 'wogs' (Beecham, 2004: 13).

In 2004, a self-proclaimed proud, longstanding Cronulla resident wrote to the *Daily Telegraph*:

> The people from this area are fiercely protective of our home and stick together because the Shire is highly regarded as a great place to live and we want to keep it that way.

It is not in any way 'rough around the edges'. The area has some of the best, most expensive waterfront and beachside real estate in Sydney, easily rivalling anything in Bondi. It is hardly like the western suburbs of Belmore and Canterbury.

Cronulla is the only beach suburb with a train station. We have had to endure a constant influx of people from other areas for a long time. If the locals could have our way, we would keep the area to ourselves (De Vere, 2004: 32).

The Cronulla beaches are indeed the only ones of Sydney's 47-odd ocean beaches that are accessible by railway. They lie on a peninsula at the southern-most end of the Sydney coastline, bounded by Botany Bay to the north and Port Hacking to the south, framed by sand dunes and bushland, with national parks north and south.

Cronulla is also something of a peninsula demographically, remarkably set apart from the cultural diversity of Sydney. The 2006 census results for Cronulla show that less than a third as many Cronulla residents were born in a non-English-speaking country than for the Sydney Statistical Division overall (7.3% compared to 24.0%). There were 1.9% recording non-Christian religion compared to Sydney's 10.9%, with, for example, 0.4% Muslims compared to 3.9% for Sydney. The proportion who speak a language other than English at home was 6.8% for Cronulla; 29.3% for Sydney. Those who speak Arabic (the most commonly spoken language in Sydney apart from English and the Chinese languages) at home comprise 0.2% of the population of Cronulla, contrasting notably with 3.9%, for the Sydney Statistical Division, 19.5 times that percentage (Australian Bureau of Statistics, 2006).

## Wog-bashing without racism

In the aftermath of the riot, moral entrepreneurs ranging from local politicians to the Prime Minister denied, in the face of the obvious, that racism was the underlying factor in these events. We need to explain this refusal to recognise blinding reality and we need to explain its purchase on common sense; if it wasn't racism, what was it? The predominant alternative offered returned to the account which had preceded the events of December 5th and rapidly supplanted the response of shock and shame over the racist riot: this narrative described how local residents had become understandably exasperated with the bad behaviour, including incivility, aggressiveness and disrespect for women, of Lebanese-background young men on the beach, and had acted out of desperation in the absence of action by the police.

Opponents of multiculturalism held its policies and values to blame in a popular philosophy that has been vying for intellectual and moral leadership in matters of ethnic relations since about 1996 (see the discussions in Poynting and Mason, 2006, 2008). This philosophy posits that multiculturalism is culpable for its moral relativism which indulges backward and often essentially misogynist cultures, instead of obliging them to integrate with civilised values or at least demonstrate civility in public comportment. The claim is commonly made by supporters of this view that the 'political correctness' associated with multiculturalism led police (and officials and media and politicians) to accord special privileges to undeserving or even deviant others, for fear of being labelled as 'racist'. Multiculturalism, it is claimed, has disparaged 'traditional' Anglo-Celtic Australian culture and downgraded associated identities, damaging national pride and national unity. Prime Minister John Howard's pointed refusal to acknowledge the racism behind the mob violence at Cronulla was bound up in this type of attacking, undermining and dismantling of multiculturalism which had been at work since the election campaign that brought him to office in 1996. It remains to be seen how much this might be reversed under the new Rudd Labor Government elected in November 2007 (Poynting and Mason, 2008; *Daily Telegraph*, 2007).

The right-wing columnists who unwaveringly supported the Howard government were in no doubt that multiculturalism, not racism, lay behind the Cronulla violence. Piers Akerman wrote, in the *Daily Telegraph* (2005: 18):

> The attack on a surf patrol on Cronulla beach a week ago was the notional trigger for Sunday's events, but the tangled roots of anger lie deep within the failed multicultural policies foisted on an unsuspecting nation decades back. Though sold with the help of such anodyne ditties as I Am, You Are, We Are Australian, it has long been apparent that many people from certain migrant groups –

notably Lebanese and Muslim – neither think of themselves as Aussies nor wish to embrace the extraordinary tolerance identified as a remarkable Australian trait.

Likewise Miranda Devine in the *Sydney Morning Herald* (2006):

> ... this week Sydney courts began to hear evidence against Arab-Australian youths charged with violent reprisal attacks after the Cronulla riots on December 11. ... Thanks to an epidemic of similar law and order problems in other Western democracies with Muslim immigrant populations, even left-wing liberals are beginning to join the dots, and question multiculturalism. It is not the 'culturally diverse community, united by an overriding and unifying commitment to Australia' as the Prime Minister, John Howard, put it in his Australia Day address, which is being questioned, but a welfare-driven ideology, corrupted by politicians chasing the ethnic vote, which has encouraged separate identities.

This sort of right-wing attack representing multiculturalism as elitist, fostering disloyalty and disunity, encouraging unacceptable otherness, and unfairly offering special privileges to indigenous and immigrant minorities at the expense of deserving and often needy mainstream Australians was the stock-in-trade of former Liberal Party candidate Pauline Hanson in 1996, and the anti-immigration One Nation party that she later founded. Though he expelled Hanson from the Liberal Party during the election campaign of that year, John Howard took pains to recognise publicly, as deeply held and genuine, the views of the up to ten per cent of voters that her supporters represented, and to defend their rights to express these against the censorship of so-called 'political correctness'. Nor did the Labor Party under Kim Beazley's leadership vigorously defend multiculturalism against these attacks. Two and a half decades of virtually bipartisan political support for multiculturalism were increasingly abandoned from then on.

The Howard Coalition successfully adopted many Hansonite approaches, most spectacularly in the 'boat people' panic and the Tampa crisis of 2001, simply rendering One Nation redundant, and the Labor Party, for want of distinguishing features, irrelevant. Hanson's supporters always resented and refused the label 'racist'and Howard himself had been deeply wounded in an earlier period in the 1980s when he was accused of racism for lending support to the claims of Geoffrey Blainey and others that the level of Asian immigration to Australia was too high. By 2001, his populist instincts (and doubtless his pollsters and advisors) told him that rankling at the 'racist' label was widely shared amongst the public. After Cronulla, Howard declared that racism 'is a word that's flung around carelessly and I'm simply not going to do it' (Kerin and Leys, 2005: 4). The causes of the riot, for him, lay in the 'large number of people and a large amount of alcohol' and 'an accumulated sense of grievance' (Howard, 2005: 18).

Thus, after some days of public remorse and shame over the anti-'Middle Eastern' mob violence, the focus of media and political attention returned to the story of the deviance and incivility of so-called 'gangs' of Lebanese or Muslim youths. The disproportionate bulk of media reports and political spin ever since has concerned the revenge riots of the Sunday night and the Monday, involving convoys of young men coming in cars from the southwest suburbs around Bankstown, Punchbowl and Lakemba, wreaking property damage and vicious assaults on presumed Anglos in beachside Cronulla, Brighton-le-Sands and Maroubra. The language of 'thugs' and 'grubs' from NSW Opposition and Government alike, returned to the terms of the moral panics over ethnic gangs which had circulated since the mid-1990s, criminalising the Arab and then the Muslim Other, and repeating the populist bidding war over law and order (Collins et al., 2000; Poynting et al., 2004). Then NSW Opposition Leader Peter Debnam echoed the tabloids in complaining that the '200 Middle Eastern thugs' he claimed were associated with the revenge attacks and were known to police, were being indulged through political correctness instead of receiving the zero tolerance treatment they deserved. He postured, that, if elected: 'at dawn ... on the 25th of March, my instruction to the police commissioner will be to take as many police as you need and charge them with anything to get them off the streets' (Clennell, 2006b). In fact, in proportion to the 5,000 or so involved in the anti-immigrant racist violence, these two hundred-odd were receiving far more than their share of police and criminal justice attention. At the time Debnam was saying this, some 51 people had been charged in relation to the original racist mob violence, and 53 in relation to the reprisal attacks (Clennell, 2006a).

It was no surprise that the right-wing commentariat claimed equivalence between the premeditated racist violence of a 5,000-strong mob on the afternoon of 11 December, and the spontaneous (though also very violent and arbitrary) revenge rampage by a couple of hundred youths that night and the next day – that's when they were not saying the 'Middle Eastern' perpetrators were worse. More surprising is that similar views were advanced by the social-democratically inclined David Burchell, sometime editor of *Australian Left Review* and now an editor of *Australian Universities Review*, in which he wrote of 'equally damaging and violent revenge attacks', which should be considered 'in the same light', and which he castigated 'Marxists' and multiculturalists for overlooking (Burchell, 2006). Burchell also incidentally referred to the motivation for the 'rally' as an 'apparently motiveless assault of a surf lifeguard' ,2006:6). There were in fact two (off-duty) surf club *lifesavers* assaulted – not one *lifeguard* (who are council employees). Moreover, it had been reported that 'police are not treating Sunday's bashing as completely unprovoked', having involved the racial taunts discussed above and some 'what are you looking at' masculine aggressiveness from the lifesavers (McIlveen and Downie, 2005: 2).

The State Opposition Leader Peter Debnam accused the Labor Government of going soft on Lebanese gangs to curry favour with constituents of its (alleged) ethnically stacked branches around Lakemba. In reality, Labor Governments for three terms of office under Bob Carr had led the charge to racialise crime and perpetrate the populist ethnic targeting of high-profile zero tolerance gestures (Poynting and Mason, 2006). This, as much as the federal government's manipulation of xenophobia over the same period, from 'Middle Eastern' boat people to the 'war on terror', contributed to the intercommunal conflict at Cronulla.

Ex NSW Police Commissioner, Ken Moroney, musing prior to his impending retirement, reflected recently that the Cronulla riots resulted from 'a lack of manners and values among the young' (Kearney, 2006: 3). Still in the office of police commissioner, he bought into the 'values debate', saying that immigrants should have the courtesy to embrace 'our traditions', and had no excuse for not learning English. He gave the example of a 'good migrant' who at least had the decency to apologise to him for talking her foreign language in front of him and his grandson in a milk bar (McIlveen, 2006: 19).

Meanwhile, in the Federal sphere, the Department of Immigration and Multicultural Affairs[1] put out a booklet, helpfully advising immigrants what manners will be expected of them in Australia (Burke, 2006). Among other things, they are counselled not to spit in the street or slaughter animals in their backyard and not surprisingly both these iconic examples of immigrant transgression can be found in *All for Australia* by John Howard's old mate Geoffrey Blainey (1984) who warned that, if we weren't careful, we'd have riots in the suburbs and blood in the streets.

The fact that politicians, senior police and immigration bureaucrats were reprising Blainey's discredited dystopia shows the extent of the systematic white-anting and dismantling of multiculturalism that had occurred over the previous decade. It was not the reality of cultural diversity, but that destructive attack on the culture and policies of Australia's ethnic affairs disposition which had been effective over thirty years – and the attendant manipulation of racism for political advantage – that led to the Cronulla riots.

# References

Akerman, P. (2005) 'Cracks then a hole between cultures', *Daily Telegraph*, 13 December: 18.

Australian Bureau of Statistics. (2006), accessed 9 June 2009, http://abs.gov.au/websitedbs/d3310114.nsf/Home/census

Beecham, D. (2004) 'Cost of the clean-up', letter to the editor, *Sunday Telegraph*, 8 February: 13.

Blainey, G. (1984) *All for Australia* Methuen Haynes, Sydney.

Brown, M. (2005) 'A day at the beach becomes a nightmare', *Sydney Morning Herald*, 12 December: 7.

Burchell, D. (2006) 'An email from the ether: after the Cronulla events', *Australian Universities Review* 48, 2: 6-8.

Burke, N. (2006) 'Migrant guide to BYO Aussie manners', *Daily Telegraph* 21 September: 38.

Carey, G. (2005) 'Cronulla – and the blues – revisited, easily recognised', *Sydney Morning Herald*, 17-18 December: 25.

Carswell, A. (2005) 'Dangerous cocktail of racism and hate', *Daily Telegraph*, 12 December: 21.

Clennell, A. (2006a) 'Police tough on both sides of Cronulla riots', *Sydney Morning Herald* 19 July: 2.

Clennell, A. (2006b) 'Police to Debnam – thug plan not arresting', *Sydney Morning Herald* 20 July: 1.

Collins, J., Noble, G., Poynting, S. and Tabar, P. (2000) *Kebabs, Kids, Cops and Crime: Youth, Ethnicity and Crime* Pluto Press, Sydney.

*Daily Telegraph* (2005) 'Gangs are the problem, cries local', *Daily Telegraph*, 12 December: 5.

*Daily Telegraph* (2007) 'Howard drops multiculturalism', 23 January. *Daily Telegraph,* accessed 9 June 2009,

http://www.news.com.au/dailytelegraph/story/0,22049,21105650-5001028,00.html

De Vere, D. (2004) 'The Bulldogs are not our team', letter to the editor, *Daily Telegraph*, 29 September: 32.

Devine, M. (2006) 'Time to confront failures, not ignore them', *Sydney Morning Herald*, 26 January: 13.

Gee, S. and McIlveen, L. (2005) 'Not on our beach', *Daily Telegraph*, 9 December: 1

Greenhill, C. (2005) 'Eyewitness to onslaught on the track', *Daily Telegraph*, 17 December: 28, 61.

Hannan, E. and Baker, R. (2005) 'Nationalists boast of their role on the beach', *Age*, 13 December, accessed 9 June 2009, http://www.theage.com.au/news/national/nationalists-boast-of-their-role-on-the-beach/2005/12/12/1134236003135.html

Howard, J. (2005) 'Call it what you will, it's hate and it's ugly', *Daily Telegraph*, 13 December: 18.

Huxley, J. (2005) 'Who'd have thought it – Blinky Bill, the face of race hatred', *Sydney Morning Herald*, 13 December: 5.

Jones, G. (2005) 'Police feared thugs would kill victims of wild attacks', *Daily Telegraph*, 1 December: 4-5.

Kearney, S. (2006) 'Ice worse than heroin, says top cop', *Australian*, 25 September:

Kennedy, L., Murphy, D., Brown, M. and Colquhoun, T. (2005) 'Race riots explode', *Sydney Morning Herald*, 12 December: 1-4.

Kerin, J. and Leys, N. (2005) 'We're not a bunch of racists, PM says', *Australian*, 13 December: 4.

King, D. (2005) 'Far-right groups admit role', *Australian*, 13 December: 4.

King, D. and Box, D. (2005) 'Lebanese bashed as mob rampages through beach suburb. Revenge attacks in race war'. *Australian*, 12 December: 6.

Lette, K. and Carey,G. (1979) *Puberty Blues* McPhee Gribble, Melbourne.

Marr, D. (2005) 'Alan Jones: I'm the person that's led this charge' *Age* December 13, accessed 1 May 2006, http://www.theage.com.au/news/national/alan-jones-i-led-this-charge /2005/12/12/1134236003153.html

McIlveen, L. (2006) 'Ken's mission to leave the law in order', *Daily Telegraph*, 25 September: 19.

McIlveen, L. and Downie, S. (2005) 'Second beach brawl – Police call for calm as locals plot revenge', *Daily Telegraph*, 8 December: 2.

Michaels, F. (2006) 'Australia: Police report reveals real instigators of Cronulla race riots', *World Socialist Website*, 30 November, accessed 9 June 2009,

http://www.wsws.org/articles/2006/nov2006/rio1-n30.shtml

Monaghan, D. and Rutherford, N. (1989) 'On the beaches', *Sydney Morning Herald*, 26 December: 20.

Moses, D. (2006) 'Pogrom talk'. *On Line Opinion* 11 January, accessed 9 June 2009,

http://www.onlineopinion.com.au/print.asp?article=4038

Murphy, D. (2005), 'Thugs ruled the streets, and the mob sang Waltzing Matilda', *Sydney Morning Herald*, 12 December: 4-5.

Overington, C. and Warne-Smith, D. (2005) 'Countdown to conflict', *Weekend Australian*: 17, 20.

Poynting, S., Noble, G., Tabar, P. and Collins, J. (2004) *Bin Laden in the Suburbs: Criminalising the Arab Other* Sydney Institute of Criminology, Sydney.

Poynting, S. and Mason, V. (2006), "'Tolerance, freedom, justice and peace"?: Britain, Australia and anti-Muslim racism since 11th September 2001', *Journal of Intercultural Studies 27*, 4: 365-392.

Poynting, S. and Mason, V. (2008) 'The New Integrationism, the State and Islamophobia: Retreat from Multiculturalism in Australia'. *International Journal of Law, Crime and Justice* 36, 4: 230-246.

*7:30 Report* (2006) 'Cronulla: six weeks on', reporter Jonathan Harley, 23 January, (june 2009, http://www.abc.net.au/7.30/content/2006/s1553586.htm

Strike Force Neil (2006) *Cronulla Riots: Review of the Police Response*, Vol. 1. Sydney: NSW Police.

*Sydney Morning Herald* (2005) 'Neo-Nazis in race riots: police', *Sydney Morning Herald*, 12 December, accessed 9 June 2009, http://www.smh.com.au/news/national/neonazis-in-race-riots-police/2005/12/12/1134235970427.html

# Notes

[1] The Department's name was changed in January 2007 to the Department of Immigration and Citizenship, thus 'dropping' the 'Multiculturalism'.

# Chapter four

# Riotous Sydney take three (Cronulla) Confessions of a beach survivor

## Wendy Shaw

There appears to be something amiss in Sydney, with no less than three sets of seemingly unrelated 'riots' in just a few years. The first in this trilogy was the so-called 'Redfern Riot' that erupted in February, 2004. The events that occurred on this day happened in the aftermath of the death of a 17 year-old Aboriginal youth who died while fleeing police. Just over a year later, in February 2005, two young 'Caucasian' males were killed when their car collided with a tree in a high-speed police chase. This event incited another set of reactions which were dubbed the 'Macquarie Fields Riots'. As with the events in Redfern, the Macquarie Fields Riots are widely regarded to have occurred because of clashes between dispossessed locals – in this case impoverished 'westies' – and police.

By contrast, the cause of the so-called Cronulla Riots and various offshoots and counter incursions that started in December 2005, remains somewhat underdetermined. The media pointed to an alleged attack on a surf lifesaver and threats to bikini-clad women by men of Middle Eastern descent, as the likely flashpoints of a string of events that were thereafter bannered as 'race riots' (King and Box, 2005: 12).

Having spent my formative years in the Cronulla area, and having fond memories of the place, I was a little bewildered when I heard about the 'riots'. Others I have spoken to since, with similar ties but who also left long ago, expressed a similar response. It was not that we were especially shocked - we were familiar with the history of young people 'going off', or letting off a little steam - but what was unexpected was the added layer of racialisation. So, rather than presenting an analysis of the 'riots', I have a different aim.

Because I grew up in the Cronulla area, this 'issue' has piqued certain subjectivities that, as a researcher on issues of racialisation and Whiteness (Shaw, 2004; 2006; 2007), have implications for my capacity to interpret these events. However rather than ask the question 'am I too close to this issue to make sound scholarly judgements', my task here is to provide a contribution to the collective understanding of the contextual history of these events. To do this, I have used an unconventional and somewhat controversial method of mining (my own) memories (Nelson, 2003). I am not assuming some kind of 'insider' position to the 'riots' – I moved away from Cronulla a long time ago,[1] but what I do have access to is my personal ('oral') history which consists of my own memories of people and places. Drawing on my experience growing up in the area, I will argue that certain cultural attributes formed in the 'good old days' have provided a foundation for the resentment, aggression and fear that sparked the events dubbed the 'Cronulla Riots'.

In my work on the concept of Whiteness,[2] I have remained aware of a range of issues about studying one's 'own kind', particularly in the case of an already empowered group. One concern with the study of Whiteness is the potential to contribute to an emerging body of narcissistic White academic writing.[3] Beyond the potential for self-indulgence lies a capacity for such work to construct a 'mutuality-of-harm hypothesis' (Wiegman, 1999), where claims are made for the *ethnic* disadvantaging of – in this case White – minorities (Wray and Newitz, 1997). There are fears that this can produce a disturbing converse politics to the study, and exposure, of the marginalis*ing*, and at times violent, powers of Whiteness. In this chapter, I step a little sideways from my work on Whiteness – on my own kind – to delve into my personal history. Although I remain mindful of the caveats about the use of memory in research,[4] and using one's own memory carries its own layer of difficulty, I have found this method useful in this particular case. Through a process of remembering, with the help of old photo albums, I have built a personal picture of the history of place. My recollections were assisted by discussions with family members (we had, obviously, a lot to say about the Cronulla Riots) and with a few friends from my Cronulla days. As I drilled down into what appeared to be a former idyllic existence, I experienced the emergence of a different picture, of long 'forgotten' moments. These jogged memories have provided me with an interesting 'take' on the phenomenon of contemporary urban riotous behaviours and their connections to broader political processes of entitlement (and non-entitlement) in a post-colonial city.

## Beach dreams

In recent times, a 'new' housing style has begun to inundate the back dunes of Australian coastal areas; some of these developments have tried to mimic the beach life of my childhood. I like to refer to these new housing estates that reference the beach houses, shacks, and imagined lives of the not too distant past as 'Fibro Dreaming'. Examples of these upmarket versions of the 'original' styles can be found on the far North Coast of NSW, and brandish names like 'Casuarina', and 'Salt Village' (Menday, 2005). A visit to the Salt Village website brings forth a selection of seductive designs, and the nostalgias they summon are enhanced by the moody strains of electro-reggae (Salt Village Real Estate, 2007).

I smile at these attempts to re-invent the ambience of times that have gone by, that have been promoted using a perceived nostalgia for what are largely imagined to be the 'good old days' of beach life. In a different, though related context, nostalgias for the good old days of imperially or colonially-referenced architectures, that serve to reinforce dominant hegemonic power structures established with imperialism and/or colonisation, have been well documented (Jager, 1986; Crilley, 1993). I too have considered the exhibition of such nostalgias expressed through desires to own and protect colonially-referenced heritage architecture, at the expense of other (migrant and Indigenous) heritages, in inner Sydney (Shaw, 2005). Musing on the notion of nostalgia, with reference in this case to imperialist nostalgia, Rosaldo has observed that:

> 'We' valorise innovation and then yearn for more stable worlds, whether these reside in our own past, in other cultures, or in conflation of the two … in any of its versions, imperialist nostalgia uses a pose of 'innocent yearning' both to capture people's imaginations and to conceal its complicity with often brutal

domination (1989: 108).

Nostalgia is not therefore neutral. Nostalgias for idealised pasts often disregard the complexities of race/class relations (Jager, 1986; Rosaldo, 1989; Jacobs, 1996). According to Bennett (1993: 235), yearning for 'more of the same', from before the complexities of contemporary life in Australia with its vexed multiculturalism and post-colonialism, can be muffled within the imaginings of the *good old days*. Even the most violent events can fade with the sweetened memory of the 'happier times' that have been lost to the harsh present, and even harsher future. Nostalgias are thus partitioned constructions with a capacity to enable the repetition of forgotten violences (Rosaldo, 1989).

In his example of the 'birthplace' of the Australian nation, The Rocks area in Sydney, Bennett (1993) has traced the fabrication of an idealised and sanitised version of colonisation through preservation and restoration. The marks that bear testimony to the real and contradictory history are not obvious, as the existing 'glittering façade … functions as an institutional mode of forgetting' (1993: 225). The new allegory is the ascent of 'a free, democratic, multicultural citizenry' (Bennett, 1993: 227). For Bennett, the absence of an Aboriginal presence, except for craft shops where traditionally-referenced 'artefacts' can be purchased, reinforces the belief in a 'European civilisation' that has tamed 'the natural'. Indigeneity, in this place, is now part of the now tamed 'natural' environment that has been overwritten by *human* (non-Aboriginal) occupation. The Rocks area had to be cleansed of those whose lives testified to the real complexity (and violence) of its history.

## Memorialising the beach

> The invention of tradition is a method of using collective memory selectively … [M]emory is not necessarily authentic, but rather useful' (Said, 2000: 179).

Returning to *my* recollections of the 'good old days' of beach life, I found images of languid summer days, of surfing and parties, of pranks and good old-fashioned fun. Although not part of a collective memory[5] as such, the following remembrances have contributed to a 'not necessarily authentic' picture of life as a former Cronulla beach dweller. Of course, beyond the nostalgia for the memories of these good old days, lurk the harsher realities of life and survival at the beach.

According to my photo albums and recollections, my home life as a child growing up in Cronulla offered a rich tapestry of experiences. With double the usual suburban block of land, my family dabbled in a range of activities: growing fruit and vegetables, pickling olives from our 'olive grove',[6] and the exploration of our little 'forest', a small stand of trees. We all loved the sea, and like many others in the area, my family had a couple of boats in the yard. My father loved to go fishing and would go 'outside' into the open ocean. He would return with a catch now impossible given the depletion of fish stocks around the coastline. Huge tuna were plentiful then, our freezer was always full of fish my dad had caught.

This was also an era of other kinds of plenty. I will not stretch the truth and say that my family was just like every other in the area, but, materially-speaking, most people seemed comfortable enough; times seemed much easier then. There were wealthy people too, who moved into the area to take advantage of the waterfronts,when I was a kid, though, many just happened to benefit from buying cheap waterfront blocks that were hard to build on. By the 1970s, teenagers were in abundance; the Sutherland Shire had a massive boom in the birth rate in the late 1950s and 1960s, which led to the construction of seven secondary schools. The area was not without its unusual 'characters' as well: there were old fishing folk, and the 'hermits' who allegedly inhabited caves near Kurnell (where Captain Cook landed and planted the flag). The hermits were, in some ways, the bogeymen of the area and we kids were told to avoid them. Somehow though, the whole lot of us from wealthy to vagabond, were all just 'locals'.

I learnt from a very young age that some differences were tolerable, but a lot were not. When my mother enrolled me at primary school and wrote 'naturalist' as my religion, I was somewhat marginalised. Taking 'healthy' foods to school (such as 'brown' bread sandwiches, nuts and dried fruit) did not help in an era of white bread, cream buns, chips and lollies. Later, my father became unpopular through his desire to stop the development of Sylvania Waters[7] because of the ecological importance of the mangroves as fish nurseries.

The neighbours thought we were a bit 'unusual', but we won them over by hosting big 'cracker-nights' (with fireworks). We could stage a huge bonfire at our place, and my slightly 'mad scientist' dad would entertain with all sorts of dangerous but highly controlled visual spectaculars. As a kid, this seemed like the wildest night of the year and of course this kind of use of fireworks is now illegal; there is simply no replacement for 'cracker night' in a suburban back yard.

When we moved from the Frank Lloyd Wright 'inspired' house that my parents built, the new owners did not like its unique timberwork and large windows. They modified it to look more like the others in the area (1950s brick or fibro bungalows or 'cape cod' two-storey houses). The double-sized block of land was subdivided, and a box house was built on top of my forest. But we had moved on and our next house – where I would spend my teenage years – was a little closer to what would become the most important feature of my existence: Cronulla beaches and most specifically, Wanda surf culture.

As teenagers, we were encouraged to 'Take a Walk on the Wild Side' by Lou Reed, and lived to other soundtracks of rebellion. It did not pay to be *too* different, but difference could be camouflaged and I learnt that the key to survival was to blend in, or leave as I eventually did. In the meantime, to fit into surf culture, I became a bit of a delinquent. I learnt that the height of 'cool' was to 'get really out of it'; for some the drug of choice was alcohol, for others, alcohol was mixed with smoking marijuana. Driving while inebriated was even cooler: I learnt the hard way but fortunately, the terrible car accident resulted in just a few broken bones – it should have been much worse. My mother always referred to those days as my "naughty time" and overall, I escaped too much trouble.

The police did not fuss too much about little things like drink driving (or even minor collisions) in those days. They were facing what was widely regarded to be a much bigger problem: 'heavy' drug supply and use. The rise of heroin use while I was still at secondary school became a stark reality with the first death of a student at my school from an overdose. By the time I left school, some young men I knew locally were facing imprisonment. Teenage pregnancy was also on the rise and even though this was the 1970s, the young mothers did not usually keep their babies which were 'put up' for adoption.

For the most part, my memory is that teenagers and young adults had unprecedented freedom: we were children in an era renowned for its prosperity and most of us had a comfortable life. We had part-time jobs and cash flowed. I worked on the check-outs in local supermarkets but my favourite part-time job was at a cake and pie shop in the shopping strip, which was handy to the beach. In those days, we – the surfing crowd – could afford the extras of the low cost lifestyle associated with the beach, some of my cohort moved into low-rent beachside flats and these became the places of non-stop parties.

So for many us teenagers of the 1970s (some of whom would become the parents of the 'rioters'), these were very good times indeed; the days of plenty, of hedonistic freedom and few responsibilities. Our carefree existence occurred largely before the bite of depleting water supplies, the loss of mangroves (and their fish nurseries) and deep-sea fish stocks. This was a time before urban consolidation and high rents, huge mortgages and interest rate blowouts, and a threatened disappearance of the great Aussie dream of a house in the suburbs. These were the days before a range of societal shifts, of multiculturalism and Native Title, 'political correctness' and the spectre of 'terrorism'.

I was fortunate that I missed the big jolt, the culture shock and attrition of a lazy beach culture. In 1977, my parents sent me away to Newcastle University to 'expand my horizons'. I left the idyllic surf culture life for a new set of values inspired by Prime Minister Gough Whitlam's vision of a chaotic and free tertiary education. I moved to a 'working class' city that was about to be devastated by de-industrialisation. As I became duly politicised in Newcastle[8] I kept in touch with some of my old friends, but this connection soon unravelled and I began to question the unquestionability of homogeneity. What I had forgotten was that we resisted anything that was different to our thoroughly embedded Cronulla beach culture, from the perspective of my new life, I realised that I had led a sheltered life and had blindly accepted the conformity of resistance to difference.

Dredging deeper, I remembered other details about my youth. With its high proportion of teenagers, the Shire's surf culture included a form of beach apartheid (Durrheim and Dixon, 2001) which although not overtly racialised, was territorial: you were either one of us, or you were against us. The train, which terminated at Cronulla, brought carriage-loads of visitors who came to spend a day at 'our' beaches. Many of the teenagers and young adults who visited were marked with 'difference', and were therefore fair game to their surfie counterparts. 'We', as in 'surfies' (males with female supporters) particularly hated 'westies' (people from Western Sydney) and the groups of youths who came in from other suburbs, to go to the cinema or the beach *by train*, were labelled 'westies' or 'bankies' (that is, from Bankstown), regardless of where they had come from.

Particularly vulnerable were the visually obvious 'westies': anyone sporting untanned skin, a distinctive haircut (especially one lacking sun-bleached 'rats tails') and/or tattoos, risked ridicule. There were many 'fights' around the train station but train travellers were not the only targets; I remember watching groups of young men attack vehicles (usually 'panel vans') adorned with airbrushed scenes of erotica and surf images. Real locals all knew that these vehicles were not from the area – their owners were trying too hard; they were inauthentic enough to deserve to have their offending images vandalised, and not because of the often rather derogatory objectification of women on display. The identifications of beach culture were very specific indeed.[9]

The safety of the known and of the beach culture was a very strong identification for many. Some of us ventured out of the immediate area for entertainment, we (girls) tried ice-skating at the (now demolished) Prince Albert Park Ice Rink at Central Station. Some of my girlfriends would go to 'discos' on the other side of the George's River and to the city to shop in the boutiques. As we got older we would go and see bands play, in those days, 'surfie chicks' seemed to be welcome in city bars and pubs. Sporting our long sun-bleached hair, we would offset our tans with 'pot-o-gloss' makeup and cool new clothes, and we would dance in our spangly platform shoes. The surfie boys were less inclined to leave the immediate area, and rarely travelled by train, retribution for the war with 'westies' could happen at any time, particularly outside the safety of surfie turf. When they did travel, it was 'up' or 'down the coast', within the sanctuary of their stereo-blasting station wagons. I remember car trips to beaches such as Gari, Era, Burning Palms and Voodoo within the Royal National Park south of Sydney.

During a discussion with another 'Cronulla survivor', I was reminded of one particularly bleak time in the early 1980s, when I visited old friends only to find a new and unexpected form of bigotry. This time it was the response to the emergence of the AIDS epidemic. For some their new parenthood had become a rationale for a rabid, almost violent form of homophobia. I remember thinking 'they have really changed', but it was probably me that had changed. Meanwhile, there was still a culture of dangerous anti-social behaviours, such as 'getting really out of it', driving and the occasional pub brawl, which still seemed normal. As I recalled these details, I remembered one of the reasons I agreed to move away from my beloved Cronulla beach. During the last blast of school days I was assaulted and at the time I was so stunned that I agreed to leave everything behind, including my family. I later found out that my parents had become concerned about the kind of culture within which I had become so entrenched and this – to them – was the last straw. They were very relieved when I agreed to move to Newcastle.

Nearly three decades later in November 2005, I bumped into one of my old school friends. It was a strange experience; we had not seen each other since school and he too had left the area soon after completing high school. We exchanged snippets of our adult lives and eventually he recounted some of the violence he had endured during our school days. I had not known about the years of abuse he had suffered because of his alleged homosexuality. I remembered the odd jibe and an occasional laugh at his expense, but overall he seemed to take it in his stride; he was a 'good sport' – he seemed popular, he was a good-looking, blonde surfer. During our lengthy conversation, he confessed that he had hated school life – it had been hell for him. I was shocked that I had no idea about the extent of this bullying and that it had gone on under our noses. We lamented our collective past with mixed feelings, and parted with sadness. Then, just a few short weeks later, the 'Cronulla riots' happened.

In the aftermath of the riots, while gathering my stories, I began to think that some of the cultures of violence I had chosen to forget over time had finally surfaced in a more collectivised way. 'Bashings' have always happened at Cronulla as part of the ongoing turf war between locals and 'westies'. I remember hearing about earlier encounters in the '60s, when groups of 'sharpies' arrived at Cronulla railway station and the laid-back surfie boys would turn into warriors. Of course, this had until now been mostly 'men's business', but from the media footage of the 'riots' this too had changed as the media-consuming public watched the venting of angry young women as well as men on their television screens.

Like all idyllic existences, life in Cronulla had a dark underbelly and it was the brutality that has long lurked that set a scene for the events that followed. The 'race riot' aspect of what occurred was, however, a recent addition to the territoriality that I had witnessed in my youth. The addition of a layer of racialisation to the existing territoriality demonstrated a localised smouldering about a much wider set of politics, which eventually caught fire. The events at Cronulla were a local manifestation of these more fear-ridden times, of vote-catching border security, the 'war on terror', and the consequent rise in Islamaphobia (Dunn, 2004). The localised 'fight response' may have existed for at least two generations, but the recent battle resonated with a newer politics of entitlement to urban space. As with the battle to preserve entitlements to inner Sydney landscapes to the exclusion of 'migrant' and Indigenous heritages, Cronulla's (imagined) 'good old days' provided an easy anchor for what appears to be under threat, and worthy of defending (Shaw, 2005).

## Conclusion: Riotous Sydney

As I mentioned in the introduction, it has not been my intention to analyse the so-called 'Cronulla riots' but to offer a personal account of my 'good old days' as a gesture to the need for a more thoroughly researched historical geography of place. I have traced my experiences of revisiting my days of freedom and plenty spent as a teenager at Cronulla. Using my own stories, I hope to have demonstrated the ease with which our pasts can be mythologised into 'good old days', creating a sense of loss with many potential implications. One is the ignition of resentment and a consequent ascription of blame. In the case of Cronulla, a newer group of (unwanted) visitors, who currently hold an unpopular status in the political climate, were easy targets for blame.

The 'Cronulla riots' shocked many, in Australia and elsewhere. This outbreak of flag-wielding bigotry seemed far more horrific, and rankled much more, than the retaliation responses by those targeted. The then NSW Police Commissioner Moroney described the beach event as 'un-Australian' (King and Box, 2005). In response, and by way of explanation for what was widely perceived to be uncharacteristic behaviour, the mass media, politicians and police variously constructed excuses: it was a 'one-off', or an anomaly. In other words, in the national imaginary, the riots in Cronulla were a mistake – this behaviour was 'out of place' (Cresswell, 1996), an alcohol-induced accident where kids at the beach just 'went off'. On the other hand the violence associated with retaliation by 'men of Middle Eastern appearance' was horrifying, but much less unexpected.

The unexpectedness of the violent behaviour at the beach, particularly in what is widely recognised as a comfortable area, sits in stark contrast to the other recent Sydney riots, which occurred in 'troubled' areas, with 'other' (to the mainstream) groups. Redfern, in inner Sydney and Macquarie Fields in the stigmatised western suburbs, are already 'othered' places. Riots in places of severe disadvantage, compounded by racialisation in the case of Redfern, are not only more expected (Keith, 1988), they are almost *accepted*, as somehow 'natural' (Anderson, 2000). Compared to Cronulla,

Redfern and Macquarie Fields almost hold the *right* to riot; the 'rioting' response, when expressed by already othered entities, has not unsettled the Australian psyche in quite the same way as the 2005 Cronulla events. Cronulla is a place that sits easily at the heart of the geographical imagination of 'decent Australianness'; it is a 'good', 'White', (and now) 'middle class' area.

The dominant image of a laid-back beach place celebrates an image of healthy *goodness* about Australia, and of Australians, as happy-go-lucky bronzed Aussies, where all (who fit in) deserve a 'fair-go'. But the 'riots' shattered this illusion, and revealed a hint of a much wider, national rise of revanchist resentment (Smith, 1996) against an increasingly apparent, and seemingly privileged, other (see Mickler, 1998). In a nation where the poor and/or non-bronzeable (racialised) others have exhibited riotous behaviours for tangible reasons – such as responses to the controversial deaths of young people – the 'protests' at Cronulla remain vague, but suspiciously more than innocent yearnings for a gentler past. Rather, they are yearnings for a not-so-innocent belief system about entitlement fed by an idyll of 'the good old days' of unquestioned and largely unchallenged privilege.

## References

Anderson, K. (2000) '"The beast within": race, humanity, and animality', *Environment and Planning D: Society and Space* 18: 301-320.

Bennett, T. (1993) 'History on the rocks', in Frow, J. and Morris, M. (eds.) *Australian Cultural Studies: A Reader* Allen and Unwin, Sydney: 220-240.

Bonnett, A. (2000) White Identities: Historical and International Perspectives Prentice Hall, Harlow.

Cresswell, T. (1996) *In Place, Out of Place: Geography, Ideology and transgression* University of Minnesota Press, Minneapolis.

Crilley, D. (1993) 'Architecture as Advertising: Constructing the Image of Redevelopment', in Kearns, G. and Philo, C. (eds.) *Selling Places: The City as Cultural Capital, Past and Present* Pergamon Press, Oxford.

Dunn, K. (2004) 'Islam in Australia: contesting the discourse of absence', *The Australian Geographer* 35, 3: 333-53.

Durrheim, K. and Dixon, J. (2001) 'The role of place and metaphor in racial exclusion: South Africa's beaches as sites of shifting racialization' *Ethnic and Racial Studies* 24, 433-450.

Fine, M., Wise, L., Powell, L. and Mun Wong, L. (1997) *Off White: Readings on Race, Power, and Society* Routledge, New York.

Jager, M. (1986) 'Class definition and the aesthetics of gentrification: Victoriana in Melbourne', in Smith, N. and Williams, P. (eds.) *Gentrification of the City* Allen and Unwin, Sydney: 78-91.

Jacobs, J. (1996) Edge of empire: Postcolonialism and the City Routledge, London.

Keith, M. (1988) 'Racial Conflict and the 'No-Go Areas' of London', in Eyles, J and Smith D. (eds.) *Qualitative Methods in Human Geography* Polity Press, London: 39-48.

King, D. and Box, D. (2005) 'Revenge attacks in Sydney race war', The Australian 12 December: 12.

Lette, K. and Carey, G. (1979) *Puberty Blues* McPhee Gribble, Melbourne.

Menday, L. (2005) *Assessing the 'Principles' of an Australian New Urbanism: a case study of Casuarina Beach* unpublished Honours Thesis, School of Biological, Earth and Environmental Sciences, University of New South Wales.

Mickler, S. (1998) The Myth of Privilege: Aboriginal Status, Media Visions, Public Ideas Fremantle Arts Centre Press, Fremantle WA.

Nelson, K. (2003) 'Self and social functions: Individual autobiographical memory and collective narrative', *Memory* 11, 2: 125-136.

Rosaldo, R. (1989) 'Imperial nostalgia', *Representations* 26: 107-121.

Said, E. (2000) 'Invention, Memory, and Place', *Critical Inquiry* 26, 2: 175-192.

Salt Village Real Estate (2007) 'Salt: a village by the sea', accessed 9 June 2009, http://www.saltvillage.com.au

Shaw, W. (2004) 'Riotous Sydney? Neo-colonial geographies and Aboriginal Redfern', a paper given at the *Institute of Australian Geographers Conference* Adelaide.

Shaw, W. (2005) 'Heritage and gentrification: remembering 'the good old days' in postcolonial Sydney', in Atkinson R. and Bridge G. (eds.) *The New Urban Colonialism: Gentrification in a Global Context* Routledge, London.

Shaw, W. (2006) 'Decolonizing Geographies of Whiteness', *Antipode* 38, 2: 851-869.

Shaw, W. (2007) *Cities of Whiteness* Blackwell, Oxford.

Smith, N. (1996) The New Urban Frontier: Gentrification and the Revanchist City Routledge, London.

Wiegman, R. (1999) 'Whiteness studies and the paradox of particularity', *Boundary* 2, 26, 3: 115-150.

Wray, M. and Newitz, A. (1997) *White Trash* Routledge, New York.

# Notes

[1] I left the area in the late 1970s but visited regularly until the sale of my 'family home' in 2004.

[2] I am highly critical of the use of the term 'Whiteness', and its unification under a banner of ethnicity is part of the reason for my critique. I have argued that Whiteness is a racialised/ethnicised construction that has been mobilised in the consolidation of power (Shaw, 2006).

[3] I agree with Bonnett (2000), who cites Wray and Newitz (1997) and Fine et al. (1997) as examples.

[4] I would hasten to add that gathering the memories of others is a far less fraught process than gathering our own. Allowing for the potential of lapses and inaccuracies of recollected events, and embellishment, is much more difficult to gauge while 'interviewing' oneself. For a discussion of the cultural and social context of autobiographical memory, see Nelson (2003).

[5] Because these 'memories' have benefited from the contributions of others they do have a collective aspect.

[6] My parents were a little unusual in this regard. Along with the majority, we were as 'Anglo' as the rest but we experimented in all sorts of home-based activities that included a little Southern-European influenced 'subsistence' agriculture, and bulk-buying.

[7] Sylvania Waters is a suburb that was built on the mangroves of Gwawley Bay. 'Sylvania Waters Pty. Ltd' bought the site in 1960, and began a four stage process of filling in the mangroves, and building a series of concrete canals that became desirable waterfront house blocks. It was later immortalised in the somewhat controversial reality television program 'Sylvania Waters'.

[8] The relatively new University of Newcastle campus had become very politically-oriented by the late 1970s. It had a strong 'green' politics and the influences of Marxism, Feminism, Aboriginal land rights, Queer politics and counter cultures, such as collectivised households.

[9] This included a lexicon of Cronulla-specific nomenclature. Kathy Lette and Gabrielle Carey provide some of these in their novel, 'Puberty Blues'.

# Lines in the Sand

## Part two

### *'We grew here, you flew here'*: nation, ethnicities and belonging

One of the most remarkable features of the Cronulla riots was how what was initially a localised, minor event quickly turned into event of great national significance. Fights between young men, sometimes fuelled by cultural differences, alcohol and territory, happen almost every weekend at Sydney's beaches; and that's usually where they end. As this section demonstrates, the lead-up to the riots, the protests themselves and the following revenge attacks managed to weave together complex perceptions about local and national belongings which entailed specific claims about inclusion and exclusion.

Kevin Dunn argues that the riots, and the media and political debates about them, represent contested performances of nationalism. He shows how the discussion of the initial conflict was rapidly framed as a fight about an Australian way of life, of which particular social actors – not just residents – felt very possessive. Icons of Anglo-Australian nationalism: lifesavers, flags, sporting paraphernalia and so on, were used on the day of the riots to express their investments in such a nationalism. Dunn emphasises the performative nature of this process – in contrast to a focus on the nation as an imagined community – to illustrate the constructed and fluid nature of nationalism; Australian nationalism tends to be relatively benign, but can become strongly normative and exclusionary in particular spatial and temporal contexts. In response, those who were subject to attack asserted, often aggressively, counter-nationalisms and local identities, but, in the end, Dunn claims, these only affirmed the dominant Anglo-nationalism.

Geoff Brahm Levey and Dirk Moses take this argument in a different direction by drawing a powerful and provocative parallel with anti-Semitism. They compare the 'Muslim question' in contemporary Australia with the 'Jewish question' in Nazi Germany, as the creation of a dangerous, unassimilable Other which needs to be dealt with. Levey and Moses remedy the ahistorical approach to the riots by providing a sweeping foray into the history of nineteenth and twentieth century Europe and post-war Australia. They use this history to argue that the Cronulla riots were effectively a 'pogrom' directed at Muslim Australians, premised on a questionable claim about a core culture which, despite the Prime

Minister's protestations, reveals the persistent place of racism in Australian society.

The rapid and powerful reference to nationalist symbolism in the riots is examined carefully in Affrica Taylor's insightful discussion of the cultural significance of the beach in Australian national identity. She argues that the riots can be read as 'an ardent defence of the dream of quintessential Australian bodies and beaches', and explores this by stressing the territorial and corporeal dimensions of that dream. Taylor emphasises the need to take a 'relational' approach to questions of identity and thus question the rioters' perception of themselves as 'already essentially' Australian; their identity is performed primarily through its enmeshment with others – other cultures, other organisms, other things. This allows her to map the complex relations between local and national identity and what she sees as an act of 'proprietorial enclosure'.

The embodied aspects of belonging are also the centre of Amanda Wise's discussion of the riots. Wise, like Shaw, grew up in Cronulla and this personal perspective adds enormous depth to her analysis of the phenomenological experience of the locals' responses during the riots. She argues that grappling with questions of embodiment is necessary to explain how local 'discomfort' escalates into riotous behaviour, particularly amongst local males. Wise describes the contrasts between Anglo and Leb bodies on the beach, drawing on the notion of the habitus to draw out the differences in the uses, appearances and meanings of the bodies on the beach. Significantly, Wise demonstrates the long history of violence amongst Anglo youth in the Shire to counter simplistic assumptions about violence being a feature only of young men of Middle Eastern background. Wise also talks about the problems of civility in encounters between disparate bodies, forging an understanding of what she calls the 'interethnic habitus'.

Andrew Lattas develops a similar interest in questions of interethnic relations and etiquette, but from the unusual perspective of Greek migrants in the Shire. This group, he points out, has an ambivalent relationship with Lebanese migrants and he lists some of the jokes Greeks tell about the Lebanese. He draws on interviews and on postings on an internet site for Greeks. As in the introduction, Lattas finds Elias' work on the 'civilising process' productive for understanding the relations to issues of national belonging and integration for competing migrant groups. He argues that 'Lebanese behaviour' is often taken by Greek migrants as a warning of 'the dangers of refusing assimilation'.

# Chapter five

# Performing Australian nationalisms at Cronulla

## Kevin M. Dunn

### Ways of life and performances

On the Friday before the Cronulla riots, Sydney's daily tabloid newspaper the *Daily Telegraph* (2005: 1) carried the banner headline: 'Not on our Beach: Cronulla police vow to defend Australian way'. The article was principally a report on how police would not tolerate violence on the beach, but the reference to the Australian way of life gave a clear sense that certain ideas about nationalism were at stake. Such references to Australian ways, values or culture have been exposed in critical literature as often being clandestine calls for Anglo supremacy (Hage, 1998; Johnson, 2002; Maddox, 2005). As I demonstrate in this chapter, performances of Anglo-Australian nationalism were frequent throughout the build-up to and immediate aftermath of the Cronulla riots. More broadly, the riots and their aftermath demonstrate the contest between different versions of Australian nationalism.

A local newspaper account of the day of the riot is evocative of the setting, politics and dynamics.

> A ute [utility¹] had a barbie [a mobile hot plate] on the back, its owner handing out free snags [sausages] and boxing kangaroo tattoos. Even dogs were wearing green and gold coats. The salty air oozed with patriotism … But as the crowds grew, the clouds cleared, the day became hotter and the consumption of beer increased, the stench of racism became stifling. Chants of 'Lebs go home' and 'Aussie Aussie Aussie, Oi Oi Oi', warmed up the well lubricated crowd (Stringa, 2005: 2).

The rioters had claimed possession of key icons of Australian nationalism: the barbecue, the boxing kangaroo, utes, the colours green and gold, beer, national songs and sporting chants. These performances of nationalism, and the reactions to them, provide an insight into contemporary Australian nationalism and its future directions. In this chapter, I undertake a performative analysis of the everyday nationalisms in evidence at the riots and also apply this analytical frame to the 'revenge attacks' and the anti-racism initiatives that followed. The empirics for this chapter are the eye-witness reports as recounted in newspapers in the weeks after December 11, 2005. My aims are to demonstrate the utility of performative theory for analysing competing nationalisms, and to identify the progressive political resources within the riot and its aftermath. A handful of scholars have reflected on how, rather than indicating a failure of multiculturalism, the Cronulla riot has asserted its importance, and argued for its enhancement (Babacan, 2006).

## Performance theory and nationalism

Nationalism is contested and dynamic. Some decades ago, Anderson (1983) referred to how nations were socially imagined, that they were constructed out of the thinking and actions of people in the present and of the past. His underlying counterpoint was a critique of the common sense understanding that nations were fixed, that national cultures were natural or superorganic (Duncan, 1980; Jackson, 1989:16-9). Intellectual discomfort with the idea that nations comprise a fixed set of cultural features (such as language) or shared biology (race, blood, genes) reaches back as far as the 1880s (Renan, 1882). A century later critical theorists such as Gilroy (1987) pointed to the narrowness of popular expressions of national identity in the United Kingdom, and how this was linked with racism against non-Whites.

In the last ten years, there has been an evolving scholarship on the narrowness of Australian national identity in the public imaginary (Hage, 1998; Johnson, 2002; Phillips and Smith, 2000). However, over the last three decades, settler societies like Australia and empire nodes like the United Kingdom have moved to give official recognition to the cultural diversity among their national citizenry. In Australia, this embrace of diversity has taken the form of multiculturalism, which adds another layer of national identity to earlier White Australia and assimilationist identities. Rather than being a sedimentary layer that covers the older identity, the previous layers in this case continue to be visible; nations are marked pages onto which new cultural impacts are written (Winchester et al., 2003: 24-30). Recognition of this layering provides a basis for analysing the changing and contested nature of national identity.

Performative theory is a conceptual framework which facilitates the recognition of the dynamism of national identities. Performance theory, influenced by the work of Butler (1990), can be usefully applied to debates about national identity (Dunn, 2005). Performative theory acknowledges that there are certain dominant constructions of culture and that these constructions are norms for performances of nationalism. In the Australian context of December, 2005, there were at least two substantive nationalisms (Zevallos, 2005: 46-7): one was the recently developed multiculturalism, with its official state sanction since the 1980s, the other was Anglo-nationalism, empowered by requests that non-Anglos assimilate and relying on a widespread assumption that social harmony depends upon cultural uniformity (Dunn et al., 2004: 416-8; Jaysuriya, 2005: 11). Assimilationism in this context can be assumed to mean conformity to Anglo ways of life, although the cultural inflection of the desired norm is usually left un-stated. According to performative theory, these norms do not retain their currency simply through official sanction, or through the statements of opinion leaders, they need to be performed by everyday people. Assimilationism needs to be repeated in Parliament, on talk-back radio, in sports changing rooms and around dinner tables; these recitations of the norm give it authority as in a sedimentary-like manner each reiteration reproduces the norm. In the same way, multiculturalism must be 'performed' through diverse cultural expressions and landscapes.

The process of forming normative (dominant) identities locates a fundamental power at the level of the individual. Individuals have the ability to confirm but also to trouble the norm - to present an alternative nationalism. An example was the refusal of most post-war migrants from southern Europe to relinquish their cultural heritages and assimilate into Anglo-Australianness; these resistances helped build a new national norm of multiculturalism. Another source of dynamism, anticipated through performative theory, flows from the disjuncture between simplistic norms and individual performances. The unrealistic and narrow nature of all nationalist norms means that citations are doomed to never fully match the norm, which draws attention to the short-comings of the norm.

## Performing Anglo-nationalism

In the week leading up to the violence, a text message circulated, mostly among Anglo youth, around the southern beaches and then throughout Sydney. There were at least 270,000 transmissions of this and related messages (Strike Force Neil, 2006: 35 – also known as the *Hazzard Report*). It read:

> Aussies: this Sunday every Fucking Aussie in the shire [the Sutherland area] get down the north Cronulla To help support… Leb and wog bashing day. Bring your mates down and lets show them that this is our beach and their never welcome back.. Fuck the lebs/wogs., lets kill the cunts! Tell everyone spread the word… Fire up Aussies… Sunday midday don't forget…Forward this to all you know and help us protect our brothers and sisters…lets claim back our shire…

The text drew a stark dichotomy between Aussies and Lebs – and is a common performance of nationalism in Australia, usually manifest in everyday speech as a division between Aussies (meaning Anglos) and 'ethnics'. This division has a dramatic influence on national belonging, enhancing the substantive citizenship of those who can claim the mantle of Aussie, and degrading it for those who cannot use that descriptor. In the public imaginary (and across many communities) the popular image of an Aussie is an Anglo. The text was a performance that draws upon and enhances that dichotomy, in which Anglo-Australians are Aussies and Lebanese-Australians are wogs, ethnics and not-Aussies.

In the riot Anglos deployed the dominant icons of nationalism, including national songs and sporting chants. In one incident, after two girls of Middle Eastern descent were assaulted by a group of

Anglo girls, the surrounding crowd shouted 'kill the Leb bitches' and sang 'I am, you are, we are Australian' (McIlveen, 2005: 6) – a song which, paradoxically, celebrates the culturally diverse nature of Australia. The crowd also sang the national anthem (Advance Australia Fair), the unofficial anthem (Waltzing Matilda) and a sporting chant made popular at the 2000 Olympics: 'Aussie, Aussie, Aussie ... Oi, Oi, Oi'. A journalist writing for the *Sydney Morning Herald* reflected on the juxtaposition of the national anthems and the thuggery.

> Sometimes when a victim was cornered, the mob started singing Waltzing Matilda, the first time the unofficial [national] anthem has been used as a weapon. Advance Australian Fair was similarly employed against obstructing police, and the usually good-natured 'Aussie Aussie Aussie' chant in the mouths of Cronulla youths assumed a Berlin 1936 tone (Murphy, 2005: 4).

These songs and chants were only usable by this crowd, in this way, if the definition of Aussie was reserved for those in the assembly who were mostly Anglo-Australian.

The presence of strong visual Anglo indicators among the rioters reinforced the dichotomy. Overtly Anglo-Celtic performances of nationalism by Cronulla rioters included identifications such as cricket equipment (batting pads, clothing and bats), and rugby league team jerseys. However, the principal Anglo icon was the Australian flag. Many of those undertaking racist assaults wore the flag around their necks or as capes (Kennedy et al., 2005: 4). Clements (2006:15) argued that those surfies who wrapped themselves in the flag were asserting their White power.

Everyday Australian nationalism is usually perceived and expressed as a sense of quiet pride rather than a display of ostentatious patriotism. Not many political leaders would literally wrap themselves in the flag in the manner of Pauline Hanson, the initial leader of the One Nation Party, who also often gave prominence to the Union Jack in the top corner of the flag emphasising the *Anglo* aspect of her Australian nationalism, nonetheless, the flag often features as a back-drop behind politicians. The use of the Australian flag is a crucial point of difference between everyday Anglo-nationalism and the nationalism of Hanson and the Cronulla rioters. As I discuss later there was a good deal of media and political criticism, including from the Premier of NSW, of the supposed misuse of the Australian flag at Cronulla. However, what is notable is how comfortable Anglos felt using the flag in this way because of their claim on it. These specifically Anglo performances entrenched Australian-ness (the flag, the anthems and chants) as Anglo, and therefore Lebanese-Australians as not Australian.

Poynting reflected on how Anglo-Australians felt empowered to 'take the law into their own hands' against an ethnic minority, the normative context being one in which Lebanese Australians, and Arabs and Muslims more generally, were being demonised by media, politicians and law enforcement agencies (Poynting, 2006: 33-4). Claims of national identity are unequally empowered across time and space, and access to certain performances is unevenly shared across different cultural groups.

In one of the earliest instances of racist violence on the day, a Muslim girl was chased along the beach by a group of young Anglo-Australian men. A 13-year-old trainee lifesaver was reported to have yelled out 'Get her!' (Murphy, 2005: 5). Her hijab or headscarf was ripped off and she ran to the Surf Life Saving Club to find safety while the headscarf was borne off as a souvenir. Performance of her culture, in this case dress, was the means by which hatred was converted into violence against a person; the racist victory came with the removal of the offending cultural performance, the hijab, defined as non-Australian.[2]

Another incident occurred when a youth shouted 'Fuck off, get the fuck back to Lebanon' (Kennedy et al., 2005: 4) to a swimmer who was then chased by a 200-strong mob, and took refuge in a public hotel where police and security held back a crowd that swelled beyond a thousand. Newspaper reports indicate that from that point, sections of the crowd roamed the streets around Cronulla seeking targets; at the railway station, men of 'Middle Eastern appearance' were attacked, and police had to protect other travellers who may have looked Lebanese to the mob: 'The victims were simply chosen because of their Middle Eastern appearance' (Strike Force Neil, 2006: 8,31). Two young men on a train were set upon by about twenty rioters; the assault was captured in detail by a photographer for the *Daily Telegraph*, and the images dominated the front page of the newspaper the following day, the photographer intervened, pulling off attackers, ahead of the police (Aston, 2005: 5). Again, the targets of the violence were determined physically, in this case by their skin colour. Racist violence is a performance of exclusive nationalism which identifies and attacks performances that are considered to be non-normative. Since non-normative performances trouble the norm and suggest alternatives, their punishment is generally an important part of the process of protecting norms.

Norms are often narrow and unrealistic, so anxious attempts to preserve them can have a destabilising effect. The punishment of non-normative performances can become seen as foolish, or nefarious, and this can also undermine the norm. For example, Australia's organised racist groups occupy a fringe position in Australian politics; in general, levels of support for multiculturalism and tolerance make it difficult for these groups to establish a mainstream hold. As discussed below, support for multiculturalism (as indicated by positive attitudes towards cultural diversity) is strong, while belief in racial hierarchy and separatism is confined to about one-in-eight Australians (Dunn et al., 2004: 420). Yet this minority represents a substantial pool of supporters for organised racist groups and far right parties.

The call to arms which led to the riot was an opportunity for these groups: those present included the Patriotic Youth League and the Australia First Party[3]. Patriotic Youth League posters had been plastered throughout the area, with the message 'Aussies fighting back' (Stringa, 2005: 3), Australia First party representatives handed out stickers that stated 'Stop immigration now', and leaflets declaring 'Immigration out of control' and 'Your teachers are lying to you' (Murphy, 2005: 4; Stringa, 2005: 3). The crowds' chants of 'No more Lebs' and 'Lebs out' matched the politics of Australia's racist organisations and Cronulla provided a unique opportunity for organised racist performances to edge towards normalisation if only within that spatial and temporal context. It is in this peculiar context that so many young Anglo-Australians participated in exclusionary politics, however, the overtly racist nationalism of the performances created a troubling effect as it focused attention on the exclusionary nature of Anglo-assimilationism.

The then Prime Minister, John Howard, was quick to deny that the riots indicated a problem with racism in Australia, and pointed instead to a handful of law breakers. This denial had an air of the unreal about it as in the face of such obvious racism the defenders of Anglo-nationalism were compelled to either deny the undeniable, or to dismiss the rioters as a despicable aberration. Howard also pointed to Lebanese anti-social behaviour as a cause, and how 'a group of people broke the law the previous weekend when they assaulted two life-savers' (Levett, 2005: 1),[4] his implication being that the 'underlying cause' of the riots was a lack of respect for Australian values by those against whom the riot was targeted. Nonetheless, the reactions to the riots were themselves very interesting performances of nationalism.

## Getting even? Failed counter nationalisms

Performance theory implies that non-normative actions and statements are political resources; in some circumstances, such performances can trouble norms, but that is not necessarily the case. Immediately following the violence, some victims stated they would seek revenge: a victim interviewed in Sutherland Hospital stated 'We are going to have the last laugh. That is exactly what is going to be happening. I got beaten up by 50 people. I am half Lebanese, part-Aboriginal [Indigenous Australian]. I am more Australian than the Anglos' (quoted in Kennedy et al., 2005: 4). Others at the hospital stated: 'Today the beach might be theirs. Tomorrow it will be ours' (quoted in Brown, 2005a: 7). These quotations, and the text message quoted earlier, demonstrate how the ethnic battle-lines were clear for both the Anglo-Australian rioters and for those Lebanese-Australian youth considering retaliation. The comments demonstrate a strong sense of confidence and belonging among those affected by the riot: a claim to nation and locality: Australia and the beaches were as much theirs as their antagonists'. Ultimately however, the 'us-and-them' language and the revenge performances served to confirm hierarchies of citizenship that privilege Anglo-Australians.

On the evening of the beach violence more than 40 vehicles assembled at Arncliffe and Punchbowl in Sydney's south and west and drove to the eastern suburbs as a show of force and to exact revenge (Strike Force Neil, 2006: 45-46). In the beach suburb of Maroubra 50 cars had windscreens smashed, a car was bombed by a molotov cocktail, and local pedestrians of Anglo appearance were assaulted. At the Returned Services League (RSL) Club in Brighton-le-Sands, men of 'Middle Eastern descent' scaled the roof, took down the Australian flag, and a crowd of perhaps 150 men burnt it (Strike Force Neil, 2006: 45-46; Higgins, 2006: 6; Wallace & Brown, 2005: 7). It is noteworthy that the Australian flag was a target of the retaliation and that this performance served to affirm the Anglo ownership of the flag and alienated non-Anglos from this icon of national identity.

In the next few days, violence spread to other parts of Sydney, notably in Auburn in central western Sydney – an area with a large Muslim population (23%) but which is culturally very diverse (Dunn, 2004a: 342). On the evening of Monday 12 December, gun-shots were fired outside a primary school in south Auburn where Christmas carols were being sung, and parents and children were abused by men of Middle Eastern appearance (Baker, 2005: 5; Morris, 2005a: 5). During the next evening the hall of a Uniting Church in Auburn was firebombed, and burnt to the ground and another Anglican church in Auburn had its windows smashed (Cubby, 2005: 7; Watson and Gee, 2005: 5). In the first few nights of that week, as many as 400 police patrolled flashpoint areas, and local commands were asked to regularly patrol places of worship. The focusing of revenge attacks on religious targets demonstrates that these protagonists perceived a cultural basis to their grievance and saw Christians as their foe. Insofar as these performances were political interventions they were failures and only served to confirmed the nationalist norm of a Christian, Anglo Australia.

## Performances of multiculturalism and anti-racism

Newspaper headlines immediately after the riot stated: 'Our Racist Shame' (Kennedy et al., 2005: 1) and 'Our Disgrace: Beach race riots shame Australia's values' (*Daily Telegraph*, 2005b: 1). These headlines drove attention to racism as a problem of society as a whole,[5] some locals were reported to have wept at the sight of the riot, and what they saw as the misuse of the Australian flag. An anti-racism street performance a week later in the Sydney CBD, featured a line of protestors with the flag wrapped around their heads, covering their faces (Frew, 2005: 4); this performance was a resistance to what was seen as blind Anglo-assimilationism. At the scene of the riot, a brave anti-racist wore a T-shirt that read 'I'm ashamed to be an Australian in Cronulla. December 11, a day of racism' (Norrie, 2005: 7). Talking about racism at, and after, the riots was risky, on the day of the riot, and in defiance of a chant 'Fuck off, Lebs', a young man grabbed the megaphone saying that the chant was racist, he was struck in the forehead by a beer bottle and stumbled away bleeding.

As mentioned, the then Prime Minister was quick to deny that the riots were a reflection of racism in Australian society (see Poynting, 2006: 33-34) and denied there was 'underlying racism in Australian society' (quoted on Australian Broadcasting Commission radio news, 2005). At the local level, the NSW Parliamentary representative for Cronulla stated 'There were some drunken louts who have indulged in racist remarks but this [Cronulla] is not a racist community' (quoted in Davies and Porter, 2005: 6). However, the then Labor NSW Premier, Morris Iemma, referred to the events as 'the ugly face of racism'. Some Islamic representatives were more direct. Kuranda Seyit, the Director of the Forum on Australian-Islamic Relations, argued that the riots showed an '...underlying racism running deeply in the Australian psyche. It's been simmering for a few years but I think the latest incident here – people have really let loose their inherent racism' (quoted in Davies and Porter, 2005: 6). The riots exposed the presence of racism, and the Prime Minister's denial in the face of the images and display appeared forlorn.

Less than one month before the riots, Australia had hosted a football World Cup qualifier in Sydney in which Australia won qualification against Uruguay in a tense and thrilling match watched by millions on television. Football is probably the most culturally diverse of all the organised sports in Australia (Warren et al., 2002). The *Sydney Morning Herald* editorialised that the result, and the popular support for the team, revealed how Australia's multicultural society had exceeded the sum of its cultural heritages.

In a multicultural nation in a fractured world, the Socceroos can bring together the sum of their parts: Muslim, Catholic, Orthodox, Anglican. German, Lebanese, Polynesian, Croatian, Italian, Melanesian, Greek. It is a rich tapestry but last night they – and we – were one thing only. Australian. (*Sydney Morning Herald*, 2005: 12)

This example is counter evidence to the narrow nationalism discussed earlier and opinion surveys have consistently found that a majority of Australians (around 80%) value cultural diversity and support multiculturalism (Dunn et al., 2004: 416-20); most however also recognise that there is a problem with racism in Australian society. Prime Minister Howard tried to use the former datum to counter the latter, stating that: 'If you have 81 per cent of the population tolerant and supportive of ethnic and racial difference then you can't simultaneously have underlying racism' (quoted in Dodson et al., 2005: 1). But, clearly, both of these attitudes and both nationalisms co-exist.

## Outcomes and revelations

The riots and subsequent events have had some effects that would please racist organisations: Muslims have been left fearful and their sense of belonging degraded, a Lebanese-born resident attending a peace rally at Belmore Park told a reporter how it had made her fearful of others, and that her Australia-born children and grandchildren did not feel comfortable enough to attend the peace rally (Frew, 2005: 4). This anxiety is similar to how Muslims felt following other moments of crises, such as during the Gulf Wars and after the 11 September, 2001 terror events (Dreher, 2005:10-11; Human Rights and Equal Opportunity Commission (HREOC),

1991:387-388, 2004:54-57; Poynting and Noble, 2004:6-8). The Anti-Discrimination Board of NSW (2005) reported a surge in discrimination experienced by people of Middle Eastern appearance following the riots. In the weeks following, the beaches were White, and some young Anglo-Australians made it clear that non-Whites and Muslims were not welcome (Brown, 2005b: 1). Madona Kobayssi of the Muslim Youth Summit, and a resident of Bexley, said that the riots had made her feel a stranger in her own country; she was too fearful to use public transport, fearing racist violence because she 'doesn't have blonde hair and blue eyes' (quoted in Marcus, 2005: 10). Again, we see how physical features, and dress, are important performances that are used to restrict citizenship in times of inter-communal tension. As in Britain, anti-Islamic racism in Australia depends heavily on traditional and physical indicators of difference, such as skin colour or dress (Dreher, 2005:11-14,20-1; Dunn et al., 2007; Hopkins, 2004:269; HREOC, 2004; Modood, 2005:12).

The day after the riots, the Premier of NSW hastily arranged a meeting of ethnic leaders, Cronulla representatives and government officials. The delegates agreed to work to find solutions (Trembath, 2005: 4) and generated cross-cultural initiatives and events in the following weeks. There were meetings between local surf leaders and Islamic representatives, including the involvement of the latter in the launching of a new rescue boat by Wanda Surf Club (Allely, 2005:4), some apologies from local leaders involved in the riots,[6] and statements to the effect that the beaches were for all Sydney people to use. There were also joint communiqués from Sydney celebrities from the fields of film, sports and popular music (Cubby, 2005: 7; Gee, 2005: 9; Watson, 2005: 1,42,43) and the National Union of Students (the peak University student union in Australia) arranged a peace and harmony rally in the Sydney CBD.

There were also many interfaith meetings and statements against racism: worshippers of the Omar Mosque in Auburn walked to the Harold Wood Uniting Church (the site of the arson attack) to hold a solidarity meeting where a crowd of 500 heard from Muslim, Christian and Jewish speakers, including the President of the Uniting Church in Australia, the President of Australian Federation of Islamic Councils, and a representative of the Executive Council of Australian Jewry (Baden, 2005: 5;  Cubby, 2005: 7). Catholic, Muslim and Buddhist leaders met and condemned the violence, reminding people that had Jesus Christ been on Cronulla Beach on 11 December 2005 he too would have been bashed because he was of Middle Eastern appearance (Morris, 2005a: 5). In Christmas sermons Catholic priests asserted the importance of tolerance and other Christian leaders made similar calls for peace (Morris, 2005b: 2; Trembath, 2005: 5). A dawn prayer service, organised by an Anglican minister and attended by 200 people along with Muslim representatives was held at North Cronulla at the scene of the riot (Trembath, 2005: 3).

Some commentators have interpreted the Cronulla riots, and debates and events thereafter, as symptoms of the failure of multiculturalism; others see the dominance of Anglo-assimilationism. Looking at these events as contested performances of nationalism provides a more nuanced vista. While the riots were patently racist and the rioters gave voice to the culturally inflected nature of Australian assimilationism, this outburst was also contrary to the usually unstated presence of Anglo-ness in debates about national identity and values.

Since the riots, there were efforts by some commentators to concentrate critical attention on the actions of young Muslims. This re-targeting of blame could be seen as an attempt to recuperate the normative status of Anglo-nationalism and distract attention from the performances of the 5000 (mostly) Anglo rioters, their exclusionary chants, and their deployment of Australian icons. However, the iconography and performances of the riots are etched in the public mind, and they have linked assimilationism with racist Anglo-nationalism.

Multiculturalism should emerge emboldened by these performances which have troubled the normality of assimilationism, although the revenge attacks by some Lebanese-Australian youth were performances that had the opposite effect, redirecting attention away from the Anglo rioters. The statements condemning racism and the ecumenical and cross-cultural initiatives that followed 11 December, 2005, were performances that helped sediment multiculturalism as the only workable nationalist norm. The racist performances of nationalism at Cronulla should, in all likelihood, provide long-term scope for performances of multiculturalism, reiterating the need for expressions of national identity and citizenry that are culturally diverse.

# References

Australian Broadcasting Commission (2005) *ABC Radio News* 12 December.

Allely, S. (2005) 'New boat helps float friendship', *St George and Sutherland Shire Leader* 20 December: 4.

Anderson, B. (1983) *Imagined Communities: Reflections on the Origin and Spread of Nationalism Verso*, London.

Anti-Discrimination Board of NSW (2005) 'Race discrimination on the rise', *Media Release: 23 December* Anti-Discrimination Board of NSW.

Aston, H. (2005) 'Angry group assaults pair on train' *Daily Telegraph* 12 December:

*Australian* (2006) 'Editorial: Iemma talks tough: but he must ensure the law is universally enforced', *Australian* 18 January: 13.

Babacan, H. (2006) 'Has multiculturalism failed us? Rethinking multicultural policies in post-Cronulla Australia', in Gopalkrishnan N & Swee-Hin, T (eds.) *Proceedings of the National Symposium Responding to Cronulla: Rethinking Multiculturalism, Griffith University, 21 February, 2006* University of the Sunshine Coast: 59-75.

Baden, S. (2005) 'Police guard churches as tension rises', *Sydney Morning Herald* 15 December: 5.

Baker, J. (2005) 'Smouldering suspicion as a community mourns its hall', *Sydney Morning Herald* 15 December: 5.

Brown, M. (2005a) 'A day at the beach becomes a nightmare', *Sydney Morning Herald* 12 December: 7.

Brown, M. (2005b) 'Beneath the calm, a nasty undertow still threatens' *Sydney Morning Herald* 26 December: 1.

Butler, J. (1990) *Gender Trouble: Feminism and the Subversion of Identity* Routledge, New York.

Clements, K. (2006) 'Cronulla: Understanding the violence and conflict', in Gopalkrishnan N & Swee-Hin, T (eds) Proceedings of the National Symposium Responding to Cronulla: Rethinking Multiculturalism, Griffith University, 21 February, 2006 University of the Sunshine Coast: 6-17.

Cubby, B. (2005) 'Religious leaders embrace for peace – and point finger a radio station', *Sydney Morning Herald* 17 December: 7.

*Daily Telegraph* (2005a) 'Not on our Beach: Cronulla police vow to defend Australian way', *Daily Telegraph* 9 December: 1.

*Daily Telegraph* (2005b) 'Our Disgrace: Beach race riots shame Australia's values', *Daily Telegraph* 12 December: 1.

Davies, A. & Porter, J. (2005) 'United in Condemnation, divided over the causes' *Sydney Morning Herald* 12 December: 6.

Davis, R. and Stimson, R. (1998) 'Disillusionment and disenchantment at the fringe: explaining the geography of the One Nation Party vote at the Queensland Election', *People and Place* 6, 3: 69-82.

Dodson, L., Timms, A. and Creagh, S. (2005) 'Tourism starts counting the cost of race riots', *Sydney Morning Herald* 21 December: 1.

Dreher, T. (2005) *Targeted. Experiences of Racism in NSW after September 11, 2001* University of Technology Sydney Press, Ultimo.

Duncan, J. (1980) 'The superorganic in American cultural geography', *Annals of the Association of American Geographers* 70, 2: 181-98.

Dunn, K. (2004a) 'Islam in Australia: contesting the discourse of absence', *Australian Geographer* 35, 3: 333-53.

Dunn, K. (2004b) *Attitudes Towards Islam in Australia* Australia-Indonesia Institute, Canberra.

Dunn, K. (2005) 'Australian public knowledge of Islam', *Studia Islamika* 12, 1: 1-32.

Dunn, K. (2009) 'Public attitudes towards hijab-wearing in Australia', in Dreher, T. and Ho, C. (eds) *Beyond the Hijab Debates* Cambridge Scholars Press, Newcastle: 31-51.

Dunn, K., Forrest, J., Burnley, I. and McDonald, A. (2004) 'Constructing racism in Australia', *Australian Journal of Social Issues* 39, 4: 409-430.

Dunn, K., Klocker, N. and Salabay, T. (2007) 'Contemporary racism and Islamaphobia in Australia: racialising religion', *Ethnicities* 7, 4: 564-589.

Frew, W. (2005) 'Out in force to foster harmony', *Sydney Morning Herald* 19 December: 4.

Gee, S. (2005) 'Good sports showing the back to the beach', *Daily Telegraph* 23 December: 9.

Gilroy, P. (1987) *There Ain't No Black in the Union Jack* Hutchinson, London.

Hage, G. (1998) *White Nation: Fantasies of White Supremacy in a Multicultural Society* Pluto Press, Annandale.

Higgins, E. (2006) 'ALP "soft on ethnic criminals"', *Australian* 18 January: 6.

Hopkins, P. (2004) 'Young Muslim men in Scotland: Inclusions and Exclusions', *Children's Geographies* 2, 2: 257-72.

Human Rights and Equal Opportunity Commission (1991) *Report of the National Inquiry into Racist Violence in Australia* Australian Government Publishing Service, Canberra.

Human Rights and Equal Opportunity Commission (2004) *Isma ϵ Listen: National Consultations on Eliminating Prejudice Against Arab and Muslim Australians*, Human Rights and Equal Opportunity Commission (HREOC), Sydney.

Jackson, P. (1989) *Maps of Meaning: An Introduction to Cultural Geography* Unwin Hyman, London.

Jaysuriya, L. (2005) 'Our shared, core values are but a myth underpinning this new racism', *Sydney Morning Herald* 17 December: 11.

Johnson, C. (2002) 'The dilemmas of ethnic privilege: a comparison of constructions of 'British', 'English' and 'Anglo-Celtic' identity in contemporary British and Australian political discourse', *Ethnicities* 2, 2: 163-188.

Kennedy L., Murphy, D., Brown, M., Colquhoun, T. (2005) 'Our Racist Shame' *Sydney Morning Herald* 12 December: 1, 4.

Levett, C. (2005) 'Asian leaders quiz PM over riots', *Sydney Morning Herald* 15 December: 1.

McIlveen, L. (2005) 'An ugly descent into mob thuggery', *Daily Telegraph* 12 December: 1-3.

Maddox, M. (2005) God Under Howard: The Rise of the Religious Right in Australian Politics Allen and Unwin, Crows Nest.

Marcus, C. (2005) 'Anxious Madona feels cut off from Australia', *St George and Sutherland Shire Leader* 13 December: 10.

Marr, D. and Wilkinson, M. (2003) *Dark Victory*, Allen and Unwin, Crows Nest.

Modood, T. (2005) *Multicultural Politics: Racism, Ethnicity and Muslims in Britain* University of Minnesota Press and University of Edinburgh Press.

Morris, L. (2005a) 'Riot and attacks a blemish, says Pell', *Sydney Morning Herald,* 21 December: 5.

Morris, L. (2005b) 'Churches urge peace and unity', *Sydney Morning Herald,* 23-24 December: 2.

Murphy D. (2005) 'Thugs ruled the streets, and the mob sang Waltzing Matilda', *Sydney Morning Herald* 12 December: 4-5.

Norrie, J. (2005) 'Locals talk of fear and disgust after violence of bloody Sunday', *Sydney Morning Herald* 12 December: 7.

Phillips, T. and Smith, P. (2000) 'What is "Australian"? Knowledge and attitudes among a gallery of contemporary Australians', *Australian Journal of Political Science* 35, 2: 203-224.

Poynting, S. (2006) 'Cronulla: Understanding the violence and conflict', in Gopalkrishnan, N and Swee-Hin,T (eds.) *Proceedings of the National Symposium Responding to Cronulla: Rethinking Multiculturalism,* Griffith University, 21 February, 2006 University of the Sunshine Coast: 32-7.

Poynting, S. and Noble, G. (2004) Living with Racism: The Experience and Reporting by Arab and Muslim Australians of Discrimination, Abuse and Violence Since September 11, 2001, *Report to the Human Rights and Equal Opportunity Commission,* Centre for Cultural Research, University of Western Sydney.

Renan, E. (1882 reprinted 1990) 'What is a nation?' in Bhabha, H.K. (ed.) *Nation and Narration* Routledge, London: 8-22.

Sheehan, P. (2006) 'How the politics of sheer populism led to racial riots', *Sydney Morning Herald* 16 January: 9.

Smith, S. (2005) 'Chasing the 'race' and 'ethnic' votes: profiles of minor parties and their positions within the Australian political landscapes of 'racism', 1999 and 2003 New South Wales state elections', in Khoo, T. (Ed.) *The Body Politic: Racialised Political Cultures in Australia,* Proceedings of the Australian Studies Centre Conference, Brisbane: University of Queensland Australian Studies Centre and Monash University National Centre for Australian Studies. Accessed 20 April 2006 from http://www.asc.uq.edu.au/bodypolitic/.

Strike Force Neil (2006) *Cronulla Riots: Review of the Police Response,* Vol. 1. Sydney: NSW Police.

Stringa, P. (2005) 'Darkest day for so-called patriotism: boozed-up crowd erupts', *St George and Sutherland Shire Leader* 13 December: 2-3.

*Sydney Morning Herald* (2005) 'Editorial', Sydney Morning Herald 16 November: 12.

Trembath, M. (2005) 'Shame transformed into healing of scars', *St George and Sutherland Shire Leader* 20 December: 5.

Wallace, N. and Brown, M. (2005) 'Cronulla train bashing accused released on bail', *Sydney Morning Herald* 23 December: 7.

Warren, J., Harper A. and Whittington, J. (2002) *Sheilas, Wogs & Poofters: An Incomplete Biography of Johnny Warren and Soccer in Australia* Random House, Sydney.

Watson, R. (2005) 'Enough is enough: League stars line up against violence', *Daily Telegraph* 15 December: 1, 43.

Watson, R. and Gee, S. (2005) 'Anger ignites an unholy war', *Daily Telegraph* 15 December: 5.

Winchester, H., Kong, L. and Dunn, K. (2003) *Landscapes: ways of imagining the world* Pearson/Prentice Hall, Harlow.

Zevallos, Z. (2005) '"It's like we're their culture": second-generation migrant women discuss Australian culture', *People and Place* 13, 2: 41-48.

# Notes

[1] A utility [ute] is a motor vehicle with a flat-bed rear for transport.

[2] This contrasts to the 'Public Attitudes Towards Islam in Australia Project' finding that 81% of respondents were not bothered by Muslims wearing hijab (Dunn, 2004b, 2009).

[3] The Australia First Party was founded by a former One Nation Party activist in 2002. The One Nation Party (ONP) was jointly founded by the more well known Pauline Hanson, but dipped from the political landscape since the 1990s (Davis and Stimson, 1998; Smith, 2005). Some argue that this is because the mainstream parties, more specifically the Federal Liberal leadership, captured Hanson's political platforms and much of the ONP constituency (Marr and Wilkinson, 2003). During 2005-6, the Australia First Party had been attempting to re-register as a political party, and maintained a platform of discriminatory immigration.

[4] The *Hazzard Report* for the New South Wales Police Service refuted this characterisation of the earlier incident between an off-duty Caucasian lifesaver and an Australian of Middle Eastern appearance. Strike Force Neil described it thus: 'The incident was started by two young men objecting to the other staring at him. An argument took place and insulting and indecent remarks were made by both young men. A fight followed and was

was on ethnic deviancy, with media opinion pieces and talk radio
concentrating on those youth involved in the revenge attacks. It was
asserted that the government and police had been going soft on ethnic
gangs in the Lakemba area [in the Bankstown LGA of western Sydney],
and that youth from these gangs were the cause of the incivilities that had
generated the race riots (*Australian*, 2006: 13; Higgins, 2006: 6; Sheehan,
2006: 9). Such criticisms of Lebanese youth had been relayed on talk radio
in the lead up the riot, with criticism of 'out-of-control Lebanese Muslim
gangs who hold us … in contempt' and attack 'ordinary Australian girls'
(Maddox, 2005: 166). The *Hazzard Report* (Strike Force Neil, 2006: 7-8,27-
8,33-34) apportioned a deal of blame for the riot to talk radio and tabloid
newspapers, who were criticised for disseminating inaccuracies about
events leading up the riot, using racist language, and inciting racist violence.
[6] A former Cronulla Rugby League professional, and surf club member led
the crowd in chants of: 'No more Lebs', and 'No Lebs in Sutherland Shire',
and in his oration to the crowd stated: 'We've put up with this for five or
six years. Enough is enough. We're sick of them putting it on our girls...,
we're not going to cop it any more. This is what our grandfathers fought
for … we don't need Lebos to take it away from us'. This role model later
made apologised to the Lebanese Muslim community, expressing his
embarrassment and shame, as did others who stated that the protest had
'escalated out of control under the influence of right-wing racists, from
outside this community, and alcohol' (Watson and Gee, 2005: 5).

# Chapter six

# 'The Muslims are our misfortune!'

## Geoffrey Brahm Levey and A. Dirk Moses

The Cronulla Riots have been understood principally in terms of ethnic conflict and White Australian racism. In this chapter, we introduce a comparative dimension by briefly examining pre- and post-Nazi anti-Semitism in Europe and Australia. As non-Christians, the presence of Jewish minorities posed challenges for their Christian hosts that bear comparison in many respects with western Muslims today; we will argue that these comparisons help to reveal the deep societal and cultural dynamics at play in the Cronulla riot and its 'reception'.

We begin by examining the German nationalist reaction of historian Heinrich von Treitschke to Jewish emancipation in the late nineteenth century, and ask after the parallels with the Australian nationalist reaction to Muslim immigration. Secondly, we argue that 'pogrom' is a better term than 'riot' for the events of December 2005 by considering anti-Jewish violence in Imperial Russia as well as lynching of Black men in the United States. Then we turn to the question of Jewish immigration and assimilation in post-war Australia; was Australia in the 1950s so different to Germany in the 1880s in its ethnic self-understanding? Finally, we consider the reaction to suggestions of racism in the Cronulla riots, and how the invocation of 'core values' masks deep tensions in Australian norms and expectations.

### 'A word about our Jewry'

In 1880, Heinrich von Treitschke (1834-1896) wrote a much-discussed article entitled, in English: 'A word about our Jewry'. This article bears a remarkable resemblance to the conservative media commentariat's views about Muslims in Australia today. Striking the pose of the neutral observer, Treitschke noted that the philo-Semitic public culture was changing and proposed to explain why. He did not oppose the new anti-Semitic tone emerging in Germany because, in his view it meant that finally, open discussion of a real problem had commenced: 'the instinct of the masses has in fact clearly recognized a great danger, a serious sore spot of the new German national life; the current expression of 'the German Jewish question' is more than an empty phrase' (Treitschke, 1880/1995: 343).

The framing of the 'Australian Muslim question' after Cronulla proceeded in the same way. For many newspaper columnists and media commentators, as we will see below, the Anglo-Australian violence expressed the righteous indignation of the Australian masses, and political correctness could no longer blind us to this fact. We were told that the events permitted us, finally, to talk openly, and without fear of being labelled a racist, about the problem of Muslims. Treitschke's answer was no different from the demand made of Australian Muslims:

> What we have to demand from our Jewish fellow-citizens is simple: that they become Germans, regard themselves simply and justly as Germans, without prejudice to their faith and their sacred past which all of us hold in reverence; for we do not want an era of German-Jewish mixed culture to follow after thousands of years of German civilization (Treitschke, 1880/1995: 343).

What was it about these Jews that offended Treitschke? Above all, it was their perceived sense of cultural superiority and their 'stubborn contempt for the German *goyim* [gentile]', which manifested itself in dishonest business dealings and domination of the press. The latter, he wrote, led to the perversion of public opinion, because Jewish journalists slandered the nation, writing 'without any reverence, like an outsider, as if mockery of Germany did not cut deeply into the heart of every individual German' (Treitschke, 1880/1995: 344).

No-one in Australia claims that Muslims or Arabs dominate journalism, but the feeling among conservatives that 'cultural elites' denigrate the nation and mock ordinary Australians echoes Treitschke's criticism of the media's alienation from the sentiments of the vast majority of common people. These critics maintain that the press has been hijacked by a dangerous and culturally alien element that undermines the substance of the nation. What is more, from the conservative columnists' perspective, these Anglo cultural elites prevent open discussion of the 'Muslim problem' by mobilising political correctness; they are said to be pro-Muslim, the functional equivalent of Trietschke's 'Jewish press'.

Populist commentators here also share Treitschke's objection to immigrants' demand for equal treatment. For instance, he complained, Jews wanted Christian pictures removed (presumably from public buildings), and the Sabbath celebrated at mixed schools (Treitschke, 1880/1995: 345). The Australian outrage at Muslim requests such as short periods of gender segregated swimming in public pools expresses the same impatience.

Treitschke was no radical anti-Semite compared to some contemporaries who wanted to reverse Jewish emancipation (i.e., granting of legal equality). He was prepared to acknowledge the efforts of some Jews to assimilate, for instance, by campaigning against usury (money lending) among fellow Jews. This distinction between good and bad immigrants is repeated here in the separation between 'moderate' and 'radical' Muslims; what distinguishes the two categories is the perceived preparedness of the former to integrate.

But does this distinction obtain in reality? Resistance to full assimilation is the problem for Australia's nationalists, for them, any residue of cultural difference is interpreted as 'radical'; hence the hysteria about Muslim women wearing head coverings. Although such dress harms no-one, it is considered offensive, even 'confronting', as the former Prime Minister John Howard put it (*Age*, 2006). Treitschke expressed the political emotions of the issue in the following terms: the 'reason for the passionate anger in our days' was the immigrants' 'lack of respect' for the locals. That is why, he reported, that he heard men in even 'the best educated circles' say 'the Jews are our misfortune!' (Treitschke, 1880/1995: 345). Reading many Australian columnists, it is easy to detect the same message about Muslims and Arabs.

The Nazis made this phrase – 'the Jews are our misfortune' – notorious in their propaganda, but it is doubtful whether Treitschke would have supported their genocidal policies; he was a nationalist who wanted Jews to assimilate, not a totalitarian fanatic who advocated their expulsion or murder. His anti-Semitism thus omitted some of Adolf Hitler's lurid phantasms, such as the infamous passage in *Mein Kampf* where the author worries about Jewish men preying on fair German maidens: 'The black-haired Jewish youth lies in wait for hours on end, satanically glaring at and spying on the unsuspicious girl whom he plans to seduce, adulterating her blood and removing her from the bosom of her own people' (Hitler, 1940: 448).

Such primal anxieties about race and sex are common in all societies. Consider the ritualised sadism of lynching in the South of the United States, replete with castrations and other torture, which often attended rumours of Black men raping White women (Gilmore, 1998; Whites, 1998). The Nazis took these anxieties to the extreme, but was Australia immune from a moderate version of this when Lebanese-Australian gang rapists were sentenced to unprecedented jail terms, longer than for murder (Crichton, 2002: 1)? Were not these sentences redemptive punishments? Was the outrage at these terrible crimes *not only* an understandable expression of indignation at gang rape, *but also* symptomatic of the fear that, so to speak, 'black-haired Arab youths lie in wait for hours on end, satanically glaring at and spying on unsuspicious Anglo girls'?

## Pogroms

If Treitschke did not explicitly approve of violence or legitimise fears of racial defilement, his intellectual justification of anti-Semitism was of a piece with elite reactions to pogroms against Russian Jews and lynchings of African Americans during his lifetime. Government officials and newspaper editors in both these cases would consistently ascribe the violence of the majority against a hapless minority to an understandable, if extreme, reaction to 'Jewish domination and exploitation' or against some Black crime, criminalising the victims of mob violence rather than the mass of people who perpetrated it. Because the Australian media's reaction to the Cronulla riots was the same, it is worth considering whether 'pogrom' is a more appropriate word for the violence.

The term derives from the Russian word for thunder (*grom*) and the verb *pogromit*, which means 'to smash' or 'to conquer'. The word became associated with attacks on Russian Jews during the nineteenth century, and more recently on Roma ('Gypsies') in contemporary Europe. Significantly, while Imperial Russian authorities themselves usually referred to these attacks as disturbances, disorders or riots, contemporary observers and later historians have used the term pogrom (Klier, 1992: 34f; Barany, 2002). If we also class American lynchings as pogroms, the scholarly literature on the topic concurs in listing the following generic, historical features:

- They customarily occur when established social and ethnic hierarchies are disturbed by economic change and immigration.
- Press campaigns against these developments are a prerequisite.
- Local frictions, different in circumstance, take place over the terms of civic inclusion and exclusion of immigrants and minorities.
- Contrary to popular opinion, they were not organised by state authorities.
- They are not caused by prejudice *per se*, and police inaction.
- Lower classes of the majority population are anxious that their ethnic status, which assigns them a higher rank than the minority, is threatened.
- Pogroms are not a constant feature of multi-ethnic societies, but occur in times of social stress. In Russia in 1881/82 and 1905/06, for instance, the authority of the state was weak, and many worried that Jews, who represented a new liberal order, would dominate. The question of 'who is in charge' or 'for whom does the state govern' becomes paramount (Rogger, 1992: 314-372; Hoffmann et al., 2002; Rohrbacher, 1993).
- The minority is seen as an aggressor against society, as a guest who abuses the hospitality of the host, who betrays the society by exploiting or abusing its members. Although the descendants of African slaves could not be described as guests

GEOFFREY BRAHM LEVEY AND A. DIRK MOSES

or immigrants, the notion of outsiders violating the ethnic
hierarchy was evident when Whites in the American South
complained about 'defiance by the Negroes', and express alarm
at their supposed 'threatening attitude' (Vinikas, 1999: 536).

• The point of the pogrom is to put the subordinate minority
group back in its place, the violence is not just instrumental
(i.e., looting shops), it is also symbolic. The message is: 'This is
our country. Don't behave as if you own the place. Stay in your
(subordinate) place!'

• After the pogrom, elites justify the violence by defaming the
character of the victims.

Significant differences can be discerned between the extent of
violence in Russian and American pogroms in the late nineteenth
and early twentieth centuries and the Cronulla incident. The former
often claimed hundreds of lives at a time, with significant property
damage while no-one was killed or even seriously injured in
Cronulla. Pogroms became routine in Russia and the United States
because Christians had been allowed to get away with the violence
on previous occasions; no pogroms occurred in Russia in places
where authorities would not tolerate them. Happily, police
intervened in the violence in Cronulla, and the courts prosecuted
offenders afterwards; does this mean that the pogrom analogy is
overdrawn?

We need to ask ourselves what would have happened had the
police and later, the courts not intervened so forcefully; it is likely
that some of the victims would have been very seriously injured if
not killed. The passions aroused on Sydney beaches, and the other
features of Cronulla, then, do bear a disturbing resemblance to a
pogrom. Although Muslims and Arabs occupy a different space in
the economic system to Jews in Imperial Russia and Blacks in the
Southern states, they are nevertheless cast as social enemies by
media commentators who routinely complain about their supposed
welfare parasitism and anti-social behaviour. In addition, a crisis of
consciousness was cultivated in Australia by a government that
painted asylum seekers and local Muslims as terrorist security
threats.

For their part, some Arab Australian youths violated conventional norms of behaviour at the beach prior to the riot; whatever the provocation though, did it warrant the extent of the wanton brutality of 11 December? After all, *anyone* with 'Mediterranean looks' was attacked, irrespective of whether they were members of gangs, including women wearing hijabs. This targeting was very discriminating in its indiscriminateness and for this reason the excess of violence and rhetoric cannot be explained by inter-gang rivalry or youthful machismo.

After the pogrom, the entire Arab Australian and Muslim Australian community was subject to a relentless campaign of vilification. By mid-January 2006, media and political hysteria about the gangs of south west Sydney and the supposed impotence of police was growing. However the tendency to denigrate Arab Australians had begun earlier (Sheehan, 2005a and 2005b); before Christmas 2005, News Limited and many Fairfax writers began decrying Lebanese-Australian men as members of 'gangs' while the youths of Anglo-Cronulla were described as merely 'beachgoers' (Norton, 2005). By identifying the Lebanese-Australian community's supposed inability to integrate, by focusing on the bad beach behaviour of youths 'of Middle Eastern appearance', they suggested that the denizens of Cronulla were unduly provoked. The editors of the Australian made this point plain when they argued 'there is a degree of racism' in all societies and people - that is apparently an anthropological constant - so that the efforts of many to end racism is 'an exercise in fanaticism'. The fanatics were not the neo-Nazis but those who opposed them, the anti-racist 'cultural elites'.

Moreover, according to the same commentary, the ethnic self-defence of the native born was said to be a natural and normal response which should not be pathologised by what that newspaper inanely called 'the multiculturalism industry' (*Australian* 2005a). The problem, we are led to conclude, was the supposed inability of Lebanese-Australian youths to assimilate.

An argument against the 'Cronulla pogrom' proposition may be that Russian and American pogroms were enforcing an explicitly racist hierarchy in which pogroms were supposed to keep subalterns in their place, whereas in multicultural Australia there is equality before the law and a stated ethos of equal respect for all people. While this may be true on paper, the widespread incidence of Australian flags being wrapped like superman capes around the rioters suggests otherwise. The rioter's self-understanding needs to be taken more seriously if we are to appreciate the inner nature of national identity. They were not simply guarding their beach against unwelcome intruders, they were also defending the nation against its perceived colonisation by foreigners ('Lebs' and 'Wogs'). The infamous text message says it all: 'Come to Cronulla this weekend to take revenge. This Sunday every Aussie in the shire get down to North Cronulla to support the leb and wog bashing day'.

## A word about Jewish immigration to Australia

Two years before the Jews of France first won their emancipation, up to a dozen Jews arrived in Australia on the First Fleet as convicts (Levi and Bergman, 2002). Most of the convicts were eventually emancipated and to their credit, no Australian colony, state, or territory has ever needed to emancipate its Jews. Jewish free settlers and emancipated convicts enjoyed all the rights and opportunities of their far more numerous Christian counterparts (Getzler, 1970). Like their French and German co-religionists, the small Jewish community in the Australian colonies and later in the new Commonwealth of Australia assiduously integrated and acculturated to the local way of life. One of them, John Monash – the son of German-Jewish immigrants – went on to become commander of the Australian Corps in World War I. Another, Isaac Isaacs, became the first Australian-born Governor-General (1931-36). Yet neither the Jews' presence in Australia since the beginning of European settlement, their successful integration, or their attainment of high state office mattered during the 1940s and early 1950s when the Australian government succumbed to popular prejudice and restricted the immigration of European Jewish refugees.

Immediately after the war, the new Department of Immigration under Minister Arthur Calwell introduced a humanitarian program by allowing some 2,000 Holocaust survivors to come to Australia as part of the family reunion program. Vigorous opposition to the program had developed by 1946, as historian Suzanne Rutland (2001: 52) records: 'Alarmist headlines and anti-refugee articles and cartoons filled the press. It was claimed that Jewish migrants were enjoying preferential treatment in securing passage to Australia and were aggravating the housing shortage'. The concept of 'queue-jumping' evidently has a long lineage in the Australian imagination, but this was not the only concern. 'Yellow press' outlets like *Smith's Weekly* claimed that the Jews were disloyal, a claim largely based on apprehension about 'Jewish terrorism' in Palestine, where Great Britain was the Mandate power. Senior British officials had been assassinated by Zionist militants in Palestine, and the King David Hotel was bombed in July 1946, leading to violent anti-Jewish rhetoric in both Australia and Britain (Rubinstein, 1991: 387f.). A letter sent in 1946 to Prime Minister Chifley by an H. Osborne, who included a copy of an article claiming that Jews in Palestine refused to serve British troops in cafes and spat on British troops and civilians in the streets, captured the popular mood:

> In view of this cutting and recent outrage in Palestine will you issue instructions that no more Jews be allowed into Australia. It is public knowledge that the Minister for Immigration favours Jews and Jews in Melbourne boast that they can obtain any assistance from him. Alien Jews are nearly all Zionists and are against we British. (quoted in Rutland, 2003: 60).

Yet another complaint was about Jewish business acumen, echoing Treitschke's complaint about the business and professional acumen of German Jews. Jack Lang thundered in Federal Parliament: 'Although thousands of soldiers are unable to enter business in our country because of rationing and other controls, most of these aliens slip straight into business when they leave the ship'. Even respectable newspapers joined the chorus of disapproval: the *Canberra Times* complained about black market activities of Jews and their supposed ungovernability (Rubinstein, 1991: 385). In this vein, the traditional charge that Jews were unassimilable was raised; the Liberal Member for Henty in Victoria, H.B. Gullett, for instance, declared that 'We are not compelled to be a dumping ground for people whom Europe has not been able to absorb for 2000 years' (Rutland, 2001: 53) and similar sentiments were common in the RSL (Rubinstein, 1991: 386). Jews then, were regarded in terms that were eerily similar to the attitudes towards Muslims in Australia today: as queue jumping refugees, economically parasitical, clannish, and associated with terrorism. 'Frequently the [Jewish] terrorist violence in Palestine', one historian noted, 'was linked, irrationally but potently, to the prospect of Jewish refugee migration to Australia' (Rubinstein, 1991: 388). The same could be said of Muslim refugees to Australia since the Tampa affair in 2001.

Calwell believed that Australia's need for increased immigration might founder on the backlash against Jewish immigration. He thus set a quota of no more than 25 percent of Jews being allowed to travel on any one vessel sailing to Australia, effectively stymieing Jewish arrivals. In his autobiography, he would later explain the need for a Jewish quota in terms now reminiscent of John Howard's 1988 statement on the need to slow Asian immigration. (Kelly, 1992:423). According to Calwell, allowing boatloads of Jews into Australia 'would have created a great wave of anti-Semitism and would have been electorally disastrous for the Labor Party' (quoted in Rutland, 2002: 163). Acquiescence obviously is one way of responding to popular prejudice, another of course is to combat it.

## Racism, core values and the 'Muslim question'

For this reason, the central issue debated in the media about the Cronulla riots – that of whether they represented racism or a cultural clash – is at once wholly bogus and very revealing. The reluctance of Australians to acknowledge racism among themselves tends to be based or defended on three assumptions: one is the defensive assumption that 'we' – a tolerant, easy-going, and peace-loving people, as former Prime Minister John Howard liked to say – simply aren't capable of such dastardly prejudice. The historical record, as in the Australian response to Jewish immigration in the 1940s just canvassed, clearly shows otherwise.

A second assumption driving the denial of racism appears to be the common equation of racism with a specifically biologically-based prejudice; an equation doubtless informed by nineteenth century associations of race with bloodlines and physiognomy and in the popular imagination, with their visitation on American Blacks and European Jews in the twentieth century. This narrow conception of 'racism' flies in the face of how the term has come to be legally and commonly used; the *Anti-Discrimination Act 1977* (NSW), for example, is not unusual in defining 'race' broadly, as including 'colour, nationality, descent and ethnic, ethno-religious or national origin'. Yet even using a biological conception of race, one would be hard-pressed to deny racism at work in the Cronulla conflagration: after all, from various quarters, people *were* targeted on the basis of their physical appearance, among other things.

The third assumption behind the denials of Australian racism relates to a misbegotten sense that racial prejudice is indelible. The *Australian* initially took this stance, insisting that racism had nothing to do with the Cronulla episode and, we were told, such talk showed only the contempt of 'Howard haters' for ordinary Australians. To make its case, the newspaper proposed a distinction be drawn between 'prejudice directed against migrants, which time heals, and racism, which festers for centuries' (*Australian* 2005b). The trouble with this distinction is that it simply ignores how the category of 'race' denotes the marking out of those deemed to be alien, unassimilable or beneath respect at any point in time, which is of course how racism works. Who is considered acceptable and who is considered unacceptable changes over time according to governmental and popular sentiment (de Lepervanche and Bottomley, 1988; Stratton, 2000: 195-219), one need only trace the history of the 'White Australia' policy, for example, and the shifting definitions of who is 'White' – or White enough – to see this.

Presumably, it was out of some realisation of these various points that not even the *Australian* could keep denying the obvious and in its 22 December *volte face* suddenly saw racism as ubiquitous and natural and as noted, tried arguing instead that the real problem lies with those who condemn these 'understandable' reactions of many Anglo-Australians. A year on though, there were again voices wishing above all else to preserve the nation's honour against the stain of racism (eg. Switzer, 2006).

To be sure, thuggery figured in the riots, which is a matter of law enforcement. Doubtless too, the riots contained elements of a clash of cultural norms in Australian society and here, the appropriate solution is acculturation. The engine room of acculturation; especially for the second generation, has always been schools and it is appropriate to ask why our schools may be failing in the case of some section of migrant groups. But the Cronulla pogrom was much more than thuggery or a lack of acculturation, such characterisations miss the thick symbolism that was manifest throughout the episode, and the fact that so many of the culprits were 'clean skins' with no prior record of misdemeanour and who afterwards could barely understand or articulate what moved them to be involved. For example one of the apprehended, who kicked his victim to the ground and incited a screaming crowd to gather around the man, was a JP Morgan financial analyst and classical pianist who came from a family with 'strong Christian values' (*Sydney Morning Herald,* 2006: 1).

As the media reaction to the episode confirms, the underlying dynamic of the Cronulla riots goes to the heart of how Australian society frames its 'core culture' and who is admitted into it; and thus how it looks upon and treats its minorities. All this is very much despite the spirit and terms of Australian multiculturalism. Conservative commentators see the problem as one of minorities simply not respecting or heeding the core culture when in fact, the problem runs much deeper than this – in two ways.

First, as in other liberal democracies, there are deep tensions within the prevailing Australian self-understanding of its own core culture (Levey, 2008). On the one hand there are the liberal democratic norms frequently cited as part of Australia's political and cultural inheritance; such as liberty, equality, toleration, reciprocity and respect for democratic processes and institutions. On the other hand, there are the national-cultural or lifestyle norms having to do with the Australian way of life and captured by the sentiment 'This is how we do things here!' When members of the political community are steeped in the same national culture, it is easy to assume that liberty and equality also are being honoured since everyone wants to do much the same thing; but when some members observe different practices and traditions, as they do in culturally diverse democracies like Australia, then the attachments to the 'national culture' and the commitment to liberal democratic values do not always coincide. Yet both dimensions are claimed to be part of the core culture. To the customary exhortation of our politicians and media commentators: 'If you choose to live here then observe our core values!' the appropriate response must be, '*Which* values?' The norms regarding how the Anglo-Celtic Christian majority look, speak, behave and lead their lives? Or the core values involving liberal democratic norms? And if the latter, then why doesn't the value on liberty and equality entitle citizens to live differently from the Anglo-Celtic Christian majority where there is no harm involved?

The tendency of national cultural majorities to conflate their own cultural and lifestyle norms with the expression of liberal (and universal) values has beset social relations in modern states. The problem was in evidence in the late eighteenth century during the European debates over the extension of civic equality to the Jews, when their fitness for citizenship was challenged on the grounds that they separated themselves from their fellows through their kosher dietary laws and by marrying their own, were unable to make good soldiers because they were too short and unable to fight on the Sabbath, or were disloyal (Mendes-Flohr and Reinharz, 1995: sections II and III). Today, we see the same dynamic at work regarding Muslims. For example, the *Australian*, Liberal backbenchers Bronwyn Bishop and Sophie Panopoulos and endless letter writers to editors describe the veil, hijab, or burqa worn by some Muslim women as a 'mark of separation' and therefore unacceptable (e.g. *Australian, 2006*).

The second profound problem with the insistence on respect for the core culture is, perhaps, even more vexatious than the first. Even where cultural minorities or their members *do* assimilate and integrate, they are rejected or made to feel unwelcome. This was the experience of Jews in Treitschke's Germany and in Australia during the 1940s. In both cases, the main problem was precisely the fear that Jews were *too good* at integrating. The socioeconomic and cultural situation of Muslims may presently differ in this regard, but there is little reason to suppose that assimilation or integration will bring easy acceptance.

But perhaps the most telling sign of the depth of the problem of cultural exclusion and double standards is the inability of leaders and commentators from the dominant cultural majority even to see that it exists. Instead, they defensively interpret criticisms and frustrations of the way they relate to or treat minorities as a threat to their cultural dominance and values (Albrechtsen, 2005). In this respect, it is not surprising that the official website of The Knights Party, USA – the political wing of the Ku Klux Klan – featured these responses to the Cronulla riot in its 'international news affecting White Christians world wide' forum (Knights Party, 2005). In their eyes, such criticism requires virile reaffirmations of 'our core values' and reminding minorities of their 'place'. So the cycle continues and the problem festers.

## Conclusion

What we witnessed in Cronulla evidences a complex of issues. It is clear to us, however, that deep and longstanding social and political dynamics were in play behind the pogrom and its treatment by the media. Unless and until our political leaders and nationalist opinion makers begin to appreciate this complexity and indeed, their own deep complicity in it, then inter-ethnic relations will continue to be a sore, and sometimes explosive, point in this country.

## References

*Age* (2006) 'Muslim garb "confronting": PM', *Age* 27 February: 1.

Albrechtsen, J. (2005) 'Racism is repulsive, but so is self-loathing', *Australian* 14 December: 10.

*Australian* (2005a) 'The racism furphy', *Australian* 22 December: 15.

*Australian* (2005b) 'Racism not endemic', *Australian* 14 December: 15.

*Australian* (2006) 'The veiled conceit of multiculturalism', *Australian* 24 October: 15.

Barany, Z. (1992) *The East European Gypsies: Regime Change, Marginality, and Ethnopolitics* Cambridge University Press, Cambridge.

Crichton, S. (2002) 'Sword of justice fells worst rapist', *Sydney Morning Herald*, 16 August: 1.

De Lepervance, M. and Bottomley, G. (eds.) (1988) *The Social Construction of Race* Sydney Association for Studies in Society and Culture, Sydney.

Getzler, I. (1970) *Neither Toleration nor Favour: The Australian Chapter of Jewish Emancipation* Melbourne University Press, Carlton, Vic.

Gilmore, G. (1998) 'Murder, Memory and the Flight of the Incubus', in Cecelski, D. and Tyson, T. (eds.), *Democracy Betrayed: The Wilmington Race Riot of 1898 and its Legacy* University of North Carolina Press, Chapel Hill.

Hitler, A. (1940) *Mein Kampf* Reynal and Hitchcock, New York.

Hoffmann, C., Bergmann, W. and Walser Smith, H. (eds.) (2002) *Exclusionary Violence: Antisemitic Riots in Modern German History* University of Michigan Press, Ann Arbor.

Kelly, P. (1992) *The End of Certainty*, Sydney, Allen and Unwin.

Klier, J. (1992) 'The pogrom paradigm in Russian history', in Klier, J. and Lambroza, S. (eds.), *Pogroms: Anti-Jewish Violence in Modern Russian History* Cambridge University Press, Cambridge.

Knights Party (2005) 'Official web site of the Knights Party', accessed 12 June 2009, http://www.kkk.bz/international_news_affecting_whi.htm

Levey, G. (2007) 'Multiculturalism and Australian National Identity', in Levey. G. (ed.), *Political Theory and Australian Multiculturalism* Berghahn Books, New York: 254-276.

Levi, J. and Bergman, G. (2002) *Australian Genesis: Jewish Convicts and Settlers, 1788-1860* Melbourne University Press, Carlton, Vic.

Mendes-Flohr, P. and Reinharz, J. (eds.) (1995) *The Jew in the Modern World: A Documentary History*, 2nd edn. Oxford University Press, Oxford.

Norton, A. (2005) 'If there is prejudice, there is also tolerance' *Australian* 22 December: 13.

Rogger, H. (1992) 'Conclusion and overview', in Klier, J. and Lambroza, S. (eds.), *Pogroms: Anti-Jewish Violence in Modern Russian History* Cambridge University Press, Cambridge: 314-372.

Rohrbacher, S. (1993) *Gewalt im Biedermeier: Antijüdische Ausschreitungen im Vormärz und Revolution* (1815-1848/49) Campus Verlag, Frankfurt am Main.

Rubinstein, W. (1991) *The Jews in Australia: A Thematic History vol. 2* William Heinemann, Melbourne.

Rutland, S. (2001) 'Subtle Exclusions: Postwar Jewish Emigration to Australia and the Impact of the IRO Scheme' *Journal of Holocaust Education* 10, 1: 50-66.

Rutland, S. (2002) 'Postwar Jewish 'Boat People' and Parallels with the Tampa Incident' *Australian Journal of Jewish Studies* 16: 159-76.

Rutland, S. (2003) 'Postwar Anti-Jewish Refugee Hysteria: A Case of Racial or Religious Bigotry?' *Sojourners and Strangers: Journal of Australian Studies* 77: 69-79.

Sheehan, P. (2005a) 'Nasty Reality Surfs In as Ugly Tribes Collide' *Sydney Morning Herald* 12 December: 11.

Sheehan, P. (2005b) 'Little punishment for real thugs' *Sydney Morning Herald* 19 December: 9.

Stratton, J. (2000) *Coming Out Jewish* Routledge, London.

Switzer, T. (2006) 'Beach violence not a symptom of rampant racism', *Australian* 11 December: 8.

*Sydney Morning Herald* (2006) 'Life in tatters as court mops up after lifesaver attack', 20 January: 1.

Treitschke, H von. (1880/1995) 'A word about our Jewry', in Mendes-Flohr , P. and Reinharz J. (eds.), *The Jew in the Modern World: A Documentary History* 2nd ed. Oxford University Press, Oxford: 343-346.

Vinikas, V. (1999) 'Specters in the past: the Saint Charles, Arkansas, lynching of 1904 and the limits of historical inquiry', *Journal of Southern History* 65, 3: 535-64.

Whites, L. (1998) 'Love, hate, rape, lynching: Rebecca Latimer Felton and the gender politics of racial violence', in Cecelski, D. and Tyson, T. (eds), *Democracy Betrayed: The Wilmington Race Riot of 1898 and its Legacy*, Chapel Hill: University of North Carolina Press: 143-162.

# Chapter seven

# Australian bodies, Australian sands

## Affrica Taylor

Relations between Australian bodies and Australian sands loom large in the national imaginary. Exemplified in Max Dupain's famous 'The Sunbaker' photograph (Dupain, 1937), the powerful bond between Australians and the beach is a recurring trope within national imagery and narratives. This association with the beach is built upon longstanding and shared first-hand experiences. Accessible to the vast majority of the population, who live in urban coastal regions, the beach remains unrivalled as a weekend and holiday destination, going to the beach is widely regarded as integral to Australian lifestyle and closely associated with sunshine, freedom and leisure (Game, 1991; National Museum of Australia, 2006).

In a recent study of beach culture, Booth (2001: 1) observes that for Australians who are 'surrounded by beaches', the beach simultaneously offers geographical and cultural enclosure. This relationship between geography and culture concerns me in this chapter, and I locate it in the nexus between the beach itself, embodied beach experiences and representations of national identity.

Experientially, historically and affectionately registered, the relationship between Australian bodies and Australian sands is circulated and reinforced through a vast archive of familiar images. From the stock-in-trade reconstructions of Captain Cook disembarking upon the sands of Botany Bay, to the plethora of post-Federation images of 'bronzed Aussies' relaxing on sun-drenched beaches, representations of bodies-on-the-beach have been consistently deployed to signify Australian identity. The legendary figure of the lifesaver, arguably the most recognisable Australian beach body, is regularly touted on civic occasions to embody the Australian spirit (such as the opening of the Sydney

Harbour Bridge in 1932 and the Sydney 2000 Olympics closing ceremony). Through repeated promotion and exposure, iconic images of idealised surf lifesavers' bodies have been imprinted upon the popular imagination as quintessential Australian bodies (Saunders, 1998) and the territory of the beach as a quintessential Australian site (Booth, 2001).

It was within the context of this national imaginary of quintessential Australian bodies and sands, that the Cronulla riot was triggered by a physical altercation between a group of Australian youths from Middle Eastern backgrounds and two Anglo Australian surf lifesavers. Using the riot as my springboard, I set out to de-centre the national imaginary of the 'bronzed Aussie' as the prototypical and self-evidently authentic Australian subject. I challenge the validity of any notion of an essentialised Australian identity and its associated entitlements, through tackling the exclusionary White masculinist framing of this imaginary. In order to do this, I track the trajectories of some Australian body/sand relations across a network of nature/culture semiologies and geo-historical territorial events, relocating these semiotic and territorial networks of beach relations within the unsettled cultural politics of national belonging, in which the spectrum of non-indigenous Australian-ness remains a radically open and contested field of struggle (Anderson and Taylor, 2005). I recast the array of disparate bodies on beaches that I have selected for this study, in all their heterogeneous associations, as variously engaged in performances of Australian belonging.

## Defending the dream?

The Cronulla riots can be read, literally, as an ardent defence of the dream of quintessential Australian bodies and beaches. As proclaimed in the widely circulated mobile phone text message, this was a territorial gatekeeping event of intensely disputed Australian belongings. 'This Sunday', it read, 'every Fucking Aussie in the shire, get down to North Cronulla to help support Leb and wog bashing day... Bring your mates down and let's show them this is our beach and they're never welcome back' (cited in Jackson, 2006). In response, an estimated 5,000 predominantly young white men

112

converged on the beach. By late morning, as the press images of the day demonstrate, they had formed a massive crowd of Australian flag bearing and wearing bodies (see for example *The Age*, 2006).

Exclusionary nationalist slogans were written upon the beach itself, as well as on the clothing and skin of many in the crowd. The bold lettering in the sand declaring '100% AUSSIE PRIDE' echoed the sentiments of 'White pride', a battle cry that was chanted throughout the day. The nationalist inscriptions, chants and flags simultaneously marked the (White) 'Aussie' men as self-appointed custodians of the nation and demarcated the beach as their sovereign territory. This articulation of White, male 'Aussie' bodies with 'Aussie sands' reiterated an assumed-to-be natural order of association.

In the process, the simultaneously semiotic and material 'defence' of Cronulla enacted what Whatmore (2002:61) has described as a 'provisional moment' of 'proprietorial enclosure'. White nationalist proprietorialism, the presumption of White male ownership, was provisional upon a number of historically continuous and widely accepted semiotic and material regimes of body/sand relations. It was also provisional upon a plausible formulation of 'Lebs and wogs' as inappropriate 'others', whose presence could be deemed as a serious threat to the integrity of this beach as a national space (Hage, 1998).

During the riot, the mob attacks on those of 'Middle Eastern appearance' functioned as a physical and symbolic expulsion of 'non-Aussies' from the assumed-to-be quintessential Australian space of the beach. The 'bashings', as purification rituals, were a central dramatic component of the white nationalist defence of the beach. Moreover, the raw corporeality of these violent attacks was a necessary ingredient in the performance of a national identity authenticated through oppositional definition and justified through heroic defence. In other words, the legitimacy of the White defenders' embodiment of Australian-ness was contingent upon purging those deemed-to-be un-Australian 'Leb and wog' bodies.

As a discursive and embodied hyper-performative event, Cronulla exposed the resolutely inter-corporeal and inter-textual tensions that underpin national identity politics. It has prompted me to deliberate upon the territoriality of all struggles to belong, as well as upon the ways in which present-day struggles are haunted by past events. Thus for my purposes, this Cronulla event becomes an 'extroverted' site of time/space convergence (Massey, 1993). I use this locus of constellating relations as a springboard to explore lines of connection with other key bodies and sites from other moments in Australia's nation-building past. From this 'provisional moment' of 'proprietorial enclosure', I trace a network of beach relations within the uneven landscape of Australian belongings.

## Relational Thinking

The relational approach that I am taking involves more than just establishing a series of historical and place-based connections and associations with the Cronulla riots. It is a way of reconsidering identity and agency. It addresses the limits of individual autonomy by paying more attention to human inter-subjectivities, or to what we might call, following Butler (2004a: 25), our mutual enmeshment with each other. As Butler reminds us, we can only ever know ourselves through each other: we are neither fully known to ourselves nor totally self-determining because we continually 'perform' ourselves for each other and through each other. In a blending of Butler's understanding of the limits of autonomy with Althusser's (1971) notion of the interpellation of individuals as national subjects, those who were interpellated by the rallying call to 'every fucking Aussie in the shire' and their 'mates' to 'get down to North Cronulla' as being hailed into 'doing' this national identity performance (bashing 'Lebs and wogs') with and for each other. This relational emphasis is a significant shift away from accepting the rioters on their own terms, as self-evidently, independently and already essentially 'Aussies'. While not denying the profound racism of the event, this same relational emphasis also steers me away from a definitive appraisal of 5,000 self-determining individual white racists spontaneously joining forces through malevolent intent. Instead, it prompts me to trace the threads of their 'enmeshment' with others in order to suggest a complex web of collectively racialised agency.

Moreover, not all of these others with which we are enmeshed are human. Like Whatmore (2002), who transported the notion of human/non human hybridities from Actor Network Theory (Latour, 2005) and feminist science studies (Haraway, 1991) into human geography, my approach acknowledges the affect, effect and actancy of a range of non-human elements, things or physical environments upon the meaning-making processes and 'social fabric' of our lives. Such acknowledgements are part of an effort to decentre the human and dislodge a resolutely anthro-centric notion of agency. By flagging that it was not only the relations between the self-proclaimed 'Aussies' and the 'Lebs and wogs' that mattered in the Cronulla flare-up, but wider networks of body/sand relations, I have gestured towards a 'hybrid geography' (Whatmore, 2002) of human/non-human provisionalities. In the second part of this chapter I will investigate a fuller set of historical, geographical, discursive, human and non-human relations that underpinned the event.

Through remaining open to the complex mergings and inter-determinancies of our lives, relational thinking/writing necessarily involves complicating binary orderings (Allen, 1999). For instance, the beach (as passive nature) is not set up in binary contradistinction to the human activities (as productive culture) that occur upon it. Rather, and as foreshadowed in the consideration of non-human agency, the neat nature/culture divide is blurred by investigating the inter-determinancy of Australian bodies and sands. The sets of meanings ascribed to nature, or in this case discourses of the Australian beach, remain a consistent point of interest. This is because the semiology of the beach is co-implicated in the construction of the authentic Australian subject and must therefore be understood, at least partially, as a cultural construct.

This is not to say that the beach is only a human concept. As Latour (1998) points out: 'The weakness of semiotics has always been to consider meaning production away from what the nature of entities really are'. Through taking a relational approach to bodies and beaches, in which the elemental nature of the beach itself is one of the 'players' (rather than a set on which human activities take place), I attempt to acknowledge that the elemental nature of the beach has affect and is partially determining of human experience and meaning-making. In other words, a relational approach tries to take note of the fact that not only do humans act on the beach, but the beach acts on humans. It is this boundary-blurring generative interaction that is the focal point of my study.

A relational approach also challenges the 'us' and 'them' binaries of identity. Referring to previous commentaries about Cronulla, I have begun to interrupt the invariant oppositional distinction between the assumed-to-be authentic or real (White) Australian and the judged-to-be essentially un-Australian 'Leb and wog' others by refocusing upon the dynamic processes through which the fiction of the 'real' (White) Australian is produced. In the Cronulla case, those self-appointed 'Aussies' were compelled to position the 'Lebs and the Wogs' as the un-Australians in order to affirm themselves as the 'real' Australians. This way of thinking foregrounds the inter-subjective performativity of *all* Australian identities.

By recognising the limits to autonomy and taking these inter-determinancies seriously, relational thinking leads us to confront the ways in which we are simultaneously vulnerable to and responsible for others (Butler, 2004b), casting such thinking within the spectrum of ethics. Drawing upon Levinas' philosophy that 'self is not a substance but a relation' - relational thinking leads us to acknowledge, as Rose (2004:13) puts it, that 'life with others is continually entangled in responsibility'. Moreover, for Rose, as she articulates an ethics of decolonisation, this includes taking responsibility for past relations. This decolonising ethics requires us to simultaneously acknowledge our inter-subjectivities and our inter-temporalities and becoming cognizant of the ways that colonial relations (regardless of our efforts to disavow them) continue to inhere in the present and to shape our lives.

As I move to further relational considerations of Australian bodies and sands, I trace connections between differently marked bodies and identities in different times and beach environments, between bodies, senses and non-human elements, and between hegemonic and counter-hegemonic representations of belonging. These interlocking trajectories can be understood as a series of nestings or articulations with the territorial struggles at Cronulla. It is important to reiterate that they are not intended to function as crude causal explanations of the event. Rather they seek to evoke an appreciation of the web of inter-relations and effects that constitute our lives as provisional and contingent. They represent an attempt to take account of our convergence with all manner of others, events and discursive regimes and thereby to encourage a more 'extroverted' consideration of identity.

Networks of relations are characteristically unwieldy. In an attempt to steer a pathway through this complexity, I have identified two trajectories which articulate with the events at Cronulla. They are neither definitive nor discrete trajectories: the first, 'staking out Australian sands', registers several significant historical nation-building performances enacted on the beach. The second section is a selection of emplacement performances, or snapshots of the ways in which certain bodies come to be regarded as Australian through appearing to be 'in place' on the beach. I call these 'embodying Australian beaches'.

## Staking Out Australian Sands

The inaugural beach flag staking, under the direction of Captain Cook, took place on Eora sands, or what was named by the colonists as Botany Bay. The flag was the British Union Jack and the staking symbolically marked Eora country as the sovereign British territory of New South Wales. This initial proclamation and the ones that followed were predicated upon the legal fiction of 'terra nullius': the determination that this was a land belonging to no-one. Successive re-enactments of that staking have been performed to reiterate British occupation and to mark the white settler 'origins' of the nation. From the moment that this staking and its concomitant territorial renaming inscribed the [perceived] emptiness (Ryan, 1994) as British territory and as a white place, symbolic and material struggles over the meanings, ownership and control of Australian places had begun.

Since the White Australian policy days of Federation, volunteer surf lifesavers have patrolled Australian sands and commanded

status as the undisputed guardians of urban beaches. Their ritualistic
stakings of familiar red and yellow 'swim-between' flags have been
peaceful acts 'for the public good'. For a hundred years, they have
ceremonially traversed the sands and occupied the beaches in quasi-
military style. They have performed countless drills and parades,
simulated and real surf rescues. They have demarcated the safe from
the dangerous beach zones and maintained watch rosters. They have
staged thousands of massed club carnivals. Their high profile has
been felt on all city beaches. Within the tradition of volunteerism,
and in line with the duties of those in the armed service, surf
lifesavers have occupied beaches in order to 'protect the public'.
Their vigilance in monitoring dangerous nature (the rips and the
sharks) and regulating human bodies (determining who can swim
where and when) is regarded as a necessary civic service. They are in
charge of maintaining beach order by controlling the dangerous
excesses of beach nature and the bodies that inhabit it.

While associations with the inaugural colonialist stakings might
not have been foremost in the minds of the Cronulla flag bearers,
flag-bearing white nationalism was openly defended in terms of
fighting for the sanctity of Australian surf lifesaving and ANZAC
traditions (see White, 2007). In this heroic imaginary, the staking out
of Cronulla beach territory was folded into those other beach
offensives that are popularly upheld as epitomising the spirit of
Australian national identity: the military landing at Gallipoli and the
surf lifesaver patrols on Australian beaches. Foldings of beach
defence and landings, flag-bearing patrols and militaristic marchings,
even some resonances of national security and border protection
can be traced across Australia's semiotic and material sands to the
Cronulla event.

## Embodying Australian Beaches

Given that 97% of Australians have their ancestral origins outside of
the Australian continent, getting out into nature and developing a
relationship to it is a well-trodden route through which many non-
indigenous citizens seek to naturalise their belonging and attain the
status of 'real' Australians. This is exemplified in the 'White native'
status of characters such as The Man from Snowy River, Crocodile

Dundee, The Bush Tucker Man and Steve Irwin, secured in each case through enacting a repertoire of bush-savvy encounters with dangerous nature. Each one of these 'White native' media personas has been constructed around fearlessly mastering wild nature. Demonstrating a high degree of being 'at home' in essentially wild nature provides the means by which fictional or real bodies come to be identified as 'true-blue' and to embody the bush legend.

For the urban majority, however, the city beach remains the preferred place for encountering nature. Here nature can be embodied through close to home, pleasure-based and sensory experiences of sun, surf and sand. Commonly dressed in scant casual attire for leisure, recreational or sporting purposes, somatic beach experiences are maximised through direct skin contact with sun, saltwater and sand. The urban beach provides an intimate interface of pleasure-seeking sensory experiences and multiple non-human elements.

Unlike distant outback or interior 'wilderness' natures, which are rarely visited and remain the imagined locus of unpeopled and exotic 'other' natures, urban beaches are semi-domesticated playgrounds. Highly encultured, they are groomed, patrolled, netted, flagged and raked; urban beaches provide an interface between the wild nature of the sea and the built environment. In proximation to 'civilisation', many are encroached by high rise or surburbia, adjacent to shopping centres and flanked by cafes. For their blending of attractive natural and cultural qualities, they are subjected to regular human visiting; they become familiar and popular places, heavily peopled neighbourhoods.

Never fully tamed, the urban beach is also respected for its dangerous edges: its rips, dumping waves, blue bottles and shark attacks. As a rich sensory and yet never entirely predictable experience, the beach remains a site at which Australians might anticipate bodily immersion within a nexus of elemental nature, sensory pleasure and the visceral thrill of mediated danger.

The nature of city beaches also creates a set of opportunities for ritualising national belonging. As Game (1991:169) explains: 'it is an everyday affair, an "other" that can be incorporated. We can be natural at the beach, put ourselves in the place of nature'. She points out that the familiarity of urban beaches, constructed through repeated returns, are echoed in the elemental dynamics of the beach itself, in the 'waves repeating themselves over and over'. Moreover, the urban beach is not only familiar territory through being '*lived* in'. As a dynamic environment, with shifting sands and a rhythmic patterning of waves, it also offers 'an endless possibility of new origins with each return'.

For non-indigenous Australians, collectively seeking belonging in the aftermath of (often suppressed) Indigenous dispossession (Gelder and Jacobs, 1998), the beach functions as a desirable site of unambiguous Australian nature with qualities that promise to assuage anxieties around origins, displacements and belongings. Through repeated visitations and pleasurable embodied experiences, non-indigenous Australians are able to rehearse their origins. This rehearsal has a cumulative effect: the more one feels 'at home' on the beach, the more one feels like an Australian. For subsequent generations of immigrants, these rehearsals are a pedagogical process, often beginning early, regular childhood visits imprint layered body memories of salt water, waves, sand and sun. Through immersions, revisitations and sensory imprintings, beach play becomes 'second nature' for many urban children and naturalises a passageway into Australian adulthood.

Entangled with these lived experiences of embodying Australian beaches are the semiotic regimes which idealise and reify the relationship between certain kinds of bodies and sands. Max Dupain's iconic 'The Sunbaker' (Dupain, 1937) image is a case in point, as a celebrated example of nature/culture semiology, this oft-cited photograph exemplifies the imaginary of quintessential Australian body/beach symmetry. It implies a perfect fit: the salt-encrusted, sunburnt and yet White, male sunbaker's body is marked by the same beach elements that it inhabits. The proximities between the body and the sand underscore its naturalisation – suggestive of what Crombie (2004) claims to be Dupain's promotion of environmental nativism.

Crombie (cited in Perera, 2006) has located this kind of racial prototyping evident in Dupain's work as part of a larger eugenics and body culture movement that first emerged in Australia between the two world wars. In its efforts at generating a new kind of naturally emplaced and racially embodied nationalism, this nativist movement explicitly deployed the white, bronzed Australian surfer's body as its archetype (White, 2007).

Of course, the possibilities for securing 'White native' status through promoting the bronzed body of the surfer as archetypically Australian is conditional upon the successful displacement of any Indigenous bodies from the national imaginary. For such purposes, the beach becomes a kind of palimpsest, a tableau on which the images of Indigenous bodies have been progressively overwritten and thus obscured by the naturalised White ones. In her playful image 'The movie star: David Gulpillil on Bondi Beach' (Moffat, 1985), Moffat draws attention to the ways in which White emplacement is contingent upon Black displacement by re-presenting the seemingly 'unnatural' and 'out of place' Black body on an urban beach. Marked as a explicitly hybrid body; simultaneously Black, traditional, contemporary and urban, the actor David Gulpilil appears as a humorous anathema, strangely ambiguous and misplaced in the 'quintessentially' Australian beach environment.

In the national imaginary, the beach-emplaced national body is not only racialised as White, it is also gendered as male. In her reflections on lifesavers as national icons, Saunders (1998:96) refers (with irony) to the selective idealisation of lifesavers' bodies as 'specimens of superb manhood'. The process through which these bodies have come to represent the pinnacle of Australian masculinity has a long history – a history of differentiated superiority. An understanding of the primacy of the male lifesaver's body in relation to other lesser bodies (male and female) is lauded in Russell's 1910 description:

> The lifesavers represented the very highest class ...the Samurais, the oligarchs, the elite. They strut the beaches with superiority that is insolent, yet at the same time, tolerant of the shortcomings of lesser breeds – a gladiator caste, envied by all the men, adored by all the women (National Museum of Australia, 2006: 5).

Texts such as these have selectively eulogised homogenous representations of 'superior' athletic, White, male body prototypes for at least a century. Across this same timespan, the embodied beach experiences of the heterogeneous population never quite match the image. There are wide gaps between the idealised semiology of Australian beach embodiment and the lived realities of it: such gaps underpin the aspirational as well as the differential nature of Australian belongings that were played out at Cronulla.

Many of the body/text networks I have outlined above come to nest within a key image of a young man at the riots. Below the slogan 'We grew here! You flew here!' his bare torso was inscribed with the Cronulla postcode '2230'. The writing on his body declares that he is not just rightfully 'in place' but more emphatically 'of the place'. 'We grew here' invokes the pedagogy of his beach belonging, '2230' that he embodies the local beach. Read across the '100% Aussie' writings in the sand, the writings on his and many other 'local' bodies function inter-textually as a form of cross-referencing. In tandem, they narrate a symbiotic relationship: these bodies belong to the beach and the beach belongs to them. By implication, this is an exclusive relationship. There is no space for others.

Local status is not only delineated by geographical proximity, but it is also differentiated in oppositional and inter-temporal terms: 'we grew here' [unlike you who only recently] 'flew here'. According to Graham (2005), the editor of the *National Indigenous Times*, this proprietorial white-settler slogan was countered in Koori networks by the quip 'we growed here, you rowed here', drawing attention to the strategic amnesia of the White postcolonial 'custodians' as well as the hollow basis of their originary claims. Whether or not the 'home grown' boys were cognisant that prior ownership claims constituted an appropriative form of native land rights status, 'being here first' was clearly offered, in their own case, as a valid basis for their proprietorial rights.

This sense of natural entitlement, spelt out in uncompromising terms on the young man's body, is reinforced through his seamless articulation with those masculinist semiotic regimes of White native nationalism I traced across the bodies of the sunbaker and the lifesaver. Burnt by the sun, draped in the flag; his athletic, semi-naked body is accommodated within the national imaginary of quintessential Australian-ness.

So many body/nature tracings can be read off this body across time and place, across beach cultures and rituals and across racialised and gendered performances of Australian belonging. And yet this is such a parochial image of essentialised identity claiming originary status. Just like the short-lived '100% Aussie pride' sand writings, erased by tides, this body inscription: 'We grew here you flew here' is both transient and transparent, it belies its anxious denials of earlier dispossessions.

## Conclusion

Throughout this chapter, I have been working against the parochial and racial demarcations brandished in the riots. Through taking a relational approach I have sought to scramble the binary logics that structure life as a heroic struggle between the forces of good and evil, that circumscribe the local as a space to be defended against invaders and reduce the complex cultural diversities of Australian social fabric to an essentialised dichotomy between authorising white custodians and inappropriate others.

Seizing on Cronulla as a flash point of 'proprietorial enclosure', I have countered these defensive local responses by opening up to the array of heterogeneous relations that constellate around any such event. These networks of relations constituted the riot as a 'provisional moment'; without them, things would not have worked out as they did. This outward movement of relational thinking counters parochialism in two ways: firstly, it involves insisting, as Massey (1993) does, upon the 'extraverted' nature of all local places and events, seeing them as locales of time/space convergences: not only connected to other places, times and events but partially constituted by them. The second way in which relational thinking counters parochialism is by looking beyond 'us' and 'them' to the array of complex inter-connections between us. Instead of promoting the self through essentialising difference, as in 'I am "naturally" better (more Australian) than you', it emphasises the webs of exchange through which we come to understand ourselves and each other. Examples of these inter-temporal, inter-corporeal, inter-textual and inter-subjective relations are woven throughout my reflections on Australian bodies and Australian sands.

My tracings are far from complete. The wide horizons of relational thinking are messy and unwieldy. Even my attempts to frame them around the Cronulla-related body/sand relations have been partial. Because my attention was focused upon the White nationalist actions at Cronulla, I traced those particular exchanges through which White subjectivity has come to be seen as the originary and authentic Australian identity. This led me to follow the intersecting trajectories of White territorial stakings and beach embodiments. My mediated ramblings have precluded a consideration of the networks of relations that configure around Lebanese Australian bodies and sands. Nor have I paid attention to any of the post-Cronulla reconciliation efforts. Events such as these produce new configurations of relations involving different sets of actors, historical and geographical convergences, discursive intersections and layered semiologies.

Founded upon strengthening relationship and engaging with difference, they tap into the kind of ethics that relational thinking promotes. As Latour reminds us when reflecting on the social fabric, 'Strength does not come from concentration, purity and unity, but from dissemination, heterogeneity and the careful plaiting of weak ties' (Latour, 1998). When nation-building is viewed relationally and the national space reimagined as one of open-ended difference, plaiting becomes a new kind of metaphor for linking all kinds of Australian bodies with Australian sands.

# References

*Age* (2006) 'Riots in Sydney', 13 December, accessed 9 June 2009, http://www.theage.com.au/ftimages/2005/12/12/1134235988898.html

Allen, J. (1999) 'Spatial Assemblages of Power', Massey, D., Allen, J. and Sarre, P. (1999) (eds.) *Human Geography Today* Polity Press, Cambridge, Oxford, Malden: 194-218.

Althusser, L, (1971) *Lenin and Philosophy and Other Essays* Monthly Review Press, New York.

Anderson, K. and Taylor, A. (2005) 'Exclusionary politics and the question of national belonging: Australian ethnicities in multiscalar focus', *Ethnicities* 5, 4: 460-475.

Booth, D. (2001) *Australian Beach Cultures: The History of Sun, Sand and Surf* Routledge, London.

Butler, J. (2004a) *Undoing Gender* Routledge, London and New York.

Butler, J. (2004b) *Precarious Life: The Powers of Mourning and Violence* Verso, London and New York.

Crombie, E. (2004) *Body Culture: Max Dupain, Photography and Australian Culture, 1919-1939* National Gallery of Victoria with Peleus Press, Mulgrave Vic.

Dupain, M. (1937) *The Sunbaker,* Art Gallery of South Australia, accessed 9th June 2009
http://www.artgallery.sa.gov.au/TLF/801ph8/image.html

Game, A. (1991) *Undoing the Social* Open University Press, Milton Keynes.

Gelder K. and Jacobs, J. (1998) *Uncanny Australia: Sacredness and Identity in a Postcolonial Nation* Melbourne University Press, Carlton South, Victoria.

Graham, C. (2005) Blog entry, 13 December, accessed 11 December 2006, http://www.crikey.com.au/articles/2005/12/13-1550-5006.html

Hage,G. (1998) White Nation: Fantasies of White Supremacy in a Multicultural Society Pluto Press, Sydney.

Haraway, D. (1991) *Simians, Cyborgs and Women: The Reinvention of Nature* Free Association Books, London.

Jackson, L. (2006) 'Riot and Revenge', *Four Corners*, ABC, accessed 11 December 2006
http://www.abc.net.au/4corners/content/2006/s1590953.htm

Latour, B. (1998) 'On actor network theory: A few clarifications', Nettime Mailing List Archives, accessed 9 June 2009, http://www.nettime.org/Lists-Archives/nettime-l-9801/msg00019.html

Latour, B. (2005) *Reassembling the Social: An Introduction to Actor-Network-Theory* Oxford University Press, Oxford.

Massey, D. (1993) 'Power-geometry and a progressive sense of place' in Bird, J. et al. (eds) *Mapping the Future* Routledge New York and London: 59-69.

Moffat, T. (1985) *The Movie Star, David Gulpilil on Bondi Beach*, National Gallery of Australia, accessed 9 June 2009
http://nga.gov.au/Federation/Detail.cfm?WorkID=177494

National Museum of Australia (2006) *Between the Flags: 100 Years of Surf Lifesaving*, National Museum of Australia Press, Canberra.

Education at National Museum of Australia (2007) 'Rips, rescues, recreation and riots: Australian beach culture', accessed 9 June 2009,

http://www.nma.gov.au/shared/libraries/attachments/schools/resour
ces/surf_lifesaving/surf_lifesaving_activity_1/files/17379/Surf_Lifesa
ving_Rips.pdf

Perera, S. (2006) 'Race, Terror, Sydney, December 2005' *Borderlands* 5, 1: 1-
21, accessed 9 June 2009,
http://www.borderlandsejournal.adelaide.edu.au/vol5no1_2006/perer
a_raceterror.htm

Rose, D. (2004) *Reports from a Wild Country: Ethics for Decolonisation* UNSW
Press, Sydney.

Ryan, S. (1994) 'Inscribing the emptiness: Cartography, exploration and the
construction of Australia', in Tiffen, C. and Lawson, A. (eds.) *Describing
Empire: Post-colonialism and Textuality* Routledge, London and New York:
115-130.

Saunders, K. (1998) '"Specimens of superb manhood": The lifesaver as a
national icon', *Journal of Australian Studies* 56: 96-108.

Surf Lifesaving NSW. (2006) 'Surf lifesaving on the same wave with
Australia's multicultural communities', accessed 6 December 2006
http://www.surflifesaving.com.au/SurfLife_CMS/News/061123-
OTSW.htm

Whatmore, S. (2002) *Hybrid Geographies: Natures, Cultures, Spaces* Sage,
London.

White, C. (2007) 'Representing the nation: Australian masculinity on the
beach at Cronulla', Proceedings of the Everyday Multiculturalism
Conference, accessed 9 June 2009,
http://www.crsi.mq.edu.au/news_and_events/documents/CameronW
hite_000.pdf

# 'It's just an attitude that you feel': inter-ethnic habitus before the Cronulla riots

## Amanda Wise

"They play soccer and kick sand all over people, they make rude remarks to women, they intimidate everybody" said Campbell. Girls in bikinis are called sluts and whores, the gangs play loud music and leave rubbish on the beach, local residents say. Bartlett (2005)

I was in Queensland the week leading up to the Cronulla riots having a break after a conference to spend some time in the sun. The first I heard of the riot was at breakfast in our Maroochydore hotel. I was horrified at the apocalyptic newspaper images of drunken surfie boys spewing forth some of the nastiest racism I've witnessed.

This was more than just professional interest, I grew up in the Shire in the 1970s and 1980s and spent a good portion of my youth on the beach at Cronulla. I left in the early 1990s for many reasons, but mainly because of the sexism and conservatism that were omnipresent. Although I had moved out of the area, a number of my family and friends remain there and were upset when I was quoted in newspapers as being critical of the racism displayed by the rioters. Although disapproving of the racism, they felt the riots were a result of long suppressed tension which had been brewing for years, yet was never officially acknowledged or dealt with. Their view was that 'politically correct' academics like me simply denied their experiences of anti-social behaviour by young men of Middle Eastern[1] background over a number of years.

Talking to my family and Cronulla friends about the 'cause' of ill-feeling that led to the riot, it seemed they found these feelings difficult to articulate, traversing between observations about everyday discomforts and stereotypes of 'Middle Eastern youth'. Because it links to other work I have been doing, I became interested in the extent to which they emphasised everyday discomforts experienced in shared spaces such as the beach or park. There were a few themes that emerged prominently during these conversations; boisterous soccer played amidst sun-bakers; groups of 'Leb' boys who were rowdy and aggressive; the 'pack' style of fighting they perceived 'Leb boys' to favour; and sexist remarks, 'looks' and harassment of young women. I focus here on the first three themes. I do not deal with sexual harassment as Judy Lattas's contribution to this volume analyses the intersections between gender, race and harassment. I argue that the escalation from 'discomfort' to riot had to do with the intersections between the phenomenological experience of incompatible embodiment and everyday ritual, and larger moral panics surrounding Islam and Arabic-speaking youth.

## Beach Rhythms & Embodied Difference

"Its just an attitude that you *feel*" is how a talk-back radio caller tried to explain her discomfort with men of Middle Eastern appearance on Cronulla beach in the years leading to the riots. Many of the statements from 'Shire types'[2] about Middle Eastern youth employ similar language, evoking notions of *'feeling'*[3] intimidated, uncomfortable or threatened around young Middle Eastern men. Such accounts are at least as common as first-hand experiences of violent anti-social behaviour. However, they speak with a level of intensity which suggests these 'feelings' need to be taken seriously if we are to understand and prevent further racialised conflict. I argue they are attempting to describe unconscious 'feelings' sometimes associated with differing *'technique du corps'* (Mauss, 1979), or 'interethnic habitus' (Wise, 2005; forthcoming, 2010). I argue that differently habituated masculinities and modes of using space can cause some of the discomforts that 'shire' types try, but usually fail, to articulate without falling into racist evaluations.

Summer at Cronulla has a relaxed feel. Tanned bodies spread out along the beach as if in mass meditation. The voices and movements of others on the beach seem absorbed by the sand and wind and surf such that one can feel almost alone despite being amidst hundreds of others. Anglo boys cluster in small groups, sometimes mixed with girls. The surfer boys are easy to pick out, you see them when you drive past the car-parks which stretch from Wanda to North Cronulla. Morning and afternoon, lone figures are dotted along the road leaning on the white railing assessing the waves, others are pulling on wetsuits and unloading boards, marked out by their sun-bleached hair and tanned torsos. Long-time surfers are easy to spot with their muscular upper body. Many develop a particular gait; even away from the beach they hold their arms in a way that it's easy to imagine a surfboard tucked under. Surfing is a solitary sport and one which these boys seem to embody in and out of water.

Surfer boys personify the idealised Anglo body. With a few exceptions (which I'll speak to later) these bodies are typically affectively contained. There are few expressive gestures and their speech is clipped, using as few words as possible. Yep. Righto. Mate. Interactions with other bodies are similarly circumscribed by codes of masculinity. 'Chilled out' is how they might be described by some; 'cold and unresponsive' by others. For many 'Shire types' such bodies are experienced as an excess of *presence*. Male 'Leb' bodies, on the other hand, are stereotypically expressive bodies; their bodies move outward, connect with others, and demonstrate emotions in obvious ways. Boisterous, rowdy and aggressive is how they are sometimes described.

Anglos, especially the young, also present a unified colourscape of beach clothing: bright, light and pastel. Black (except for bikinis) is uncommon. Young men have a uniform of knee-length boardshorts and particular brands are prominent; Billabong, Rip Curl, Quicksilver.

It's easy to pick out the 'Leb' kids, they differ in body size and type, dress, bodily disposition and group size. The Anglo and Leb groups cluster differently: Anglo families visiting the beach typically consist of the nuclear family, possibly a grandparent or two; young friendship groups tend to be smaller, commonly with a gender mix. 'Shire' boys are often there to surf or ride boogie boards and will group in clusters of three or four.

The photo taken at North Cronulla on a summer's day before the riot shows the different patterns: amidst clusters of Anglo bikinis and board shorts are three groups of young men of Middle Eastern appearance. At the back of the sand on the way to the kiosk is a group of about fifteen young men playing what looks to be a game of soccer. They stand out with their size and their haircuts; a few of them sporting the 'undercut' style; sides shaved, longer on top, they are nearly all wearing black football shorts which are typically much shorter than board shorts and have elastic waists. Closer to the water is another cluster who appears to be in their early teens, wearing black Adidas-style shorts, their father looks on as they play soccer between the mid-section of the sand, close to the flags. They are enjoying themselves, but their number and boisterousness could easily be irritating if they enter the sunbakers' zone. This is another point of difference: Anglo-Australians tend not to 'do' things on the beach. Activity takes place in the water. With the exception of young children, the sand is for 'relaxing'.

Soccer on the beach at Cronulla came up in news reports about the 'causes' of tension and it emerged in interviews conducted by community and youth workers, reports to council and discussions with council lifeguards. Indeed, it started the initial altercation between the off-duty lifesavers and the 'Leb boys' prior to the riot. Council lifeguards informed me that soccer in the crowded section near the flags had become a problem in recent years and resulted in verbal exchanges when it spilled onto other users. They said they had, in previous years attempted to section off an area away from the flags in order to accommodate soccer players and other users. Unfortunately this caused a secondary set of problems when hot after a game, the soccer players would swim in the water adjoining the sectioned off area. This resulted in tension when lifesavers asked them to swim between the flags.

The soccer is typically casual, involving groups of young men of Middle Eastern background ranging from pre-pubescent to late teens playing in the vicinity of the flag area either on the shoreline or on the dry sand. The games are usually good natured, if boisterous, the tension points occur when the beach is crowded and balls go astray; bouncing into other users, or when players get overexcited in chasing a ball through the crowd, kicking sand along the way. This behaviour is read as 'uncivil' by Anglo beach users, as this *Sydney Morning Herald* blogger shows:

> I have also seen them totally disrespect other people, kicking around a soccer ball in the middle of a packed beach, to the point where a child of no more then 5 years old was hit in the face. They didn't even care that a child was hurt, as long as they were having fun. (Steve 2005)

Anglo experiences of 'Leb' difference on the beach range from 'feeling uncomfortable' to intense irritation in situations such as these soccer incidents. They represent a continuum which has its roots in the notion of what has come to be known as 'habitus'. Related to Mauss's notion of *'techniques du corps'*, habitus is 'embodied history, internalised as a second nature and so forgotten as history … the active presence of the whole past of which it is the product' (Bourdieu, 1990a: 56). Habitus refers to the embodied dispositions that 'internalise our social location and which orient our actions', a mastery of the implicit principles of the social world, manifest 'in our actions, our modes of appearance and through a bodily *hexis* or bodily bearing – posture, manners, ways of speaking and dressing' (Noble and Watkins, 2003: 522). Bourdieu has termed this mastery of the social world a 'feel for the game' (Bourdieu, 1990a: 66). Because of their embodied nature, habitus and *hexis* have the capacity to induce affective responses to inter-subjective encounters with those around us and to our social and material environment.

The notion of habitus is linked to the concept of social field. Although Bourdieu rarely deals with ethnicity, it is implicit in his scheme, that, cross-cutting other fields, ethnicities themselves can function as fields within which hierarchies exist, and which nest an ethnically framed habitus. Habitus, therefore, is bound up with power and with the embodied practice, classification and sense-making of everyday life. Like shopping centres and other public places, a beach is a situation of enforced togetherness. Cultural norms involving specific rituals and codes for the management of such situations are embodied in our habitus which (re)produces these rituals at the pre-conscious level. Extending the notion of habitus to the discomforts experienced in the crowded public beach suggests that certain behaviours are noticed more where the actors

AMANDA WISE

involved are differently embodied and where codes and ritual norms are not shared.

In a highly individualised Western context, civility requires that strangers maintain a separateness in crowded places. Rituals for the maintenance of self-containment in public spaces involve what Goffman calls 'civil inattention', which refers to those micro-rituals employed to achieve a sense of staying unknown in public places. It represents a 'competence to refuse relations without creating non-persons' (Hirschauer, 2005: 41). Goffman describes an example of civil inattention on a footpath: 'After a quick but open glance at a proper distance, the participants' looks are lowered for each other, and raised again only at the moment of passing…. Gazes should…neither signal a 'recognition', promising an openness for contact, nor should they be full of distrust and hatred' (Goffman, 1963:84). This management of strangeness is a normalised non-relation (Hirschauer, 2005) designed to maintain a sense of apartness in a context of enforced togetherness.

These rituals for managing such situations help explain some of the irritation at soccer on the crowded beach. When young men enter the 'zone' of other users without signalling in the way Goffman describes, it is experienced by Anglos as an act of incivility. In turn, habitus reminds us of the extent to which such experiences are not conscious, but embodied ones which function at the subconscious level. The discomfort of differing bodily practices such as those around 'rowdy' Lebanese youth on the beach signal the fact that we actually 'feel' bodies 'out of place'. Rodaway (1994) describes such spatial bodily encounters as experienced through our haptic sense system, which involves our tactile, kinaesthetic and proprioceptive senses, and makes the surfaces of our bodies porous and permeable. Our haptic senses allow us to perceive weight, pressure, balance, temperature, vibrations, presence and orientation in space (Fisher, 1997). Through the haptic system we receive and perceive the environment, on the skin and inside our bodies. For these reasons, touch is one of the most intimate and reciprocal of senses, for to touch is always to be touched and can evoke a whole gamut of emotions from desire, caring and love to disgust, revulsion and hate (Rodaway, 1994: 41). Western bodies often feel

132

uncomfortable in crowded spaces because their culturally attuned sense of interpersonal distance is much greater than other cultures. Personal space is 'an extension of the self's presence in space, and violation of this space by another is felt to be like the violation of the body itself' (Rodaway, 1994: 59). So psychically, habitually and historically engrained is this spatial and bodily order, that the disorder can produce a sense of bodily threat and a sense of shock, especially when there is no accompanying apology or acknowledgement of transgression.

Such encounters produce a sense of *dis-ease*. Many commentators dismissed Anglo beach users irritated at young men playing soccer in their midst as prejudiced, however this irritation had as much to do with subconscious expectations about how public spaces such as the beach should be used and shared, about the kinds of bodies one might expect and how they should move and cluster.

## Towel as Chair

Rituals of civility in crowded places are also made manifest in the design and management of spaces. The placement of towels and culturally imbued rules of ambulation around them tells us a lot about how Anglos unconsciously produce and 'feel' freedom on the beach.

Sydney's beaches can get crowded on weekends and holidays during summer. Despite this, there is a rhythm and orderliness about the beach; people move at a certain pace, and children playing are often reprimanded if they bother others. When the beach is not too crowded, sunbakers keep a large distance between themselves and others, when it is crowded, the distance between where people 'set up camp' is closer, but maintained. The space for playing and running about is normally along the firm wet sand at the shoreline. Care is taken not to kick or shake sand on others. If there is a wind, those packing up to leave will shake their towel down-wind from neighbouring sunbakers. People avoid moving within the space of other 'campsites' as stepping on another's towel is considered an act of infringement upon another's private space. These are practices which have to be learnt, indeed, Anglo children are trained in these practices from a young age.

Frivolity is confined to sanctioned spaces; in the water, on the firm sand at the shoreline, in the 'no man's land' of the dry sand at the rear of the beach and in the green zone parks which border the beach. These rules apply especially for activities which involve fast movement, flying objects, and running. Prior to the riot, one caller to radio broadcaster Alan Jones (2005) supported the public protest being called for, complaining about 'Middle Eastern' youth on the beach: "We sat down on a picnic blanket and they kept kicking balls at us!"

Movement between towels in the crowded mid-section of the sand is usually confined to children playing near their parents. Adult movement through this zone would normally only involve walking to and from the water, change-rooms or kiosk, or leaving the beach.

The spatial arrangement of towels can be read as 'comfy chairs'. Sennett talks about the convergence of notions of freedom with the development of orderly public space and argues that this produces bodies closed to difference and averse to 'social touching'. The layout and rituals attached to towels represent the material manifestation of bodies trying to be private and self-contained in a public space. Towel sites circumscribe the boundaries of public sociality on the beach.

Sennett argues that certain forms of self-containment emerged in the West in the 19th century concurrent with an increasing quest for 'individualised comfort' in the material and social world.; this individualisation of bodies was increasingly spatialised and impacted upon the design and use of space. He uses the evolution of the 'comfy chair' as a manifestation of the 'containment' of bodies. Eighteenth century chairs were 'social chairs', typically without arms and designed to allow movement of the body so people could talk to those around (Sennett, 1994: 340). By the nineteenth century, a version of the 'comfy chair' similar to today's lounge had evolved, which the occupant could sink into, feeling enveloped, but no longer able to easily interact. This containment moves to the street where 'people began to treat as their right not to be spoken to by strangers, to treat the speech of strangers as a violation' (1994: 341-

343). Sennett argues that 'urban spaces take form largely from the ways people experience their own bodies' (1994: 370). In urban design, unobstructed movement becomes synonymous with freedom.

The spatial arrangement of towels on the beach and codes of movement around them can be read as akin to 'comfy chairs', they represent manifestations of how Anglo beach users 'feel' and reproduce a sense of freedom in spatially individualised terms. Despite the crowded space, the layout and codes of organisation which help to sustain unobstructed movement, and rituals which 'manage' the civil non-relation with other users maintain the myth of 'freedom' and a sense of 'aloneness in a crowd', and produces a feeling of relaxation and comfort. The beach has come to personify freedom in the Australian imaginary; photos of Australian beach scenes in tourism and promotional literature are nearly always empty or contain few people. Rituals of civil inattention can be seen as maintaining the myth of aloneness and freedom at the beach.

Drawing together these threads, dis-ease exists for several reasons. First, it arises from the disjuncture around ethnically different habitus and unconscious expectations of what should happen within the beach space. The rituals, rhythms and codes of movement through space can be seen as a means of producing a sense of ontological certainty, a subconscious sense of expectation and confidence at the orderly flow of the world. Noble terms this 'comfort' which is related to Giddens' notion of ontological security but is more social, sensual and affective, 'grounded in the routines and spaces of daily existence'. He characterises 'comfort' as involving a 'background mood of well-being, trust and confidence' and the "fit' we experience in relation to the space we inhabit and the practices we perform' (Noble, 2005:113-4). Second, boisterousness on the beach is experienced as intrusive; without the ritual of civil inattention, this is experienced as an act of incivility, where the boys 'have not recognised me as a person'. Third, since habitus is tied up with affect, running into someone's towel can be *felt* as threatening in an embodied sense. In this context, *feeling* uncomfortable as a result of displacement from one's comfort zone can create a sense of empathy with rumours of serious anti-social behaviour leaving Anglos receptive to moral panics about Middle Eastern youth.

## Fighting the good fight

One of the justifications for the riot made by Shire youth and shock jocks was the apparent attack on two off-duty lifesavers. As with any such situation there are conflicting reports about who was involved, and what started the fight. It was reported in various news outlets following a media release put out by the NSW Police Service. The fight was characterised by the rioters and the press as the 'straw that broke the camel's back', and another example in a string of incidents involving group violence and young men of Middle Eastern background. The following is a first-hand account of that day from a blog site which parallels the description of the same event in the *Hazzard Report* (Strike Force Neil, 2006: 26).

> Two Life guards and another guy were talking.. When a group of lebos overheard them say "those fucken lebos".. or something along those lines. So of course.. what do you expect them to do? Nothing? So they start talking to the guy... then one of the life guards said "you don't belong here" or something
>
> So they smashed him... then the guy who was talking with the lifeguard... was saying please stop... and tried stopping it... but by then they were pissed.. And bashed him too.
>
> A group of Aussies on the beach got involved maybe 10-20... so 5 leb cars came down.. to smash the Aussies who jumped in.... (Anon, 2005)

The racist remarks which sparked the fight and the group fighting which followed suggest that Anglo and 'Leb' boys emphasise different notions of respect and loyalty and have sometimes incompatible moral codes of fighting which articulate with the performance of culturally defined masculinities. One comment that came up among the 'Shire types' were perceptions about 'immoral' codes of fighting favoured by Lebs. They were disdainful towards what they viewed as an unmanly form of unbalanced fighting where several Lebs would join in to fight a single Anglo. Group fighting, revenge attacks and use of weapons are similar threads, the following post to a bulletin board is a typical 'Anglo' view.

> ...everytime we try to have a little party (we being 16) with a group of friends a group of 20yr old lebanese always rock up and gate crash...this then leads to fights but you can never fight a leb they are dirty filthy cheating bartsards they carry around knives and if you do next week they come back with 20 of their couzins to get their revenge. (Brent, 2005)

What underpins this animosity towards how 'Lebs fight'? On the face of it, fighting in any form is a site of excess beyond ordered social codes, yet it actually involves a strict set of moral codes and should not be viewed as being divorced from social norms. Men of Anglo-Celtic background often reference the 'digger' ideal, characterised by the lone, brave, yet fair soldier, typically of authentic working class or country stock: what was a classed discourse has become an ethnicised one. For Anglos, the 'fair fight' is an important frame of reference: Fair fights are 'even fights', numerically matched and physically matched in terms of combatant size and weapons. The bare fist fight is seen as the 'fairest' fight, whereas fights involving weapons are seen as cheating or unmanly; most importantly, a combatant with a weapon should never fight one without. Physical matching also refers to body size: a big bloke shouldn't fight someone much smaller, men should not fight women, nor should one fight someone much older or younger. In terms of their participation, 'mates' should stand around in support, but should not join in unless the other side increases its numbers.

Of course Anglo men don't always 'fight fairly': there are numerous reports of anti-social behaviour as serious as anything committed by 'Leb boys'. Nonetheless, notions of 'the good fight' differ distinctly across cultures and contexts. As Poynting et al. (1999) have shown, for young men of Arabic-speaking background there is no more moral cause than to fight to support your mate if he is attacked. This is seen by the Arabic speaking young men as quite different from their Anglo counterparts, who they perceived as lacking a sense of mateship and reluctant to join a fight in support of their mates. This work also emphasises the extent to which the 'wounds' of racism impact, how this creates a sense of defensiveness which can result in violence.

Eiad Diyab: We knew always there was racism, but we never knew it was to this extent. I mean, all your life you've been - you've been raised to be Australian. I mean, you carry the Australian flag. When you go to sports events and all that, you're happy to be Australian and all that. And all of sudden people reject you. "Go home!" They shout your names. Like, "Go home, you Middle Eastern Lebs," or whatever. "Go home." I mean, that's a shock to us. "Go home." **I mean, like, you get cut inside your heart, you know.** Like you feel like you're not part of society no more. [my emphasis] (Jackson, 2006)

Diyab evokes the almost physical pain of racism; his feeling of utter displacement is palpable when he talks about how it feels to be told you don't belong. As Poynting et al. (1999), have shown, the deep wounding of racism can create a disposition of violent and group-oriented defensiveness among alienated young men and produces a sense of protest masculinity in response to that racism.

Here, though, I want to unpack the idea that Lebs are 'more violent' than Anglos. I also argue that, in addition to codes of fighting, there are sanctioned places for aggression and that Anglo 'fighting spaces' tend to be separated from the everyday, rather than absent altogether. One sanctioned 'space of violence' for Anglos is the pub which is a space of intense interaction and alcohol consumption. Tomsen's research in drinking venues in Newcastle explores masculine cultures of drinking-related violence and he argues there is little support for a direct cause-effect relationship between alcohol and violence. Tomsen posits instead that drinking-related violence is a result of a number of intersecting factors: much drinking-related violence takes place in situations of intense interaction among young males; drunk and disorderly behaviour and low-level violence are often experienced as a pleasurable and valued activity and fights are often deliberately begun for trivial reasons, are characterised by escalating confrontation over male honour and are highly meaningful in terms of protecting masculine identity. Fights typically occur around taking 'exaggerated offence at some minor act of nuisance behaviour' such as 'cheating at a game of pool, approaches made to girlfriends, squabbles over bumping and spilt drinks' (Tomsen, 1997: 94-95). The most common encounters were with figures of authority, particularly door staff and bouncers, often involving refusal of entry or ejection from premises; the more extreme of these can also be read as expressions of 'protest masculinity'. Drinking time and rowdy behaviour, loudness, swearing, arguments and fights are viewed as a 'time out' period, a release from social constraints involving a sense of delight in the resulting disorder (Tomsen, 1997:96-97).

What is striking about Tomsen's study of working class Anglo pub violence is the similarity with the parameters of 'Leb' fighting; principally emanating from forms of protest masculinity. Where do 'Leb boys' typically fight? In situations of intense interaction. What 'sets them off'? Situations which involve the defence of male honour, especially involving girls and figures of authority. Fighting for young Anglo and 'Leb' males alike is a kind of sport, part of an enjoyable social outing; fighting for 'Leb' boys can also be seen as 'time out' from restraints imposed within a strict parental context. What is different however, is the social spaces and sanctioned forms of fighting.

For Anglos, fighting most often occurs in situations such as the pub or is channelled into 'safe' zones such as on the sporting field. This 'sectioning off' into specialised domains is no historical accident. Elias argues that since the fifteenth century, Western civilisation has seen a separation and repression of the affects, and the modulation of affects related to aggression. He argues that 'it is well known how violent manners were in the fifteenth century, with what brutality passions were assuaged' (Elias, 2000: 168). This occurred for various reasons, but had most to do with a shift towards centralised forms of power from smaller units of towns and villages under a feudal system. As central authority (at its apex under the system of nation states) grows, people are forced live in relative peace with each other because of their increasing interdependence and physical power is increasingly monopolised by central authorities. The pleasure of violence is channelled into specialised spaces and times; Elias gives the example of the rise of boxing and organised sport as evidence of this channelling of violence into sanctioned spaces and of how affects associated with violence are channelled from participation to spectating. In this way, 'belligerence and aggression find socially permitted expression...and

are expressed especially in 'spectating' …in the imaginary
identification with a small number of combatants to whom
moderate and precisely regulated scope is granted for the release of
such affects' (Elias, 2000: 170).

Tomsen's description of sanctioned violence in drinking spaces
represents one trajectory for the modification of aggressive affects.
Elias helps us understand the impulse towards aggression amongst
young men, and how arbitrary the 'special' spaces are that evolve to
channel this aggression. Tomsen's work is particularly meaningful in
relation to one of the most common arguments about the Cronulla
riots; that 'Anglo' fighting is somehow not as bad as the aggression
of Lebs which often takes place in daylight hours in public spaces
and typically does not involve alcohol. Then Prime Minister Howard
argued that the Anglos involved in the riot were not necessarily
racist and that it was primarily a result of them 'having had too
much to drink' and being worked up by the crowd - as though that
excused their behaviour (AAP, 2005). In what appears to be a set of
double standards, the 'alcohol was to blame' argument was used for
Anglos to explain away anti-social behaviour, whereas petty
aggressive behaviour by Lebs on the beach in the years leading up to
the riots was read as evidence of a widespread incivility amongst an
entire ethnic group. There is, however, a long history of Anglo
violence in Cronulla which the selection of headlines below
demonstrates.

## Disappearing Bodies

'All Out War Against Bodgies' (12 December 1957)

'Louts Brawl in Streets' (18 July 1962)

'Youth Mobs Defy Law in Wave of Terror' (7 November 1962)

'"Surfies" Go on Rampage' (29 May 1963)

'Police Blitz on Hoodlums at Cronulla' (9 October 1963)

'Cronulla on Alert on Beach Louts' (29 October 1969)

'Police Make Swoop on Caringbah-Cronulla' (10 November 1971)

'Suburb under Siege: Quiet Cronulla or Just Waiting to Erupt?'
(22 February 1984)

'Cronulla's Weekend of Shame' (14 February 1984)

'Reign of Terror by Drunken Hooligans' (26 June 1985)

'Mounted Police Patrol Cronulla Beach' (15 November 1990)

'Police Crackdown: Gang Violence on the Beaches of Cronulla' (7 October 1993)

'Beach Crime Wave' (31 October 1994)

'Mayor's Firm on Her [Cronulla] "Bronx" Slur' (1 November 1994)

'MP Calls for More Police' (25th January 2000)

'Gang' Brawls worry Cronulla Restaurateurs' (4 April 2000)

'Hotheads a Danger to Summer Fun' (24 October 2000)

'Public Anger Rises; MP Calls Rally on Crime' (8 March 2001)

'Violence at Cronulla: Brawl and a 30cm Knife' (9 October 2001)

'Task Force Help: New Elite Squad Ready for Summer at Cronulla' (4 December 2001)

'Hoon Gates: Boom Lowered at the Beach' (8 August 2002)

'Drunk Kids blamed for Australia Day Battle' (1 February 2005)

All these headlines from the local Shire paper the *St George & Sutherland Shire Leader*[4] report violence and anti-social behaviour in Cronulla from the mid 1950s until the early 2000s. What is interesting about the reporting is how certain bodies 'appear' and 'disappear' over this time, intersecting with moral panics of the time.

With a couple of exceptions, until the early 2000s, the anti-social behaviour was committed by perpetrators without a named ethnicity. Where a descriptor beyond 'lout' or 'hoodlum' was used, it tended to be a youth sub-cultural tag. In the late 1950s this coincided with a broader panic about 'bodgies' (Moore, 2004) while in the 1960s the reporting focused on 'surfies'. Through these reports is a consistent theme of alcohol-related violence, vandalism and anti-social behaviour, particularly on Friday and Saturday nights. This was most apparent during the 1980s and 1990s.

Another dominant theme was the 'outsider' status of those involved. Until the late 1990s hooligans were only occasionally named as 'not from around here'. As far back as 1962, the paper made the point that arrested hoodlums were from 'Earlwood' ... 'congregating in their cars outside a coffee shop' (Anon, 1962: 1), however, these were 'Anglo' outsiders – working class 'westies'. In the 1990s, 'outsiders' began to take on an ethnicity. Initially these were simply people 'coming in on the train', but were then named as 'gangs' of Pacific Islanders fighting with 'gangs' of Middle Eastern youths. From the 2000s the reporting focused on Middle Eastern youths: and being an 'outsider' or 'not from around here' eventually came to mean 'not Anglo'. It is not surprising that the escalation of 'naming' coincided with wider national and international moral panics about Middle Easterners; Islanders, meanwhile, disappear from the reports. Despite this focus on ethnicised outsiders there remained a consistent reporting of alcohol-driven anti-social behaviour on Friday and Saturday nights, yet these reports rarely mention ethnicity or the fact that those involved were mostly 'locals'. This occurs as recently as Australia Day 2005 when up to 2000 drunken locals were involved in brawls in Dunningham Park after an outdoor event (Leto, 2005: 1). There are ongoing reports of fighting outside the 'Northies' pub, vandalism in the mall, blood-splattered ATMs and so forth.

I would like to return to the notion of interethnic habitus to ask why is it that certain bodies become more present to us at certain moments. Habitus, of course, is not simply a given. Although Bourdieu never really deals with race, he never lets us forget that habitus embodies relations of power, this helps to explain how it is that certain kinds of bodies become more 'present' in certain contexts. Bodies which are experienced as 'matter out of place' can become 'Panic bodies' (Lupton, 1999) especially when they permeate personal space and fail to engage rituals of non-recognition in the context of shared urban zones. I want to argue that on top of taken-for-granted rituals are discourses which make certain bodies more visible in public space. The experiences of discomfort are real, and have to do with differently habituated bodies and expectations surrounding how they should behave in certain places. But these experiences are made more intense when they intersect with moral panics; in this case young men of Middle Eastern appearance. There exists a continuum where Anglos who have had 'petty' discomforts involving minor ritual transgressions (boisterousness which invades personal space etc), who have not had much contact with cultural diversity, and who are surrounded by negative discourses, are more vulnerable to moral panics. While most beach users have not directly experienced violent anti-social behaviour, when they hear about such behaviour it *'feels'* real or at least distinctly possible.

## Conclusion

The Anglo rioters at Cronulla on December 11 clearly had some fantasy that their actions could free their beach of the discomforting strangers. Having been taught a lesson about codes on 'our' beach, those Lebs who came back would know they had better behave and that past beach practices would no longer be tolerated. However, the desire to cleanse the area of uncomfortable difference is a dangerous and ultimately ineffective quest for freedom.

Sennett (1994:371-2) argues that 'without significant experiences of self-displacement social differences gradually harden because interest in the Other withers'. He muses about the possibilities for modern rituals – not rituals that seek to erase or cleanse, but those that turn the body outwards. These are 'rituals which...[do not] destroy the dominant order, but which create a more complex life for the bodies in the dominant order sought to rule in its own image ... without a disturbed sense of ourselves, what will prompt most of us... to turn outward toward each other, to experience the Other'? In this light, we need to resist a paranoid impulse for a sense of comfort based in order and singularity. Those involved in developing interventions need to be wary of expecting too much of strategies which seek to Anglicise Middle Eastern bodies, such as the training program for Muslim lifesavers which took place in the summer of 2006/7. Such initiatives can and do have positive effects and should not be avoided, but organisers need to be aware that such interventions should place as much emphasis on making Anglo bodies more open to difference, rather than simply training Lebs to behave 'more like us'. Community-based interventions are more important than ever, but must always run in parallel with programs designed to intervene in larger discourses and they need to engage the hearts and minds of both sides in these conflicts.

# References

AAP (2005) 'PM refuses to use racist tag', *Sydney Morning Herald* 12 December: 1.

Anon (1962) 'Youth Mobs Deny Law in Wave of Terror', *St George and Sutherland Shire Leader* 7 November: 1.

Anon (2005) These comments were made on a web site that no longer exists

Bartlett, L. (2005) 'Cultures on the edge', Standard [Hong Kong] 16 December, accessed 9 June 2009, http://www.thestandard.com.hk/news_detail.asp?we_cat=9&art_id=7956&sid=5928362&con_type=1&d_str=20051216&fc=10

Bourdieu, P. (1990a) *The Logic of Practice* London, Blackwell.

Bourdieu, P. (1990b) *Outline of a Theory of Practice* Cambridge University Press, Cambridge.

Brent (2005) 'Cronulla Race Riots', 8 December, accessed 16 March, 2007, http://aussieseek.proboards25.com/index.cgi?board=main&action=print&thread=1134269912

Collins, J., Noble, G., Poynting, S. and Tabar, P. (2000) *Kebabs, Kids, Cops and Crime* Pluto Press, Sydney.

Connell, R. (1995) *Masculinities* Allen and Unwin, Sydney.

Elias, N. (2000) *The Civilizing Process*, revised edition, translated by E. Jephcott, Blackwell, Oxford.

Fisher, J. (1997) 'Relational aesthetics: Towards a haptic aesthetic', *Parachute* 87: 4-11.

Goffman, E. (1963) *Behaviour in Public Places* Free Press/ MacMillan , New York.

Hirschauer, S. (2005) 'On Doing Being a Stranger: The Practical Constitution of Civil Inattention', *Journal for the Theory of Social Behaviour* 35, 1: 41-67.

Jackson, L. (2006) 'Riot and Revenge', *Four Corners, ABC*, Sydney, accessed 9 June 2009, http://www.abc.net.au/4corners/content/2006/s1588360.htm

Jones, A. (2005) 'Alan Jones Show', *2GB*, 7 December.

Leto, A. (2005) 'Drunk kids blamed for Aust Day battle', *St George and Sutherland Shire Leader* 3 February: 1

Lupton, D. (1999) *Risk* Routledge, London.

Mauss, M. (1979) *Sociology and Psychology* Routledge & Kegan Paul, London.

Moore, K. (2004) 'Bodgies, widgies and moral panic in Australia 1955 - 1959', Paper presented to the Social Change in the 21st Century

Conference, Centre for Social Change Research, Queensland University of Technology, 29 October.

Noble, G. (2005) 'The Discomfort of Strangers: Racism, Incivility and Ontological Security in a Relaxed and Comfortable Nation', *Journal of Intercultural Studies* 26, 1: 107-120.

Noble, G. and Watkins, M. (2003) 'So, How did Bourdieu Learn to Play Tennis? Habitus, Consciousness and Habituation', *Cultural Studies* 17, 3/4: 520-538.

Poynting, S, Noble, G. and Tabar, P. (1999) '"If anyone called me a wog, they wouldn't be speaking to me alone" *Journal of Interdisciplinary Gender Studies* 3, 2: 76-94.

Rodaway, P. (1994) *Sensuous geographies* Routledge, London.

Sennett, R. (1994) *Flesh and Stone* W.W. Norton & Company, New York.

Steve (2005) 'SMH News Blog: Puberty Blues all over again', 21 December, accessed 16 March, 2007, http://blogs.smh.com.au/newsblog/archives/your_say/003037.html

Strike Force Neil (2006) *Cronulla Riots: Review of the Police Response*, Vol. 1. Sydney: NSW Police.

Tomsen, S. (1997) 'A Top Night: Social Protest, Masculinity and the Culture of Drinking Violence', *British Journal of Criminology* 1: 90-102.

Wise, A. (forthcoming, 2010) 'Sensuous Multiculturalism: The embodied habitus and interethnic living in Ashfield', *Journal of Ethnic and Migration Studies*.

Wise, A. (2005) 'Hope and Belonging in a Multicultural Suburb', *Journal of Intercultural Studies* 26, 1: 171-186.

# Notes

[1] I use terms such as 'Middle Eastern youth', 'Leb boys' to reflect colloquial usage. They are of course deeply problematic descriptors from a sociological viewpoint..

[2] 'Shire Types' is one colloquialism often used to describe Anglo, working and lower middle class 'types' seen as typical of the Shire. The term connotes an inward looking 'white bread' suburban outlook and tastes.

[3] I use quotes around the word 'feeling' to signal the embodied nature of 'feeling' intimidated or uncomfortable.

[4] A couple of the earlier pieces are from the *Leader's* predecessor, the *Observer*.

# Chapter nine

# From *Turko* to Lebo: the Cronulla riot and the politics of Greekness

## Andrew Lattas

The riot at Cronulla beach in 2005 exposed divisions amongst migrants in terms of their allegiances and it highlighted different ways in which migrants align themselves with the Australian nation.[1] Many older migrants from the south of Europe felt sympathy for those who were attacked because they happened to look 'Middle Eastern'; watching the riot on television, older Greek migrants were distressed by pictures of drunken Aussies unable to contain their contempt for those seen to be from the Middle East. These ugly scenes of nationalism, of crazy Australians (*τρελή Αυστραλή*) on the rampage, evoked painful memories of their own harassment at work and in public places and some older Greeks took joy in the revenge attacks by Arab youths, exclaiming 'καλά τους κάνανε' (Good what they did to them).[2] However, this sympathy is only half the story; many European migrants sided with the outraged 'Aussie' residents, and joined in criticising 'Lebos.'[3]. Even Greeks who had suffered abuse at Cronulla, voiced their anger at being mistaken for a 'Lebo' criticising Aussies not for the legitimacy of their animosity but for their lack of ethnic subtlety, for their inability to distinguish Greeks from Arabs.

Whilst many older Greeks sympathised and saw the new migrants as being persecuted for their cultural identity in much the same way as they had been, this was less so for younger Greeks reared in Australia. Many of them saw the riot as something the Lebs had brought upon themselves and this was so even for some who had experienced Aussie prejudice first hand. One youth who went to an inner-city high school described how Aussie kids called him a greasy wog, and he would retaliate by calling them convicts and skips. He noted, however, that at school most abuse was now directed at the Lebs commenting that they deserved it.

The riot reveals changing definitions of Greekness and changing forms of nationalism in Australia. In the common enemy of the Arab a newfound cultural unity is affirmed between Aussies and homegrown Greeks. Always denying that it is racist, this new cultural nationalism trades on a civilisational logic, where Australia is seen to be involved in a global partnership with America and Britain to uphold western values of freedom, democracy and respect for women. This cultural nationalism trades on Australia as a target in the global war on terror. It also trades on national pride in Australia's military expertise and low casualties in the Allies' wars against Islamic extremists in Afghanistan and Iraq.

Within Australia, the war on terror has done more than empower an alliance of Aussies with British and Americans. In appealing to a civilisational logic, the global conflict with Muslim extremism draws Christian European migrants into a cultural nationalism that celebrates Australian values as upholding democracy on a world stage. For then US President Bush and then Australian Prime Minister Howard, this global defence of democracy and humanitarianism was rendered as defending the existence of civilisation itself in a violent world. For many Australians, participation in the conflicts in Iraq and Afghanistan has resurrected national pride in a military history of fighting overseas to defend western civilisation. The Anzac spirit has been a core part of Anglo-Australian nationalism (Kapferer, 1988; Morris nd).

Today, Australia's participation in military clashes with Islamic militants has forged a new nationalism that incorporates many southern Europeans into a cultural alliance with Aussies and which has mobilised many Christian southern Europeans into becoming the new vigilantes for a logic of cultural assimilation. Here migrants themselves affirm the limits of multiculturalism and join Aussies in policing its boundaries. For example, recently, inner-city Sydney councillors of southern European background, complained about shops whose signs were not in English, claiming this promoted segregation.[4] On the national news, some Greek migrants supported

Prime Minister Howard's speech to the Hellenic club in Canberra which called on migrants to speak English before arriving in Australia (Mathews, 2006). Paradoxically, few Greek migrants could speak English when they arrived in Australia and many still cannot speak English even after a long residence.

How has the co-opting of Greeks happened? The new alliance of southern European migrants with the dominant Anglo culture draws partly on the fact that many migrants come from homelands that had a long tradition of colonial control under the Ottoman Empire. In the Greek community, this historical memory and cultural opposition to the Muslim Other is reproduced in everyday forms of teasing between adults. It is also kept alive in socialisation practices: children who are greedy, aggressive or bad tempered will be scolded and called Turko (Τούρκο). Such children are called upon to distance themselves from the Muslim Other as the ultimate symbol of an unfeeling, ungenerous, violent brute who cannot be reasoned with and who does not engage in civility. The Turk is an άγριος άνθρωπος, a wild person, and a possibility within each individual that must be subdued and transcended. Here, a civilising process played out to incorporate Greek children into the etiquette of everyday life finds new resonances in the contemporary clash of civilisations and the nationalism this entails.

In Australia, a general opposition to the Muslim Other is sustained through fear of Lebanese gangs and their involvement in drugs and shootings, the raping of 'Australian' girls; and boatloads of refugees which, according to Government ministers, may contain terrorists (Hage, 2003; Poynting et al., 2004). A Christian solidarity has emerged which experiences not just a clash of civilisations or cultures but which understands the world, in a similar way to President Bush, as struggling for the very existence of civilisation. Here the brutality of terror by overseas Muslim extremists is localised by being read as played out on a smaller scale in the crimes of Lebanese gangs and in the bad manners of Muslim youth (Poynting et al., 1998; Lattas, A, 2007; Lattas, J., 2007). In interviews with residents and visitors to Cronulla, the word 'respect' continually comes up as the reason for hostility to Muslims, for it is in bad manners that a new-found moral anger and nationalism is forged as a civilisational struggle.

One mature-aged Greek lady described new Arab migrants as 'ἄσχημοι ἄνθρωποι' (ugly people). The word ἄσχημοι means ugliness but here it refers not to physical ugliness, but a moral and social ugliness. She described how in the units where she lived she often heard a Muslim man's arguments with his wife, on one occasion, neighbours called police to end his abuse. Such uncomfortable incidents could be dismissed simply as domestic disputes that reflect poorly on individual participants, but she read them as indicative of a collective ethnic temperament. This is despite the fact that she divorced her own husband for violent abuse; and even though uncomfortable domestic scenes can be witnessed in the Greek community where yelling can be part of everyday gender negotiations. Such forms of social amnesia, or wilful forgetting, facilitate the construction of the otherness of the Muslim in a context where Greeks share many cultural practices with Middle Eastern migrants.

Many older migrants living in Cronulla were afraid to speak to me. One elderly Maltese woman complained of 'bloody Muslins' but refused to say any more, her Greek neighbours were initially keen to speak but became frightened of saying the wrong thing or keeping alive the harm it was doing to local businesses and the area's reputation. Migrants I spoke to who had lived for a long time in the Shire felt accepted, despite the text message that sparked the riot referring to a wog bashing day, most knew the riot was not directed at them. Indeed some felt secure enough to walk around witnessing the riot: Joltz, a Cronulla resident and an administrator of the internet music site GreekCity, described in a community forum how he had strolled around wearing a t-shirt featuring his Greek identity and had felt no hostility. Other residents and visitors who were there on the day of the riot or who sought to defend it as form of protest were sincere when they claimed they harbored no resentment towards other migrants.

A number of residents, including a Greek resident, who were keen to defend their suburb, suggested I expand my study to Bankstown where I would get first hand accounts from people who had day-to-day dealings with Arab migrants. I was told only those who had to wage everyday combat with these people could give me the truth about them. Residents were angry at what they saw as the media's unfair portrayal of the riot as arising from their racism, feeling it ignored their claim that, since many rioters came from the western suburbs, hostility towards Lebanese was not just a local issue. On the internet site, GreekCity, many younger Greeks sided with the rioters and even before the riot, many GreekCity contributors were voicing antagonism to Lebanese migrants. Here, the Arab Other was used to reposition Greekness in Australian society. GreekCity plays Greek music over the internet and hosts Community Forums where all kinds of issues are discussed in English, contributors often use Greek words and colloquialisms as badges of authenticity to show their familiarity with Greek culture. One discussion on the site covered dating Lebanese men; one contributor, in disbelief, asked if the initiator of the topic was 'on drugs' and asked her to write on a more sensible topic. Others, mainly men, felt the need to lecture on the dangers of such liaisons: one writer explained how there were two kinds of Lebanese, and Greek girls should make sure they choose those who come from *οικογένεια*, which refers to the moral socialising space of the family which produces domesticated Lebanese subjects capable of integration with others.

On GreekCity, there are many jokes about Lebanese migrants and the caricatures of ethnic hostility surfaced well before the riot. Lebanese jokes are popular not just amongst Aussies but among non-Arab migrants, nevertheless, I was surprised to read them on GreekCity. In another time, similar jokes were told about Greeks, especially on themes dealing with smell, hairiness and stinginess. In these jokes, there is a logic of caricature, characterising the Lebanese as having: a pack herd mentality, low IQ, poor education, tacky sense of dress, and idiosyncratic family relations; other jokes are about their propensity to steal cars, aggressiveness, territoriality and unfamiliarity with sex.

Q: Why did the leb cross the road?

A: To bash the chicken.

Q: Why did 50 lebs cross the road?

A: The chicken was winning.

Q: Why do lebs have big noses?

A: Because air is free.

Q: Why dont lebs where underwear?

A: Cause ADIDAS dont make them

Q: Why do lebs have so many children?

A: Because ADIDAS doesn't make condoms.

Q: What do you call a leb who has had an abortion?

A: CrimeStopper

Q: What do you call a leb that passes his English test?

A: A cheat

Q: What's the difference between a lebbo and yoghurt?

A: yoghurt has a decent culture.

Q: What is 8 blocks large and has an I.Q of four?

A: Lakemba, Bankstown, and Punchbowl.

Q: Why can`t lebs make ice cubes?

A: Because they always forget the recipe.

Q: Why do lebs wear thick gold chains?

A: So they know where to stop shaving.

Q: Why didn't the lebanese olympic boxing team compete in Sydney 2000?

A: They found out you have to fight one on one.

Here Greek migrants inflict on newcomers the comic abuse they suffered themselves and, in doing so, mark out and celebrate how they are now positioned differently. They are no longer a subordinate group to be mocked, but are sufficiently empowered with *national belonging* to mock the manners of those who do not know how to assimilate, who lack the finesse and desire to make themselves true Australians (Hage, 1998).

Most of the hostile discussions on the GreekCity forums were directed at young Arab men but there were comments about Lebanese women being butch and possessive, reinforcing a general construction of Arabs as aggressive. Well before the riots, there were discussions about why Lebanese behaved rudely and were prone to violence. Russel (27/10/01) warned against tainting one group with the same brush, but noted:

> The Arabs are quite a cultured and refined race usually, but in australia they have imported all the outcasts and misfits. They are all low class and ignorant and resort to violence like animals. I think this is where the problem emanates from. The south African solution may be appropriate for the Lebanese problem of australia.

The attempt to avoid a wholesale racial condemnation of the Lebanese leads to a more subtle class explanation of Australia's Lebanese problem. There is a covert scientisation of race and ethnicity going here, which is not so much biological but, as Habermas (1971) recognised, a way of rationalising the social. It is an example of how 'sociological' analyses become part of popular culture and confer the authorising aura of reason on beliefs, values, practices and social relationships. Nevromakimou, another contributor to the forum made this attempt at sociological subtlety (2/1/02):

> Lebs come from a socialy disorientated society. The usually come from a disfunctional family and their learned behaviour of being bashed by abusive parents or drinking alcohol excessively is passed on. Thos lebs which have grown up from a happy family and healthy social life are great people and I know many of them. lebs are also pack hunters like wolfs are, but if you get one alone their wimps :eek: :eek:

Here welfare discourses of disadvantage are layered onto an underlying biological determinist view where race has not completely disappeared, for Lebs share an underlying animality, a collective pack mentality. They are redeemable, in that like wild dogs they can be domesticated by family, by οικογένεια. However, they preserve their domestication as long as they remain isolated from each other. When together, there emerges the violence of an evolutionary heritage, a collective wolf pack consciousness. It is as the symbolic opposite of a culture of individualism that Lebs become the opposite of civilised society. In jokes and discussion, contributors saw their herd mentality and low IQ as evidenced not just by their gangs but in their preference for brand names.

GreekCity contributors rejected the charge of racism despite topics such as, 'Lebs, What The Hell Do They Want?' It was started by Joltz, who lived at Cronulla and after witnessing the riot first hand, claimed: 'the Aussies have it right this time. In the history of Australia, ive never seen the people (the people, not the government) turn on a certain race, and deservadly so.' He described how young beach goers were quietly minding their own business when a group of Lebs arrived and began playing soccer. Carried away by the game, they kicked their ball and sand onto others. Joltz acknowledged this was accidental, but 'this group ... did not care or respect the others using the beach.' Reflecting the moral outrage of many, Joltz criticised how they attacked the life saver who asked them to settle or move down the beach.

> Ridiculous. A lifesaver is a guy giving up his own time, volunteering at the beach to help others. One day it could be you or your child that he pulls out of the water. This pathetic and cowardly attack angered the community and rightly so. A week later, one of the lebs was caught by police and charged, so the vendetta begins, the hard dumbfucks 'declared' war on Cronulla beach and 50 lebs marched down the beach to bash some Aussies up. Thats when the community took matters into theyre own hands and declared war back.

> Its not the first time this has happened at Cronulla and not the first time its happened in Sydney by a ethnic group targeting others. Saturday at cronulla was peaceful, i was walking around there with my dog on the beach and streets in my Greek jersey and no one flinched or said anything to me. The Aussies werent targeting wogs, they were targeting middle eastern appearance, altho abit silly cause some europeans could look middle eastern, but regardless, we know they had declared war on the lebs or immigrants from the middle east.

> And I for one totally agree, its time us as Australians stood up for ourselves, and told these fucks to fuck off.

> When our parents came to Australia we may have been called a wog or what not, but it stopped there, the Greek, Italian, German, Spanish etc etc immigrants that arrived in Australia post ww2, helped build our great country, they worked hard and looked after theyre family and remembered their heritage and culture, and Australia accepted that.

> As descendants of Greeks or any other European nation we accepted

Australia and built the country as the lucky country, were all educated here, bred here, work here and admit it or not we all love it here and have things so much better than anywhere else in the world.

When someone attacks our way of life we fight back cause we know whats right and wrong. The lebanese community did the same to us Greeks in Brighton, they even went into the newspapers saying that Brighton is lebanese, always has been and will be taken back off the Greeks, when they got fucked in Brighton they moved down to cronulla, and now they will fuck off somewhere else to, what they need to accept is that theyre Australian the same way we accept it.

Here Greeks are the symbolic opposites of Muslims, celebrated as an example of assimilation, of migrants who know how to move upwards by and redefining themselves as Australian. Joltz contrasted the multicultural tolerance of other migrants to the intolerance of the Lebanese. Greeks, Italians and Chinese were all said to welcome people into their neighbourhoods and 'dont rise up and kick aussies or others out of theyre areas.' But anyone walking through Bankstown was said to receive intimidating stares and needed to keep looking behind their back.

Its plain and simple, these lebs that parade around Sydney thinking theyre in beifuknrut telling communities that this is theyre area need to fuck off out of the country, and the same goes for anyone who doesnt think theyre Australian.

With Joltz, we have an example of young Greeks embracing and loving Australia and its peaceful way of life. They belong to Australia so fully they can confidently tell others to assimilate or leave. According to Joltz, migrants have to stop trying to make Australia into Lebanon, Italy or Greece: 'if your not ready to accept that you share this country with others then your no different to being one of those rascist lebs and ill gladly join in a fight to kick your asses.' Lebanese are defined as the true racists, as exclusionists seeking the security of their own neighbourhoods. Such discursive inversions are common in the contemporary era where racism masquerades as anti-racism, where it projects the charge of racism onto minority groups when they seek solidarity and autonomy from the dominant culture. Aborigines are often accused of this reverse racism when they seek refuge and intimacy in their own neighbourhoods (Brunton, 1993; Hanson, 1996; Morris, 2004).

The critique of the Lebanese also claims that they have not left behind the divisive attitudes that created their war torn homelands. Interviews with Cronulla residents and visitors reveal, among Aussies and migrant youth, a shared celebration of Australian culture as a relaxed state of mind and a construction of Arabs as angry (Lattas, A., 2007; Lattas, J., 2007). For Joltz, knowing how to enjoy a laid-back life-style is what separates those who truly belong to Australia from those who don't. Described as having 'the best diverse culture anywhere in the world,' Australia is celebrated for merging many ethnic groups to build a great country, with an 'awesome "fuck it" attitude'. Here, there was no danger of people trying to take over parliament or picking up a gun to begin a fight: 'no way, we will be more like "fuck it id rather watch the origin"[5].' The relaxed pleasures of Australians depoliticises them, they have too much of the good life to become revolutionaries and their commitment to sport defines their contented state of being (Lattas, J., 2007). Joltz continues:

> 'Fuck it' It represents our true meaning in Australia, if the Greek community was told lets go to bansktown and fuck em up, were [we're] like 'fuck it lets eat some yeeros', we know when to stop and how to seperate right from wrong, but the lebs, they just keep coming in a war they cant win and thats why bankstown is such a shithole the type of peopel they are reflects the area they live in, and until they change and accept theyre Aussieness, will they be welcome in Australia in the mean time until they change we wil fight for our way of life but we wont force change on others 'fuck it'

HBK (12/12/05) agreed with Joltz, adding, 'i was at the beach last week and i nearly had a punch up with them. there garbage people.' He lamented how when Aussies see Lebs, they think it's true of all wogs. He was angered by this confusion, describing Lebs as acting like the biggest dickheads, swearing at girls and other people and trying to start fights over nothing: 'there dumb cunts. but what the aussies did yesterday wasnt right but really do u blame them?' HBK wanted to distinguish Greeks from Arabs: 'one thing i don't want is that muslim cunt on tv talkin 4 the wogs, we should have a wog representative, cos these lebbos cunts arent wogs their fukn arabs'. Sokrates aka Kypreo praised HBK. He resented how Aussies use to call Greeks Wogs and now mistook them for Lebs when in fact Greeks had been going to Cronulla for years and rarely had problems: 'The fact is Lebo's never have respect for anyone and now ppl are beginning to fight back against a tirade of abuse that the Lebo's have inflicted on others for many years.' The riot is seen as popular justice, justifiable anger. It is righteous revenge for the petty humiliations of the past that will restore the moral dignity of the dominant community.

Many GreekCity contributors sided with the Aussies who rioted and expressed anger at the failure of Arabs to assimilate, which they contrasted with their own success. 'Explore' voices Greek participation in this national anger at the disrespect shown by Muslims in affirming a separate cultural identity.

> As a Greek Australian I consider it my duty to pressure the Arab Minorities to assimilate into the Australian Society and respect its culture, whilst still keeping their identity (just as we have). Realistically Arabs shouldnt feel hard done by: In a Christian Majority our children arent even allowed to colour in Christmas Cards etc in the public school system as not to offend the Muslim Minorities (figure that one out).

> MESSAGE TO MUSLIMS..........ITS NOT THE TOWELS YOUR WOMEN WEAR OVER THEIR HEADS OR YOUR UGLY SOUNDING LANGUAGE THAT AUSTRALIANS HATE.........ITS THE DISRESPECT THAT SOME OF YOU SHOW TOWARDS AUSTRALIAN VALUES THAT ARE GIVING ALL MUSLIMS A BAD NAME.........RESPECT AUSTRALIA OR FUCK OFFFFFFFF

When Explore criticises an education system in which he claims children cannot enjoy Christmas for fear of offending Muslims, it is Greeks who reposition themselves as part of a neglected Christian majority, dominated by a political correctness that empowers non-Christian minorities. Explore is a young Greek migrant taking on board a new found duty to pressure new migrants to assimilate. This desire not just to uphold but to proselytise 'Australian values' participates in a desire for what Hage (1998) has called 'governmental belonging', the authority and cultural capital that comes from being, if not part of the governing cultural elite, then closely aligned with it, participating in its hegemony. There is symbolic capital in Greeks affirming that they are now good homegrown Aussie citizens which they prove by pressuring other migrants into adopting Australian values. There is pleasure and pride in helping to do the governmental work of assimilation, incorporating others into the etiquette of national manners and respect for the dominant culture. Today racism masquerades within the etiquette of a cultural nationalism that discovers and deploys a civilisational logic in the minutiae of everyday life.

A long time ago Elias pointed out how the civilising process went hand in hand with the growth of state power. Etiquette allowed the formation of forms of solidarity between diverse elites of different nations; etiquette incorporated them into a common aristocratic culture of disgust. For Elias, the civilising process was later deployed to transform the culture of the lower classes whilst manufacturing new distinctions for the upper classes. Today this civilisational process is used to measure national belonging as the pacification of foreign subjects and the disorder of their ethnic subjectivity, etiquette measures their degrees of compliance and resistance to assimilation.

The word respect, which so often features in this debate, is the cunning of recognition, where migrants are called upon to demonstrate the extent to which they allow themselves to be interpellated by respect for Aussie culture (Althusser, 1971; Povinelli, 2002). How migrants fit into the dominant culture, with the appropriate forms of deference, is measured by getting rid of the towels on their heads and keeping quiet their ugly language. There is a hypocrisy in this newfound Christian solidarity, in Greeks conveniently ignoring how many of their mothers and grandmothers choose to wear 'towels' on their heads and still do not speak English even after a long residence. Not learning English protected many Greeks from the assimilating requirements of the dominant Anglo culture. This hypocrisy of young Greek-Australian is a form of 'bad faith (Sartre, 1958). It is also a form of social amnesia; a wilful forgetting that allows them to ignore their shared heritage with Arab migrants and align themselves with the Christian civilisational logic of a global Anglo alliance.

Many GreekCity contributors defended the Shire from accusations of racism. Explore claimed to be a regular visitor who knew the Shire well.

> As an Australian very proud of his Greek background (have never hidden this fact) as an early teen would hop off the train at cronulla staton with surfboard under arm . I never once experienced racism in any way or form , and was treated by the locals the same way as any other grommet that came from the 'outside' to enjoy their beach.
>
> Why? because i respected the culture. If a lifeguard ever requested something of me for the sake of other peoples safety I would gladly oblige. Most of those people are there saving peoples lives on a voluntary basis , and under no circimstances should be told to fuck off or punched out . Disrespecting an Australian icon in this manner in my opinion is showing disrespect to the whole Australian way of life.

Explore's prideful homily reflects on how being a good migrant in contemporary Australia requires distance from a self-defeating culture of 'protest masculinity' (Connell, 1995; Lattas, J., 2007; Poynting, et al., 1998; Redmond, 2007). Disrespect for lifesavers shades into disrespect for 'the whole Australian way of life.' Here the son of Greek migrants re-echoes the moral authority of national Liberal politicians who have called on Muslims to assimilate and respect Australian values or 'clear off'.[6]

According to Explore, some non-Arab migrants mistakenly saw the riot as an attack upon them and even participated in the revenge attacks. He acknowledges that there had been 'a few random assaults of anyone Non Anglo . . . but these were the actions of pissed yahoos and did not represent what the protest was about'. As proof of Aussie acceptance of Greeks, he invited anyone to go to a Greek club on a Saturday night where they would find 'plenty of pissed yahoos'. Many Cronulla residents pointed to their patronage of local Greek restaurants and other small business as proof that their anger against Muslim visitors could not be labelled as racism. As Explore put it:

> Cronulla wasnt about racism, Cronulla was about anger. Imagine spending 1 million to buy a house in South Cronulla only to be too afraid to take your power walk in a bikini top along the beach because some Leb (not all) would call you a 'Sharamouta'. Imagine being

assaulted by a group of youths in your own local park because u politely asked them to move their game of soccer over a few metres after having a soccer ball land in your potato salad (lol aussies) a hundred times. This is what the riots were about.

Alot of the old timers (including my old man) reacted by saying 'Bloody Australi ' but lets face it people, Australia is a great country, as Greeks we have been accepted into this society and are very much respected members holding high positions in every proffesional field and even government positions. I dont agree that we live in a highly racist society (Greece is a far more racist place, Greeks didnt even want the Pontians to enter their borders a few decades ago).

The Lebanese are constructed as not knowing how to use respect to take advantage of the social mobility that defines Australia as a great country. They do not know how to relax and allow others to relax. They do not respect the property, leisure, and women of a coastal middle class. Explore criticises his homeland as more racist and turns against his father's outrage at the 'Bloody Australi.' Cronulla was not about racism but the anger of ordinary people who had enough of their peaceful everyday worlds being disrupted and their women abused (Lattas, J., 2007).

Here young Greek-Australians participate in the cunning of recognition formed from the praise and censure given by the dominant culture to migrant groups depending on their successful assimilation. It is no accident that in 2006, Prime Minister Howard singled out Greeks as a brilliant example of ethnic integration. Such praise rests on suppressing recognition of other aspects of Greek culture for which Muslim groups are criticised. In the same month as Howard's praise of Greek assimilation, the Immigration Minister's Parliamentary Secretary, Andrew Robb, called on Muslim religious leaders to preach in English as part of the struggle against terrorism and to promote cultural understanding. Perhaps neither Howard or Robb had visited a Greek Orthodox Church in which services are conducted in Greek. It is no accident that the then Prime Minister's praise for Greeks coincided with a situation in which many Greek-Australians felt the need to participate in the popular moral backlash of a whiteness that constructs itself as the victim of political correctness.

In Australia there has emerged a migrant desire to do the dirty work of enforcing assimilation into so-called Aussie values, rescuing Anglo-Saxon culture from the cost of coercively enforcing its way of life. The reward for being recognised as successfully assimilated is to be given the function of cultural policing, creating self-governing migrants, migrants who police migrants. At the national level, this strategy was operating when government backbencher, Sophie Panopoulos (Yaxley, 2005), of Greek background, attacked fellow Liberal backbencher and Greek, Petro Georgiou, over his attitude to immigration. For an Aussie politician to have launched this attack would have been symbolically more difficult than for a fellow migrant. Panopoulos labelled Georgiou and other Liberal MPs who disagreed with the Government's policy of mandatory detention 'political terrorists' seeking to hold the Government to ransom. These dissenting government MPs were unhappy with keeping women and children in detention centres and with detaining people for long periods. But for Panopoulos, Australia risked becoming a 'soft touch' on refugees, the nation's humanitarianism was being exploited.

Sophie Panopoulos is most famous for calling for a ban on Muslim schoolgirls wearing headscarves to school. The scarf was described as curtailing women's rights, in contrast to a nun's habit which did not 'represent the uncompromising retrograde curtailment of women's rights as does the hijab.' According to Panopoulos: 'Women have fought too hard in this country to allow political correctness to silence any criticism of women-hating ideologies.' (ABC, 2005).In parliament, when Labor frontbenchers yelled out 'where's your hijab?', Panopoulos replied: 'Never in your life, mate.' Seeking to entrap her in Greek cultural heritage, Panopoulos uses a quintessential Aussie style to assert where her 'true identity' lies.

Many Greek women wear headscarves in public as a sign of modesty or respect for relatives who have died, it symbolises the self-effacing modesty of mourning womanhood. Such aspects of Greek identity which mirror Middle East cultures are conveniently forgotten, a social amnesia grips the minds of the policing sons and daughters of Greeks. Proud of their assimilation, they take up the onerous responsibilities of their newfound regard in the dominant culture. The cunning of recognition involves responding to being interpellated by the dominant culture, with young Greeks discovering their identity in the cultural capital of Anglo nationalism. There they discover their national value and civilised sense of ordered being through policing the disorderly subjects and subjectivities of recent migrations, whose disorder is measured by their desires for cultural autonomy. When fellow Liberal Bronwyn Bishop described the headscarf as an 'iconic item of defiance' in the 'clash of cultures' (*Age*, 2005), Panopoulos had already understood what was being asked of her. In the minutiae of everyday life - in etiquette, manners, language and dress - the dominant Anglo culture discovers its informal citizenship tests and ethnic allies who assume the symbolic cost of policing cultural compliance as a measure of pacification, civilisation and national belonging.

For contemporary Greek-Australians, Lebs or Muslim migrants operate as a symbolic other of ethnic loyalties gone wrong. 'Lebanese' behaviour is read as a moral warning of the primordial dangers of refusing assimilation. As a symbolic other, the Arab has been reinvented for Greeks, the Turko has been transformed into a Lebo, into the danger of how not to be a migrant.

## References

*ABC* (2005) 'Minister tells Muslims: accept Aussie values or "clear off"', *ABC News Online* 24 August, accessed 10 June 2009, http://www.abc.net.au/news/newsitems/200508/s1445181.htm

*Age* (2005) 'Bishop backs headscarf ban', *Age* 29 August.

Althusser, L. (1971) *Lenin and Philosophy* Monthly Review Press, New York.

Brunton, R. (1993) *Black Suffering, White Guilt?* Institute of Public Affairs, West Perth.

Connell, R. (1995) *Masculinities* Allen and Unwin, Sydney.

Elias, N. (1994) *Civilising Process* E. Jephcott (trans.), Blackwell, Oxford.

Habermas, J. (1971) *Toward a Rational Society* Beacon, Boston.

Hage, G. (1998) *White Nation* Pluto Press, Sydney.

Hage, G. (2003) *Against Paranoid Nationalism* Pluto Press, Sydney.

Hanson, P. (1996) Maiden Speech delivered in federal Australian parliament on 10 September 1996, accessed 10 June 2009, http://www.australian-news.com.au/maiden_speech.htm

Howard, J. (2006) Speech to Hellenic Club, Canberra, accessed 10 June, 2009 http://greekconsulate.org.au/catalog.php?id=454

Matthews, G. (2006) 'Testing times for 'Australian values', *Green Left Weekly* issue #685 27 September, accessed 9 June 2009, http://www.greenleft.org.au/2006/685/8111

Kapferer, B. (1998) *Legends of People, Myths of State* Smithsonian Institution Press, Washington.

Lattas, A. (2007) '"They always seem to be angry": the Cronulla Riot and the Civilising Pleasures of the Sun', *The Australian Journal of Anthropology* 18, 3: 301-320.

Lattas, J. (2007) 'Cruising: "moral panic" and the Cronulla riot', *The Australian Journal of Anthropology* 18, 3: 320-335.

Lees, J. (2006) 'Language of sense or stupidity?' *Daily Telegraph* 23 October, accessed 9 June 2009, http://blogs.news.com.au/dailytelegraph/yoursay/index.php/dailytelegraph/comments/language_of_sense_or_stupidity/P20/

Morris, B. (2004) 'Abolishing ATSIC in the Enabling State', *The Australian Journal of Anthropology* 15, 3: 303-28.

Morris, B. (Nd) *'Egalitarianism and the genesis of ANZAC'* Seminar paper, Department of. Anthropology, University of Sydney.

Panopoulos, S. (2005) 'Islamic fundamentalism - Speech', House of Representatives, Grievance Debate, 5 September, accessed 9 June 2009, http://parlinfo.aph.gov.au/parlInfo/genpdf/chamber/hansardr/2005-09-05/0171/hansard_frag.pdf;fileType=application%2Fpdf

Povinelli, E. (2002) *The Cunning of Recognition* Duke University Press, Durham.

Poynting, S., Noble, G. and Tabar, P. (1998) '"If anybody called me a wog they wouldn't be speaking to me alone": Protest masculinity and Lebanese youth in western Sydney', *Journal of Interdisciplinary Gender Studies* 3 2: 76-94.

Poynting, S., Noble, G., Tabar, P. and Collins, J. (2004) *Bin Laden in the Suburbs: Criminalising the Arab Other* Sydney Institute of Criminology, Sydney.

Redmond, A. (2007) 'Surfies versus Westies: Kinship, Mateship and Sexuality in the Cronulla Riot' *The Australian Journal of Anthropology* 18, 3: 336-350.

Sartre, J-P. (1958) *Being and Nothingness* Methuen, London.

Yaxley, L. (2005) 'Sophie Panopoulos criticised over "political terrorist" tag', *ABC Radio* 15 June, accessed 9 June 2009, http://www.abc.net.au/pm/content/2005/s1393119.htm

# Notes

[1] Though there is not a high number of Greek migrants living in Cronulla and the Sutherland Shire, this is not so for other Southern Sydney suburbs of such as Botany, Canterbury, Kogarah, Marrickville and Rockdale.
[2] One of those arrested for the revenge attacks was the son of Greek migrants.
[3] As elsewhere in this book, the terms of representation are problematic. "Lebanese" is a short hand derogatory label for new migrants from Jordan, Syria, Palestine, Iraq and Iran and especially for Muslim migrants. 'Lebo' plays on 'Abo', the abusive term by Aussies for Aborigines. Some of the caricatures used in jokes and abuse against Aborigines have been redeployed against Muslims.
[4] Marrickville councillor, Victor Macri, argued: "If they are offended by the English language, they should seriously consider where they live," (Lees, 2006)
[5] State of Origin, a major Rugby League match in Australia
[6] See comments by Brendan Nelson (ABC, 2005).

# Lines in the Sand

## Part three

## Boys behaving badly? Gender, culture, territory

Many chapters have already indicated that the riots can't be understood properly without grappling with questions of gender, especially the specific aspects of masculinity at stake during the conflict. Many commentators interpreted the incidents primarily in terms of a 'boys behaving badly' framework, even if it received a particular spin when cultural differences were added. As the introduction noted, masculine violence, even when it doesn't involve questions of ethnicity, is a recurring feature in beachside areas.

This section takes this set of issues and explores them in greater detail. Andrew Jakubowicz discusses the cultures of masculinity and their interaction with class, ethnic and local cultures in the course of the riots. He puts the conflict between young men at Cronulla in the context of the masculine competitiveness and sexual politics enshrined in the sporting arena, especially in the game of rugby league. Jakubowicz uses a number of infamous incidents in rugby league as well as the riots and revenge attacks to explore the media's role in communicating ideas about masculinity, ethnicity and violence.

Clif Evers explores the other side of this equation – male surfing culture. Evers, himself a surfer and immersed in the surf and culture at Cronulla, examines the dynamics of 'localism', the territoriality and 'cultural laws' that underpin surfing culture. Evers argues that the everyday practices of localism played a crucial role in the riots, and also worked to weave together larger communal, national and international issues. Evers also draws on the notion of habitus to explore the relation between these cultural rules and everyday practices as ways of inhabiting the social space of the beach. Evers evokes what he calls the sensual economy of masculinity that binds surfers together with stronger affective ties; these same ties also produce a very tough stance towards outsiders. Localism entails an ethos of care, but it's an ethos which doesn't exempt violence.

Judy Lattas offers an equally nuanced analysis of gender issues in understanding the tensions that produced the riots. Rather than accepting at face value or dismissing the claims that Lebanese men harassed young Anglo women, she steers a balanced approach to what is an overlaying of issues around ethnicity and gender. Rather than focus simply on masculinity, she suggests that women's experience also has to be taken into account here. She teases out the complex issues at stake in the mix of gender and ethnicity at Cronulla – the perception by young men of Middle Eastern background that they are rejected by Anglo women on racist grounds problematises who we think of as possessing or not possessing power. Importantly, she uses the conflict to pose very difficult questions for feminists, who have been criticised by right-wing media for 'betraying' the victims of sexual harassment and rape by marginalised ethnic youth.

Fig 1: Photograph by Dean Sewell / Fairfax Photos

Fig 2: Photograph by Andrew Meares / Fairfax Photos

Fig 3: Cronulla Beach, photograph by
Amanda Wise

Fig 4: Photographer
Noel Kessel / Newspix

Fig 5: Photograph by Andrew Meares / Fairfax Photos

# Masculinity, culture and urban power: the Cronulla conflicts and their amplification in popular media

## Andrew Jakubowicz

Male bonding in 'gangs', 'tribes' and 'packs', often enhanced by chemical expanders (alcohol, marijuana, 'speed', 'ice') has long been a part of late adolescent localism in Australia, part of the learned cultures of place. Such bonding often translates into territorial conflict over scarce and valuable public resources, such as the beach. The Cronulla events exemplify the way masculinity and ethno-cultural identity can be spatialised, especially as part of a broader narrative of inter-group tensions. This chapter uses media accounts to interrogate explanatory discourses for the riots from a gendered perspective, and sets these against the context of institutional masculine competitiveness displayed in rugby league football

### Masculinities

In the wake of the riots, there has been widespread discussion about the causes, effects and implications of the events (Gopalkrishnan and Swee-Hin, 2006; Norton, 2006). One of the recurrent themes has been the cultures of masculinity and their interaction with class, ethnic and local cultures (Poynting, 2006). This chapter examines three ideas of masculinity that are embedded in the political discourses of social control generated by responses to Cronulla as a political event. As the public display of identity affirmation that followed the riots was to demonstrate, local self-perceptions linked the ocean, the surf, lifesaving, the flag, the land and the national colours of gold and green in an intimate association.

The Cronulla events were quintessentially political, in the sense that politics can be understood as the process through which societies determine the allocation of scarce goods – in the case of Cronulla the scarcity was use of an accessible beach during the hot summer days[1]. While the point of the political issue can be easily identified, it is important to note that the political struggle was constructed by the various participants within a history of prejudice and apprehension, and unequal capacities to make use of the resource under contestation. Where the city is a system for the distribution of opportunity, the political struggles associated with these contests carry other trajectories of previous engagements – of gender, place and 'race'.

The discourses of masculinity that provide explanations for the events also have their own histories. Each discourse revealed both a utopian face and dystopian face, which were intimately interconnected. Each discourse of masculinity also carried a racialised aura, in that no discussion of what it means to be 'manly' is possible without being located in a culture; in a multicultural society any exposition of culture requires a process of differentiation from the other to provide local meaning.

One way of understanding the polysemic nature of masculinity discourses can be found in the exploration not of the riots, but of another shared experience of racialised, class-inflected and spatially located gender politics, National Rugby League (NRL) football. In Australian society, masculinity is closely associated with physical prowess, and in Sydney the dominant arena for such expression remains rugby league, and, in particular, the weekly competitions held as part of the national competition.

## On the field

Rugby League has been the focus of allegations of sexism and violence against women for some years; teams had been investigated for gang-rapes and individual members had been charged with brutality against women. This issue exploded in 2004, especially in relation to out-of-town training camps which were opportunities for 'bonding': expressions of deep masculine commitment, where the physical perfection of the team underpinned its need to demonstrate mateship. In these incidents, mateship was demonstrated by communally mating with the same woman; in some teams the tradition was long established that the men, sexually attractive to the women who followed the teams, would share a woman for sexual purposes, thereby expressing camaraderie. Previous scandals led the NRL to post a code of conduct and retain feminist Catherine Lumby as 'a specialist adviser to the game in the area of gender politics'. Commenting on the investigation that cleared one team – the Canterbury Bulldogs – of allegations, Lumby said:

> ...the core attitude is that, you know, we need to ensure that women are treated with respect, care and concern in every situation, whether that's in a sexual situation or whether it's about someone having a drink in a bar. We know, we know that rape is beyond the pale, but it's also not acceptable to denigrate women, treat them like objects, harass or assault them in other contexts (Nolan, 2004).

The first public coming together of standard bearers for the ostensible antagonists in the Cronulla events, the Cronulla Sharks and the Canterbury Bulldogs, took place in May 2006, six months after the riots. The teams clashed at the Homebush Bay Telstra stadium, the 'Dogs' home ground. Blogs were running hot with comment about potential disruption in the lead-up to the game; and with the history of violence that existed, the Bulldogs declared the day of the game 'Support Police Day', offering cut price tickets to police and their families, while also hosting the annual Queensland versus NSW Police League match. Outside the stadium the police presence was subdued but strong, with riot vans, police horses and dogs, and back-up teams waiting to intervene if violence occurred.

League stars are role models, heroes, and sometimes villains in the popular media; when the Sharks and the Dogs met on 21 May 2006 each brought a history directly implicated with the sex and violence scandals of the code. They each also 'stood for' the diversified but almost tribal community that backed them. The Dogs are a working class team from the Canterbury Bankstown suburban cluster, originating among ex-servicemen and workers in the inner-west of Sydney in the 1930s. The team had a few early victories then nothing until a surge of grand finals in the 1980s and 1990s; it won the grand final in 2004, the same year its members were investigated by police for allegations of sexual harassment. During 2005 its game against the Eastern Suburbs Roosters was marred by crowd violence, prompting state legislation against football hooliganism.

Despite the rocky period associated with that investigation, the team had retained its major sponsorship from Mitsubishi, while many of its players carried personal sponsorship deals. If players scored in a match the announcement would always include their sponsor's name, for example Subway sandwiches sponsored the Muslim player Hazem El Masri (complete with a person dressed in a giant bread-roll costume wandering around the sideline. The local Subway franchise offers a special line in Halal food). The Dogs team that day included El Masri and a host of other young men of immigrant background – mainly from the Pacific islands. Tries went to Utai, Holdsworth, El Masri and Tonga, with El Masri starring with six goals; one of the Dogs' most public supporters is Sheikh Taj Al Hilaly, imam at the main Lakemba mosque, and at the time the so-called Mufti of Australia.

The Sharks were formed in the mid-1950s as the suburbanisation of the peninsula was accelerating; strongly supported by the local council, its Anglo-Australian middle class environment produced solid teams but never a grand final winner. In recent years it has also recruited a significant group of Islanders – from New Zealand and Tonga especially, However, the dominant image of the current team is White; scorers in the May 21st game were Simmons, Bailey, Covell, Bird and Hilder – with its one 'non-Anglo star', Tevita Latu, sacked immediately after the Dogs game for assaulting a young woman near a nightclub, where he had been 'commiserating the loss' (ABC, 2006).

Each team also has a 'cheersquad', young women (mainly professional dancers) who perform at half-time, and hang around as 'eye-candy' before the game. They provide role-models for the adoring hero-worship stance that is still apparently the appropriate attitude for women towards the players, this is clearly endorsed by the clubs and the League, despite the Lumby critique. Masculinity carries many inflections.

MASCULINITY, CULTURE AND URBAN POWER

During the 2004 fracas over the sexual harassment allegations against the Bulldogs, Sydney radio commentator Alan Jones, who had a history of anti-Muslim sentiment and was a key 'stirrer' in the December 2005 events at Cronulla (Strike Force Neil, 2006) was forced to admit that only El Masri was above suspicion in the case, due to his well-known abstemious Muslim behaviour. El Masri is a heroic figure for Dogs supporters, especially for the strong Middle Eastern community. As the star goal-kicker for the team and its only Muslim representative, he carries a heavy responsibility and has taken a firm public position against gang violence and sexual harassment, distancing himself from the 'blokey' culture of popular masculinities and the stereotypical anti-woman representation that became associated with young Middle Eastern men after the Sydney gang rapes of 2002, and the 2005 riots (attributed in the press to the sexually-charged harassment of Anglo women by Middle Eastern men from the west of Sydney).

The masculinity stories are a major focus for the media accounts of the riots, as the male body and its behaviour became a site for articulating the core values of Australia.

## On the beach: political violence and multiculturalism

Values are ostensibly at the heart of the political engagement with the Cronulla events. John Howard (2005), then Prime Minister who was overseas at the time, commented:

> most Australians .... want a nation where, irrespective of our background and always accepting the right of people to retain affection for their own culture and to honour it as well as their own religion and to honour that, we should encourage to the maximum extent possible, everybody to become part of the integrated Australian community, that's what I mean and I think any emergence of so-called ethnic gangs is a manifestation of tribalism and something which in different ways, we should try to discourage.

Media stories and audience participation indicated that three discourses about values were vying for definitional priority:

1. The White Australian defence of the beach was the consequence of an upsurge of anger following years of intimidation by

organised gangs of Muslim youth, experienced as anti-White racism by local people;

2. It was White racism against the despised 'outsiders', who nevertheless had every right to share the space claimed by the Whites as their own, and

3. The situation should be described and defined as the outcome of criminal activity by anti-social 'thugs' under the influence of alcohol and egged on by outside agitators.

As governments have backed away from public affirmations of 'multiculturalism', a symbolic vacuum has emerged through which Australia's diversity must still be conceptualised, analysed, integrated and communicated. The Federal government announced its concern with the confusion about the term multiculturalism, with no clear preference for an alternative *(Australian* 4 November 2006) until the January 2007 replacement with 'citizenship'.

The specific history and cultures of the suburbs of Cronulla and Lakemba (the epicentre of Lebanese Muslim settlement) then come into play. These suburbs reflect the different trajectories of contemporary Sydney, where ethnic concentrations have become rather more marked than in the past, and where socio-economic and political power have fused in increasingly segregated settings (Dunn et al., 2006). Even the Cronulla beach – a long stretch of sand running north-south – had become more demarcated in the same way. The northern end is White, the realm of men with surfboards and women in bikinis, the south, especially on weekends, is where 'the wogs' went for their picnics. For decades it has attracted fully-dressed families from the west, with their barbeques and picnic tables, extended groups of old and young, who, though they rarely entered the surf, enjoyed the ocean breezes as a relief from the heat of the inland suburbs.

Cronulla has had a culture of White separateness for generations, the setting for the coming of age novel and film of the 1970s, *Puberty Blues* (Lette and Carey, 1979) and its description of the sexist rites of passage among Anglo-Australian youth. Cronulla has been a centre for drug abuse, teenage drop-outs and born-again Christianity. The suburban train line ends at Cronulla – after which there is a river and the bush or the ocean. Over four in five Cronulla residents, who are older than the Sydney average, were born in Australia, compared to three in five in greater Sydney. The top five countries of birth of the remainder are the UK, New Zealand, Italy, Germany and South Africa. It is a place where Christians live, slightly more Protestants than Catholics and is wealthier, better educated, with higher disposable incomes and more expensive properties than elsewhere in Sydney. Its geography lends it a certain isolation. If you are young, local, White and male, Cronulla is about as quintessentially Australian as it can be imagined. Indeed then Prime Minister Howard (2001) referred to it as the place he uses to understand what Australians are thinking:

> It represents an area of Sydney which brings together all of the great aspirations of the mainstream of the Australian community. This part of Sydney which I know so very well, has always represented to me what middle Australia is all about. And if you listen to the people of this part of Sydney you've got a pretty good idea of what the people of Australia are thinking and what the people of Australia want from their leaders.

Lakemba, heartland of Lebanese Australia, is rather different. It sits in the declining industrial inner-west of Sydney, part of the 'Green Crescent' of suburbs with high numbers of Muslim residents. It is polyglot, serving as a crossing place for many ethnicities, a place other Sydneysiders drive through or past, en route to somewhere else. Only just over one third of the population is Australia born – the top five countries of origin being Lebanon, Vietnam, China, Greece and Fiji. The top four religions are Islamic, Catholic, Orthodox and Buddhist. It is poorer, with cheaper property prices, and a bulging youth cohort; there are fewer professionals and managers, more tradespeople and labourers. If you are young, non-Anglo and male, it is also turf – but turf without the beach, and framed by protocols of public behaviour. The space is contested by many 'gangs' – with Lebanese and Pacific Islanders the strongest forces, and inter-gang violence occurring within as well as between communities. It has been identified as a centre for the distribution of methamphetamines ('ice') and targeted by the NSW police Middle East squad (NSW Police Force , 2007)

# Media and socio-cultural power

Studies of the relationship between media and racial or ethnic groups in Western societies demonstrate the ways the media reflect the structure of social power within a society, and thus reflect its wider ethnic relations. The media work with a set of assumptions about news values and social hierarchy, and locate minorities within narratives generated by these assumptions (Downing and Husband, 2005; Stephanie, 2005; Wilson et al., 2003). Minorities rarely appear unless they are of importance to the dominant groups and their interests – either as resources to meet their needs (food, music), items of exotic interest (strange countries, extraordinary feats) or threats (crime, public disorder). Minorities are integrated into narratives of crisis, where a wider sense of fear and apprehension is given specific existence through personification by ethnicity or race. Yet they are not silent or passive recipients of such narratives – they also produce their own, and contest those in the mainstream media.

As Hunt (1996:17) points out in his analysis of the 1992 Rodney King race riots in Los Angeles,

> These [media] texts are necessarily polysemic because contradictory semantic fields exist within cultures. That is, television texts inevitably activate particular, socially situated ways of seeing, memories capable of generating differential audience interpretations of decoding. Often these memories are of other specific media texts, texts that somehow position audiences in social space, ... the television experience is a dialogic one, an ongoing dialogue between immediate texts and intertextual memories... Hegemony theory ... [is a] framework [which] recognizes that media texts work to interpellate and influence (i.e. position) audience members; but it also recognizes that the process is inherently unstable and unpredictable, That is, cultural struggle is ongoing; it is not decided in advance.

In the Australian environment there has been a growing controversy about the way in which the mainstream media deal with race. The first Gulf War acted as a trigger, when the media were accused by anti-war activists of war-mongering and racism against Arabs, while some media (especially the national broadcaster the ABC) evoked the ire of government and pro-War groups for its apparently pro-Arab perspective (Jakubowicz, 1994). Although there had been earlier exploration of these tensions, following anti-Asian waves of moral panic during the 1980s (Jakubowicz, 1990), the shift in focus to Arab and Muslim communities after 1991 inaugurated a reign of folk devil creation that has become almost overwhelming (Poynting et al., 2004). Studies of the media and its engagement with Arabs and/or Islam in Australia have shown the systematic practices associated with the marginalisation of these groups from the 'mainstream'. The semantic structures employed by the media consistently locate these groups outside what it means to be Australian, using them as a countervailing component in stories of the truly national and the foreign.

The marginalisation of ethnic others as part of the media's expression of their national commitment has been a consistent element in Australian cultural politics for over a century. Laurie notes in his analysis of early twentieth century media accounts of immigrants and race, that:

> ...press reports between 1919 - 1929 which defend the White Australia policy, express negative attitudes towards Asia and Asians, especially the Japanese, and oppose the arrival of non-British migrants, notably Italians. There is a chilling similarity between the politically motivated use of xenophobic fear of migrants in the 1920s, based on concern that they were racially and culturally inferior and would not assimilate, and the current belief that asylum seekers undermine Australia's security and way of life (Laurie, 2004: 420).

More recently, Manning (2003) has shown how the systematic placement of certain concepts repeated in stories about Arabs and Muslims has constituted an impenetrable wall of scapegoating, such that there is almost no space for a non-threatening Arab voice to be heard. Manning talks of this journalism as 'dog whistling', that is, the constant use of a semantic code that triggers hostile responses in a significant readership, but can be denied by editors and journalists when challenged by minority groups and researchers (Manning, 2004). Lygo (2004) makes a similar case in his analysis of the 2001 MV Tampa rescue of a group of refugees in Australian waters, most of whom were Muslim refugees from Afghanistan and Iraq, that was important in framing Australian media approaches to asylum seekers. He argues that the media followed the government's lead, and systematically worked to frame asylum seekers as negatively as possible and to portray Australia as a nation under siege from terrorists, illegal refugees, and Muslim jihadists. The building of a fear culture then becomes a sustained and self-justifying process, in which the media locates all others as outsiders. When the outsiders are allowed to speak it can only be to defend themselves against the media's principled inquiries into their bonafides and testing of whether they are truly Australian in their culture and commitment. An attempt by the NSW Anti-Discrimination Board (2003) to tackle this range of media biases was scuttled by a political-media campaign, orchestrated by the Premier's office and the *Sydney Morning Herald* journalist Paul Sheehan, which led to the demise of Board chair Chris Puplick and the subordination of the ADB to government dictates. From that point on there was no official resistance to the worst excesses of the media (Jakubowicz, 2002).

## The media roles

The perspective that defended the Cronulla Whites was carried in the first few days, fed and amplified, by the popular media; it reflected and reinforced the sense of unease that locals had about their space being invaded. The narratives in the blogs, and vox pops drawn on by newspapers such as Sydney's *Daily Telegraph*, and its News Ltd stablemates the Melbourne *Herald Sun* and the Brisbane *Courier Mail*, began from the assertion that young Australians had been trying to enjoy their traditional lifestyle on Cronulla beach. In their view, groups of Muslim Lebanese young men had been visiting the beach in packs, ogling young Australian women and addressing them loudly and lewdly, reflecting their supposedly well-known sexist attitudes – a view reinforced by the Prime Minister when he said, 'there are within some sections of the Islamic community, an attitude towards women which is out of line with the mainstream Australian attitude' (Howard, 2006) and echoed by conservative commentator Keith Windschuttle (2005) explaining Cronulla as a clash of cultures.

In the dominant narrative of these events, these values, un-Australian to the core, were at the heart of the problem. They had been paraded to the public over the previous four years in the reporting of the lurid trials of a number of Lebanese and Muslim men convicted of raping a number of teenage 'Aussie' women. Locals felt the presence of these men to be malevolent and when the men were confronted and told their behaviour was intolerable, the story goes, they reacted violently. They returned with their friends, men with criminal and violent histories, who justified their boorishness by claims to cultural superiority as Muslims and Lebanese. On a hot day, with a lot of anger, alcohol and resentment around, the invasion by those of Middle Eastern appearance was too much – and in defence of place, history and the inviolability of their women, the local boys stood up to their enemies, and war began. Then, in a cowardly riposte, the narrative goes, those of Middle Eastern appearance returned over the next two nights in darkness, in their hotted-up cars, to destroy the place – a sure sign that they were not Australian, and they were acting out of the feared phenomenon of 'tribalism', an anti-social primordial group identification.

The countervailing discourse argued a different scenario: the Cronulla beaches had been the protected space of young White males, where they could ride their surf boards, ogle the blonde young women on the sand who reciprocate by fawning at their heroes, and indulge themselves in various recreational drugs. When men of Middle East appearance and their families appeared, they are viewed with suspicion, made to feel unwelcome, and hectored until they depart. Their women, dressed in hijab, were offensive, the northern part of the beach had long been staked out by locals, and anyone, especially 'hooked nosed monobrows', as one Lebanese blogger described himself, are resented. One hot day this got out of hand and young men of Middle Eastern appearance attacked some young off-duty lifesavers who had made disparaging remarks about Muslims, the epitome of White male arrogance. The White boys rallied their clan; a week later some five thousand White boys, with help from some women, and lubricated with alcohol, egged on by the once obscure but now spotlit neo-fascist groups, beat the Middle Easterners in view of the TV cameras, following a week of SMS texting and call-back radio-sponsored demands for vengeance. These events form part of the omnipresent harassment of Muslims in Australia, a residue of the policies and mind-sets of White Australia, a *weltanschauung* (the 'we grew here, you flew here' brigade) that cannot cope with the presence of the 'Other'. The Anglos behaved as they would – especially given their use of alcohol which is forbidden to Muslims. The events at Cronulla called forth a repressed anger on behalf of those of Middle Eastern descent at this treatment, and while the reactive violence and property damage by Muslim youth cannot be justified, their behaviour was comprehensible in the heat of the moment and in the face of the provocation to their honour.

The first two discourses were repeated in the media, and in more flamboyant forms, filled the blogs and listservs of White and Muslim cyberspace. At the same time an official government and police discourse was immediately put into place, seeking to defuse the conflict and also to marginalise the participants, so that their claims to representing Australianness on the one hand, and Lebanese superiority on the other, would not be legitimised – a position amplified in the October 2006 report by the police review under Norm Hazzard that pointed to the role of talk-back radio as an instigator of the violence (Strike Force Neil, 2006). It was crucial for government that hostility against Muslim communities not be fed by the media, and at the same time alienation from the government among Muslim communities and the broader society not be intensified by their apparent failures to act. Yet given the history of commitment to 'Australian values' by the national government, it could not be seen to be deserting its heartland and core supporters.

Government spokespeople were hampered by their pre-existing script – that Australia was not racist, a position reiterated by the then Prime Minister. This had also been his position when he had reluctantly conceded that Australian multiculturalism was an acceptable if low key policy position back in 1999; it had also been the Labor Opposition's position when it disavowed any policy statement on multiculturalism in 2000 and had not developed one by the time of the riots five years later (Jakubowicz, 2002) nor indeed by the Federal election of 2007.

The Prime Minister's first comment on the riots was to condemn the behaviours as aberrant, and to deny that racism was widespread in Australia, even if the events were fuelled by racism.

His victory in the election of 2004 had been built on an assertion about Australian nationalism that was in part defined by it not being about race. He claimed the peaceful absorption of races had become the hallmark of Australian modernity: 'I believe yesterday's behaviour was completely unacceptable but I'm not going to put a general tag [of] racism on the Australian community ... I do not accept there is underlying racism in this country' (*Sydney Morning Herald* 2005:1).

## Conclusion

The role of the media in communicating, amplifying and reinforcing ideas about folk devils, through the creation of moral panics, is well documented (Ball-Rokeach, 2001; Cutcliffe and Hannigan, 2001). Amplification of apprehension on all sides, polarisation of views and mobilisation of action all require active media involvement. In the Cronulla case, the expansion of digital technologies magnified the process. While it is important to distinguish between technologies used by the general population (cell phones, emails, etc) and media with editorial managers deciding what was to run (newspapers, talk-back radio, television, online newsletters, websites, blogs), the speed of transmission of information soon meant that they were inextricably intermingled.

Thus newspapers were trawling blogs looking for comments, while blogs sucked down content they agreed with or wanted to argue with from the online versions of the mainstream media, while radio was reading out SMS messages (some 270,000 SMS messages were sent in the days before the riots). Some mainstream commentators also ran blogs attached to their columns, which were linked in convoluted strings of assertion and response. Talk-back radio hosts – a number of whom actively stoked the hysteria by calling on listeners to respond to the SMS messages being circulated and reading them on air a number of times – played a central role, both in relation to mobilising the Anglo-Australian masses and conveying their views on events to politicians with whom they were influential. For Muslim youth the many Muslim on-line forums provided venues for their anger and frustration, where the various politico-religious tendencies in the communities struggled for positions from which they could 'explain' the situation, and calm or inflame their followers.

Cronulla; as a series of events in a political relationship of class, race and gender in a globalising city offers a way of viewing the fractures within Australian society. There continue to be analyses of the consequences and implications and of the responses by government and communities. The dynamic of the struggle over that sandy place – it's hard to launch surfboards from a beach where other people want to play soccer or play soccer where other people are hanging out to go into the surf – demonstrates that the struggle for spatially rationed scarce urban resources will become an increasingly omnipresent feature of Sydney, with the privileged ever more protective of, and the disadvantaged ever more hungry for, those rationed benefits the city provides.

# References

*Australian Broadcasting Commission* (ABC)(2006) 'Sharks sack Latu over alleged assault', 23 May, accessed 9 June 2006, http://abc.net.au/news/items/200605/1645669.htm?nsw

Anon (2006) Cronulla 2230: Win Back Australia!, accessed 9 June 2006, http://www.downundernewslinks.com/Cronullagame/boardgame.htm

Ball-Rokeach, S. (2001) 'Scholarly milestones essay', Mass Communication and Society 4, 1: 3-18.

Cutcliffe, J. and Hannigan, B. (2001) 'Mass media, 'monsters' and mental health clients: the need for increased lobbying', *Journal of Psychiatric and Mental Health Nursing* 8, 4: 315-321.

Downing, J. and Husband, C. (2005) Representing Race: Racisms, Ethnicity and the Media Sage, London.

Dunn, K., Forrest, J. and Pe-Pua, R. (2006) The Racism Project accessed 9 June 2009, http://www.uws.edu.au/social_sciences/soss/research/challenging_racism

Gopalkrishnan, N. and Swee-Hin, T. (Eds.)(2006) Responding to Cronulla: Rethinking Multiculturalism Multi-Faith Centre, Griffith University and Nathan; Centre for Multicultural and Community Development, University of the Sunshine Coast.

Howard, J. (2001) 'Speech on Cronulla', accessed 10 January 2007
http://www.pm.gov.au/news/speeches/2001/speech1281.htm

Howard, J. (2005) 'Media conference', 12 December, accessed 10 January
2007 http://www.pm.gov.au/news/interviews/Interview1723.html

Howard, J. (2006) accessed 10 January 2007
http://pm.gov.au/news/interviews/Interview1779.html

Hunt, D. (1996) *Screening the Los Angeles 'Riots' : Race, Seeing, and Resistance*
Cambridge University Press, Cambridge.

Jakubowicz, A. (1990) *Racism, racist violence and the media* Human Rights and
Equal Opportunities Commission, Sydney.

Jakubowicz, A. (2002) 'White Noise: Australia's struggle with
multiculturalism', in C. Levine-Rasky (Ed.) *Working through Whiteness:
International perspectives* State University of New York Press, Albany.

Jakubowicz, A. (Ed.)(1994) *Racism, Ethnicity and the Media* Allen and Unwin,
Sydney.

Laurie, R. (2004) 'Reporting on race: White Australia, immigration and the
popular press in the 1920s', *Journal of the Royal Historical Society of
Queensland* 18, 10: 420-431.

Lette, K. and Carey,G. (1979) *Puberty Blues* McPhee Gribble, Melbourne.

Lygo, I. (2004) News Overboard: The Tabloid Media, Race Politics, and
Islam Southerly Change Publications, Melbourne.

Manning, P. (2003) 'Arabic and Muslim People in Sydney's Daily
Newspapers, before and after September 11', *Media International
Australia* 109: 50-70.

Manning, P. (2004) Dog whistle politics and journalism: reporting Arabic
and Muslim people in Sydney newspapers Australian Centre for
Independent Journalism, Sydney.

Nolan, T. (2004) 'NRL admits to League's attitude problem towards
women', *The World Today, ABC*, April 28, accessed 9 June 2009,
http://www.abc.net.au/worldtoday/content/2004/s1096545.htm

Norton, A. (2006) 'Disliking making a fuss [Electronic Version]',
Policy:Centre for Independent Studies, 4. accessed 9 June 2009,
http://www.cis.org.au/Policy/autumn06/autumn06_04.pdf

NSW Police Force (2007) A Safe and Secure New South Wales - Annual
Report 2007-2008 NSW Police Online, accessed 9 June 2009
http://www.police.nsw.gov.au/__data/assets/pdf_file/0012/146001/
2007-08_NSWPF_Annual_Report.pdf

Poynting, S., Noble, G., Tabar, P. and Collins, J. (2004) *Bin Laden in the suburbs: criminalising the Arab other* Institute of Criminology, Sydney.

Poynting, S. (2006) 'What caused the Cronulla riot?', *Race and Class* 48, 1: 85-92.

Stephanie, L. (2005) Media and Minorities: The Politics of Race in News and Entertainment Rowman and Littlefield, Lanham.

Strike Force Neil (2006) *Cronulla Riots: Review of the Police Response*, Vol. 1. Sydney:NSW Police.

*Sydney Morning Herald* (2005) 'Hundreds ready for racial brawl', December: 1; 13

Wilson, C., Gutierrez, F. and Chao, L. (2003) *Racism, Sexism, and the Media: The Rise of Class Communication in Multicultural America* (3rd ed.) Sage, Newbury Park.

Windschuttle, K. (2005) 'Explaining Cronulla as a clash of cultures', *Australian* 16 December: 14.

# Notes

[1] A sense of competition captured in the fictitious 'Cronulla 2230 – win back Australia' board game that was, for a while, linked to the website of the right-wing organisation, Australia First. The game, also known as 'Cronulla Monopoly', involves buying property in the Shire to help fund extremist political groups, and it includes 'Aussie Luck Cards' which contain racist references (Anon, 2006).

# Chapter eleven

# 'The local boys': violence, care, masculinity and the riots

## Clifton Evers

Cronulla is a good place to go surfing. Shark Island is the premier wave of the area and is revered throughout the surfing world for the intensity of its hollow rides. It's a wave that rises, warps, peels and mutates over a shallow slab of rock and the blokes who ride 'the island' are gutsy, tough and respected by other surfers. The danger, relief, 'stoke' [joy] and pride experienced in the line-up of Shark Island bonds together a particular group of blokes – the 'local crew'. The local crew believe they have priority to waves and a sense of entitlement, in surfing culture this process of dominating a territory and imposing its cultural laws on others is known as 'localism'.

Localism operates from a paranoia that surf-spots are under siege from 'outsiders' (Scott, 2003). It works at a micro level similar to the way nationalism does at the macro, in that it creates an 'us versus them' situation in which the 'them' is never as good or as right as 'us' (Swoboda, 2000). Surfers have a long tradition of spray-painting 'Locals Only' on footpaths and walls to let people know that particular beaches and pieces of turf are 'theirs'. Cronulla has a history of localism because its surfing culture runs deep.

My aim in this chapter is not to examine the cause of the riots, but to look at the role localism played in the events. Drawing on three decades of surfing I will provide an account of the everyday practices of localism and how it worked as a site within which larger communal, national and international issues were played out. The masculine bonding that localism fosters led to local surfers participating in the violence that took place at Cronulla, even though some of them may not have intended to be racist. This bonding is a form of mateship that functions as a type of *care* that accommodates violence.

At times the men involved in the riots came to function as representatives of Australian masculinity, and inherited the role of guardians of Australian 'turf' – the beach, values and women. Within this context the surfer's practices of localism and masculine bonding take on importance in relation to the riots, but they also have ramifications for understanding the behaviour of young men beyond surfing.

## Cronulla

At dawn on December 11, 2005 I'd been for a leisurely surf amongst the small beach-break waves at Cronulla. A mate phoned that afternoon, and explained in an agitated voice that a huge brawl was taking place. People were being bashed and cars destroyed by a large crowd; he screamed down the phone-line that the 'Lebs' were getting 'done over'. The next day I read in a newspaper that up to 5000 people had gathered in Cronulla to protest 'offensive' and 'unacceptable' behaviour by groups of young Lebanese-Australian men. The behaviour was described as harassing local women, littering, reckless car driving, loud music, boisterousness, and being dressed inappropriately (Poynting, 2006: 87).

During October, police had been called to Cronulla three times to break up altercations between groups of reportedly 'Arab' youths and local men. The last straw, it seems, was the reported bashing of three North Cronulla volunteer lifesavers by Middle Eastern youths. This event was a trigger for the demonstration.

The day of the riot began with barbecues and beer in the sun on the beach. Australian flags were waved about, draped over people's shoulders, hung from balconies, or temporarily tattooed onto people's bodies with water-based stickers. By the afternoon many families went home, and large groups of men began to get drunk. Slogans appeared, painted on t-shirts or naked torsos: 'we grew here, you flew here', 'Love Nulla Fuck Allah', 'Wog-Free Zone', 'Lebs Go Home' and 'Osama Don't Surf'. The crowd set upon anyone of 'Middle Eastern appearance', while chanting 'kill the Leb'.

The way the demonstration escalated into a riot was surprising to many, however fighting 'outsiders' for turf is not unusual at Cronulla.[1] From the 1950s to the 1970s, tension between surfers and members of surf lifesaving clubs – 'clubbies' – lead to fights over use of the beach; there are also many stories about surfers fighting rockers and bikers.

Over the last few years, it has been Lebanese-Australian men's turn. These blokes favour particular cars, sports, food and ways of dressing; even their bodily posture is read for its cultural coding: how they stand, walk and sit. What informs their choices and bodies are their ethnic and class backgrounds. Some Cronulla locals claim that these men are being 'un Australian' because they do not act like them; those who come to the beach are supposed to obey local rules and values, but they are rules and values made by others.

A popular discourse in the Australian polity constructs people of 'Middle Eastern appearance' as key 'Others' in the national imaginary (Hamilton, 1990). This is particularly the case in light of September 11, Iraq, Afghanistan, Tampa, the London bombings, and the Bali Bombings (Perera, 2006). Lebanese-Australian men were set up as a 'dangerous Other' against whom our backyards must be protected (Betts and Healy, 2006; Poynting et al., 2004). Many of the Lebanese-Australian men who go to Cronulla are Christian, but this does not seem to matter. As Ahmed observes, within the current international political context 'Muslim' is often conflated with 'Middle Eastern' and 'terrorist' and 'illegal immigrant' (Ahmed, 2004, pp. 75-76). The effect of this 'Otherness' means that when the Lebanese-Australian blokes arrive at Cronulla Beach they're under a watchful gaze from the locals. It's hard not to step on anyone's toes when they go to the beach.

It is significant that the riot took place on a beach. Beaches like Cronulla are the 'stage upon which our national dramas, big and small, are played out' (Engberg, 1994: 19); they are where people celebrate Australia Day.[2] The Australian beach has become representative of 'nationalism rather than national identity' (Morris, 1992). The conservative federal government, headed then by Prime

Minister John Howard, entrenched the nationalism at the beach by creating a climate of fear, mistrust, and tension over threats to Australia's coastal borders. As Perera (2006) explains,

> Since 2001, the Australian beach and shoreline have been refigured as the frontline against the incursion of a new threat in the form of refugees and asylum seekers ... [and] ... reimagined as the homeland in the context of the war on terror.

Cronulla is one of the 'whitest' parts of Sydney (Forrest and Dunn, 2006), yet many Australians of migrant backgrounds have enjoyed going there. A train-line and road connects Cronulla directly with the western suburbs, which is made up of a large immigrant and low socio-economic population, particularly those not of Anglo-Celtic descent. When these 'westies', 'outsiders' and 'touros' go to the beach they are marked by racial, class, religious, ethnic and cultural differences. These can be as simple as different food, clothing and music. The increasing diversity of those using Cronulla beach saw some people claim that the riots were reclaiming 'Australia' and 'Australianness'. 'Taking back our shire' or 'claiming back the beach' circulated in SMS text messages, on talk-back radio and during the events. As one resident claimed, 'This place has changed in the past 30 years and now the young ones are taking it back' (*Age*, 2005: 4).

Some of the media, like shock jocks Alan Jones and Ray Hadley of radio station 2GB, read the attack on the lifesavers as an attack on Australian masculinity. No-one was going to push around 'genuine Australian blokes'. The relationship between Australian-ness, masculinity and the surf was an important factor in the riots. Moffit (1973: 50) illustrates this relationship when he writes about a surf lifesaver:

> Vic Rushby, surf club captain, was my first Australian Hero: tall and grey as a digger monument, straight as steel, iced saltwater in his veins ... strong as granite: austere, inviolate ... like a Viking in the surfboat.

This imaginary of Australian manhood has been set up as the guardian of the beach. Surfing tradition reifies this image of manhood (Evers, 2004; 2005; 2006).

According to Saunders, since the early twentieth century there has been a shift from the bushman to the digger to the surf lifesaver as representing the 'continuing image of Australian masculinity – able-bodiedness, heroic sacrifice and racial purity' (1998: 96). As White (1981: 155) observes, the lifesaver became a figure in whom 'Australians could ... identify nationhood with an ideal type of manhood'. The nature of the Anglo-Australian body in this masculine guardianship and manhood 'compounds the effect of exclusionary violence and xenophobia' on the already 'racially contested white site of the Australian beach' (Perera, 2006).

When the surfers joined other local men in the riot they liked to think that they were letting everyone know that they were still 'real' men like the diggers of WW1, and were not to be pushed around by these 'Lebs'. This was evident in a text message circulated prior to the Cronulla riot: 'Who said Gallipoli wouldn't happen again! ... Rock up 2 Cronulla this Sunday were [sic] u can witness Aussies beatin Turks on the beach.'

The men who took part in the riots on December 11, 2005 wanted to reclaim what it means to be an Australian man in the face of immigration and multiculturalism. Yet, in presenting the incident between the lifesavers and Lebanese youths as an attack on an Aussie icon, the Australian media forgot to mention that the lifesavers had provoked the Lebanese youths by taunting them with 'Lebs can't swim' and that the lifesavers were not actually on duty or in uniform at the time.

## Local Boys

The egalitarian image of Australian beaches is a myth and in its place are complex culturally informed sandy games of assimilation and exclusion. Surfers are very familiar with these games. Every day people negotiate unwritten rules and jostle for privilege at the beach and a piece of turf. Some groups wind up with the best trees for shade while others are consigned to a sandy desert. Surfers like myself know how to read the waves and rips, what to wear, who we're allowed to look at and how to look at them and how to avoid stepping on someone else's turf.

When I paddle around the surf or walk along the beach, nobody questions what I'm doing there. But if I was a girl without a 'perfect' figure, a tourist family, or one of the Lebanese-Australian blokes it wouldn't all seem so obvious, the rules could seem strange and frightening. Ideas about where you walk, swim, surf, how you dress, what kind of games you play and the food you eat on the beach have evolved to fit a particularly Anglo-Australian middle class view of the world. Inexperienced beachgoers and newcomers transgress beach rules, often unintentionally, because these practices are unfamiliar.

Cronulla beach is carved up through the cultural know-how of the space and rules. This know-how and the policing of its rules is a process surfers call 'localism'. The surfers will try to protect 'their' beach and way of life from others and to do this they use verbal and physical intimidation. No rules are posted, so the locals can be despotic and aggressive to get across the message that they're at the top of the pecking-order, and you're not. The fine-tuned local know-how affords these surfers privileges; they will hang out next to the best beach facilities, and claim rights to car parks, waves, park benches and girls. If people move too close to where they hang out they'll begin talking in a loud and offensive manner – borders can be acoustic. Sprawling over a large area is also a useful marker of turf.

To belong as a local, and feel comfortable in this space, my mates and I spent many years becoming intimate with the complex rules of the territory. We soak cultural rules into our skin and develop an approved persona, tastes, values and know-how. The rules are largely unstated because we have incorporated them into our flesh. The rules become 'normal', and feel 'natural' even though they're not. They also appear to be the only way things can be done, even though they aren't. This shared, embodied history is what Bourdieu (1984) calls the 'habitus', the way individuals are corporeally informed by social positions and expectations. Our bodies speak of their pasts in everyday actions – gestures, manners, and small ways of being and inhabiting social space.

The feeling of belonging as a local, and one's dedication to it, is emphasised most when the group faces a common threat. That threat can be imagined or real. Even if my mates and I *think* someone is trying to change the rules or claim that they have as much right to a picnic bench, a wave, or is chatting up a local girl we'll stare down the intruder. It's an intimidating prospect because we'll all rise at once to back each other up if we need to. We don't do this because of some violent 'hyper-masculinity' or because there's an essential violent masculine archetype deep inside us that drives us. We do it because of what our bodies have gone through together. We have developed a form of *care* that doesn't exclude violence. It's a misguided form of care perhaps, but care nonetheless. The surf sessions, afternoons at the pub, fights, and so on that my mates and I experience as 'local boys' are collaborative. They are a mixed assortment of touch, smell, sight, sound, and taste that spill all over each other (Leonard, 1997: 6).

The boys also bond with the geographical turf. We band together to fight 'dodgy development approvals' and 'sewage outfalls' (Doherty, 2003: 11). I have bonded with some surf spots to the point where it is now hard to tell where my body begins and the local environment ends. Surfers form a relationship with the local weather patterns, sea-floors, jetties and rock walls (Preston-Whyte, 2002) Knowing how to ride 'with' a wave at a particular spot is a clear marker that you're a local. The environment and how it works becomes so ingrained as part of 'the boys' that we can tell the different surf seasons by the way our body feels. A sensory relationship exists where I feel the natural and the cultural entwine as my 'habitat'; this sensory relationship turns a beach into 'my turf'.

A sensual economy not only connects me with the environment but also ties me and my mates and together, and teaches us how to behave in situations. The way our bodies learn and bond is through feelings; the boys share interest, excitement, enjoyment, fear, shame, pride, anger and so on. When we surf waves we experience varying combinations of feelings that keep us coming back for more, but so does the sharing of these feelings with each other. Stoke [joy] can fly through the air just by a look. It reaches the point where it's as if my mate's blood is mine. The brotherly love that you feel is physical – as long as the touching stays in the 'right' places; homophobia is rife in the surfing culture. Sedgwick (1985) explains this kind of bonding as 'homosociality', the way heterosexual men show physical affection and emotional intimacy for one another, while rejecting homosexual desire. In a homosocial setting the male body is protected from homoeroticism by a plethora of rules. This bonding enables my mates to say 'I love ya man' when we're drunk, change in close proximity, and go on 'boys' own' surf trips without being called 'a faggot'.

Blokes use touch, looks, nods and so on to transfer respect, trust, shame, disgust and pride. We have special handshakes and feelings pass through our skin to recall experiences we've had together. During the riot the locals put their arms around each other, slapped each other on the back and gave high-fives. These actions are techniques used to express pride in others for taking part, trust in their solidarity, and to confer that you belong. Pride tells you that you measure up, that the way you're acting, feeling and thinking are 'approved'. I spent years earning my 'right to belong' until the day I got a pat on the back from a revered older bloke to let me know that I did. It can feel like you're getting a knighthood.[3]

But pride isn't the only feeling associated with belonging, so is shame. Probyn (2000) writes of how 'shame' is also used to set up who is allowed to belong and how one is allowed to act. The shame experienced when you fail to back your mates up forces you to 'fix' your values, loyalty and abilities. Shame is meant to make you think about who you care about – those who are the 'same' as you or the 'Others' – and to get a sense of what not belonging feels like.

My mates and I have tattoos announcing permanency and authenticity on our chests, necks, backs, arms and shoulders. After the riot many young men from the area tattooed the Southern Cross, the Australian flag and the postcode (2230) on their bodies (Gee, 2006:13). However, before somebody can belong they're expected to take some 'rubbishing'; a key rule of localism is that when a newcomer wants to join in it has to be on our terms and if he steps out-of-line he'll be mocked, abused or even beaten up. Cruelty acts as a test; it's called 'paying your dues', and teaches his body what is 'right' and 'wrong'. He develops a script much the same way that a dancer learns their steps – acquiring a biological memory of what behaviour, beliefs and tastes are accepted, and what are not.

Young blokes are emptied out and punched into shape. It's a process of bastardisation and bullying that one grows to accept and, in turn, perpetuate because 'that's how you learned and it did you no harm'. If his body can weather this cruelty because he wants into the group badly enough - he'll eventually belong.

I grew up in a space where violence was an instrument used to shape what I see, and how I know certain things. My body has learned to react in certain ways to particular triggers rather than others so I have a habit of resorting to, and justifying, violence as a way to put things 'right' when I feel that they aren't. I haven't seen a lot of violence in the surf, although I've been in a few fights. But the violence only has to happen sometimes to engender the pain, shame, guilt, humiliation and ridicule that communicates what's allowed to happen and what isn't, and who sits where on the pecking-order.

Since my mates grew up within the same economy they will feel angry when I'm feeling angry and things can get out of control for no apparent reason. My mates and I mistakenly assume we have been provoked when in actual fact it is our own triggers and familiarity with violence that are the problem.

The bonding local blokes go through means they're expected to stick up for each other and to chase off outsiders. Blokes tend to hate who their mates hate, and when their bodies have bonded with each other and their turf they sometimes act first and think later. At Cronulla this bonding as the 'local boys' means backing each other up to chase off the 'dangerous Others'. Taking part in what happened on December 11, was a way for local blokes to express care for and protect those bodies, turf, beliefs and practices they believed were under threat. Larger communal, national and international discourses of fear of cultural difference, disseminated by the media and government, also fed this concern.

Ironically, groups of Lebanese-Australian blokes use similar methods to local surfers to get a sense of belonging, and to set up turf where they feel comfortable, and where their know-how is privileged. Mateship, localism and bonding aren't the preserve of White Australians. According to Randa Kattan (Higgins and O'Brien, 2006), the executive director of the Arab Council of Australia, there is an old Arabic saying: 'Me and my brother against my cousin, me and my cousin against the world'.

At Cronulla, Lebanese-Australian men intentionally contested rules like what sports could be played where. Their taste for particular cars, sports, food, and ways of dressing were read not simply as different and as their form of belonging, but as an obstinate refusal to 'toe the line'. Even their culturally developed bodily posture was interpreted as arrogant, rather than the subservience and deference they were meant to show to 'real' – read Anglo-celtic ('local') – Australian men.

Through acts of their own masculine bravado the Lebanese-Australian blokes exploited their difference to confirm their status as the 'dangerous Other'. They intimidated locals passing through a car park they had colonised and several of the Lebanese-Australian blokes used racist taunts to invert the gaze, 'normal' routines, and authority of the local boys. It was the same racist tactic some locals were using to exclude them. As Hage (2006: 2) writes

...the division of people as good and bad relies on a common racist conception of racism as always white ... [however], everybody can be racist. White people of a European background do not have a monopoly on racist beliefs and attitudes; it is a feature of all cultures.

People interpret such gestures as a threat to their safety in light of what they could, though not necessarily, lead to. Some locals began to feel like a fish out of water in their own backyard.

Over several evenings after the initial riot, young men of Middle Eastern appearance drove into Cronulla and surrounding suburbs in what has become known as 'the revenge attacks'. These men attacked anyone appearing to be Anglo-Australian with knives, baseball bats, or bare hands, leaving some unconscious and others with knives still stuck in their bodies. They slashed tires, broke windscreens and smashed. The attacks were revenge for making them and their families feel unsafe at Cronulla; again, it was a violent marriage of masculinity and care. Girard (1978) refers to such retaliation as 'mimetic rivalry', the reciprocity of violent acts in situations of conflict such that each act of vengeance mirrors the act of the opponent.

## Protecting Women

All the men involved valued a version of masculinity where care and violence are not mutually exclusive and where they work to support each other so they can bond. The men involved in the Cronulla riot and the revenge attacks related their masculinity to an ability to fight for a piece of turf, and to belong. This relationship between masculinity, localism, violence and care came to the fore when all the men involved in the violence claimed that they wanted to get revenge for harassment of their women.

In this logic, women were positioned as property, a piece of turf, a common phrase expressed during the riots was: 'we are protecting our women'; after the riot local men said that they wanted to get revenge for harassment of their women (Jackson, 2006). Taking part in the riot was a way for local men to counter a perceived threat to their 'authority' to look after 'their' women and they did it in the way they were most familiar with – violence. Anti-Muslim and anti-Arab sentiment had been rising since a series of gang-rapes in Sydney's west by some Arabic-speaking men (Collins, 2005); urban myths claim violent and rapist attitudes are endemic to Lebanese or Arab or Muslim culture.

The Australian-Lebanese, however, draw on the same trope of caring for 'their' women: 'We had to respond … Your mum, your sisters and all that, they're going to be scared to walk in the street. Because there's no-one to protect them' (Jackson, 2006).

There was little, if any, reflection by any of the men who committed the violence on their own behaviors and attitudes toward women, which regularly include objectification, misogyny and sexual harassment at Cronulla. While girls now surf, little else has changed since the film *Puberty Blues* (1981) exposed the hidden realities of gendered relations in the surfing subculture, including underage sex, harassment, and gang rape. Today, even though a leering look may seem trivial to some men, '[M]any women interpret a 'minor' or 'everyday' form of unwanted sexualized attention or aggression within the context of other, more serious possibilities' (Mason, 2002: 84).

# Respect

Since the riot many families from non-English speaking backgrounds have been too scared to return to Cronulla. Instead they favour Brighton-le-Sands, a neighbouring beach that 'might as well be on another planet' (Verghis, 2005). Brighton is not a surf beach and is far more ethnically diverse than Cronulla.

Local surfers claim that to be welcome at 'their' beach all you have to do is give respect. As Richard Marsh, an ex-professional surfer and 'born and bred' local at Cronulla said 'This is our backyard. The day of the incident was simply locals trying to get a respect issue across, regardless of race' (Leitch, 2005: 39).

According to the rules of localism if you give respect you'll get it, but that's not really true. The respect flows one way because the local Anglo-Australian way is considered the authentic one. Other cultural ways of doing things can be exercised, but they will only be tolerated rather than viewed on an equal footing. This tolerance relied on the outsider being subservient to local rules, but as Preston King points out: 'There is something intolerable about the concept of 'tolerance'. For if one concedes or promotes a power to tolerate, one equally concedes a power not to tolerate.' (1997: 6).

Localism's version of respect sets locals up as legislators and guardians of their own laws, and perpetuates a narrow set of rules about how things can be done. Those who are not respected are those who begin to develop a will of their own and to move beyond the turf that is allotted to them, as Lebanese-Australian men did. Little effort was made to understand how they might see and feel things differently, or have different needs or even have a similar understanding of masculinity. They had no rights unless locals gave them some, so they tried to earn those rights in a way they were familiar with – violence.

The form of respect peddled by advocates of localism continues to disguise and reproduce a real inequality. What happened at Cronulla on that hot Sunday was a violent spectacle that made all too clear the 'us and them' mentality localism fosters, and how it can act as a conduit for racism to enable some to belong at the expense of others. The masculine bonding of mateship that localism reifies, which is called an Australian value, slipped into a form of care that uses violence to work.

Ishiwata (2002) argues that any local/global distinction is becoming increasingly frustrated. People settle, move and resettle; the movement of people blurs traditional cues of belonging. There are flows of material, values and know-how across national borders that take the local into the broader world, and the broader world into the local (Appadurai, 1996). The world is getting smaller, so it will become increasingly important to orientate ourselves towards this future of change. Rather than a guarded retreat from new relationships, there's also the opportunity to seek them out and to confront each on its own terms. When we do so, locals would do well to remember the original Hawai'ian term for surfing: *he'enalu* which not only means to slip or glide along a wave, but also to suspend judgement and confer together (Leonard, 1997: 12).

## References

Ahmed, S. (2004) *The Cultural Politics of Emotion* Edinburgh University Press, Edinburgh.

*Age* (2005) 'War of Words', *Age* 12 December: 4.

Appadurai, R. (1996) *Modernity at Large: Cultural Dimensions of Globalization* University of Minnesota Press, Minneapolis.

Betts, K. and Healy, E. (2006) 'Lebanese Muslims in Australia and Social Disadvantage', *People and Place* 14, 1: 24-41.

Bourdieu, P. (1984) *Distinction: A Social Critique on the Judgement of Taste* Harvard University Press, Cambridge, MA.

Collins, J. (2005) 'Ethnic Minorities and Crime in Australia', paper to a Public Seminar organised by the Office of Multicultural Interest Western Australia.

Doherty, S. (2003) 'Editorial: Localism is a dirty word', *Tracks Magazine* November: 11.

Engberg, J. (1994) 'Flotsam and Jetsam', in Engberg, J. (ed.) *The Beach* (exhibition catalogue), Heide Museum of Modern Art, Heidelberg, Victoria: 19-26.

Evers, C. (2004) 'Men Who Surf', *Cultural Studies Review* 10, 1: 27-41.

Evers, C. (2005) *Becoming-man, Becoming-wave* unpublished doctoral thesis, University of Sydney.

Evers, C. (2006) 'How To Surf', *Journal of Sport and Social Issues* 30, 3: 229-243.

Forrest, J. and Dunn, K. (2006) 'Racism and Intolerance in Eastern Australia: A Geographic Perspective', *Australian Geographer* 37, 2: 167-186.

Gee, S. (2006) 'Postcode of pride or a symbol of provocation', *Daily Telegraph* 31 May: 13.

Girard, R. (1978) *Things Hidden since the Foundation of the World*, Bann, S. and Metteer, M. (trans) The Athlone Press, London.

Hage, G. (2006) 'Racism Is Not Simply Black and White', *Online Opinion* 16 June, accessed 9th June, 2009, http://www.onlineopinion.com.au/view.asp?article=4577

Hamilton, A. (1990) 'Fear and Desire: Aborigines, Asians and the National Imaginary', *Australian Cultural History* 9: 14-35.

Higgins, E. and O'Brien, N. (2006) 'Kid Gloves Syndrome', *Australian* 28 January, accessed 9 June 2009, http://www.icjs-nline.org/indarch.php?article=779

Ishiwata, E. (2002) 'Local Motions: Surfing and the Politics of Wave Sliding', *Cultural Values* 6, 3: 257-272.

Jackson, L. (2006) 'Riot and Revenge', *Four Corners*, Australian Broadcasting Commission, March 13, accessed 9 June 2009, http://www.abc.net.au/4corners/content/2006/s1588360.htm

King, P. (1997) *Toleration* Frank Cass, London.

Leitch, T. (2005) 'Cronulla Conflict', *Australia's Surfing Life Magazine* January: 36-38.

Leonard, A. (1997) *What Surfing Feels Like* unpublished honours thesis, University of New South Wales.

Mason, G. (2002) The Spectacle of Violence: Homophobia, *Gender and Knowledge* Routledge, New York.

Moffit, I. (1973) 'March Past of an Image', *Walkabout* 39: 50.

Morris, M. (1992) 'On the Beach', L. Grossberg, C. Nelson, and P. Treichler (eds.) *Cultural Studies* Routledge, New York: 450-478.

Perera, S. (2006) 'Race, Terror, Sydney, December 2005', *Borderlands*, 5, 1, http://www.borderlands.net.au/vol5no1_2006/perera_raceterror.htm

Poynting, S., Noble, G., Tabar, P. and Collins, J. (2004) *Bin Laden in the Suburbs: Criminalising the Arab Other* Institute of Criminology, Sydney.

Poynting, S. (2006) 'What Caused the Cronulla Riot', *Race and Class* 48, 1: 85-92.

Preston-Whyte, R. (2002) Constructions of surfing at Durban, *Tourism Geographies*, 4,3: 307-328

Probyn, E. (2000) 'Sporting Bodies: Dynamics of Shame and Pride', *Body and Society*, 6, 1: 13-28.

*Puberty Blues* (1981) Dir. Bruce Beresford. Limelight.

Saunders, K. (1998) 'Specimens of superb manhood: the lifesaver as national icon', *Journal of Australian Studies* 56: 96-108.

Scott, P. (2003) 'We Shall Fight on the Seas and the Oceans ... We Shall', *M/C: A Journal of Media and Culture*, 16, 1, accessed 9 June 2009, http://journal.media-culture.org.au/0302/05-weshallfight.php

Sedgwick, E. (1985) *Between Men: English Literature and Male Homosocial Desire* Columbia University Press, New York.

Swoboda, G. (2000) 'Tribal Pissings', in Young, N. (ed) *Surf Rage: A Surfer's Guide to Turning Negatives into Positives* Nymbodia Press, Angourie: 74-84.

Verghis, S. (2005) 'Welcome to Cronulla – unless you'd fit in better at Brighton', *Sydney Morning Herald* 13 December, accessed 9 June 2009, http://www.smh.com.au/news/national/welcome-to-cronulla--unless-youd-fit-in-better-at-brighton/2005/12/12/1134236005935.html

White, R. (1981) *Inventing Australia: Images and Identity 1688-1980* Allen and Unwin, Sydney.

# Notes

[1] See Amanda Wise, this volume.
[2] Many Indigenous Australians, see it as a day to mourn their colonisation.
[3] Nick Carroll, in private communication to the author, 30 June, 2006.

# Chapter twelve

# 'Bikini vs Burqa' in contemporary Australia: a feminist response to the Cronulla riots

## Judy Lattas

> Girl 2...last year, the school holidays, there were like a lot more, you know, Lebanese people, and then after the riots they just stopped coming
>
> Girl 1 I like it now there, without them, I feel safer, like...
>
> Girl 2 yeah, you always get comments before
>
> Girl 1 yeah, like you, you walk around on the beach and they'd be like, whistling at you, or telling you to cover yourself up, that you were ugly or, or that you were hot and that you should go to their room. What was that about?

'What was that about?' wonders one schoolgirl I talked to on the sand at North Cronulla, four months after the events of December 2005. One of the problems at the heart of the Cronulla riots concerned the reports of young women of Western appearance (the 'Aussies', often meaning White Australians) about their recent experiences at the beach. Groups of young men of Middle Eastern appearance (the 'Lebs', meaning Lebanese-Australians)[1] were harassing them sexually, approaching them as they hung out in their beachwear and abusing the women if they tried to ignore them.

The question – not only for this schoolgirl, but for writers and teachers in response to the riots - was what to *make* of these reports. Should they be dismissed as the allegations of racists, given their use in justifying the riots? As nothing out of the ordinary, given old-fashioned Aussie sexual harassment? As 'further proof' of Muslim immigrant misogyny? As the failed practice, or failed myth, of

Australian multiculturalism? My suggestion in this chapter is that none of these responses will do, and that if we are ever to work out a better response, we must overcome what Ghassan Hage (2003) has called our 'exighophobia': the unwillingness to try to understand what is going on, especially as it might risk recognising the humanity of all involved. Feminism is not innocent of this widespread unwillingness and recent shifts in the idea of freedom for women, I believe, make it imperative for us now to make an effort to overcome it.

It is necessary to call up these shifts – a certain twisting and turning of the Women's Liberation idea of sexual freedom – before I move to my contribution on events at Cronulla.

The first part of this chapter explores some of the political context with which the stories of the women at Cronulla must contend. This context includes popular discussion of the current affairs of the time, such as the moves made by the West against the Taliban in Afghanistan, and the moves made by the Howard government against certain immigrant communities in Australia. In texts available publicly, this was a conversation that appeared in the form of internet blogs and opinion pieces in major Australian newspapers. Gender and more specifically a concern about the status of women's sexuality, and the status of Western feminism, emerges as a key point of interest in this popular discussion.

In the latter part of my paper I offer my thoughts on the empirical research that I have conducted at Cronulla. On a number of occasions throughout 2006 and as part of a single project I collected responses from locals at the beach, and followed this up with interviews and correspondence.[2] In particular I found accounts of incidents in which female Aussies would be harassed by male Lebs in the form of come-ons, routinely accompanied by the insult that they were sluts or whores. This is a common story that has become a popular explanation for why the rioters acted as they did (e.g. JustPhil, 2006). While this claim has been widely questioned as an explanation for the rioting, the complexity of the reality that it cites has not been explored.

The issues of sexual morality and modesty in dress that feature in these accounts are ones in which there is much at stake, in the cultural rivalries of West and non-West, and in the political rivalries of Right and Left.

## Bikini vs. Burqa: the cultural stakes

The phrase 'Bikini vs. Burka' is in the title of a paper by American Henry Makow, posted on his Save the Males website. For Makow 'Bikini vs. Burka' names two extremes of the appearance of womanhood, two possibilities that identify something crucial about women today and that 'say a great deal about the clash of so-called "civilizations"' (Makow, 2002). Women in the West, the argument goes, are deeply implicated in the advance of what we now call 'raunch culture' (Levy, 2005). Makow was writing some years before the introduction of the term, but this is what he means. He writes that for the American woman, 'As an adolescent, her role model is Britney Spears, a singer whose act approximates a strip tease'. Her opposite is the 'Muslim woman shrouded in a burka…One woman is totally hidden from the public; the other is totally exposed.'

There are two apparent value systems counterpoised against one another here, and Makow does not defend the one that represents the West, or more particularly, represents America now. Save the Males is a right-wing anti-government site that perpetrates the suspicion that America has been taken over by a conspiracy of Jewish bankers, corrupt politicians, and man-hating feminists. To Makow, 'Feminism is another cruel New World Order hoax that has debauched American women and despoiled Western civilization'. Freedom for women is not a value that he holds dear and one might think that it is not a value held dear by the political administration that he opposed either; George Bush owed his ascendancy to the religious Right in America, as much as to the 'New World Order' neocons. But in places like Afghanistan and the Middle East, the spectacle of the liberated Western woman has served the ideology of 'freedom' well. And on the domestic front, the 'Babes in BushWorld', as Chaudhry (2005) calls them, are at the very 'centrefold' of Republicanism. In a post 9/11 world, 'feminism' has been drafted into the 'War on Terror' (Lattas, 2006).

Makow's anti-government stance and his anti-feminism allow him to entertain the validity of the non-Western paradigm. The burqa for him is one extreme of a pole drawn between pornography and marriage and while he stops short of endorsing the requirement of obedience and self-effacement that it represents, Makow defends the Muslim's protection of marriage, saying 'The role of woman is at the heart of any culture. Apart from stealing Arab oil, the impending war in the Middle East is about stripping Arabs of their religion and culture, exchanging the burka for a bikini' (Makow, 2002).

This idea of exchanging the burqa for a bikini has found resonance on the internet. On one Islamist site, the question is asked, 'Why does "Women's right" always involve the removal of her clothes? Hence, expect the bikini to replace the modest Islamic dress'. Abid Ullah Jan (2006) comments:

> Now that Muslims' 'horrific treatment of women' is common knowledge, dieting and working out to wear a string bikini has become a patriotic act.... It might be hard for the cultural imperialists of the West to digest, but the undeniable reality is that Islam doesn't offer choices when it boils down to the right to wear Burqa or bikini. It is not the eyes of a woman in purdah but the anxious darkly circled eyes of a girl with anorexia nervosa -- the woman trapped inside -- that needs to be liberated from the invisible cultural confines of the west. The Burqa and the bikini represent opposite ends of spectrum. We need to find out which one actually exert a noose-like grip on the psyche, social and physical health of girls and women before jeering at others or internationalising our values.

## Violence and silence: the political stakes

In Australia in 2005, the violent confrontations between groups of youths in the Cronulla riots highlighted the elements of culture and gender that we are concerned with here. Because Cronulla is a beach, and the beach is emblematically Australian, the bikini took its place in the symbolic landscape of these confrontations in a palpable way. It was an undercurrent of the tensions that had built up between the Cronulla locals and the Lebanese beachgoers, revolving around accounts of the sexual harassment of Aussie women. It is this part of the story that prompted *Age* editor Pamela

Bone (2005) and *Sydney Morning Herald* columnists Miranda Devine (2003) and Paul Sheehan (2006) to question why feminists in Australia have not taken to the podium on such issues of culture and gender. Why have they not risen to decry the misogyny and criminality of these latest reports of offences to women? Why did they not seize the microphones when young Aussie women were subjected to the brutality of the 'ethnic gang rapes' in Sydney? Their answer is that feminists have been silenced by 'political correctness'.

Despite its malign intent, I take up this charge against feminism because I think it is a challenge that we would do well to make our own. The work done in Australian studies on the intersections of gender, race and culture has been important, but it has a limit. The limit is reached when it comes to confronting, for feminism, cases of harm in which the offenders would be members of a subordinate masculinity, and the victims members of a privileged femininity. In relation to Cronulla, this limit on scholarship has left us with few resources to bring to crucial national debates that concern us centrally as feminists and that are building daily in intensity and risk.

There is a growing chorus of right-wing voices on the theme of feminist self-censorship. As long as its challenge remains unanswered, the question from the right about a response from the left acts as a rhetorical one. It works to confirm the left's unwillingness to speak up for Australian women when the perpetrator of harm is Black (e.g. Aboriginal family violence), or Muslim (e.g. Lebanese and Pakistani-Australian gang rapes in Sydney, and the Sheik Faiz Mohamad and Sheikh Taj Al Hilaly comments on women and modesty: see Kerbaj, 2006). My point is that we need to build a body of feminist work that is capable of tackling these situations in a careful analysis, and it is to this body of work that I commit my research. I will start with *Sydney Morning Herald* opinion writer Miranda Devine. Her commentary on the 'ethnic gang rape' cases identifies feminism as most deserving of public censure in its 'betrayal' of the female victims and their defenders.

> When Crown prosecutor Margaret Cunneen and Superintendent Kim McKay addressed a conference on the prevention of violence against

women earlier this year, they didn't expect a hostile response from any of the feminists present. After all, they had successfully prosecuted a series of gang rape trials in which the young female victims were degraded like animals. ...instead, a 'small but vocal group' in the audience angrily asserted that the gang rape cases were 'nothing but racist prosecutions', that Skaf would not have received such a long sentence if he hadn' tbeen Lebanese.

This is how an influential part of Sydney's legal and media circles thinks; many, to their eternal shame, are women, for whom a politically correct stance on multiculturalism is more precious than feminist principles or the safety of young women and girls. It makes them uncomfortable to acknowledge the fact that young Muslim men have been roaming around Sydney gang raping non-Muslim women, or as the rapists like to say, 'Aussie pigs' and 'sluts' who ask for it' (Devine, 2003).

Devine's view on this case was taken up by others internationally (e.g. Pawlik, 2004). Nationally Pamela Bone, the late associate editor of the *Age*, wrote a piece entitled 'The silence of the feminists' which continued Devine's theme (Bone, 2005a). In this and another on female genital mutilation she condemned Australian feminism for lapsing into silence with the passing of its more intrepid second wave (Bone, 2005b).

In relation to Cronulla, Ho has recently explored this public damning of Australian feminists for not coming to the anti-Muslim party. In making way for the voices of Muslim women to be heard, she restates the left-wing truths that 'Muslims don't have a monopoly on misogyny' and that 'Crime is not caused by your ethnicity' (2006). I do not dispute these truths. I am unsatisfied, however, with the argument that the right way to deal with gender and race, here, is to keep them properly separate.

Ho was struck, she says, with 'how *gendered* these racial tensions became' at Cronulla; Sheehan is wrong, she says, to insist 'on representing rape as if it were a racialised crime' (2006). I submit, however, that this may be how phenomena such as these are experienced originally: as gendered and racialised together. Of course, this point has been made before; most eloquently in Australia by Roberta Sykes (1997), but also by others contributing to the growing body of feminist work on intersectionality. It is rarely made, however, with reference to the experience of sexual harm when the offenders, not just the victims, are members of a subordinated racial or ethnic group. The simultaneously gendered and racialised experience of sexual harassment is suggested in my empirical research, as it follows in this chapter and in other publications (Lattas, 2007; 2009). As a matter of principle, if gender and race are treated in isolation – as they are in cases that are politically sensitive in this way - we run the risk of missing the complexity, the distinctiveness and the operative context of each spate of harm.[3]

Specifically on Cronulla, it is Janet Albrechtsen who leads the chorus on the Australian left's 'blind spot'. In her article she quotes an email that she has received from a colleague whose family lives in Brighton-Le-Sands. As a key to the story of nearby Cronulla Albrechtsen offers her friend's personal account of sexual harassment there:

> This young woman recounted that all of the girls in her family (except the youngest) have been 'subject to harassment inflicted by groups of these men -- comments on our appearances, racist comments on our Australian background, unwanted touching, being followed while walking home by groups of men in cars (I was once followed all the way home -- have never been so scared in my life), sexually explicit remarks while alone, with friends or with boyfriends, unwanted called-out invitations to have sex with groups of them, etc' (Albrechtsen, 2005).

Albrechtsen characterises the left's inability to acknowledge this targeting of women as a by-product of its perverse need to see mainstream Australia as the aggressor. It is 'a form of elitist self-loathing', she says. This self-loathing triggers a reflex which automatically constructs the cultural other as a victim. This other cannot be seen as aggressive in its gender harms, as long as it is held to be the subject of race harm in Australia; 'culture is talked about only as an excuse for abhorrent behaviour', writes Albrechtsen, 'so that the offender becomes the victim'.

Some Australian feminists have been deconstructing the binary categories of 'offender' and 'victim' for years (e.g. White women as colonisers; Black men as violent family members). Few, however, have wanted to tackle Other on Other, especially Black on White sexual aggression with the kind of feminist commitment, qualified by a post-colonialist consciousness of race oppression, which is required (Awkward, 1995: 96).

To my knowledge, it is only Poynting, Noble and Tabar (1997) who have come close to an undertaking like this in Australia. Their work takes up Connell's on 'protest masculinity' (1995:109-119), recording the views of some Lebanese-background youths from South Western Sydney. Whilst the discourse of these youths is deeply at odds with itself, it confirms a certain resentful attitude to Aussie women – and to Aussie men in relation to Aussie women – which is at the heart of what I wish to explore in my analysis. Two short statements, drawn from their empirical work and attributed to 'Mohammed', capture this attitude and its contradictions. Firstly, the authors report that 'Mohammed ... resented "Aussie" boys because of "the way they get girls sometimes" (Poynting et al., 1997: 11) . Mohammed disliked being overlooked by the girls he might want, in favour of boys of a privileged ethnicity, the Aussies. Secondly, the authors explain that 'respect is denied the dominant "western" culture and in particular [denied] to "Australian" girls because, Mohammed explains, "I found them very easy, you know what I mean?"'. Here, in contrast with Lebanese girls (whom Mohammed knows 'can't go out' and 'have a shit life', the Aussie girls are easy to get, but made contemptible for this (1997: 13).

I note that Poynting has signalled his intention to renounce the critical analysis of Lebanese masculinity referred to above.[4] Poynting's *mea culpa* (his sense of having contributed to Lebanese suffering, in providing this critical analysis) appears to validate the charge of self-censorship that is mounted by the right. However, it also underlines the very tricky nature of this effort to acknowledge a problem that is so often held up to confirm and promote a racist view.

## 'Race' and the Slut Archetype: (You're coming on to every man, so) why not me?

Girl 3I remember walking ...with my friend 'Stella'[5]...and a group of

guys up in the car park who looked to be of Lebanese origin
…started yelling out to Stella… Stella's blonde and good
looking…you know, 'what's your name' and all this sort of stuff. And
then we kept walking and we were quite nervous… and then they
started sort of yelling out abusive stuff, because she didn't turn
around and acknowledge 'em… swearing, like, 'fucking turn around
you slut,' rah rah rah

JL oh

Girl 1 yeah, generally when, um, like the guys try and get girls'
attention, it starts out like, 'oh come-on, come-on, come over here'
sort of thing, and when you don't respond it turns to abusive, like
'fuck you, you're a slut'…'we didn't like you anyway' sort of
thing…it's really common.

This account was given by a group of three locals whom I
interviewed at Cronulla.[6] The word that strikes a listener to these
stories of harassment, of course, is the word 'slut'. Emily White
writes about 'The Slut Archetype' in her book *Fast Girls*. As a
category, she argues, the slut 'has all the characteristics of a Jungian
archetype'; it resides in the unconscious and has a mythic structure
(White, 2002: 55). The word is a condensed form of a story about
women and their sexuality that gets told over and over, not just in
pornography but in everyday life. 'Slut rumors hinge on the fear of
female sexuality and its mystery; they evoke fear of the woman with
a hole at the center of her body that is infinite, the black hole of
feminine space into which a man could disappear' (White, 2002: 58-
9). It is the story of the mythical woman 'who can take an infinite
number of men inside her' – and she not only *wants* it, she wants
*more* (White, 2002: 64). Teenagers raised on modern horror movies
know that this is the woman who must be killed in the story, the
one who indeed invites 'her own violent end' by her sluttish
behaviour (White, 2002: 71-2).

Efrat Tseëlon's phrase for the impossible position that women
can be put in, here, is 'the modesty paradox'; 'the woman is
constructed as seduction – to be forever punished for it'. There is an
associated paradox of femininity that she calls 'the beauty paradox'.
Here, says Tseëlon, 'the woman embodies ugliness while signifying
beauty' (Tseëlon, 1995: 5). Both paradoxes feature commonly in the
first-hand Cronulla accounts.

The repetition of the word 'slut' and its correlation with deserved violence are evident in the stories of Cronulla lifesavers I interviewed:

**Male** lifesaver 1 they just don't have much respect

Female lifesaver 1 yeah calling girls names, kicking sand at them when they wouldn't talk to 'em, getting into fights with the locals...kept calling us sluts cause we're not covered up...Like you're not trying to provoke them or anything you're just trying to do your patrol...

Male lifesaver 1 some of the words, like...'dirty Aussie sluts' or 'you deserve to get raped'.

Female lifesaver 1 ...with Australian guys it's more like whistling at girls and stuff like that, but with Lebs, like, it's insulting them

Male lifesaver yeah. It's like...Australian guys, or like any other type of guys...whistling, sort of saying 'hey, how's it going good looking' or something like that, but these guys are going, like, 'you dirty slut, come over here so I can rape you'...[7]

Here a distinction is volunteered between the come-ons of Aussie men, and those of Lebs. Others I spoke to were reluctant to implicate the Lebs without implicating the Aussies, but still felt a difference in quality. An email from a local informant (whom I had interviewed earlier in the project) reflects on the experience, and 'the beauty paradox' that is encountered: the girls are simultaneously hailed as attractive young women, and jeered as repellent, ugly 'dogs'.

When these boys approach girls like ourselves, we are usually a bit stand-off-ish to give them the indication that we are not interested. The guys usually try and get your number or ask you to go somewhere with them. At this stage we usually begin walking away and say no, or "i've got a boyfriend, so thats probably not a good idea", at this stage guys have began calling us "sluts" or generally degrading us in some way, "we didnt want you anyways your dogs" etc etc. This kind of thing seems malace however it doesnt seem that big a deal to the girls, becasue you just think of them as (colloquially speaknig) losers...there is this almost "expectation" that (if any guys at all) are going to talk to you or try and pick you up they will be of middle eastern decent ...That is not to say that australian guys don't do it, becasue they do aswell.[8]

What I want to hone in upon here is this recognition of the girls that the men 'of middle eastern decent' seeking to pick them up are already significantly reduced in power, as subjugated masculinities; or, '(colloquially speaknig) losers'. The approach of these men and how it will play out is already known. In another part of this same email, the informant says that 'girls living down near the beach or who hang around down at cronulla are used to this behaviour. There is a stigma attached to middle eastern guys in a way, becasue they are known to approach girls so confidently and at times forcefully'. The approach is aggressive, but the girls clearly recognise that it is also *defensive*. 'I suppose we just kind of take it in our stride and don't talk it seriously becasue they are only expressing their own insecurities', she wrote. The young men fully expect the young women to ignore them; they anticipate and are ready to be rejected. Their confidence is a bravado that contains and is fuelled by the knowledge that they will be rejected.

It is at this point in my analysis that I want to introduce the aspect of race – or more precisely, the 're-ethnicised' identity taken on by a post-migration generation and experienced in terms of race – which I maintain is a crucial part of this story.

The young men believe that the reason they will be rejected is that they are, as they say, Lebs. They know that it is a disadvantage in Australian society, to be 'wogs', and to be 'the worst of the wogs'[9], as they are currently held to be. They know that there is 'a stigma attached to middle eastern guys' that will rule them out, and rule them out specifically in the eyes of the girls at the beach. This is objected to bitterly. It is where the distinctive anger and protest of Leb masculinity comes in, expressed in the rhetorical menace of the implied pick up question of *why not me?* The question, which cannot be voiced - except in the insistent repetition of the unproductive come-on - demands an answer, which also cannot be voiced. There is a loading of felt injustice in the *why not me* that is also crucial to the story and it is articulated repeatedly with the spitting out of the word *slut*. It is the supposition *you're coming on to every man (so why not me)?*

*You're coming on to every man* is what ramps up the question of *why not me* and it is what yields the 'racist' insult anticipated in the rejection. If you are coming on to every man, but not to me, then

210

you are excluding me from the category of every man (because I am Lebanese). The ancient myth of the woman who can take every man inside of her, who will not discriminate and will not say no, who provokes her own punishment by being so sexually open, carries here an implication of 'racism'. To the Middle Eastern men she is racist, for excluding them from 'every man', while the woman brands them as racist, for calling her a (Aussie) 'slut'. She defends herself from the idea that her rejection of them may be racist by her register of the insult of 'slut'. For one young female surfer, this is what it came down to:

> Surfer 2: I've actually been called a slut ...some guys say, 'hey, come over here' and like, just trying to ignore them, walking off, and like having them say, 'hey, get back here, don't you turn your back on me'...And I mean, you don't know how to handle it. But I was actually thinking about it the other day, and you do get, like you get whistled at by the white Caucasian male...especially when they're in cars and that...you still feel a bit violated, but it's not the same, kind of, thing. It's a bit different when you get called a slut... I was trying to think, maybe it is me being racist. But I think it, pretty much, did come down to getting called slut.10

As Tseëlon (1995) points out, of course, the slut story is as old as the first woman; as old as Pandora, Lilith, and Eve. In her naked sexuality the woman is condemned and only redeemed - in part - by modesty and an asexual maternity. Women have been called sluts, effectively, for centuries, and long before 'the clash of so-called "civilizations"'. It is a disciplining device that girls even use on each other, as White's (2002) work in American high schools illustrates. Why is it important, now, to distinguish between the forms of sexual harassment that draw on this archetype of the slut in the contemporary Australian context? Because young women in Australia today are being made to bear an unfair burden of Muslim male resentment at the exclusion they feel here. The powerful myth of the slut is intensifying and channelling the affective charge of this felt exclusion onto the exposed bodies of young Aussie women, and they are at a loss with how to deal with it.

A pivotal, indispensable point in my understanding of this form of sexual harassment, then, is that young men of Middle Eastern background have a very strong sense of being rejected by mainstream Australian culture. This is played out repeatedly in the attempt to pick up Aussie women on the beach. Ethnic tensions at Cronulla are worked out in everyday gender interactions, as they are at other places around the world. The young women I spoke with at Cronulla were keen to point out that all kinds of men in Australia engage in sexual harassment. The incidents involving these groups of young men however, were distinctive in their defensive-aggressive intensity. In my analysis of these incidents, I am arguing simply that there is no easy way of saying who has more power in gender relations that involve disadvantaged men and privileged women. These relations need to be addressed carefully and fairly, if we are to avert further confrontations. Most importantly, young men of Middle Eastern background need to feel included in Australian culture.

If right-wing pundits are the only ones able to recognise and articulate the role of 'race' in this intensification of sexual harassment, then their distortions of the realities I have found at Cronulla will have several consequences. The first is that the left, especially feminism, in Australia will be further discredited in popular consciousness for its unwillingness to intervene. The second is that the right's unqualified construction of the 'powerful enemy male perpetrator' versus the 'powerless and unsuspecting female victim' will go unchallenged. Thirdly, young women will not be helped by feminist knowledge. Sharon Marcus for example, rejecting the idea of 'rape as a fact of patriarchy', offers a discursive analysis of its social scripts (Marcus, 1992). Marcus proposes an important and complex analysis of what she calls the 'rape script'. It is with her work in mind that I have sought to recognise, rewrite and rebuff the 'sexual harassment script' as it is playing out in terms of race on Sydney beaches. I have developed this argument elsewhere (Lattas, 2009); my point here is simply that we need to challenge the popular categories through which these debates are played out. Similarly, in relation to fashion items like the bikini, feminism has also contributed a highly nuanced opus on dress and desire. It is necessary now to put that knowledge to work in offering women some practical help in pursuing their sexual freedom in relative safety. The Sydney invention of the 'burqini' happily resolved the 'bikini vs burqa' opposition – the 'choice' between

Western ideals of female 'exposure' and traditional Muslim expectations of 'concealment' – for some female recruits to Cronulla lifesaving (Teutsch, 2006). The 'modesty paradox' remains however for young women in Australia, and without some help in negotiating the bikini's articulations and seductions – especially in the climate created by the Sheik's comments, as volunteered below by some off-duty female lifesavers - they will be put further at risk of aggression in their participation in the advance of raunch culture.

Lifesaver 1:   ... they sort of refer to you as like ...

Lifesaver 2:   meat

Lifesaver 1:   yeah...and it's like they just expect you to pore over them...

Lifesaver 2:   I was actually told about...I think it's in the news, about how, a, Muslim Sheik,

Lifesaver 1:   yeah, said something about how

Lifesaver 2:   we walk around like this, we deserve to get raped and all this.

Lifesaver 1:   ... it's a different culture, like, it's, yeah, we dress in bikinis, their religion doesn't believe in that... I'm not an Australian born, my parents are actually Greek...so I can understand both sides of it, where, being raised on an Australian beach...we wear our cossies, we feel comfortable in it, you know, it's no big deal, it's how we live. Whereas to them, seeing a girl in a cossie, they immediately stereotype, then there's, oh my - you know - God, some easy meat, because we're not covered up.[11]

My feminist inclination is to defend the bikini for these young women, whilst working to wrest its meaning away from both patriarchal and 'patriot' interpretations. As an icon of Australian culture, its representation of the good life cannot be left in the hands of either right-wing opinion makers, or Aussie male rioters. 'Cronulla' has become the quick way of referring to a crucial moment in Australian history, when the idea of sexual freedom for women pushes at the limits of tolerance. These limits are being experienced at the level of individual psychology and of mass psychology in politico-cultural terms; as allegiances either for or against Western values, and it is potentially very destructive (Willis, 2003). It is only by joining in the public debate on the nature and the importance of these incidents of sexual harassment, I contend, that events at Cronulla can be worked through in ways helpful to both sets of 'victims': the young women at risk of gender harm, and the young men at risk of further cultural exclusion as they act out, in psycho-sexual terms, the anger of feeling rejected. Neither gender nor culture can be considered in isolation and while the politicisation of 'raunch culture' highlights their mutual implication, activists on the left side of politics – most importantly feminists - need to be ready to respond.

# References

Abid Ullah Jan. (2006) 'The Choice Between Burqa and Bikini', accessed 9 June 2009 http://www.allaahuakbar.net/womens/choice_between_burqa_and_bi kini.htm

Albrechtsen, J. (2005) 'Racism is repulsive, but so is self-loathing', *Australian* 14 December, accessed June 2006, http://www.theaustralian.news.com.au/common/story_page/0,5744,1 7559578%255E32522,00.html

Awkward, M. (1995) Negotiating difference: *race, gender,* and the politics of positionality University of Chicago Press, Chicago.

Bone, P. (2005a) 'The silence of the feminists', *Age* 4 February, accessed 9 June 2009, http://www.theage.com.au/news/Pamela-Bone/The-silence-of-the-feminists/2005/02/03/1107409981815.html

Bone, P. (2005b) 'The bravest women in the world', *Age* 8 August, accessed 9 June 2009, http://www.theage.com.au/news/pamela-bone/the-bravest-women-in-the-world/2005/08/07/1123353210652.html

Chaudhry, L. (2005) 'Babes in BushWorld', *In These Times* 28 October, accessed 9 June 2009, http://www.inthesetimes.com/site/main/article/2371/

Connell, R. (1995) *Masculinities* Allen and Unwin, Sydney.

Devine, M. (2003) 'Betraying the rape victims', *Sydney Morning Herald* 30 November, accessed 9 June 2009, http://www.smh.com.au/articles/2003/11/29/1070081589026.html

Diken, B., and Laustsen, C. (2005) 'Becoming Abject: Rape as a Weapon of War', *Body and Society* 11, 1: 111-128.

Hage, G. (2003) '"Comes a time we are all enthusiasm": Understanding Palestinian Suicide Bombers in times of Exighophobia', *Public Culture* 15, 1: 65-89.

Ho, C. (2006) 'Cronulla, conflict and culture: How can Muslim women be heard in Australia?' UTSpeaks public lecture 5 September, accessed 9 June 2009,
http://www.communication.uts.edu.au/social_inquiry/research/utspea ks_cronulla_conflict_culture.pdf

JustPhil (2006) posted: Sun Feb 26, accessed 6 June 2006,
http://www.publicdebate.com.au/forums/viewtopic.php?p=86314&si d=dbb21559711f8269c8ade2cc9bc282f6

Kerbaj, R. (2006) 'Muslim leader blames women for sex attacks', *Australian* 26 October, accessed 9 June,
http://www.theaustralian.news.com.au/story/0,20867,20646437-601,00.html

Lattas, J. (2006) 'Uncovered meat' in *Punchin' Judy: A Women's Studies blog* accessed 9 June 2009,
http://wpmu.innovation.cfl.mq.edu.au/talkingpoint/2006/11/06/pun chin-judy-a-womens-studies-blog/

Lattas, J. (2007) 'Cruising: "moral panic" and the Cronulla riot', *The Australian Journal of Anthropology* 18, 2: 320-335.

Lattas, J. (2009) '"Stop!": the undirected scripts of sexual morality', in Dreher, T. and Ho, C. (eds.) *Beyond the 'hijab debates': New conversations on Gender, Race and Religion* Cambridge Scholars Press, Cambridge.

Levy, A. (2005) *Female Chauvinist Pigs* Schwartz Publishing, Melbourne.

Makow, H. (2002) 'The Debauchery of American Womanhood: Bikini vs. Burka', accessed 9 June 2009,
http://www.savethemales.ca/180902.html

Marcus, S. (1992) 'Fighting Bodies, Fighting Words: A theory and politics of rape prevention', in Butler, J. and Scott, J. (eds.) *Feminists Theorize the Political* Routledge, New York: 385-403.

Pawlik, A. (2004) 'Feminists Pave the Way for Women to be Raped', 14 January, accessed 9 June 2009,
http://www.faithfreedom.org/oped/AmberPawlik31229.htm

SBS Television *Dateline* (1995) 'Women in war', *Dateline* 9 September.

Poynting, S., Noble, G. and Tabar, P. (1997) 'We Stay Lebanese Together', *Education Australia* 37: 10-13.

Sheehan, P. (2006) 'A shameful silence on women's rights', *Sydney Morning Herald* 24 July, accessed 9 June 2009, http://www.smh.com.au/news/opinion/a-shameful-silence-on-womens-rights/2006/07/23/1153593209660.html

Sykes, R. (1997) *Snake Dreaming* Allen and Unwin, St Leonards.

Teutsch, D. (2006) 'Tide has turned as Muslim lifesavers start training in burqinis', *Sydney Morning Herald* 12 November, accessed 9 June 2009, http://www.smh.com.au/news/national/tide-has-turned-as-muslim-lifesavers-start-training-in-burqinis/2006/11/11/1162661949135.html

Theweleit, K. (1987, 1989) *Male Fantasies* [2 volumes] Conway, S., Carter, E. and Turner, C. (Trans.) Polity Press, Cambridge.

Tseëlon, E. (1995) *The Masque of Femininity* London, Sage.

White, E. (2002) Fast *girls: teenage tribes and the myth of the slut* Scribner, New York.

Woods, G. (1969) 'Some aspects of Pack Rape in Sydney', *Australian and New Zealand Journal of Criminology* 2, 2: 105-119.

Willis, E. (2003) 'The Mass Psychology of Terrorism,' in Aronowitz, S. and Gautney, H. (eds.) *Implicating empire: globalization and resistance in the 21st century world order.* Basic Books, New York: 83-94.

# Notes

[1] Please note that all such terms are problematic and often fluid or contested. 'Aussies' usually means White Australians or those of Anglo or European background, but in this case people of Indian or Asian heritage were still 'Aussies' for the purposes of being distinguished (or distinguishing themselves) from 'Lebs'. Similarly, 'Lebanese' could often refer to anyone of 'Middle Eastern appearance'). So these are popular categories often in contrast to the more complicated reality of them often having multiple or overlapping identities.

[2] Research project 'Respect for women' on Sydney beaches: a study of gender and culture in contemporary Australian popular culture' (Macquarie University Human Ethics Committee Reference No.: HE24FEB2006-R04503).

[3] In Bosnia-Herzegovina, for example, the distinctiveness of rape in war became an issue of utmost importance. Initial efforts to get rape listed in

mass occurrence; the genocidal character of forced pregnancy; the asymmetry of its 'warfare' (Diken and Laustsen, 2005). When compared to something like marital rape, even the psycho-sexual dimensions of rape in war are exceptional, while related (Theweleit, 1987, 1989). Martial rape is nearly always gang rape. Gang rape, in turn, has distinct forms and rationales for its brotherhoods (the football team, the motorbike club, the blood ties of family or ethnicity, shared underdog or outsider status). In the 1960s, 'pack rape' in the new suburbs of Western Sydney was scripted primarily in terms of class, masculine prestige and the youth rebellion of the time. (Woods, 1969). Sexual harassment too, I suggest, could be usefully differentiated. It would not take much to distinguish its individualised and privatised white collar forms from what I am addressing at Cronulla.

[4] This in his most recent presentations, and in email advice to me from Scott Poynting (2 July, 2006): 'The mea culpa for the protest masculinities stuff is due towards the end of the year (as a book chapter in a book on migrant masculinities).' In proceeding in this research, I am mindful of the men's studies concern of Michael Awkward (1995: 96): Without a feminist imperative, an interpretation that focuses on 'subordinate masculinities' is perhaps as likely as any unrepentant form of androcentrism to seek to justify, excuse or explain away instances of male transgressions against women.

[5] The name of the friend has been changed to protect her from being recognised.

[6] Transcript of interview of three friends, two females, one male. Conducted 15 April, 2006, in the park at North Cronulla.

[7] Transcript of interview of two lifesavers. Conducted 8 April, 2006 at Cronulla, northern beach.

[8] email received 05/07/06.

[9] Australian slang for migrant (from 'Western Oriental Gentleman'), often second or third generation.

[10] Transcript of interview of two local female surfers. Conducted 19 November, 2006 at Cronulla, northern beach.

[11] Transcript of interview of two local female off duty lifesavers. Conducted 19 November, 2006 at Cronulla, northern beach.

Lines in the Sand

Part four


In the wake of the riots:

responses and repercussions

As the introduction suggested, the repercussions of the riots are still being worked out in terms of broad issues of policy and the Australian public's ambivalent relationship with multiculturalism. This is in no small part due to rapid and often extreme responses to the riots amongst police and politicians. As Chris Cunneen demonstrates, the NSW Government introduced legislative amendments to its law enforcement legislation to improve the police force's capacity to respond to incidents that threaten public order, partly because the police were roundly criticised for a poor response. As a consequence new police powers were introduced that, Cunneen argues, challenge the principles on which the justice system works and offer a 'blunt instrument' for dealing with complex disturbances of social order.

Paul Tabar returns us to questions of community leadership. The riots, he argues, brought out conflict *within* the Arab and Muslim communities, and exacerbated the ambivalent position of community leaders, especially within the Muslim groups. The riots initially produced a unified response, but differences between Muslim and Christian leaders soon emerged, especially around claims of racism. More importantly, Tabar suggests, the riots uncovered generational and class differences within communities and struggles over their leadership, involving questions of what he calls 'ethnic capital'. This analysis suggests there are major changes ahead not just in terms of policy and practices of multiculturalism, but also the emergence of new voices of community activism.

An afterword from Ghassan Hage contemplates the riot and the revenge attacks as not so much an expression of a crisis of multiculturalism or monoculturalism, but of the dead-end way we have of polarising these categories and using them to think about the contradictions facing 'White colonial cultures' across the world. Hage argues the central issue is not assimilation, not just because the Lebanese boys are actually well assimilated (perhaps too well assimilated!), but because those that attacked them were, he claims, more interested in asserting their power to make these boys assimilate. The resulting violence is thus a struggle between forms of agency, a struggle which points to the need for a different way of conceiving and living relations within culturally complex societies.

# Chapter thirteen

# Law, policing and public order: the aftermath of Cronulla

## Chris Cunneen

The December 2005 riots at Sydney's southern beaches disturbed a view of Australia as a prosperous, racially tolerant and successful multicultural society. Thousands of young white Australians were shown draped in flags reclaiming 'their beach' from other Australians of different cultural backgrounds. Mostly those targeted were of 'Middle Eastern descent' and in particular, Lebanese Muslim Australians. The images of young people engaged in this racist demonstration and subsequent violence were powerful expressions of a contemporary Australian nationalism concerned with who is included within the boundaries of nation and with the excluded and who can be publicly vilified and violently assaulted because of their ethnicity or religion.

Following the riots at Cronulla and other Sydney beaches, the NSW Government introduced a raft of legislative amendments with the expressed aim of preventing and controlling large-scale public disorder incidents through the *Law Enforcement Legislation Amendment (Public Safety) Act 2005*. In addition to the new laws there has also been discussion and trials relating to various enhancements in police hardware to respond to public disorder. This chapter will discuss the new approaches to policing and the legal framework within which they have occurred post-Cronulla.

To begin with, it is worth noting the legal system tends by its very nature to depoliticise and dehistoricise our understanding of the background and motivations involved in large scale public disorder and riots. The positivist nature of the law does not distinguish between the motivations of the law breakers in the sense that a drunken brawl, a political protest or a racially motivated attack might all constitute 'affray' or 'riot', providing the elements of the offence are proven. For example it has been previously noted in relation to hate crime that 'while "hate" may well be the most important factor for both the victim and the perpetrator, it has historically been a matter of principled indifference for the official actors in the formal criminal justice system' (Cunneen et al., 1997:1). As Owen (2006:9) has noted in relation to the Macquarie Fields riots in 2005, the characterisation of protestors and riots as criminal disavows questions relating to motives and belief. The term 'criminality' tends to preclude the need for any further explanation (see also Cunneen et al., 1989) and policing, criminal law and penal sanctions become blunt instruments of public policy. Law and order rhetoric replaces the need for more considered understandings of the motivations and dynamics involved in public disorder.

## Lockup and Lockdown

The new measures introduced in the *Law Enforcement Legislation Amendment (Public Safety) Act 2005* introduced new police powers, new offences and increased penalties for some existing offences. A new offence of 'assault during public disorder' was created, which carries a higher penalty than that for general assault: the maximum is seven years imprisonment where the assault causes actual bodily harm, compared to a maximum of five years for a similar common assault. There are also substantially increased maximum penalties for affray (up from five years to ten years imprisonment) and riot (up from ten years to 15 years imprisonment). The changes express the sentiment that the government is tough on law and order and are in line with a dominant governmental view that increasing penal sanctions has the effect of reassuring community fears. Little thought appears to be given to whether the new penalties have any deterrent effect, or whether the escalating scale of punishment holds any real proportionality to the seriousness of the offence.

Other changes introduced by the Act centred on creating special powers in relation to targeted areas; these provide substantial enhancements to police powers over citizens, irrespective of whether or not they are involved in public disorder. Police have the power to impose an emergency closure of licensed premises and liquor outlets, and to establish emergency alcohol-free zones. The legislation removes the presumption in favour of bail for certain public order offences.

However, it is the 'lockdown' powers which are most extreme and demonstrate the greatest potential to override the rights of people to go about their daily business. The Commissioner of Police can establish special 'lockdown' zones, the potential size of which is ill-defined. A few streets? A residential or commercial block? A neighbourhood? A suburb or locality? A region? They are all possible 'zones' for a lockdown. After the lockdown has been declared, police can establish roadblocks where police may stop and search persons and vehicles and require persons to disclose their identity. The legislation allows police to confiscate and search mobile phones and other communication devices for text messages and to confiscate vehicles in cases where the driver has been, or is likely to be, involved in public disturbances.

Furthermore, police can prevent entry into or exit from the authorised zone. The lockdown can last for up to 48 hours on the authority of the Police Commissioner, or can be extended by the Supreme Court. This power to control movement of individuals in large designated areas has fundamental implications for freedom of movement. It creates a relationship between police and citizen whereby police are more like a military-style force controlling an occupied population.

Specific offences under the new legislation include failing to comply with police directions relating to the emergency liquor restriction, drinking or possessing alcohol in an emergency zone, or failing or refusing to disclose your identity. However, it is not so much these offences created under the legislation that are the concern, it is more the substantial extension of police powers to interfere with the freedoms of citizens. The potential abuse of this legislation in terms of racial profiling and/or the targeting of young people is significant.

These lockdowns were put in place in various Sydney beach suburbs in the days following the Cronulla riot. It is telling however, that within a week of the new laws being enacted, the first use of a 'lockdown' outside of Sydney was in a public housing area, the Gordon estate in Dubbo, with predominately Aboriginal residents.

As a result of a disturbance local residents spent the first day of 2006 being unable either to enter or leave the estate in which they resided. This was an ominous beginning for the potential use of the new laws; far from being used to prevent racist attacks, the laws were being applied to Aboriginal people living on public housing estates.

The introduction of new laws and the ramping-up of existing penalties as a response to collective disorder is not a new political response. Many of the changes from the older common law public order offences to statutory offences of violent disorder, affray and riot were introduced during the latter part of the 1980s in New South Wales as a result of riots and collective disorder, much of it involving Indigenous anti-police protests in places like Brewarrina, Bourke and Redfern (Cunneen et al., 1989: 185-186).

The changes in the legislation *post*-Cronulla also draw attention away from the problems with police responses to large-scale collective disorder. The report by former assistant police commissioner Norm Hazzard into the disturbances painted a picture of a police force with poor command structures in place and confusion over various responsibilities (Clennell and Wright, 2006: 3).

## Water Cannon and Tasers

In late March 2006 the NSW government announced it was requesting tenders for the supply of water cannon to the NSW police riot and public order squad. The reason presented to the public for the need for the equipment stemmed from the racially-motivated disturbances at Cronulla. The government also claimed that previous riots at Redfern and Macquarie Fields were instances where water cannon may have been used, if available (Clennell, 2006). The previous month it had been announced that police would be trialling the use of taser guns which deliver electric shocks of 55,000 volts. Perhaps the NSW government was unaware that the US-based corporation Jaycor had developed an electrocuting water cannon where, according to the company, 'debilitating but not lethal shocks' travel through the water jet (Smith, 2003). For a state government looking to save money this might have been seen as a 'two for the price of one' bargain in the public order armoury! The then proposals for taser guns and water cannon were in addition to the arming of many Australian police services in recent years with capsicum spray. In the subsequent years most Australian police services have been armed with tasers and New South Wales police also have their water cannon.

One might question whether public disorder has reached a point in Australia where governments could justify the use of water cannon against its citizens. While water cannon are presented as a 'non-lethal weapon', they can and do cause serious injury through the blunt impact trauma from the highly pressurised water as well as injuries sustained from flying debris and collisions with cars, poles and other fixed objects. The use of taser guns has also been the subject of considerable controversy in Canada and the United States and now increasingly in Australia. A recent Amnesty International report (2005) estimated that there had been 103 taser-related deaths in North America between June 2001 and March 2005. There were also many examples of the inappropriate use of taser guns against people already restrained or in custody, and against children and people with physical disabilities. Amnesty International called for a suspension on the use of taser guns pending an independent, rigorous and impartial inquiry. More recent data by Amnesty showed that the death toll had passed 150 by early 2006 (Amnesty International, 2006). After a Victorian proposal to trial taser guns, the Law Institute of Victoria (2004) gained access under freedom of information to a Ministerial Advisory Committee report which found that there was a clear lack of scientific evaluation regarding the safety of these weapons. With the roll-out of tasers to police in New South Wales, Queensland, Western Australia and Northern Territory during 2008 and 2009 the controversy over tasers has deepened. There have been at least two deaths of individuals in Queensland and the Northern Territory after tasers have been used (McKenna, 2009).

The growing use of tasers nationally and the purchase of a water cannon in New South Wales belies a shift in attitude towards public disorder and appropriate policing. Certainly water cannon will not work in relatively closed spaces like football stadiums, nor does it discriminate well in public places where only a small number of people in a crowd may be involved in violent activity. As the Americans found in the civil rights and Vietnam War protest days, water cannon also poses a public relations nightmare for government. One might question for example the long-term effect on the public if water cannon had been used in Melbourne during the World Economic Forum demonstrations in September 2000. Perhaps more importantly, these solutions to public disorder shift attention away from the causes. It is easy to forget that recent riots in Palm Island, Macquarie Fields and Redfern all occurred immediately after there had been deaths in police custody or involving police pursuit. All three communities are among the poorest urban and rural places in Australia and with histories of volatile police relations; water cannon and tasers are unlikely to resolve the long-running problems in these communities and will, in all likelihood, make the work of day-to-day policing far more difficult.

Are we becoming a society where public disorder is more prominent? A cursory look at the last three decades suggests that incidences of public disorder have remained relatively infrequent, and perhaps less frequent now than in the past. Most large-scale public disorder has either been associated with political protests, with sporting and leisure events, or as a reaction against heavy-handed policing; very few have been associated with racist motivations such as in Cronulla. There have been riots associated with music venues such as the Frankston Hotel in Melbourne, the Star Hotel in Newcastle and the Stage Door Tavern in Sydney which have reached almost iconic status through later popularisation in rock music. There have been disturbances over the years at soccer and rugby league matches – and these continue to cause some level of concern. The longest running public conflict around leisure events was the riots at the Bathurst Motorcycle Races during the early to mid 1980s (Cunneen et al., 1989).

Police responses to these disturbances have varied from underestimating conflict, to ad hoc violent over-reaction[1], to relying on specialised police riot squads. Perhaps one lesson, which should be kept in mind in today's climate, is the danger of institutionalising conflict between particular groups and the police. Certainly the lesson from the Bathurst motorcycle races' riots was that the use of the Tactical Response Group (TRG) had limited effect on controlling the violence and instead institutionalised a pattern of anti-police behaviour. As has been argued elsewhere, in that instance the presence and use of tactical police polarised and exacerbated the situation (Cunneen et al., 1989).

## The Limits of Policing and Criminal Law in Riot Control

The heyday of TRG-type police groups was the late 1980s, so it is disturbing to see the re-emergence of the idea that heavily equipped riot police will stop public disorder. Ironically, the last time the purchase of water cannon was seriously discussed was during this period of the early 1980s and specifically in relation to the riots at the Bathurst motorcycle races. By the late 1980s the TRG in NSW and Western Australia were also routinely used in Aboriginal communities when there were disturbances. By the early 1990s, there were a number of official inquiries - particularly over the use of excessive force in Redfern (Cunneen, 1990) and as a result of a number of shootings such as that of Darren Brennan in Glebe. As a result the NSW TRG was disbanded, but today essentially the same idea has re-appeared as the Riot and Public Order Squad.

It is worth briefly outlining the main arguments against institutionalised police riot squads such as the TRG to demonstrate the limits of this style of policing public order situations. The TRG was formed in 1982 allegedly as a response to riots at the Bathurst motorcycle races (see Cunneen et al., 1989). However, their role as a specialist riot control group quickly became institutionalised within the State's policing apparatus. The group had its own executive, administrative, operational and training components and most importantly it grew in size and increased its operational duties during the 1980s.

The TRG, like the more recent Riot and Public Order Squad, was established as a fast response police tactical unit capable of being deployed anywhere in the State at short notice. It was noted after their establishment that such groups, although originally established to deal with a specific 'threat', soon develop at an operational level to incorporate many of the more usual functions of general duties policing (Cunneen et al., 1989:120). In addition the structure of groups like the TRG and the new Riot and Public Order Squad are designed to ensure that a sense of independence and elitism develops. There is a clear risk of alienation from the concerns of mainstream general duties policing.

One of the most important factors in the establishment of specialist riot squads is the implied admission that relations between the normal civil policing agencies and sections of the public have deteriorated to such an extent that a paramilitary response is necessary (Cunneen et al., 1989:121). The very nature of centralised specialist police responses means that there is no requirement to develop local relationships or networks; specialist squads respond to situations which have already been defined in advance as problematic and likely to require higher levels of force. The possibility of negotiation between community and police over acceptable behaviour and the limits of protest is removed, and the likelihood of violence substantially increases in the stand-off between riot squad and the crowd. Peaceful resolution of conflict is less likely when the training and equipment are clearly focused on the use of force.

Negotiation and consent are important components in developing community respect for police and these are undermined when a reliance on tactical police develops. Without respect, consensual policing becomes impossible and the likelihood of the necessity to rely on forced is accentuated. As Findlay has noted, 'Respect and its maintenance, along with the generation of community consent, is an essential feature of most policing structures. The maintenance of respect becomes a primary function for policing...' (Findlay, 2004:45). The alternative is the police acting in a role more like an occupying army, relying on the availability of greater force to ensure order.

If paramilitary responses to public disorder provide for a distorted view of the relationship between police and public, then the criminal law also can become significantly deformed when it is applied to collective disorder. As has been previously noted,

The application of individual criminal responsibility to collective behaviour, rests on individual identification of offenders who, while being proved to possess personal guilt, are punished to a great degree as representative of the collective disorder... While the crowd cannot stand in the dock, its spectre compounds the determination of individual criminal responsibility and the level of punishment it is deemed to deserve (Cunneen et al., 1989:123-124).

We see some indication of this with the introduction of a new offence of 'assault during public disorder', and the higher penalty it attracts compared to other forms assault. It begs the question of proportionality and social harm: should a male involved in an assault in a public disturbance receive greater punishment than a similar person who assaults his spouse and children in the privacy of his home?

However, the clearest distortions of the law are evident in the new 'lockdown' powers of police. It has been well demonstrated that police discretion has a key influence on the way manifestations of public disorder and protest are contained or escalate into riot and violence (Cunneen et al., 1989). The new stop, search and confiscation powers substantially enhance police discretion; further, the new laws shift the balance of potential criminality onto whole communities or social groups.

## Policing Racist Violence

This chapter has dealt primarily with issues relating to public disorder and criminal justice responses; it is also worth considering how the law might respond to matters of racist violence. It was just over a decade ago that the Australian Human Rights and Equal Opportunity Commission (HREOC, 1991) released its report after a national inquiry into racist violence. The Commission found that although comparatively speaking Australia was a non-violent, socially cohesive nation, racist violence was a major issue which must be confronted before it becomes a significant threat. The Commission found that racist violence particularly impacted on Australians of Asian and Arab backgrounds and that institutional racism was an endemic problem for Aboriginal people in Australia. The inquiry had arisen because of an upsurge in racist attacks against minority groups and concern over the impact of institutional racism in the criminal justice system on Aboriginal Australians.

It is worth recalling that HREOC had, as a result of its inquiry, recommended that a federal criminal offence of racist violence and incitement to racist violence be introduced. While the offences were introduced federally in the *Racial Hatred Act* (1995), they lacked criminal penalties; however in New South Wales the *Anti-Discrimination (Racial Vilification) Amendment Act* (1989) introduced a criminal offence under section 20D of serious racial vilification with a maximum penalty of six months imprisonment. Racial vilification falls into the category of serious racial vilification 'if it is aggravated by threats of, or incitement to, more serious physical harms (personal violence or damage to property)' (McNamara, 2002:133). It remains a mystery to many as to why no-one was charged under section 20D as a result of the Cronulla riots.

It is also clear that sections of the media played an instrumental role in aggravating the violence at Cronulla. The *Hazzard Report* specifically criticised talk-back radio commentators for fuelling racism, and in particular for reinforcing the view that men of Middle Eastern backgrounds were a threat (Clennell and Wright, 2006: 3).

HREOC also recommended that where racist motivation was an element of an offence it should constitute an aggravating factor in sentencing. The only Australian state to introduce racist motivation as an aggravating factor in sentencing was New South Wales; this was introduced recently, not as result of HREOC's 1991 recommendations, but as a result of the gang rapes committed by young Muslim men against (mostly) non-Muslim women. One of the perpetrators was given a total sentence of 55 years imprisonment. A further recommendation of HREOC which has been ignored is that Australian police forces monitor the frequency and nature of hate crime, however unlike many European and American jurisdictions it is not possible in Australia to determine whether official reports of racially-motivated offences have been increasing.

# Conclusion

There has been a move to a much tougher stance on public disorder and part of this has been through legislative changes that have increased police powers in the public realm and increased penal sanctions for public order offences. There have also been calls for 'technical' solutions to public disorder such as the use of water cannon and taser guns. Law and order rhetoric has apparently displaced the need for a more careful and specific consideration of how policing and the law might respond to particular types of collective disorder. Certainly in relation to racist violence, the specific recommendations of the National Inquiry into Racist Violence still have relevance today.

Of concern is that the use of criminal law is a blunt instrument in dealing with these types of disturbances. There are dangers that conflict will become institutionalised through the use of tactical riot squads and that restraint in the use of force will disappear if specialist squads are provided with hardware such as water cannon. These radical responses to public disorder seriously distort the relationship between police and communities and the role of the criminal law in prosecuting and punishing individual offenders. Given the relative infrequency of public disturbances in Australia we need to question seriously whether the 'ramping up' of the criminal justice system is in any way proportionate to the level of threat. The spectre of a police water cannon dispersing citizens in a Sydney suburb is one that would substantially and perhaps irrevocably change the dynamics of civil policing in this country.

# References

Amnesty International (2005) USA: Excessive and lethal force? Amnesty International's concerns about deaths and ill-treatment involving tasers AI Index: AMR 51/139/2004.

Amnesty International (2006) 'USA: Renewed call for suspension as taser-related deaths pass 150 mark' Press release, 28 March, accessed 9 June 2009, http://news.amnesty.org/index/ENGAMR510392006

Clennell, A. (2006) 'Voters on drip-feed as Iemma pledges water cannon', *Sydney Morning Herald*, 21 March, accessed 9 June 2009,

Cunneen, C. Fraser, D. and Tomsen, S. (eds.)(1997) *Faces of Hate. Hate Crime in Australia* Hawkins Press, Annandale.

Cunneen, C. (1990) *Aboriginal/Police Relations in Redfern with Special Reference to the Police Raid of 8 February 1990*, Report Commissioned by the National Inquiry into Racist Violence, Human Rights and Equal Opportunity Commission, Sydney

Findlay, M. (2004) Introducing Policing. Challenges for Police and Australian Communities Oxford University Press, Melbourne.

Law Institute of Victoria (2004) 'Lawyers warn against Taser guns', Media Release, 12 November, accessed 9 June 2009, http://www.liv.asn.au/media/releases/20041112_taser.html

McKenna, M. (2009) Taser death second in six months *Australian* 13 June, accessed 13 June 2009, http://www.theaustralian.news.com.au/story/0,25197,25628617-2702,00.htm

McNamara, L. (2002) *Regulating Racism: Racial Vilification Laws in Australia* Sydney Institute of Criminology, Sydney.

Owen, J. (2006) 'Moral Indignation, Criminality and the Rioting Crowd in Macquarie Fields' *Current Issues in Criminal Justice*, vol 18, no 1, July 2006, pp5-19.

Human Rights and Equal Opportunity Commission (HREOC) (1991) *Racist Violence: Report of the National Inquiry into Racist Violence* Australian Government Printing Service, Sydney.

Ombudsman Victoria (1994) Report of investigation into alleged use of excessive force by Victoria Police against demonstrators at the Richmond Secondary College on 13 December 1993 Victorian Government Printer.

Smith, G. (2003) 'The Electrocuting Water Cannon', *Village Voice* 28 January, accessed 9 June 2009, http://www.villagevoice.com/2003-01-28/news/the-electrocuting-water-cannon/1

# Notes

[1] See, for example, the report on the Victorian police reaction to the 1993 Richmond Secondary School blockade (Ombudsman Victoria, 1994).

# Chapter fourteen

# Generation, class and community leadership

## Paul Tabar

I first visited Cronulla beach with some friends some years after I had settled in the Bankstown area of Sydney in 1971. Cronulla, we were told, was famous for its long sandy beach and surfing. The place was beautiful and spacious: I'll never forget the refreshing sensations as I took a dip into the waves that day. However, the place had a peculiar feeling that made me unable to relate to it. Indeed, I felt 'out of place': the bronzed bodies of the surfers with their long blond hair and their colourful surfing boards; the flag poles dug into the sand demarcating the area overseen by volunteer 'lifesavers'; the boat turned upside down at the bottom of the look-out tower and surrounded by 'lifesavers' with their distinguished caps and tanned and well-shaped bodies; and, most significantly, the pub located nearby and separated from the beach by a road and a car park. Soon after our arrival, I realized that the beach was not somewhere I would feel 'at home' and I also came to the conclusion that I could not easily become part of the pub's life. Both places were spatially and symbolically dominated by cultural practices that were alien. On the beach, I could certainly lie on my towel and take a swim from time to time and, in the pub, I could enjoy a cold beer, but both acts were somehow 'outside' the rest of the scene, isolated and excluded.

This feeling was reinforced when some young 'Aussies' yelled at us, 'you wogs, why don't you go back home?' Our difference, we were being told, was not only hard to accommodate, it disqualified us from belonging to the nation, however, I assumed this was just part of the normal and slow process of settling in; in time, perhaps, I would be accommodated in some way. It certainly didn't occur to me that my experience would also be experienced by later, 'second generation', Lebanese-Australian migrants, nor did it occur to me that such experiences could reach a point of racial outburst. Such tensions pose challenges not just for migrant communities generally, but for those whose task it is to represent those communities and mediate between those who see Australia as their home by birthright, and those who wish to make it home.

At the time the riots broke out, I was teaching in Beirut. Colleagues and students bombarded me with questions about the events. Generally, the impression those in Lebanon have of Australia is that it is a peaceful and tolerant country and suddenly, I found myself in an awkward position. On one hand, I felt I wanted to defend the positive image of Australia, my country of choice, yet on the other news coverage of the riots made this position difficult to maintain. In the end, all I could say was that the situation was more complex than the simplistic version of the events presented on the news. A 'softer' line on multiculturalism and Australian society had replaced the much more critical view of racism I had developed as an academic in Australia. This sense of being torn between competing views of what was going on and between different audiences of the accounts of these events echoed the interest I had had for many years in the dilemmas of community leadership. As I saw the names of young community spokespeople crop up in the news, I reflected on the changes within the structures of leadership that the riots revealed.

The Cronulla riots represent a momentous event in the history of community relations in Australian society. As one journalist said: 'Cronulla was possibly Australia's biggest racist protest since the vigilante miners killed two Chinese at Lambing Flat in 1860' (Murphy, 2005). What this journalist forgot to mention however, is that the riots occurred about one and a half centuries later, and more than 30 years after the implementation of multiculturalism. This event is not just significant then in terms of a history of racist conflict, but also in terms of the government management of cultural diversity. Yet it is also significant in a third way, in terms of the development of forms of ethnic organisation.

The events of the riots have already been documented in this volume. This chapter, based on interviews with community leaders and on analysis of print media and the minutes of community organisations, examines community leadership within the Arabic-speaking and Muslim communities in the context of the riots and their aftermath. By presenting the community with a difficult challenge, the riots brought the conflicts that exist between second-generation Lebanese Muslims and the 'old' leadership of the community into the open, with the former using the riots to justify their long-standing claim to replace the latter with younger and better skilled leaders. This generational conflict, however, is articulated with class differences, religious identity and migration history.[1]

## Community leadership: history, class and generational conflict

Community responses to the riots pose a challenge to researchers in 'ethnic politics' because they bring to the surface the many fissures within what is normally constructed as an 'ethnic community' with a stable organisational structure. Previous work has demonstrated the complex nature of 'community representation' and its contradictory relations to Lebanese communities and government. Community leaders have been, intentionally or not, complicit in the criminalisation of their own constituency to maintain the legitimacy which is ultimately bestowed upon them by the State (Collins et al., 2000; Poynting et al., 2004). This work has suggested that 'ethnic politics' be best conceptualised, drawing on the work of Bourdieu, as a field in which leaders accumulate the forms of 'ethnic capital' that serve them in the process of representing others, and in being recognised by the State (Tabar et al., 2003). I want to complicate these contradictions by exploring class differentiation within the two main religious groups (Muslims and Christians) of the Lebanese-Australian community and its impact on their leadership via its articulation with generational differences. My principal claim is that while Christian Lebanese-Australians do not experience a crisis in their leadership, Muslims do because of the short period of settlement in comparison to their Christian counterparts and the stronger resistance their leaders put up against emerging middle class Muslims who aspire to become the new leaders of their embattled community. The riots provide a case study in which to examine such issues through the politics of community leadership among Lebanese-Australians.

To understand the relation between religion, class, generation and leadership, we need to understand the context of settlement. The first wave of Lebanese migrants to Australia (1880-1940) was primarily Christian who belonged to the Maronite, Melkite and Eastern Orthodox Churches. In 1954 the religious composition of the Lebanese community was 70% Catholic (Maronite and Melkite), 18.5% Orthodox, 4% Muslim and 3% Druze (Price, 1983). In the early twentieth century, the majority of Lebanese migrants who settled in New South Wales (NSW) worked as hawkers and shopkeepers, by 1947, up to 60 % were still active in commercial activities but now as either employers or self-employed (Mckay and Batrouney, 2001:556). The economic success of early Lebanese migrants in Australia does not mean that they were not affected by the 'White Australia' policy and its effects on their assimilation. In fact, this policy resulted in the nearly complete assimilation of the second and third generations of the first wave of migrants. This was assisted by the small number of Lebanese migrants and their descendants (7,000 in 1940) and their inability to form a territorial community with specific associations due to their dispersal around Australia. Second and third generation migrants were also more educated and urbanised, they were 'occupationally mobile and economically prosperous in comparison with their peddling and shop-owning ancestors. They were well represented in professional, technical and managerial positions' (Mckay and Batrouney, 2001:557). The absence of ethnic-specific churches and schools added momentum to their assimilation into the dominant culture.

The second wave of Lebanese migration to Australia (1947-1976) set up a new process of community formation, characterised by a greater number of migrants (43,000) who were still predominantly Christian and came from northern Lebanon. This period was also distinguished by the arrival of unskilled migrants needed as manual workers in the growing industrial sector of the post-World War II economy. These migrants mainly settled in Sydney and Melbourne and developed their own community organisations to deal with problems of settlement. Among the Christian migrants, the Churches of the Maronite, the Antochian Orthodox and the Melkite communities played a major role. During this period, Lebanese Muslims also established mosques as places for worship and centres for helping in the settlement of the newly arrived migrants. The community developed clubs and voluntary associations (e.g. the Australian Lebanese Association in 1956) which, in combination with the religious associations and places of worship, created the social and cultural infrastructure needed for the maintenance of Lebanese ethnicity. By the early 1970s as multiculturalism officially replaced 'White Australia' policies of assimilation and integration, additional force was given to the process of cultural maintenance through the support that federal and state governments granted to Lebanese welfare, social, religious and cultural associations.

The outbreak of the civil war in Lebanon in 1975 resulted in a third wave of immigration to Australia. At the 1996 census, there were at least 150,000 persons in Australia who were either born in Lebanon or who had parents born in Lebanon. The 1996 census also reveals that 'there were roughly similar proportions of Lebanese in each of the two main religious groups [Christians and Muslims], the largest group being Catholic (40 %), followed by Muslim (39 %) and Orthodox (10 %) (Humphrey, 2001:563). Catholics were still divided between Maronites and Melkites, but the number of Orthodox increased (from 14 % to 28 % between 1971 and 1981). While the majority of Lebanese remained Christian, there was a significant change in the number and composition of Muslims with a diversification that saw all Muslim sects present in Australia: Sunnis, Shi`is, Druze and `Alawis. There were almost twice as many Sunnis as Shi`is and they are concentrated in Sydney (around 74 % of Lebanese-born Muslims live in NSW, mostly in Sydney) which is consistent with the overall concentration of the Lebanese.

In terms of employment, the 2006 census shows that among Lebanon-born people aged 15 years and above, 45.5 % participated in the labour market and 12.1 % were unemployed, at odds with national levels (64.6 % and 5.2 %). Comparing unemployment between Muslims and Christians (taking men aged 25-64) the figures become more alarming: '47 % of Lebanese Muslims were either unemployed or not in the workforce, compared to 28 % of Lebanese Christians and 21 % of all men in this group' (Betts and Healy, 2006: 14). According to this census, the rate of Lebanon-born persons who were employed in the unskilled occupations was higher (20.6 %) than that of the total Australian population (15.1 %) (Department of Immigration and Multicultural and Indigenous Affairs, n.d.). Lebanese Muslim households have lower weekly income than Lebanese Christians and it stretches over more members. Their income per household member is half the national average (Betts and Healy, 2006: 5-7; Omar and Allen, 1996: 36-38).

These statistics have repercussions for community organisation, which tends to rely on professional, middle class migrants. Lebanese Christians who arrived post-1975 found established associations and churches to assist in their settlement whereas Muslims faced the task of establishing their own organisations and networks (Humphrey, 2001:565). Initially, the burden of these tasks was shouldered by two associations, one Sunni, the Lebanese Muslim Association (LMA), and the other, Shi`i, the Association of Lebanese Southerners. The smaller number of Lebanese Muslims and their later arrival meant that the emergence of a Muslim middle class only recently began to make its presence felt in the leadership of its community.

The recent nature of Muslim settlement and the late development of a middle class aspiring to play a role in community leadership coincided with a series of domestic and international developments which resulted in greater racism directed against the Lebanese and Muslims in particular. With the First Gulf War in 1991, Arabs in Australia, including Lebanese-Muslims, became targets for racial attacks (Human Rights and Equal Opportunity Commission, 1991). In 1998, following the stabbing of a schoolboy in south-western Sydney, the NSW government launched an attack on so-called 'Lebanese gangs', accusing the community of possessing a culture which encourages 'violence and gangsterism'. This resulted in an increase in racial attacks which were mostly borne by veiled women and youth of Lebanese background. Tabloid media and popular radio broadcasters exacerbated the racialising of criminality and made 'Lebanese' synonymous with 'Muslim' (Collins et al., 2000).

After 1998, the racial tension between 'white' society and Lebanese and Muslim communities intensified following a series of local and international events: 'Lebanese gang rapes' during 2000-1 and the 'refugee' crisis (2001) in which 'Muslims' were criticised for 'jumping the queue' and accused of smuggling Bin Laden's agents into Australia. Soon afterwards came the terrorist attacks on the USA (September 11, 2001), the invasions of Afghanistan (November, 2001) and Iraq (March, 2003) by the 'Coalition Forces' (including Australia) to 'stamp out terrorism'. In October 2001, Iraqi asylum seekers were accused of throwing their children into the sea to force their way into Australia. One year later (October 2002) another terrorist attack occurred in Bali and the radical group Jemaah Islamiah, with links to Al-Qaeda, was found guilty of this attack. In July 2005, London witnessed an attack by 'home grown' terrorists. These events intensified the racism directed at the Muslims/Arabs/Lebanese (Poynting, et al., 2004). This was the context in which the Cronulla riots broke out in December 2005. Unsurprisingly, people of 'Middle-Eastern appearance' were the target. Caught in the midst of these problems, Lebanese Muslims were institutionally less equipped to address them compared to their Christian counterparts.

## The response of community leaders to the riots

The rioters used the category of 'people of Middle Eastern appearance' during their mobilisation to 'reclaim' the beach at Cronulla. This category was perceived to include not only 'Lebs', Muslims, Arabs, Turks and Afghans, but sometimes migrants of southern European background. However, people of Lebanese and Muslim background were the main target of this campaign and of the media which supported it and this drew Lebanese community leaders together to respond to these events. They organised meetings to discuss the riots and assist in calming the situation, Muslim leaders played a prominent role because the youth involved in the riots and the retaliatory acts were perceived to be mostly of Muslim background. I will focus on the LMA because of the central role it played during these events and the fact that it represents the major class and generational conflicts affecting the current Lebanese Muslim leadership in Australia. Reference to other organisations will be made in so far as they relate to the broader changes that were affecting Muslim leaders within the Lebanese-Australian community.

The Lebanese Community Council (LCC) was the first organisation to call for a 'Community Leaders Consultation Meeting' a few days after the riots. LCC is an umbrella organisation representing (in 2006) 22 community associations, which are predominantly Sunni. During the meeting, which included local members of parliament and major Lebanese (Muslim and Christian) organisations, the attendees condemned the 'shameful' events of Cronulla and unanimously passed a resolution supporting: the NSW Government legislation 'giving Police more powers to apprehend criminals and trouble makers' (LCC, 2005).[2] This seemingly unified position adopted by the leaders of the Australian–Lebanese community masked a number of differences. These are more apparent when we consider interviews, public statements and the minutes of meetings during the crisis where tensions emerge reflecting class, religious and generational differences.

The unity presented by leaders was driven by a concern to stop the attack on their community by politicians, sections of the public and media. Damaging perceptions of Lebanese migrants and their descendants were affecting the community as a whole, but particularly the leaders whose 'legitimacy' depends on protecting their 'constituencies' from discrimination. Importantly, the position adopted by these leaders reflected their middle class outlook which is hypersensitive to discrimination because of the negative effect on their political, economic and social mobility. Research suggests Lebanese leaders are mostly drawn from a middle class background and their social status, derived partly from their leadership function within their community, would be undermined if they fail to protect 'their' community from attack. Furthermore, converting their cultural (professional qualifications) and economic (money and assets) capitals into recognised social and political capitals would be impeded by racism.

Despite this apparent uniformity, a difference can be identified between the positions taken by Muslim and Christian leaders. They show, among other things, that the former group was more explicit in identifying racism as a major problem facing the Lebanese community: a feature evident in the interviews with leaders in the LMA. Ahmad Kamal-eddine, the president of LMA at the time of the riots, said the backdrop to the riots was the way Muslims are treated by mainstream society: 'We're born here, educated, well looked after by parents like you and me, yet in society [we] are called kelaab (English rendering is 'dogs'), they make you feel like [you] don't belong' (Interviewed 5/9/06). Khaled Alam-eddine, the secretary of LMA, blamed the media for transforming racism against Muslims into a general phenomenon, declaring that the media coverage of overseas events contributed to this racism. Alam-eddine blamed the government for not providing jobs and amenities to keep 'Muslim' youth away from criminal and anti-social activities (25/8/06). Imam Taj Al Hilaly, then Mufti of Australia and Imam of Lakemba Mosque, concurred with these views and attributed the problems being experienced by Muslim youths to two additional factors: the low socio-cultural status of Lebanese Muslims who migrated to Australia after 1970, and the tension that second-generation youth experience due to the conflict between the culture of their parents and that of Australia (7/8/06). The coordinator of the LMA welfare centre, Eman Dandan, commented that:

> There has always been invisible racism in Australia, unsaid feelings towards certain communities but never expressed publicly. Cronulla riots was an aggressive and frightening expression of this feeling...There was anti-Lebanese and anti-Muslim sentiments, Lebanese and Islam merged into one (15/8/06).

The Shi'i Al-Zahra Association (2005: 15) condemned the riots arguing that they were caused by a minority of 'Australian' racists and a small number of Lebanese youth who were anti-social. It also condemned media figures who encouraged the violent attack on the community.

In contrast to the condemnation of the racist character of the riots, leaders of the Maronite Catholics tended to downplay this dimension in their statements and emphasised that the role of the

Lebanese community should be to restore 'law and order' and express 'loyalty to Australia'. Moreover, the statements published by Bishop Ad Abi Karam, the Head of the Maronite Church in Australia, and Joe Khoury, the president of the Maronite League addressed the events as if they only implicated Muslims; Abi Karam, for example, expressed the willingness of the Church to extend a helping hand to Muslims when the need arises 'for the sake of the future of Australia.' (Abi Karam, 2005a: 4-5; 2005b: 5; Khoury, 2005: 5). There is a belief among Lebanese Christians that the religious identity that they share with the 'host' society will exempt them from being a target, more often than not they blame the Muslims for being the cause of the racism directed at the Lebanese.

The difference along religious lines in the response to the Cronulla riots could also be related to their different histories of settlement and its impact on their class mobility. Because Muslim Lebanese only came in large number after 1975, a substantial middle class has only recently emerged from the ranks of second-generation Muslims and they are in no position to sidestep racial discrimination for fear of impeding their newly acquired social and economic mobility. This is a major reason why Muslim leaders underlined the racist character of the riots and rejected the position taken by their Christian counterparts which argued that these riots were simply an issue of law and order emanating from a (Muslim) lack of respect for the 'law of the land' and its 'core values'.

On the other hand, the descendants of Lebanese Christian migration are broadly distributed across the classes in Australian society (Betts and Healy, 2006: 9-14). Furthermore, the symbolic identification with the dominant 'white culture' via their Christian identity not only helped them to integrate into mainstream culture, but is used by Christian members of the third wave of migration (post-1975) to circumvent the impact of racism directed against the Lebanese community.

Community leaders who don't easily fall into these two positions belong to organisations which have a secular outlook and consider themselves to be part of either the larger Arab-speaking community in Australia, such as Arab Council Australia (ACA) or the whole Lebanese community (Christians and Muslims) represented by the Australian Lebanese Association of NSW (ALA). However, these organisations have in common with their religious counterparts their tendency not to be radical in their criticism of government policy towards racism for fear of losing funding.

On December 13, ACA (2005) issued a statement condemning all acts of racial violence 'that have been part of Sydney's social landscape since the weekend'. This non-critical position towards the government is revealed by the criticisms of the one-time ACA president, Habib Chamas:

> The Council should become self-funding. We should stop being a rented crowd for governments and ministers. At the moment, we're a government instrumentality. We don't dare to say anything. We become so small and insignificant. What keeps the Council going is the money that it gets from government departments. So we always have to please the ministers (11/9/06).

These words echo what another member of LMA said to me about its board of directors:

> They fear speaking out against the Government. Working at LMA puts a stranglehold on advocating and speaking out about injustices that take place in the government. "Can't bite the hand that feeds you", this attitude is very strong in the LMA...They invite politicians in festivals because they want their friendship and they want them to look favourably into their application for funding (Dandan, E., 15/8/06).

## Generational and class conflicts

To further understand the differences in the responses to the riots, we should also examine the generational conflicts that Christian and Muslim Lebanese are experiencing and the impacts of these on the outlooks of their leaders. Generational conflict does not feed into the competition that takes place inside the Christian Lebanese community leadership because the young descendants of the first two waves of Lebanese migration fulfil their role in society through their integration into its broader structure. Their long-standing socio-economic integration in mainstream society and the fact that their religious denomination is not specifically selected for racial targeting does not tend to mobilise them to engage in community politics. Competition among the leaders of ML and the ALA, for instance, is not based on generational differences but related to the personal ambitions of first-generation middle class Christians wanting to convert their economic capitals into social and 'political' capitals by becoming leaders.

By contrast, first-generation Muslim leaders are criticised by second-generation middle class Muslims for their poor performance in defending the 'cause' of their community. These young Muslims have emerged recently and are seeking to play a leading role in their community. This situation is manifested in the conflict within LMA and between it and the Australian Muslim Foundation (AMF) run by Mustapha Kara-Ali.

LMA was founded in 1957-58 by a few Sunni migrants who migrated from Tripoli in North Lebanon, to serve the settlement needs around work and accommodation. In 1963, it was officially registered with the government and, in 1973, acquired its current name (Marabini, 7/8/06). LMA organisational structure is three-pronged: it has a Council of Directors (CD) consisting of 15 members and the constitution states that, each year, the 5 longest-serving members must be substituted by new members elected in a general meeting. In addition, there is Majlis a-Shoura (the Consultation Council) which is made up of members of the community renowned for 'their honesty, good reputation and social standing and their seniority in serving the community'. The role of the Majlis is to be the referee when the CD fails to reach an agreement over a serious matter, such as the nomination of candidates for the LMA Council and it must be consulted when major decisions (e.g. buying a property) are taken. Finally, there exists the Mufti Office, then occupied by Sheikh Taj Al Hilaly. The Mufti is considered to be the supreme spiritual authority in Australia and could represent Majlis as-Shoura if requested by members of the CD to attend meetings. Sub-committees assist CD in its community work, including the teaching of Arabic and religion and the delivery of welfare.

There are two groups involved in the battle for LMA leadership each distinguished by class and generational differences. On one hand, there are the founders of the association who are drawn from the first-generation of Lebanese Sunni Muslims who migrated to Australia in the first waves. Most of them have a working-class background and moved into the leadership of LMA through community work, running LMA until the late 1990s. Around 2000, young mostly second-generation Muslims began to seriously compete over the leadership of LMA. Having been raised in Sydney, they spoke English more proficiently than their competitors and some of them were professionals or had their own businesses. In their contest for the leadership, the second-generation do not hesitate to highlight the poor educational qualifications of the first-generation leaders and to point out their failure to understand Australian society and undermine their leadership qualities. The current president of LMA is a solicitor who owns and runs a small legal firm; elected as a Councillor to Auburn municipality in 2003 as a Liberal candidate, he became president of LMA with the support of 12 out of 15 members of CD. The middle class character of the CD is reflected in the occupations of its members: a medical doctor, two lawyers, two IT consultants with their own businesses, a forensic scientist, an owner of a plumbing business, three accountants, a builder, two teachers, a travel agent and a liquidator. When commenting about the new leaders in LMA Zreika, the president, suggested that:

> The younger generation is more settled. They fact that they made a bit of money, it means they can release themselves from duties and spend time and effort to work for the community. Compared to the first-generation they have a different skill set …the first-generation is giving way to this new skill set (25/8/06).

The previous president of LMA (from May 2005 until mid-2006), Mr. Kamal-eddine, who runs a successful business, stated that before his term started LMA was badly managed. 'It had 20 million dollars in assets and it's not yet self-sufficient. So, we want businessmen to properly run the association' (5/6/06). He emphasised the 'business credentials of his team' by indicating those who were 'successful businessmen'. He proudly listed his achievements as LMA president: the renovation of Lakemba Mosque, the organisation of the 'Mosque Open Day' in September 2005 and the plan to increase the assets of the association by taking a decision to purchase a parcel of land located behind Lakemba

Mosque (LMA, n.d.). He emphasised the importance of having directors on board belonging to the same generation 'because they think at the same level...' (5/9/06). He is the oldest member on the current board (42 years old) while the youngest is 27.

Samir Dandan was a vice president of LMA at the time when Kamal-eddine was president. He was born and educated in Australia and also has a successful small business. He acknowledged the role of the earlier leaders: 'The older generation, when they came to this country, was hit with a lot of requirements'. These included a place of worship, the provision of halal food and Islamic burial services and the maintenance of Arab and Islamic culture. But according to him, today LMA...

> '... need[s] a different skill set, a skill set to understand how the society is put together, particularly the Australian society, how do we need to integrate within the Australian society...' (5/9/06).

This is characterised by having the ability

> 'to demand our right from [Australian] politicians while before due to the lack of communication [and] system understanding, we always have seen the elders approaching [the community's] needs and requirements from point of view of mercy. They really never understood how strong they were in terms of lobbying and power...'. (5/9/06).

Dandan describes the difference between the first- and the second-generation leaders in terms of differential skills: proficiency in Australian English, understanding of the workings of society and government, and the ability to lobby politicians instead of begging them for support. It infuriates him that, despite these important differences in skill and qualifications, '[t]he elders' generation [want] to maintain the control' (5/9/06).

Maintaining control by the 'elders' is better explained by their use of the LMA organisational structure, and the integration of the required 'skills' of the second-generation leaders without losing their control over them. Put simply, first-generation leaders dominate Majlis as-Shura which has managed to control the CD through the election of its members and the spiritual influence that the Mufti exerts. Majlis as-Shura and the role of religious Sheikhs are not in the constitution, but are additional sources of power which are invoked in line with traditional Islamic beliefs on governance. These beliefs guarantee a consultative role to reputed members of the community in the running of its affairs and a leading role to religious Sheikhs on the basis of their knowledge in theology. Through the control of Majlis as-Shura and the association between it and the Imamship, first-generation leaders managed to maintain control of the second-generation middle class Muslim leaders despite their election as directors of LMA since 2000. To run LMA strictly according to the constitution would go against an ancient practice of Islamic rule and therefore run the risk of being un-Islamic. In practice, the election of a third of CD members every year is turned into an endorsement of all the council members and used by the 'elders' to threaten the 'young' leaders with the possibility of being displaced if they reject their directions.

Samir Dandan, ex-vice president, who held his position on the board for only a year, explained the process of maintaining the upper hand over the CD:

> The Wassi (the mentor) you have are the scholars [meaning the Sheikhs], you have anyone of the 15 [board] members going to any of the scholars, and also you go to Majlis as-Shura, ... in order to see how things should be solved. And that is an area of weakness that can be exploited, either directly or indirectly by those who put them or set them for the board (5/9/06).

As mentioned above, it is the practice that the Majlis nominate or approve the nomination of the members before they get elected to CD.

In relation to the riots, Samir Dandan pointed out that if the community is not led by competent leaders, it will not be able to protect itself from racism. He argued that by preventing the young middle class from taking full charge of LMA leadership, first-generation leaders are undermining the 'fight' against racism. The coordinator of LMA concurs:

> 'people on board [referring to the new CD elected in 2006] don't have the skills to take the right approach to the real problems associated with Cronulla riots…a lot of them have no knowledge to ask [the right] questions and make the required changes' (Dandan, E., 15/8/06).

The coordinator's criticism was driven by the fact that the new CD was the product of Majlis as-Shura's intervention in the last election.

Generational difference is also used in criticising the 'old guard' by emerging community leaders from outside LMA, such as Mustapha Kara-Ali, the director of the AMF. Kara-Ali (30 years) migrated to Sydney when he was 10 years old. He is a graduate of a selective High School and the University of Western Sydney where he completed a Masters degree in Biomedical Engineering. He also has a Graduate Diploma in Media Studies, is a registered translator and is currently completing a Masters in Educational Leadership. Kara-Ali became active in community affairs which in turn led to his appointment in the Muslim Community Reference Group (MCRG) set up by then Prime Minister, John Howard, in August 2005, three months after the London bombings. Kara-Ali conceives of himself in this group 'as a representative of second-generation Australian Muslims' and is the Chairman of the Schooling and Education sub-committee within the MCRG. His membership, however, has been opposed by LMA: Sheikh Al Hilaly and his supporters threatened to withdraw from this group if he was not removed (Kerbaj, 2006b). Kara-Ali maintained his membership in MCRG and is still critical of community leadership and its inability to represent second-generation Muslim youth (Kara-Ali, 14/6/06).

One week before the Cronulla riots, a National Youth Summit was organised in collaboration with the Youth Sub-Group in MCRG and the Department of Immigration and Multicultural and Indigenous Affairs. Kara-Ali, who participated in the Summit, announced that Muslim youth

> ...feel alienated from their own community representatives who are a lot of time from ethnic councils that have come from overseas with a lot of baggage with them ... As long as these ethnic councils are there in place and are being supported by government then all that is doing is alienating the youth' (Raven and Devai, 2005).

After the riots, Kara-Ali argued that the violent 'young thugs' involved in the retaliatory acts and the religious extremists who pose a terrorist threat to Australia were recruited from these alienated young people (Kerbaj, 2006a; Crittenden, 2006). He outlined key differences between Muslim leaders:

[Second-generation Muslims] differ in their approach [from the first-generation] because naturally they are inclined to be active in the community but the gatekeepers, if you like, are not allowing for that process to take place easily because they resist anything that would radically change the structure which they are quite comfortable with (Kara-Ali, 29/8/06).

The Australian Federation of Islamic Councils (AFIC) is also criticised by Kara-Ali for failure to represent second-generation Muslim youth. He links the explanation of the riots to his analysis of the crisis in Muslim leadership:

[Cronulla] is a crisis of a community having to define who they are and what they want and how can they serve and how can they be part of this Australian community…[the riots express community failure] from the top down. That is how I see it, failure of the family structure and it is a failure of organisational structure.

Kara-Ali elaborated on this by arguing that families are represented in village associations, which in turn are represented in the LMA. The LMA could not empower the community because it prevents 'its children and grandchildren' from taking part in its leadership. For this reason, Kara-Ali argues'…there are two main communities: the younger home grown locally bred community of Muslims, and the first generation of migrants'.

## Conclusion

The Cronulla riots shed much light on issues around ethnic leadership; they highlighted religious differences between Lebanese leaders and their impact on the ways Christian and Muslim leaders dealt with the riots and their aftermath. This was linked to the differences in migration history and the development of a middle class capable of taking on leadership roles. A Christian middle class deriving from the early waves of migration had better integrated into mainstream society partly because of their small number and lack of geographical concentration.

In contrast, Muslim middle class leaders belong to the third wave of migration and their emergence occurred within the development of multiculturalism. In the context of increasing racial tension emanating from domestic and international events, this emerging Muslim middle class face a paradoxical situation: multiculturalism acknowledges their ethnic identity, but this identity is increasingly a target of racial attack. This makes the Muslim middle class more concerned about the politics of their community and critical of the current leadership for failing to protect Muslims. These tensions are evident among first and second generation LMA leaders, the main Lebanese Muslim organisation. However, further research into other organisations is an important topic for future scholarship to enable a better understanding of leadership and its interaction with community issues, class and generational differences.

# References

Abi Karam, A. (2005a) 'Interview' *El-Telegraph* 14 December:4.

Abi Karam, A. (2005b) 'Interview' *El-Telegraph* 19 December:5.

Al-Zahra Islamic Association (2005) *El-Telegraph* 21 December:15.

Arab Council of Australia (2005) *Violence is never the answer* (media release), 13 December.

Australian Arab Council (2005a) *Leadership Required to Create Calm* (media release), 12 December.

Australian Arab Council (2005b) *Race Riots No Surprise* (media release), 14 December.

Australian Lebanese Association of NSW (2005) Proposals and Recommendations Following the Premier's Meeting Held December 12, 2005.

Betts, K. and Healy, E. (2006) 'Lebanese Muslims in Australia and social disadvantage', *People and Place* 14.1: 24-42.

Cobb, J. (2005) Sydney Community Leaders demonstrate True Australian Spirit (media release), 16 December.

Cobb, J. (2005) Community Leaders, Federal Government Work on Grass Roots Solutions (media release), 17 December.

Collins, J., Noble, G., Poynting, S. and Tabar, P. (2000) *Kebabs, Kids, Cops and Crime: Youth, Ethnicity and Crime* Pluto Press, Sydney.

Crittenden, S. (2006) 'Mustapha Kara-Ali in conversation', *The Religion Report, Radio National* 19 April, accessed 9 June 2009, http://www.abc.net.au/rn/talks/8.30/relrpt/stories/s1618210.htm

Department of Immigration and Multicultural and Indigenous Affairs (DIMIA)(n.d.) *'The Lebanon-born Community'*, in Community Information Summary, accessed June 9 2009, http://www.immi.gov.au/media/publications/statistics/comm-summ/_pdf/lebanon.pdf

Humphrey, M. (2001) 'The Lebanese since 1970', in Jupp, J. (ed.) *The Australian People* Cambridge University Press, Cambridge.

Human Rights and Equal Opportunity Commission (HREOC)(1991) *Racist Violence: Report of the National Inquiry into Racist Violence in Australia* Australian Government Printing Service, Canberra.

Kerbaj, R. (2006a) 'Imams "forcing identity crisis on youth"', *Australian* 13 February, accessed 9 June 2009, http://muslimvillage.com/forums/index.php?showtopic=20028&mode=threaded&pid=301048

Kerbaj, R. (2006b), 'Shrouded in Strife', *Australian* 25 February: 26.

Khoury, J. (2005) 'Interview' *El-Telegraph* 19 December: 5

Lebanese Community Council (2005) Minutes of a meeting held on December 15.

Lebanese Muslim Association (2006) *Newsletter* March [n.d.].

Mckay, J. and Batrouney, T. (2001) 'Lebanese Immigration until the 1970s', in Jupp, J. (ed) *The Australian People* Cambridge University Press, Cambridge.

Murphy, D. (2005) 'Thugs ruled the streets, and the mob sang Waltzing Matilda', *Sydney Morning Herald*, 12 December, accessed 1 June 2006, http://www.smh.com.au/news/national/the-mob-sang-waltzing-matilda

Omar, W. and Allen, K. (1996) *Muslims in Australia* Australian Government Publishing Service, Canberra.

Poynting, S., Noble, G., Tabar, P. and Collins, J. (2004) *Bin Laden in the Suburbs: Criminalising the Arab other* The Sydney Institute of Criminology, Sydney.

Price, C. (1983) *Lebanese in Australia: demographic aspects* Australian National University, Canberra.

Ravens, T. and Devai, V. (2005) 'Fed: Muslim youth call on govt to help bridge the gap', *Australian Associated Press 3* December, accessed 9 June 2009, http://www.highbeam.com/doc/1P1-115933881.html

Tabar, P., Noble, G. and Poynting, S. (2003) 'The Rise and Falter of the Field of Ethnic Politics in Australia: the case of Lebanese community leadership', *Journal of Intercultural Studies* 24, 3:267-287.

[1] As elsewhere stated, the categories used – Lebanese, Arab, Middle Eastern – are all contested terms and are used acknowledging problems of categorisation.
[2] For positions taken by various organisations, see: The Australian Lebanese Association of NSW (2005), Arab Council of Australia (2005), Australian Arab Council (2005a; 2005b), Cobb (16/12/05; 17/12/05), Abi Karam (2005a; 2005b) and Al-Zahra Islamic Association (21/12/05).

# Afterword

# Zionists

## Ghassan Hage

I kept a straight face and nodded when Marwan said: 'Mate, Alan Jones is a Zionist. Ackerman is a Zionist... they all go on special visits to Israel. The Israelis look after them and they pay back by working hard on making everyone hate us...' But I couldn't help revealing a smile when he said: 'you're naive if you think that the Zionists miss a chance of turning people against Arabs. And so, if you ask me, the mob in Cronulla, they were all influenced by Zionists or Zionists themselves...' The thought of all those beach boys in Cronulla as Zionists was hilarious. And I was smiling what must have looked like a condescending smile. It was unprofessional of me and Marwan was rightly offended. He prides himself to be well informed and an avid reader, and he is way beyond being intimidated by anybody or anything that threatens his firm beliefs. It also helps that he is a very solidly built bricklayer twice my size: 'yes go ahead and laugh, Mr Professor, you're a fucking idiot like the rest of them'.

As an anthropologist I should treat my informant with more respect and I felt guilty. Perhaps what happened afterward was spurred on by this guilt, but following the encounter and despite my dismissive behaviour, the thought of a relation between the Cronulla event and Zionism lingered in my head and the more I thought about it the more I started to think that there might be something analytically advantageous in thinking a relationship between the two. Needless to say I was not taking seriously the relationship in the sense of 'Zionist conspiracy in Cronulla', rather my thought was pointing in the direction of the two sharing some common features or structures. Yet, on the face of it, this sounds almost as ludicrous as the Zionist conspiracy thesis. After all, what could the crowd in Cronulla share in common with Zionism? The latter is a European

Jewish nationalist movement that is today embodied in a Middle Eastern settler state that acts in its name. Cronulla was a fleeting event on a beach in Australia in which a primarily White Anglo-Celtic crowd came into being, acted out a certain politics and then dissipated.

Perhaps what initially made the thought further linger in my mind was the vague sense of an analogy at the level of my own subjective imaginary between the way I think of the Israeli state 'encircling' and 'destroying' Palestinians and the image of the Cronulla crowd encircling that lone Lebanese guy and going for him. This is very thin indeed as far as social scientific evidence goes, but it is what made the thought 'linger on' in the back of my mind not what sustained it as a serious analytic proposition. What did sustain it analytically was the idea that slowly firmed in my mind that, despite their radical differences, Zionist politics today and the Cronulla crowd are/were both manifestations of assertive monoculturalism. Zionism has been so for a long time, while assertive White colonial or post-colonial politics in the West had re-emerged, after an absence, towards the end of the twentieth century. Interestingly, in terms of skin colour and the cultural provenance of its Jewish population, Israel is, like Australia, a multicultural society. But it is also a White society in the sense that I have used Whiteness to denote the dominance of a White colonial fantasy in White Nation. Zionism remains very much grounded in this fantasy, encouraging all of the Jewish population of Israel and beyond, despite its 'multiculturality', to face the Palestinians with a shared fantasy of White colonial supremacy.

My aim in pursuing this comparison is not to engage in cheap political demagogy, not that this is beyond me if the occasion arises. Rather, I am hoping to raise an analytically meaningful set of questions about the Cronulla pogrom. I find Moses and Levey's description of it as such totally convincing and I am hoping to raise these questions in the same spirit as the many other questions raised in this book: by refusing to see them with the lens of what Greg Noble in the introduction rightly called 'pre-fab narratives of cultural conflict'. What would happen if we see Cronulla not so much as a crisis of multiculturalism or a crisis of monoculturalism but as a crisis of both: a crisis of multiculturalism creating a space for a bankrupt monoculturalism to think that it can be an alternative once again, but immediately facing its own bankruptcy.

What if we see this kind of crisis, the dead-end of the very multi and monocultural polarity, as the one worthy of cross-national comparisons rather than the incredibly vague notion that compares very different global events simply because it uses the tag 'riots' to describe them? That is, what if we can analyse Cronulla as an expression of the dilemmas and contradictions that are facing White colonial cultures globally? And finally, what would happen if we continue this comparative exercise to see the Cronulla counter-attack as also sharing some of the features of other responses by Muslims around the globe to their racialisation and marginalisation by this 'Western-multi-monoculturalism-in-crisis'?

A recent 'riot' in the Israeli town of Acre, which has a mixed Arab and Jewish population, involved a group of Israeli Jewish youth mobilizing through SMS messaging to 'reclaim' a mall from Arabs. The SMS message that was sent around is uncannily similar in its structure to the one which circulated before the Cronulla riots :

> We're putting an end to all the Arabs who hang out in 'Pisga' [Pisgat Ze'ev] and the mall, whistle at the girls, curse, threaten little kids. Anyone who is Jewish and wants to put an end to all that should be at Burger Ranch at 10 P.M., and we'll finally show them they can't hang in our area anymore. Anyone who is willing to do that and has Jewish blood should add his name to this message. (Haaretz 9/10/2008)

It is notable that, at the height of the liberal multicultural era of the 1980s when Western states were all committed to various forms of cultural pluralism, Israel was always perceived as the acceptable State of exception. For England to perceive itself as an Anglo-Saxon or Anglo-Celtic or White European state, or for France to conceive of itself as such or as a Catholic state would have been unthinkable. And if either of them did so, it would have put them outside what was acceptable in a cosmopolitan and cultural pluralism-oriented late modernity. Israel's conception of itself as a 'Jewish state' was not seen in the same light and is still considered neither archaic nor unacceptable.

Something quite fundamental happened in the late twentieth century with the globalisation of a new wave of paranoid White nationalism in which the anti-multicultural tide started to take hold and the politics of White-reassertion, along with the need to affirm 'European values', grew. Rather than being seen as the state of exception, Israel started to look as if it was the model certain dominant forces in the West were, at least subliminally, aspiring to achieve. The Israeli ethos of a besieged White colonial settler society: 'we need to assert ourselves politically, militarily and culturally because we are surrounded by barbarians and they are out to get us' started to take a serious hold in the western conception of the self; we can speak of a globalisation of a White colonial settler ethos.

Finally, it should be remembered that since 9/11, Bali and the Madrid and London bombings, Israel and the rest of the West were not only starting to share a common ethos, but they were deemed to be sharing the same enemy in Muslim fanatics, or simply 'Muslims' as they became perceived in the racial Western imaginary. As if, suddenly, there was now something in common between the Palestinians adopting an Islamicist ideology in their struggle to regain their homeland and Lebanese boys being a nuisance on Cronulla beach. In stressing the emergence of this commonality, it is important not to essentialise Zionism which would take us straight into a sublimated anti-Semitic 'transnational Jewish conspiracy' territory. The similarity between the events of Acre and the events of Paris and Cronulla are not due to 'the globalisation of Zionism', whatever that may mean, rather it is due to the meeting of two globalising processes: the globalisation of certain political and economic conditions that have encouraged an experience of the nation as precarious and endangered by many of those positioned within the dominant national culture, and the globalisation of the figure of the Muslim as a national and transnational other and the imagined 'cause' of such experience of precariousness.

It is from this standpoint then, that we can begin to talk in a creative, analytical way about a relationship between the Cronulla events and Zionism. But there is more: to the extent that a cultural analyst can capture such general moods, it can be said that in most parts of the western world the re-emergence of monocultural fantasies was not completely at ease with itself. The degree of legitimacy it was given by various national governments differed and this is where another, perhaps closer, similarity between the social conditions of emergence of the Cronulla pogroms and the social conditions of the reproduction of Zionism emerges.

Unlike places such as England, where multiculturalism continued to temper emergent monocultural tendencies, the Australia of John Howard, after ten years of a government committed to a politics of White restoration, was perhaps one of the few places in the Western world outside Israel where people were continuously and systematically invited to be 'relaxed and comfortable' in asserting White colonial 'core values' in the face of 'Third world looking people' who supposedly did not share these values and to be proud of themselves doing so.

The Cronulla pogrom, in so far as it was a racist festival of self-indulgence, is unthinkable without the broad legitimisation by government and pro-governmental media of the White politics of 'counter-victimology' that it represented. In this construction, if you feel that it is you who is being victimised by minorities, and not vice-versa as the multiculturalists like to claim, then you are probably right... don't let the multiculturalists censor you, express your outrage! This was long ago a foundational White minority Hansonite refrain, part of what I called then the ideology of 'White decline' (Hage, 2000). The Howard government, slowly and surely, ensured the propagation of this attitude throughout Australian culture by making it the very ideology of White reassertion. It is a paradoxical hybrid which not only asserted a belief in the cultural superiority of 'western' values, but which managed to fuse a sense of being threatened with a sense of domination. Indeed, the more it dominated the more it strangely convinced itself that it was under threat. It is a creative redefinition of the meaning of domination: the purpose of being in power is not to feel powerful, but to assert your claim to be a victim: powerfully! Here again is an unmistakeable whiff of Zionism! You dominate, invade, penetrate, humiliate the

Palestinian third world looking other... but at the end of the day, the problem is Palestinian/Arab aggression and anti-Semitism.

Now here is the point that could be usefully highlighted: Australia under Howard had had more than ten years of encouraged assertion of this type of White monoculturalism when the Cronulla event occurred. At the same time, and despite this, multiculturalism was too well entrenched in everyday life to simply disappear. So those Lebanese boys, mainly in their late teens and who are supposedly so un-integrated, must have grown up not just in the midst of Sydney's multicultural suburbs but also in the shadow of this aggressive reassertion of monocultural values. So why on earth are they only the product of multiculturalism? Are they not also, if not more so, the product of monoculturalism?

Marwan had a story about what happened to one of the Lebanese men who got bashed on the beach: 'after punching him to the ground, this bloke got on top of him and shoved the Australian flag in his face and said: "kiss the flag". The (Lebanese) guy said: "but that's my flag". The bloke on top him said: "No it's not. Kiss the flag".

Given the number of mythical stories that have circulated about Cronulla, I have no way of verifying that this has happened, nor has Marwan, though he firmly believes that it has. But like all mythical stories they do reveal a structure of experience well beyond the immediate event. And this story reveals how the Lebanese blokes on the beach, rightly, experience the dead-end of forced monocultural assimilationism. The assimilationist tells their Other: 'Assimilate', but if the Other says: 'but I am assimilated', the assimilationist simply ignores this and says: 'no you're not. Assimilate!' The monocultural assimilationists are never interested in the assimilation of the Other, they are interested in the process whereby they are trying to make them assimilate. This shows itself in assimilationist politics again and again, and it takes us close to how the Cronulla Lebanese boys saw themselves and how they were seen by the multiculturalists and the monoculturalists.

The cultural forms exhibited by the Cronulla Lebanese boys were clearly hybrid formations: the forms of working/under class masculinity that were put on show were a touch Lebanese, but nothing that you can find in Lebanon, except perhaps among Lebanese Australians living in Lebanon (!). It was also a touch of what one can call the Black and Latino American subaltern hype that has been globalised by the mass media through the propagation of particular type of music, clothing, walking, etc... and it was in other ways, quintessentially Australian: working class Australian perhaps, but Australian nonetheless.

But what is striking about the boys was not their working/under class hybrid culture but how at ease they were with their working/under class hybridity: they shamelessly exhibited it. They were at ease on the beach being sexist, being macho, being vulgar and being aggressive; they were really very much at home. It is in this that they placed themselves outside the multicultural-monocultural field. They did not represent a culture that one can be multicultural about, they were looking neither for 'recognition' nor for 'valorisation' and they were certainly not looking for 'toleration'. No Anglo multiculturalist looked at them and thought: 'I am enriched by your presence in my country', but they, on the other hand, couldn't care less anyway.

Paradoxically, this is where they rubbed monocultural assimilationists the wrong way and this is where the whole political hypocrisy of assimilationism emerges, for beneath the complaint that the boys were not well-assimilated and well-integrated was really the fear that the boys acted as if they were completely assimilated and integrated despite their cultural difference. And this was the monocultural assimilationist fear inherent in the 'no that's not your flag. Kiss the flag' myth: 'no you're not Australian. Become Australian'. That is, to conclude on this theme, behind the monocultural assimilationist claims that the Lebanese boys were un-integrated was the fear that they seemed over-integrated. Too integrated for their own good: no sense of their assumed marginality: arrogant. 'We don't expect you to act like this on the beach' the assimilationists were really screaming. 'Can't you be a bit shy for God's sake!' You should feel like hiding your feelings when you are desiring an Aussie chick on the beach'. For this is really what it all boils down to. A lament known even to slave owners when addressing their slaves who looked a touch too long at 'the lady': How dare you exhibit your desire! This was the problem with these boys: born in Australia, in an Australian grown (albeit hybrid) culture, they lost sense of the marginality of their culture. They were considered not-Australian without really being aware of it. They felt totally Australian. They were not looking for multicultural recognition nor were they looking for assimilationist approval. They were the very definition of an intractable cultural problem.

'So how did you feel when the riots happened?' I asked.

'In all honesty, many of my mates were shocked... we grew up having all kind of confrontations with many of these blokes... there's one of them I still see on the beach. I punched him when we was ten or eleven...' says Marwan.

Marwan speaks as if the little periodical confrontations on the beach were part of his Australian culture, so, to have a confrontation that brings all confrontations to an end was, as he saw it, kind of un-Australian. 'I was shocked' he kept repeating. To get stuck into each other ritually was fine: 'we knew it will happen again on the next-weekend', he said. It was as if somehow, for Marwan, being hated by 'the Aussies' was how he saw himself and his friends being interpellated on the beach as Australians. Strangely, it was a position he felt comfortable with, but what he couldn't cope with was that the riots were not part of the game: they were aiming to end the game and end his position within it. That took him and his friends by surprise and hurt him in ways that losing a fight on one of the routine days on the beach did not. The riots were not aiming at portraying him negatively; rather, they were aiming at terminating his very physical presence and symbolic existence on the beach.

'So what did you feel like when you saw the riots on the TV?' I asked

'I wanted to bash an Aussie...' Marwan said, without any hesitation.

'But, you just told me that many of your friends from school and on the building site are Aussies' I replied. 'Did you feel like bashing them?'

'No, not those Aussies', he replied and then repeated : 'I wanted to bash an Aussie...'

'What do you mean?' I insisted. But I must have sounded unconvincing.

Marwan gave me a pretty threatening look. 'Don't fuck around with me mate. You know very well what I mean.' And he repeated for the third time: 'I wanted to bash Aussies!'

I want to finish with this section of the interview because it gives a good sense of what it must have 'felt like' for the Lebanese boys who went out on the rampage after the Cronulla pogrom. They were out to bash and destroy and the 'Aussie Other' moves from being a kid one has punched in the past but whom one can still recognise, to a non-recognisable abstracted enemy: not those Aussies, but 'Aussies'. The sense of intimacy is gone and there is no attempt at voicing grievances, there is no attempt at positing a political goal or at being part of a political process. There is just a numb and dumb desire for and an acting out of, senseless violence.

This takes us to a final comparative element in this attempt to contextualise and compare Cronulla with other 'Zionist' global phenomena around the world: there is undoubtedly some similarity between the nature of the violence exhibited by the Lebanese boys in their 'revenge attack' following the pogrom and the nature of the violence exhibited in the attacks by the racialised Parisian youth in the suburbs during the so-called Paris riots. There is even a similarity between both and the violence that is part of Islamicist suicide bombing. I am sure there will be some simplistic people who would be happy to exploit this to say that there is a relation after all between the Lebanese boys on the beach and Islamic terrorism. Needless to say, this is hardly what I am saying. What I am positing is that all these reactions seem to share something which is akin to an ideological void: there is no politicised demand or program, just the will to hurt – not even specifically to hurt the Other who is perceived to have hurt you - and to create mayhem.

Slavoj Zizek (2008) argues that this kind of violence is 'meaningless' in a radical sense. He claims that it is a violence that takes one from the realm of the Symbolic into the Real as it aims to go beyond 'meaning' and constitutes what Lacan calls 'passage a l'acte' (literally: the move to action). I am not convinced about the meaninglessness of this violence. Coming often from the position of people facing the threat of symbolic annihilation, acting is often meant to convey just that: the very capacity to act. Far from being an action that is beyond the realm of communication, it is trying to communicate something. It is trying to say to those who are aiming to neutralise you, 'I can still make a difference'; it is trying to say to those who want to annihilate you, 'I am still alive'.

This is the politics of bare life (Agamben 1998). Far from being a given static state of being as some claim, bare life is actually a field of struggle. Big battles are waged within that field and the subjects participating in those battles can still claim their subject-hood. They say: 'I can still create damage therefore I am'. In this sphere, the will to power is reduced to its absolute minimum: the will to hurt, but it persists nonetheless as a will to power in its continual struggle to assert itself. It is in this sense that it points to a realm of life that is outside the existing symbolic order: in our case, outside what is increasingly becoming the platitudes and dead-ends of the monocultural and the multicultural alternatives. Violence becomes something waiting for a new symbolic effort that aims to capture it, domesticate it, and make it part of another governmentality.

# References

Agamben, G. (1998) *Homo Sacer: Sovereign Power and Bare Life* Stanford University Press, Stanford CA.

Hage, G. (2000) *White Nation: Fantasies of White Supremacy in a Multicultural Society* Routledge, New York.

Zizek, S. (2008) *Violence* Picador, London.

# Index

# Index

gangs, 3, 4, 25, 28, 35, 38, 39, 52, 53, 94, 101, 127, 142, 148, 152, 169, 173, 174, 175, 237

Goffman, Erving, 132

habitus, 74, 128, 131, 132, 135, 142, 165, 190

Hage, Ghassan, 16, 17, 28, 40, 76, 77, 113, 148, 151, 156, 194, 201, 219

Hanson, Pauline, 51, 80, 93

*Hazzard Report*, 1, 2, 3, 22, 44, 79, 93, 94, 136

Hazzard, Norm, 1, 2, 3, 22, 44, 79, 93, 94, 136, 180, 223, 229

hijab, 47, 81, 93, 107, 160, 161, 179

Hilaly, Sheikh Taj Al, 172, 204, 240, 243, 247

homosociality, 191

Howard, John, 7, 9, 29, 39, 49, 50, 51, 52, 54, 83, 86, 97, 104, 105, 140, 147, 148, 159, 173, 175, 178, 188, 201, 247, 256, 257

Human Rights and Equal Opportunities Commission (HREOC), 30, 31, 37, 86, 87, 228, 229, 237

Iemma, Morris, 7, 40, 45, 85

imaginary, 14, 15, 16, 17, 22, 34, 68, 77, 79, 111, 112, 118, 120, 121, 122, 135, 140, 187, 188, 253, 255

Imam Ali Mosque, 32

incivility, 4, 12, 13, 45, 50, 52, 132, 135, 140

Jones, Alan, 6, 46, 134, 173, 188, 252

Lakemba, 32, 52, 53, 94, 151, 172, 174, 175, 240, 244

Latour, Bruno, 115, 124

Lebanese Community Council, 239

Lebanese Muslim Association, 237, 238, 240, 242, 243, 244, 245, 246, 247, 248, 249

lifesavers, 1, 3, 44, 45, 53, 58, 73, 81, 93, 111, 112, 117, 118, 121, 122, 130, 136, 143, 153, 158, 169, 179, 186, 187, 188, 189, 209, 213, 217, 232

localism, 165, 169, 185, 186, 190, 192, 193, 195, 196

Macquarie Fields, 24, 38, 58, 68, 221, 223, 225

manners, 4, 5, 6, 7, 9, 10, 11, 12, 13, 14, 17, 18, 53, 54, 131, 139, 148, 151, 157, 161, 190

Maronite, 31, 235, 236, 240

Maronite League, 241, 243

masculinity, 2, 8, 38, 39, 45, 121, 128, 129, 136, 138, 139, 158, 165, 166, 169, 170, 173, 186, 188, 189, 191, 194, 195, 196, 204, 207, 210, 217, 257

Masri, Hazem El, 172, 173

mateship, 137, 171, 186, 196

Mauss, Marcel, 128, 131

migration, 9, 11, 14, 16, 28, 29, 30, 32, 36, 38, 39, 40, 51, 52, 54, 82, 93, 95, 99, 102, 104, 160, 189, 210, 234, 235, 236, 241, 242, 248

moral panic, 35, 36, 39, 45, 144, 177

Moroney, Ken, 7, 53, 68

multiculturalism, 1, 2, 7, 9, 10, 11, 14, 15, 16, 17, 24, 25, 28, 32, 36, 39, 40, 41, 50, 51, 54, 61, 64,

# Index

# Index

# Index

**SECOND LANGUAGE ACQUISITION 24**
Series Editor: David Singleton, *Trinity College, Dublin, Ireland*

# Third or Additional Language Acquisition

Gessica De Angelis

**MULTILINGUAL MATTERS LTD**
Clevedon • Buffalo • Toronto

**Library of Congress Cataloging in Publication Data**
De Angelis, Gessica
Third or Additional Language Acquisition/Gessica De Angelis.
Second Language Acquisition: 24
Includes bibliographical references and index.
1. Multilingualism. 2. Language and languages–Study and teaching. I. Title.
P115.D39 2007
418.007–dc22                    2007006868

**British Library Cataloguing in Publication Data**
A catalogue entry for this book is available from the British Library.

ISBN-13: 978-1-84769-004-3 (hbk)
ISBN-13: 978-1-84769-003-6 (pbk)

**Multilingual Matters Ltd**
*UK*: Frankfurt Lodge, Clevedon Hall, Victoria Road, Clevedon BS21 7HH.
*USA*: UTP, 2250 Military Road, Tonawanda, NY 14150, USA.
*Canada*: UTP, 5201 Dufferin Street, North York, Ontario M3H 5T8, Canada.

The policy of Multilingual Matters/Channel View Publications is to use papers that are natural, renewable and recyclable products, made from wood grown in sustainable forests. In the manufacturing process of our books, and to further support our policy, preference is given to printers that have FSC and PEFC Chain of Custody certification. The FSC and/or PEFC logos will appear on those books where full certification has been granted to the printer concerned.

Typeset by Florence Production Ltd.
Printed and bound in Great Britain by the Cromwell Press Ltd.

# Contents

# List of illustrations

## Table

## Figures

# Chapter 1
# *The Multilingual Learner and Speaker*

## Introduction

Human beings are remarkable language learners who can easily learn and master several languages throughout their lives. Most of us have met people who can switch from one language to another within the same conversation, or children as young as four of five who can use one language with their mother, another with their father, and yet another with their kindergarten teacher. Multilingualism is, no doubt, a common achievement for many people around the word.

The increasing spread of multilingualism and the importance of language within society has led several scholars to investigate multilingual behaviour over the years, as evidenced by the strong tradition of work on sociolinguistic and educational aspects of multilingualism (Abu-Rabia, 1998; Baetens Beardsmore and Kohls, 1988; Bhatia, 2004; Bild and Swain, 1989; Brohy, 2001; Cenoz and Genesee, 1998; Cenoz *et al.*, 2001; Clyne *et al.*, 2004; Cummins, 2001; Dagenais and Day, 1998; Edwards, 1994; Jaspaert and Lemmens, 1990; Kramsch, 2006; Leman, 1990; Muñoz, 2000; Oksaar, 1983; Pandey, 1991). Research on the cognitive and psycholinguistic aspects of multilingualism has instead been much slower to appear. With the exception of a few early studies (Chamot, 1973; Chandrasekhar, 1978; Gulutsan, 1976; Haggis, 1973; Lococo, 1976; Tulving and Colotla, 1970; Vildomec, 1963), it is only in the 1980s that multilinguals' processes begin to be examined closely and systematically, reaching the effect of raising a general awareness among scholars that multilinguals are learners and speakers of their own who should not be compared to L2 learners without some careful vigilance.

At present most studies on multilinguals' acquisition and production processes can be found in academic journals, edited volumes, conference proceedings or unpublished M.A. or Ph.D. theses. This book intends to pull these references together and provide a comprehensive and up-to-date overview of research conducted within the following core areas of inquiry: crosslinguistic influence, multilingual speech production, the multilingual lexicon, and the impact of bi/multilingualism on cognitive development and the language acquisition process.

Discussions in each chapter reflect the fundamental belief that research on multilingual behaviour can offer some valuable insights about the process of non-native language acquisition and speech production as a whole. On the one hand, it can no longer go unnoticed that a large part of the world's population speaks several languages on a daily basis, and a focus on L2 speakers alone is clearly too restrictive for future progress. On the other, most of today's language learners go on to learn languages beyond the second one, and L2 learner behaviour cannot adequately inform us about phenomena related to multilingualism. An increased under-standing of multilinguals' processes can therefore help us develop theories and frameworks that are comprehensive and generalizable to wide groups of individuals. Most importantly, since all humans are *capable* of learning and speaking more than two languages, they are all actual or potential multilingual learners and speakers at any given time in their lives. In fact, humans can be argued to be multilingual by default, with the option of being monolingual or bilingual depending on factors such as educational and social context, personal interest, individual motivation and so forth.

A first question rarely addressed about the multilingual mind relates to its capacity to retain and use linguistic information over time. We all know that individuals can learn a few foreign languages with ease, but we have hardly any knowledge of the possible number of languages that can be learned and maintained over short and long periods of time. The only information on the mind's potential that we have amounts to occasional descriptive reports of polyglots who succeeded in acquiring and using an unusually large number of languages in their lives. For instance, Baker and Jones (1998) report on the achievements of three remarkable individuals. The first is a certain Harold Williams of New Zealand, who allegedly mastered 58 languages throughout his life. The second is Derick Herning of Lerwick, Scotland, who won the Polyglot of Europe Contest in 1990 thanks to his knowledge of 22 languages. The third is Alexander Schwartz, who worked for the United Nations from 1962 to 1986, translating from a total of 31 languages.

These are extraordinary language learners who are a world apart from the typical learner researchers encounter in their work. Nonetheless, their impressive achievements provide us with a measure of the mind's potential to learn and maintain languages over time. From these three cases we can infer that the human mind is capable of handling an exceptionally large amount of linguistic information over long periods of time, which is a remarkable ability that theories and models of non-native language acquisition and speech production must necessarily be able to account for, regardless of how frequent or rare polyglots such as these may be in real life. While it is true that the average person will never learn thirty or fifty languages, it is the potential to learn and use language that concerns us the most here, as any model which aims to be comprehensive and generalizable must be able to describe how the mind works at its full potential, and not at its limited capacity.

Studies on multilingualism with specific reference to language acquisition and speech production are generally in short supply, but recent years has seen some positive changes in this regard. A noticeable growth of interest in these topics has emerged, as evidenced by the number of publications that have appeared in the literature within a fairly short period of time, particularly from the 1990s onwards. As is usually the case with any other emerging field of inquiry, there is a period of time in which the new field is conceived of as a mere extension of other well-established fields – in our specific case Second Language Acquisition (SLA) and Bilingualism. Any process of emergence inevitably sees opposing views fighting for space and clashing with one another, and the journey is rarely smooth. The study of multilinguals' processes is no exception.

This chapter begins by exploring some of the issues that generally surround this process of emergence. The chapter is organized in four sections as follows. The first section introduces some basic differences between Second and Third or Additional Language Acquisition and overviews the 'no-difference' assumption that shapes so many of the SLA studies currently available. These initial remarks are followed in the second section by a description of some of the terminological issues in the field, and then in the third section by a discussion on the existence of a bilingual bias in multilingualism research. An outline of the book content concludes the chapter, with a brief introduction to the topics covered in each of the five chapters that follow.

## From Second Language Acquisition to Third or Additional Language Acquisiton

For several decades, language acquisition research has attempted to uncover the mechanisms underlying the language acquisition process, aiming to provide a comprehensive account of how humans learn their first and their non-native languages. While much progress has been made, reviews of work conducted over the past fifty to sixty years (Cook, 2001; Gass and Selinker, 2001; Larsen-Freeman and Long, 1991; Mitchell and Myles, 1998) raise some concern with respect to the restricted focus that was applied. Most of the studies available focused on the acquisition of the first language or on the acquisition of the second language, while studies on the acquisition of languages beyond the L2 are rarely mentioned and are mostly missing. These reviews then tell us that most of what we know about language acquisition does not go beyond the L2, and this means that our understanding of how non-native languages are acquired is at best partial and incomplete.

Most scholars would agree that a general theory of non-native language acquisition cannot be based on L2 learner behaviour alone. A general theory must be able to explain how the mind operates when two, as well as more than two languages are involved, and must be based on the knowledge and understanding of how the mind acquires, treats, stores, organizes and uses all the linguistic information that is available to the learner, not just the information that belongs to the first or the second language.

If one were to state that learning a first language does not substantially differ from learning a second one, a chorus of objections would be raised in no time – and rightly so. Many arguments would be put forward, from the importance of learners' age for acquisition, to learners' different cognitive maturity, the presence or absence of prior knowledge in the mind and so forth. By contrast, stating, implying or assuming that the acquisition of a second language does not substantially differ from the acquisition of a third or additional language does not seem to cause much of a stir among scholars and goes frequently unchallenged. What are the reasons for this difference?

In reviewing the SLA literature it is clear that most researchers have been concerned with how second languages are acquired, and have not taken the time to place their findings and observations into the broader context of non-native language acquisition as a whole. Some may argue that this situation has arisen because a distinction between an L2 learner and an L3 or an L6 learner is in fact redundant, as the processes underlying the acquisition of all non-native languages is essentially the same. Others, on the other hand, may argue that prior knowledge and prior learning experience significantly affect the acquisition process and therefore that a distinction between types of acquisition is essential.

At present the onus of highlighting meaningful differences between the acquisition of a second language and the acquisition of third or additional languages rests upon those who actively work on multilingualism and language acquisition, who generally support the view that some differences between types of acquisition exist and should be accounted for. In contrast,

SLA scholars appear more willing to embrace a 'no difference' assumption in their work, and it is not uncommon to read statements to this effect.

The 'no-difference' assumption probably finds its origin in the widespread tendency to overgeneralize the meaning of the word 'second' in the literature (see also discussion in Hufeisen, 2000). Most people understand SLA to be a field of research concerned with how second languages are acquired, and the term 'second' is usually taken to refer to a second language as well as to any other non-native language in the process of being acquired. From this broad interpretation of what a second language is, we can infer that a large number of scholars regard the process of acquiring a second language as sufficiently similar to that of acquiring additional languages, implicitly supporting the view that a distinction between types of acquisition is unnecessary. Moreover, the 'no difference' assumption is also openly stated in the literature. Singh and Carroll (1979: 51), for instance, explain that 'there is, a priori, non reason to assume that L3 learning is any different from L2 learning. Learning a third language is [. . .] learning just another second language.' More recently, Mitchell and Myles (1998: 2) wrote that the word 'second' is an umbrella term for them, arguing that 'it is sensible to include "foreign" languages under one more general term of "second" languages, because [. . .] the underlying learning processes are essentially the same for more local and for more remote target languages, despite differing learning purposes and circumstances.' These are two random quotes from the literature, but many more comments of this kind could be easily located. My primary objective, though, is not to list statements but to explore why scholars may take this position.

There are probably several reasons that concur in giving recognition to the 'no difference' assumption, including the two following. First, the general lack of research on multilinguals' acquisition processes has made a systematic comparison between learners with and without prior knowledge of non-native languages difficult to carry out. Researchers do not have much information they can rely upon and, as a result, do not readily identify prior knowledge of non-native languages as a variable that can significantly affect and bias the results of their work. Insufficient evidence, on the other hand, also entails that scholars cannot easily engage in informed discussions on the similarities and differences between types of acquisition. Second, the field of SLA lacks a clear working distinction between those who are learning a second language and those who are learning third or additional languages. All learners are labelled as L2 learners – particularly when proficiency in the prior non-native language(s) is low – and it is usually up to the researcher to decide whether learners' prior knowledge has the potential to bias the result of a study or not. Such freedom of choice, needless to say, conflicts with the most basic principles of methodological rigour in language acquisition research.

While it may seem obvious to many that the prior knowledge of a non-native language is a variable that needs to be properly controlled, the reality is that the control for this specific variable is often poor, inadequate, if not lacking altogether. Learners' linguistic background is usually monitored with care only in the case in which learners are highly proficient in a non-native language. When, however, learners have some basic knowledge of a non-native language, the additional knowledge is typically ignored or minimized, as the following example can illustrate.

In a study on learning strategies, Nayak *et al.* (1990) compared monolin-gual and multilingual students, who were assigned to the monolingual or the multilingual group according to a seven-point self-rating scale of language proficiency. Those included in the monolingual group were described as being 'native speakers of English, with very minimal or no proficiency (ratings of 3 or below) in any other natural language' (Nayak *et al.*, 1990: 226). For Nayak and his colleagues, then, there is essentially no difference between having no knowledge, and having some knowledge of a non-native language. While one can argue against this position from various angles, on a broader level it is important to ask how one can decide who is a monolingual learner of an L2, and who is a bilingual learner of an L3. Are six months of instruction in a prior non-native language enough to be classified as an L3 learner? Are perhaps two or five years of instruction more suitable? Throughout the book it will become clear that we are not yet in the position to provide an answer to this question as there is hardly any evidence available on proficiency threshold levels in non-native language acquisition. Nonetheless, we will see that some studies have already shown that even as little as one or two years of formal instruction in a non-native language can affect the acquisition of another non-native language to a significant extent, hence some added caution with respect to subject selection procedures is indeed advisable.

Even though only time and further research will allow us to identify suitable proficiency threshold levels, in the absence of an agreed upon parameter we still have to question how most researchers have dealt with this decision so far. In reading the SLA literature, one is often under the impression that some of the second language learners used in research may have been exposed to some other non-native language in their lives. With this remark I do not intend to embark on isolating those studies which may have used multilingual learners rather than second language learners in the past, but rather to raise awareness about the possibility that third or additional language learners may have been used in place of L2 learners in some occasions. The implication of this error is that some hypotheses about SLA may turn out to be incorrect or inaccurate as learners' prior linguistic knowledge was not properly accounted for. The following two examples illustrate how frequently this situation can arise.

If we come across a study with adult Italian L1 learners of German as an L2, for instance, we can safely assume that these subjects are third or additional language learners and not L2 learners for the simple reason that the study of foreign languages, usually French or English, has been compulsory in Italian schools for several decades. Italian L1 speakers could be true L2 learners of German only in the case in which they had failed to complete compulsory education in Italy, or if they were illiterate. Similarly, if a study examines English L1 learners of French as an L2 at a Californian University, it is reasonable to wonder whether these subjects are true L2 learners, as a large number of students in California, and the United States in general, study Spanish in high school.

Scenarios of this kind are undoubtedly quite common in the SLA literature, mostly because the majority of subjects are adult university students or individuals raised in bilingual or multilingual environments. But does having some knowledge of a prior non-native language truly make a difference?

Common sense generally tells us that an individual who has gone through the experience of learning one or more non-native languages has already gained much knowledge and experience that is likely to be put to use in later learning. The transfer of prior linguistic knowledge and prior learning experience is a strong force in human cognition (Pennington, 1999; Wilson and Sperber, 2006), and when an individual engages in a cognitive task as demanding as language learning, it is reasonable to presume that prior linguistic knowledge and prior learning experience will play a role in the learning task. Since the distinction between the processes that underlie the acquisition of second or additional languages must be based on sound empirical evidence, the aim of the various chapters of this book is precisely to examine the evidence available in support of the two positions outlined (the difference versus no-difference assumption), placing special emphasis on the range of phenomena that are only possible when more than two languages are in the mind. While SLA research will clearly form a useful background for each discussion, the book will not specifically review the SLA literature as the objective is not to compare Second with Third or Additional Language Acquisition directly, but to examine the uniqueness of multilinguals' processes with respect to the acquisition and production of languages beyond the L2.

## Terminological (In)consistencies

The newness of a field goes hand in hand with a period of uncertainty about the most appropriate terminology to use. Whenever there is a need to express a new concept or describe a new phenomenon, the most frequent tendency is to borrow the terminology already used in well-established fields such as SLA or Bilingualism and adapt it to multilingualism. These borrowing strategies are usually helpful and effective, but they can also be problematic if a term starts to be used with more than one meaning. In order to avoid unnecessary overlaps, sometimes researchers resort to coining new terms altogether, but these terms are also influenced by existing ones and semantic clarity can sometimes be affected.

This section intends to illustrate the kind of terminological problems that scholars have dealt with in recent years, and are in actual fact still in the process of dealing with. Since it would be impossible to provide an exhaustive list of borrowed and newly coined terms used in the literature on multilingualism and the problems associated with each of them, the focus is purposely narrowed to four general concepts which can illustrate the type of inconsistency that have emerged. We can begin by considering the use of the terms 'bilingual/bilingualism' and 'multilingual/multilingualism' and the level of ambiguity that these terms can express.

Most people understand a multilingual person to be an individual familiar with three or more languages to some degree of fluency, and a bilingual an individual familiar with two languages, also to some degree of fluency. This is a clear and straightforward definition based on the number of languages an individual knows. In practice, when one reads definitions of bilingualism and multilingualism in the literature, it is clear that the number of languages the individual is familiar with is not central to the definition itself.

In the literature we find the terms 'bilingual/bilingualism' and 'multilingual/multilingualism' often used as synonyms, as the following examples can illustrate. The *Concise Oxford Dictionary of Linguistics*, for instance, describes bilingual communities as having 'two or more different languages' (Matthews, 1997: 39), a definition which effectively equates bilingualism with multilingualism. Myers-Scotton (2002) states that the term 'bilingual refers to persons who speak two or *more* languages' (Myers-Scotton, 2002: 1, italic in the original). As in the previous example, no dividing line between the bilingual and the multilingual individual seems to exist. Grosjean (1992: 51) also writes that 'bilingualism is the regular use of two (or more) languages, and bilinguals are those people who need and use two (or more) languages in their everyday lives.'

In reading these definitions – and many more of this kind are available in the literature – we are under the impression that the word bilingual can refer to *anything* beyond the L1, when in actual fact the prefix 'bi-' means 'two' hence a bilingual can only be a speaker of two languages and not a speaker of *more* than two languages by definition (see also discussion in Cenoz *et al.*, 2003; Herdina and Jessner, 2000). To complicate matters further, we also have to take into account the existence of the opposite phenomenon, i.e. the term multilingualism being used to refer to bilingualism. Hoffmann (2001) points out that, in the language context and the language planning literature, the term multilingualism is often used in place of bilingualism deliberately, as it reflects the distinction between a microlevel and a macrolevel of investigation. Multilingualism is preferred to bilingualism because it stresses the presence of linguistic varieties in sociolinguistic situations. Whatever the actual reasons for the use of the term multi-lingualism in place of bilingualism, or of bilingualism in place of multilingualism, the use of these terms as synonyms generates confusion in the field and one often needs to look for additional information in the text itself in order to be able to identify whether the author is talking about bilinguals or multilinguals.

Confusion can also arise whenever a term originally created to refer to bilinguals is used to refer to multilinguals even though the original premises are no longer applicable. This case can be illustrated with the use of the word 'dominance' and 'dominant' in the literature.

The relationship between the speakers' languages in terms of balance and dominance is based on the speakers' proficiency level in each language, whereby balance refers to having equal proficiency levels in two or more languages, and dominance to having one or more languages that are dominant over the other languages that are also in the mind (Peal and Lambert, 1962). The claim of balance or dominance then stems from a comparison between the individual's proficiencies in the two languages (Butler and Hakuta, 2004; Edwards, 2004). Since a bilingual is usually totally fluent in one of the two languages – typically the L1 – the question is whether the other language is in a balanced or in a dominant relationship *with* the L1.

The notion of balance and dominance and the comparative paradigm it entails works well with bilinguals but does not work equally well with multilinguals. Since an individual can be dominant in one language only in relation to other languages in the mind, it is not possible to establish a relationship of balance or dominance between languages without properly assessing speakers' proficiency levels in each language. If we consider a hypothetical speaker of five languages, for instance, it is reasonable to presume that some of his or her languages will be more dominant than others, and it is in fact not uncommon to find multilinguals being described as 'dominant' in one or more of their languages. But what does the word 'dominant' mean if proficiency in the other languages is not measured? As already implied, the term is no longer clear as the initial premises are no longer applicable, and this results in an ambiguous and imprecise use of the term as a language cannot be dominant per se but only in relation to other languages in the mind.

Sometimes even the simplest of words can create terminological ambiguity. For instance, we can consider how the language being learned is referred to in the literature. So far, researchers have referred to a second language as an L2, and to more than one non-native language as L2s or LN or LX. A third or additional language is often referred to as an L3, regardless of whether it is a third, fourth or sixth language. Some researchers label languages according to order of acquisition (L3, L4 or L6) without taking into account issues of language proficiency. This situation is further complicated when studies include bilingual adults or children. At times there is no clear distinction between a childhood bilingual learning a third language and an adult with a second language who is learning a third language: they are all considered third language learners or multilingual learners. Fuzzy boundaries are of course highly problematic as they create the potential danger of generalizing research findings that instead should be confined to a given subset of learners (see also Hoffmann, 2001).

There are also cases in which more than one new term is put forward to express the same idea. One of such cases is the name of the field itself, which has been labelled in at least four different ways: (a) Multiple Language Acquisition; (b) Multilingual Acquisition; (c) Third Language Acquisition; and (4) Third or Additional Language Acquisition. All of these terms are regularly found in the literature but none of them has fully established itself to the present day, probably due to the weaknesses that each of them hold.

The first term – Multiple Language Acquisition – is problematic in some respects, because the word 'multiple' means more than one *at the same time* as in 'multiple births', 'multiple copies', 'multiple personalities' or 'multiple choice exam'. Multiple Language Acquisition can then be argued to refer to the concurrent acquisition of two (or more) languages at the same time rather than to the acquisition of several languages at different points in time. There are many people who learn languages at different times in their lives and do not go through a process of multiple language acquisition per se. They become multiple language speakers or users as a result of having acquired several languages, but they do not acquire their languages at the same time. Multiple Language Acquisition is in my view better suited to refer to some specific types of acquisition, for instance the case of children raised speaking multiple languages at the same time, or of adults learning two or more non-native languages at the same time. In this regard it is important to stress that research has already identified a difference between simultaneous and sequential acquisition in the development of relative clause structures (see Flynn *et al.*, 2004) hence it is even more pressing that the distinction between sequential and simultaneous acquisition is clearly made.

The second term – Multilingual Acquisition – offers little continuity with the well-established terms of First and Second Language Acquisition. As an umbrella term for a field, Multilingual Acquisition seems to be imprecise and vague, mostly because 'multilingual' is a descriptive adjective that refers to the learner rather than to the language being learned. It is in fact the learner who is multilingual, and not the acquisition itself.

The third term – Third Language Acquisition – closely follows in the footstep of First and Second Language Acquisition but with a less effective result. This term is perhaps the least suitable as a name for a field because the word 'third' places major emphasis on the third language at the exclusion of all the other languages also in the mind. Third Language Acquisition is in fact no better than Second Language Acquisition, which also places major emphasis on one specific language – the second one – at the expense of all other languages.

The last term – Third or Additional Language Acquisition – is long and impractical to use, but it is the one I favour the most as it refers to all languages beyond the L2 without giving preference to any particular language. In fact the use of the word 'additional' is not new in the SLA literature and on occasion one can still come across the expressions 'second or additional language acquisition' or 'second or additional languages'. These expressions are, however, generally used with the intent to equate 'second' with 'additional' language acquisition, while the in the case of 'third or additional language acquisition', the intent is clearly the opposite.

The four instances of terminological (in)consistencies just reviewed are only a few of the examples that could be mentioned in a section on terminological issues in the field. Despite the obvious differences among these terms, they are all expression of scholars' common underlying need to be able to use terminology that is consistent and unambiguous and that can convey meaning with clarity and precision. This is essential to avoid ambiguities, but also to prevent unnecessary biases in research.

Multilingualism research has already begun to show that some factors previously believed to be of little relevance for the (second) language acquisition process can instead affect it in some meaningful ways (see also discussions in Grosjean 1998; Herdina and Jessner, 2000; Hufeisen 2000). The need for increased accuracy is therefore paramount for future progress. While terminology can only become fully established with time and with frequency of use, ambiguities and uncertainties can be minimized by providing specific and detailed information on learners' linguistic and educational background. Ideally, all of the information listed below should be provided whenever possible, as all of these parameters have already been shown to have some effect on multilinguals' cognitive and psycholinguistic processes:

- age of acquisition of each non-native language;
- sequence of acquisition of all languages;
- proficiency level in all non-native languages, and how proficiency level was measured;
- exposure to native and non-native language environments;
- classroom language of instruction for each non-native language (if learned in a formal setting);
- amount of formal instruction in each non-native language (years and hours per week);
- manner of acquisition (formal/instructed acquisition versus natural acquisition);
- context in which each language is or was used (for example at home, at school, with peers and so on);
- active or passive use of all languages;
- number of languages known to the speaker;
- productive and receptive skills for each language and how these were measured.

## The Monolingual and the Bilingual Bias in Language Acquisition Research

The SLA literature contains several discussions on the existence of a monolingual bias in second language research. The monolingual bias refers to the practice of assessing and measuring second language competence or performance according to monolingual norms, even though L2 learners or speakers are not monolingual by definition and will never be able to reach monolingual standards (Baker and Jones, 1998; Bley-Vroman, 1983; Cook 1995, 1997a; De Angelis, 1999; De Angelis and Selinker, 2001; Grosjean 1992). This section briefly reviews some aspects of the monolingual bias in second language research and considers whether some of the existing arguments are of relevance to multilingualism as well. The section further comments on the emergence of a new type of bias, namely a bilingual bias, which overshadows the identification of a range of phenomena that only multi-lingual speakers can display.

The best-known form of monolingual bias in second language research relates to the practice of using native-like norms to explain second language grammars. Bley-Vroman (1983) referred to this practice as the 'comparative fallacy in interlanguage studies'. The concept of comparative fallacy is central to both SLA and multilingualism research as it refers to any non-native language grammar that is measured against an ideal native-like norm. Given recent evidence that interlanguage grammars can be made up of combined features from the previously learned languages and the target language (Fuller, 1999), the topic is of direct relevance to multilingualism.

A comparative fallacy occurs whenever the grammar of the target language is used to determine the internal systematicity of the grammar of a non-native language. Non-native language grammars have been assumed to be independent since the early 1970s, when the similar notions of 'transitional idiosyncratic dialects' (Corder, 1971), 'approximative systems' (Nemser, 1971) and 'interlanguage' (Selinker, 1972) were originally proposed. In order to assess whether a non-native form or structure is grammatically correct or incorrect, or it is placed in its right obligatory context or not, researchers normally examine the non-native form or structure in the context in which it is used. The point of contention is that even though the non-native grammar is independent, it is measured against the grammar of the target language, as native speakers would know it, therefore against an L1-norm. Accordingly, Bley-Vroman argues that 'any study which classifies interlanguage (IL) data according to a target language (TL) scheme or depends on the notion of obligatory context or binary choice will likely fail to illuminate the structure of the IL' (Bley-Vroman, 1983: 15). In other words, an interlanguage grammar cannot be measured against a native-like norm because the L1 grammar is not an interlanguage grammar by definition. It would be the equivalent of evaluating the grammar of Italian using the grammar of French. The grammars of the two languages are similar but not identical.

Bley-Vroman (1983) offered strong arguments in support of the view that the comparison of an independent non-native language grammar with an L1 grammar can only lead to 'a comparative fallacy' in second language research. His work has raised much awareness in SLA on the comparability of grammars and linguistic products. Nonetheless, the problems he outlined continue to persist today (see also Cook, 1997a), as non-native languages continue to be compared to native-like norms on a regular basis.

Moving on to another type of monolingual bias, we find the bias associated with debates on the fractional and holistic views of bilingualism (Grosjean, 1992), both of which relate to how a bilingual person is conceptualized. According to a fractional view of bilingualism, individuals have separate competencies for their two languages. Since these competencies are implied to be similar to those of a native speaker, the bilingual is conceived as two monolinguals within the same person. The major opponent of this perspective is Grosjean (1985, 1992, 1997, 2001, 2004), who instead argues that viewing L1 and L2 competences as separate entities generates a monolingual bias in second language research. Bilinguals must be looked at from a holistic perspective because 'a bilingual is NOT the sum of two complete or incomplete monolinguals; rather, he or she has a unique and specific linguistic configuration' (Grosjean, 1992: 55; capitalised in the original). From this position, the mind of a bilingual must necessarily be conceived as an intact whole whose competencies in the two languages do not exist in separation from one another but are part of an intact system.

Even though the fractional and holistic views of bilingualism specifically refer to bilingualism and bilingual competence, these two views shape and influence how multilinguals are also conceptualized. With an increase in number of languages, multilinguals' competences are more prone to being viewed as separate and independent from one another, and not as an intact whole, as it is simply more convenient to do so. If we take research on crosslinguistic influence as an example, it is rare to find studies that examine the influence between languages from a holistic perspective. The influence is usually conceived as a phenomenon that occurs between two languages, regardless of the number of other languages that are actually in the mind and that may also contribute to the manifestation of crosslinguistic influence. I won't go into much detail about this topic at this stage as it is dealt with extensively in Chapter 2. It can nonetheless be said that viewing multilinguals from a holistic perspective is most certainly a challenging endeavour, particularly in the case in which one needs to isolate linguistic information that is specific to a given language. From a methodological perspective, the fractional view of multilingualism is undoubtedly the most convenient, as it allows one to easily separate source and target language information in empirical research. This said, one cannot ignore the fact that the mind of a multilingual contains information that belongs to several languages and therefore that the presence of linguistic information from various languages is likely to lead to a state of integration of knowledge in the mind.

Existing theoretical perspectives increasingly view languages as being interconnected with one another rather than being separate entities, as might have been prevalent in earlier thinking in SLA and Bilingualism. The question today is no longer whether linguistic information from different languages is integrated or not, but to what extent it is integrated and how this integration may affect the overall comprehension or production process. Cook's (1991, 1992, 1995) notion of 'multicompetence' is perhaps one of the best examples of a proposal which conceives knowledge as an integrated whole in the mind. In the early 1990s, Cook observed that L1 competence and L2 competence were never treated as a single system and that the field did not have a term to even describe the integration of knowledge in the mind. In order to fill this terminological and theoretical void, Cook (1991, 1992, 1995) proposed the notion of 'multicompetence' which, in his own words, defines the 'compound state of a mind with two grammars' (Cook 1991: 112). The notion is in contrast with the idea of monocompetence, which is the competence of a mind with one grammar. Cook justifies the necessity of multicompetence by providing several examples in its support and arguing (1992: 585) that 'at one level, multicompetence is undeniable; as L2 users do not have two heads, their mind must be different at some level of abstraction'. I will return to the notion of multicompetence in other sections of this book. At present I would however like to note that even though the definition specifically mentions the presence of two languages in the mind, the concept is sufficiently neutral to be suitable to describe the integration of knowledge in the multilingual mind as well.

One other form of bias which has come to light in recent years is a bilingual bias in multilingualism research. This bias is so pervasive that it is virtually impossible to list all the cases in which it can manifest itself. The bilingual bias refers to the tendency to view multilinguals as bilinguals with some additional languages rather than as speakers of several languages from the start. It also refers to the associated tendency of regarding bilinguals' acquisition and production processes as default processes for multilinguals. Taking the position that multilinguals are bilinguals with additional languages essentially reflects the underlying assumption that the additional languages are somewhat superfluous. The multilingual mind becomes a mind with two languages, to which some more languages can be added (or dropped), but the addition (or reduction) of languages is somewhat optional. Traces of the bilingual bias can be found everywhere in the literature and will be pointed out as we move along the various chapters of the book. We have already seen some definitions of bilingualism above, where the multilingual speaker is to all effect regarded as a bilingual speaker. We can see traces of the bilingual bias in the trend to regard all languages beyond the L2 as 'second' languages, or all learners with additional languages as L2 learners. Or we can see the bilingual bias every time a multilingual model is tailored to an ideal hypothetical bilingual speaker rather than a speaker of several languages.

Some authors provide coherent explanations in support of the strategy of assuming an identity of processes between bilinguals and multilinguals. For instance, in a discussion on word selection problems, Dijkstra (2003) claims that a

> straightforward extension of a bilingual model of word recognition to multilinguals (or of a monolingual model to a bilingual model) seems to suffice [. . .] Assuming that the theoretical frameworks proposed for monolinguals and bilinguals also apply to multilinguals is the most simple theoretical viewpoint, and for reasons of parsimony we should adhere to that view unless new evidence shows it is not psycholinguistically valid. Language processing in general is so complex, and multilingual processing even more, that this may be the best research strategy to follow until we have collected more evidence. (Dijkstra, 2003: 25)

While the argument that the absence of evidence constitutes evidence is an interesting one, the essential problem with this view is that some behaviours or production mechanisms may well be unique to multilinguals, and these cannot be identified if their existence is not even postulated.

From a theoretical point of view, the bilingual bias is undoubtedly most evident in psycholinguistic research where the step-by-step approach typically used to explain mental processes requires that information is meticulously broken down. An essential objective is the identification of what information is accessed or selected at any given time and which components are involved at each processing stage. To this end, assuming an identity between bilinguals' and multilinguals' processes is convenient, but perhaps not as fruitful as one would wish it to be, as the assumption inevitably holds us back in the elaboration of proposals suitable for multilinguals as well.

## Book Outline

This book is organized around four main areas of inquiry, which are crosslinguistic influence, multilingual speech production models, the multilingual lexicon, and the impact of bi/multilingualism on cognitive development. Below is a brief outline of the content of each chapter.

Chapters 2 and 3 examine research on crosslinguistic influence (CLI) with special reference to the influence of one or more non-native language on a target language. Non-native languages have been regarded as potential sources of influence for decades (see Odlin, 1989; Sharwood-Smith, 1994), yet a closer look at the evidence available shows an almost exclusive focus on L1 influence in the past. This means that our current knowledge of CLI is partial and incomplete as it is mostly restricted to how and when the native language influences a non-native one.

In these two chapters, it is argued that CLI phenomena cannot be adequately understood by looking at L2 learner behaviour alone. Humans are capable of learning more than two languages, and thinking that a bilingual or multilingual individual will rely exclusively on the L1 during the acquisition process is both improbable and unfeasible. The chapters intend to highlight how non-native language knowledge is also used and, more broadly, how it affects the acquisition and production process as a whole. Chapter 2 examines the factors that are known to trigger or hinder instances of CLI from non-native languages. The factors examined are language distance, target language proficiency, source language profi- ciency, recency of use, length of residence and exposure to a non-native language environment, order of acquisition, and formality of context. Chapter 3 looks at what can be transferred from one or more non-native languages to a target language in the areas of lexis, morphology, phonetics and phonology, and syntax.

Chapter 4 examines the few models of multilingual speech production currently available. After an initial review of two key models of mono- lingual production (Dell, 1986; Levelt, 1989), the chapter examines the models of bilingual speech production which have been argued to be able to account for multilingual speech production as well (de Bot, 1992; Green, 1986; Grosjean, 1992). Special emphasis is placed on the rigid route that some of these models propose that does not allow us to adequately account for the variability of non-native speech. Issues of comparability are also discussed, along with some possible explanations for the complexity of crosslinguistic influence phenomena in multilingual speakers. Several problems associated with these models are also raised, mostly stemming from the practice of using a model devised for one type of speaker (the bilingual) to account for another type of speaker (the multilingual).

Chapter 5 is about the multilingual lexicon. Past research on the structure of the bilingual lexicon focused extensively on establishing whether bi- linguals represent words in single or separate lexicons, and whether lexical access is selective or non-selective. The chapter provides an overview of existing research on multilinguals' lexical organization, as well as on the hypothesized changes in lexical organization over time and the role of language proficiency in bringing about these changes. The chapter additionally examines issues related to storage capacity and processing loads, and the evidence of integration and separation of knowledge in the mind.

Chapter 6 examines the effect of prior language knowledge on cognitive development and on the language acquisition process. Prior language knowledge and prior language learning experience are commonly believed to facilitate the acquisition of additional languages and exert a positive influence on cognitive development. The chapter examines this claim from various angles. First, an historical overview illustrates how research on bilingualism changed over time, from being negative about the effect of bilingualism on cognitive development, to being neutral and then positive about it. Next, the chapter examines the relationship between bilingualism, language acquisition and cognitive development by focusing on research on foreign language achievement and the role of bilingual literacy and metalinguistic awareness in the learning process. Studies developed within an information processing framework are also examined, with particular attention to claims associated with the development of cognitive skills such as the ability to discover rules in a new language, or to memorize. The chapter ends with a discussion on whether the number of languages known to the speaker can also affect cognitive development and the language acquisition process in some meaningful ways.

Taking into consideration the empirical evidence presented in each chapter, Chapter 7 revisits and answers two of the main questions posed at the beginning of the book. The first question is whether multilinguals should be considered as learners and speakers in their own right and, consequently, whether the distinction between Second Language Acquisition and Bilingualism, and Third or Additional Language Acquisition and Multilingualism is fully justified. The second question is how proficient in a non-native language L2 learners are supposed to be before they can begin to be classified as L3 learners in research. The chapter then provides a brief synthesis of the general conclusions reached, and some suggestions for further research.

# Chapter 2
# *Factors Affecting Non-native Language Influence*

## Non-Native Languages and Crosslinguistic Influence

The study of crosslinguistic influence (CLI) seeks to explain how and under what conditions prior linguistic knowledge influences the production, comprehension and development of a target language. The term crosslinguistic influence was first introduced in the mid-1980s (cf. Kellerman, 1984; Sharwood-Smith, 1983) as a theory-neutral term for the various types of influences that are possible on the target language, such as 'transfer, interference, avoidance, borrowing and L2 related-aspects of language loss' (Sharwood-Smith and Kellerman, 1986: 1). This chapter is chiefly concerned with transfer phenomena in multilinguals' oral and written production and the terms crosslinguistic influence and transfer are used interchangeably with no implied difference in meaning.

Non-native languages have been regarded as potential sources of influence for several decades (for early research, see Selinker, 1969; Vildomec, 1963) and continue to be included in most of the definitions of CLI that we find in the literature. Odlin, for instance, defines CLI as 'the influence resulting from similarities and differences between the target language and any other language that has been previously (and perhaps imperfectly) acquired' (1989: 27). Sharwood-Smith defines crosslinguistic influence as 'the influence of the mother tongue on the learner's performance in and /or development of a given target language; by extension, it also *means the influence of any "other tongue" known to the learner on that target language*' (1994: 198, italic in the original). Gass and Selinker say that 'for most researchers, language transfer is the use of native language (or other language) knowledge – in some as yet unclear way – in the acquisition of a second (or additional) language' (1983: 372).

From these definitions and remarks we can generally infer that, from as early as the 1960s, researchers have widely believed non-native languages to be potential sources of transfer. Given the amount of time that has gone by, one would also expect to find a substantial number of studies on non-native language influence in the literature, but this is not the case. Empirical studies on non-native language influence are quite rare and on the whole far less common than those on native language influence.

More empirical data on CLI and multilingualism can undoubtedly help us move beyond L1 influence towards a broader understanding of CLI phenomena, whether specifically concerned with native or non-native languages. There are in fact several advantages that can be gained from doing research with multilinguals, including the two described here. First, the study of CLI and multilingual behaviour offers the possibility to re-examine some well-established hypotheses about L1 influence in light of a third or additional language and consequently confirm, challenge, refute or modify existing theoretical claims. Second, scholars have the opportunity to explore – in some cases for the first time – those dimensions of CLI that can only exist when a minimum of three languages are in the mind, for example the simultaneous influence of two or more languages on a target language, or the interaction between non-native languages at a single point in time and over time. Essentially, whatever is associated with more than two languages allows us to raise a number of fresh questions about the mind and its processing operations.

A critical question with respect to CLI and multilingualism is whether the traditional conceptualization of transfer is sufficiently broad to include and accommodate phenomena that are specific to multilingualism. Transfer is customarily viewed as a phenomenon that concerns two languages – a source language and a guest or target language. The definitions of CLI reported earlier clearly reflect this position, as transfer is described as a process that occurs between an L1 and an L2, an L2 and an L3, or an L2 and an L1 and so forth. The possibility that the source of the influence may rest with more than one language is not contemplated and therefore not included in any of the definitions examined. But does this mean that the simultaneous influence of more than one language is not a feasible option, or that traditional views of transfer are too rigid in conceptualization and therefore not totally suitable to account for phenomena specific to multilingualism? The latter can be argued to be the most probable.

Viewing transfer as a one-to-one type of association is a logical and viable option for speakers who are familiar with two languages, but the same type of association ceases to be the only possibility when more than two languages are in the mind. In this case, there are at least two types of CLI that are technically possible. The first is the influence between the source and the target language, which is the one-to-one type of association already mentioned; the second is the simultaneous influence of more than one language upon a target language, i.e. a many-to-one type of association. This second kind of CLI occurs when two or more languages interact with one another and concur in influencing the target language, or when one language influences another, and the already influenced language in turn influences another language in the process of being acquired. In the absence of a widely accepted term for this kind of CLI I shall use the term of reference of 'combined CLI'.

Most studies on non-native linguistic influence have been concerned with one-to-one type of associations, hence with instances of transfer between two non-native languages, or between the non-native language and the native language (Cook, 2003; Kecskes and Papp, 2000; Pavlenko, 1999; Pavlenko and Jarvis, 2001, 2002). Research on multiple sources of influence has instead been much slower to appear, possibly because identifying and separating multiple sources of knowledge in production is methodologically complex and challenging. Difficulties aside, hypotheses about CLI will never be comprehensive if the mechanisms underlying the use of multiple sources of knowledge are not properly defined, and for this reason work on combined CLI seems to be an essential strand of research for future progress.

The purpose of the chapter is to examine research on CLI and multilingualism highlighting those types of behaviours that can only arise when a minimum of three languages are in the mind. Some of these will concern one-to-one types of associations, and others will concern many-to-one types of associations, as defined above. Some mention of L1 influence and L1 loss will necessarily be made where relevant, but the literature on L1 influence will not be explicitly reviewed as the chapter mostly deals with issues associated with non-native linguistic influence, language interaction and multiple sources of knowledge.

Research on multilingualism and CLI has already identified several of the factors that affect learners' reliance on previously learned languages and constrain the type and amount of influence on the target language. A number of these factors are important to explain both native and non-native language influence, while others are more distinctive of multilinguals' processes. The factors examined in the next sections with reference to non-native language influence are the following: language distance; target language proficiency and source language proficiency; recency of use; length of residence and exposure to a non-native language environment; order of acquisition; and formality of context.

## Language Distance

There is wide agreement among researchers that transfer is most likely to occur between languages that are closely related to one another than between languages that are distantly related (Ahukanna *et al.*, 1981; Bouvy, 2000; Cenoz, 2001, 2003b; Cenoz and Valencia, 1994; Chandrasekhar, 1978; Charkova, 2004; Clyne, 1997; Clyne and Cassia, 1999; De Angelis, 1999, 2005a, 2005b, 2005c; De Angelis and Selinker, 2001; Dewaele, 1998; Ecke, 2001, 2003; Fouser, 2001; Möhle, 1989; Ringbom, 1987, 2001, 2003; Vildomec, 1963; Voorwinde, 1981; Williams and Hammarberg, 1998).

Language distance refers to the distance that a linguist can objectively and formally define and identify between languages and language families. Sometimes the term formal similarity is also used to refer to a relationship of similarity between the features or components of two or more languages without necessarily implying a genetic relationship between them. A further distinction relates to the notion of perceived language distance. This is the distance that learners perceive to exist between languages that may, or may not, correspond to the distance that actually exists between them. Perceived language distance is frequently called upon in the literature on multilingualism to explain instances of crosslinguistic influences in production, hence it is the one that concerns us the most in the present section.

The notion of perceived language distance was originally proposed by Kellerman in the 1970s. Kellerman (1977, 1978, 1983) identified the importance of learners' perception of language distance with a study on idiomatic expressions conducted with Dutch L1 learners of English as an L2. The study examined whether 81 Dutch L1 speakers believed a list of 17 idiomatic expressions containing the Dutch verb 'breken' could be translated into the English L2 with the verb 'to break'. Kellerman found a difference in learners' acceptance rates of these expressions. Those whose meaning was closer to the primary meaning of the verb such as 'he broke his leg' displayed a higher acceptance rate than those whose meaning was more distant from the primary sense of the verb. For instance, the acceptance rate for 'he broke his leg' was 100%, while the acceptance rate for 'some workers have broken the strike' was a mere 11%. These results were then compared with those of Jordens' (1977), who had also conducted a study on idiomatic expressions, but with Dutch L1 learners of German as an L2. The comparison led Kellerman to propose the notion of psychotypology or perceived language distance.

In brief, Kellerman argued that transferability is influenced by two interacting constraints, psychotypology and prototypicality. Whenever a learner perceives two languages as being close to one another (psychotypology), L1 features are likely to influence L2 forms. The second constraint (prototypicality) is nonetheless a much stronger determinant of CLI with the claim that 'the less representative of the prototypical meaning a usage of a given form is, the lower its transferability' (Kellerman, 1987: 65).

In the literature on L1 influence, psychotypology is no longer regarded as a popular term and it is often replaced by expressions that include words like typological proximity, relatedness, similarity or language distance (Jarvis, 2000; Odlin, 1989; Ringbom, 1987). In contrast, in the literature on multilingualism and CLI the term psychotypology continues to appear with frequency (Bouvy, 2000; Cenoz, 2001; De Angelis, 2005a; De Angelis and Selinker, 2001; Ecke, 2001; Kellerman, 2001; Ringbom, 2001). In an effort to simplify the matter, I shall refer to learners' perception of typological proximity and relatedness using these terms as synonyms, adding explanations and clarifications where necessary. Psychotypology is therefore here regarded as equivalent to perceived typological proximity, and perceived similarity or perceived language distance.

The notion of psychotypology was not conceived with multilingual learners in mind, and was originally proposed to account for learners' perception of the transferability of idiomatic expression between related languages (Dutch, English and German). The original focus, then, was quite narrow. Accordingly, Kellerman never addressed the issue of how the notion would work with a combination of related and unrelated languages, or how it would interact with other factors also known to trigger instances of CLI in multilinguals.

As already mentioned, multilinguals familiar with related and unrelated languages are generally argued to be most influenced by the languages perceived to be the closest to the target language. However, some studies have also shown that learners rely on their knowledge of distant languages on some occasions, even when they have knowledge of languages more closely related to the target language. While this unusual behaviour highlights a general need for more studies with multilingual speakers, it also calls for some caution with respect to making statements about language distance and CLI as relatedness does not automatically imply that crosslinguistic influence will occur. Moreover, relatedness and formal similarity must be carefully distinguished, as one does not necessarily imply the other. Learners perceive relatedness and similarity at different levels, and may rely on their prior knowledge depending on how they judge the overall level of closeness between languages, or the similarity of some features of components of two or more languages. For instance, most learners would perceive the existence of similarities between French and

English words due to the high number of cognates that these languages share, but the same learners would also perceive that French and English differ considerably in their phonetic characteristics and phonological patterns.

Ringbom (2002) provides a classification of transfer based on the difference between form and meaning which is very useful in accounting for the difference between relatedness and similarity. His proposal is also the only attempt I am aware of to elaborate on the psychotypological explanation to account for multilingual behaviour and multilinguals' processes.

Ringbom (2002) believes in the existence of three levels of transfer, which he calls an overall level, an item level and a system level. The overall level of transfer refers to learners' overall perception of similarity between their languages, 'beginning from a common alphabet and phonemes in common over the division into grammatical categories (case, gender, word classes) to the number of cognates and other lexical similarities' (Ringbom, 2002: 1). Ringbom believes that learners' judgement of the overall similarity between languages has a general facilitative effect on learning, and on comprehension processes in particular. Learners' decisions are additionally based on the similarity between individual items, a reliance that, he argues, 'illustrates a principle well known in applied linguistics: that the whole is more than the sum of the individual parts: i.e. a large number of individual item similarities put together produce a more general facilitating effect on learning' (Ringbom, 2002: 2).

The second type of transfer – item transfer – is more specifically associated with the process of establishing interlingual identifications during the learning process. Item transfer may lead to positive or negative transfer in both comprehension and production. At the early stages of acquisition, learners often establish a one-to-one relationship between individual items by equating the meaning of an L2 word with that of an L1 word. Since at the early stages of acquisition learners have limited knowledge of the target language, they identify similarities between items by relying on form rather than meaning. Item transfer occurs whenever there is an underlying assumption that two items similar in form are also similar in meaning. False friends would be a typical example of negative item transfer. The incorrect associations made are usually rectified later on during the learning process, when learners begin to understand the real meaning of words and of individual items. As the knowledge of the language increases, then learners begin to re-examine the initial simplified one-to-one mapping and consequently revise the interlingual identifications originally made.

System transfer, the third type, refers to the process by which a learner identifies an identity of meaning between items, but not necessarily of form. This type of transfer is usually negative and can manifest itself in various ways, for instance in the form of semantic extensions or loan translations with compounds. Ringbom (2001) illustrates system transfer with the following example of a semantic extension. A Finnish L1 speaker with Swedish L2 wrote an essay in the English and L3 stating that *'he bit himself in the language'*. In Finnish, the word *kieli* means both 'tongue' and 'language'. The erroneous use of the word 'language' instead of 'tongue' is the result of the learner's incorrect assumption of a semantic identity between the two words. Ringbom (2001) generally maintains that transfer of meaning occurs from the L1 rather than the L2, unless a speaker is highly fluent in the non-native language. System transfer is therefore primarily a manifestation of L1 influence rather than non-native linguistic influence. Item transfer is instead more frequent because it is an expression of both L1 influence and non-native linguistic influence.

Similarly, Sikogukira (1993) highlights how similarity of form and meaning does not equally influence learners' judgements. In a study on English-French cognates with L1 speakers of Kirundi, a Bantu language, Sikogukira found that learners were more likely to reject French-English cognates whose meanings were the same or similar to each other, than cognates with different meanings. It may be recalled that cognates have four essential properties (Carroll, 1992). In addition to being always structural units, words, and sharing formal resemblance, they 'may be but need not be semantically identical' (Carroll, 1992: 93). Sikogukira (1993) generally maintained that his results were due to an underlying lack of confidence in passing judgements of acceptability on French-English cognates. He also proposed that learners do not use a blanket transfer strategy with cognates, but assess their transferability using supplementary information such as 'the category of cognates, the sense relations holding between cognates and other semantically related lexemes, and the learners' level of proficiency' (Sikogukira 1993: 110).

Learners undoubtedly perceive similarities at various levels, and form and meaning are not equally relied upon in this process. With multilingual speakers, differences can become even more prominent as the increase in number of languages provides learners with more information to draw upon and compare. The distinction between levels of transfer that Ringbom (2001) has proposed is particularly useful to begin to account for the difference between multilinguals' general reliance on one source language, and the occurrence of specific instances of transfer that involve form, meaning, or both, sometimes from distant languages.

With respect to learners' general reliance on one source language, multilinguals show a tendency to select one of their languages as their primary source of information. Chandrasekhar (1978) explained the phenomenon with the 'base language' hypothesis, according to which learners are mainly influenced by the language that most resembles the target language. More recently, Williams and Hammarberg (1998) have claimed that relatedness is only one of the factors that determine which language becomes learners' main source of information. Learners assign the role of 'main supplier' to one of their languages, and the role assignment process occurs by relying on relatedness as well as three other additional factors, which are L1/L2 status, recency of use, and proficiency level. The main supplier is the language that scores the highest on these four conditions.

So far, research on multilingual behaviour has confirmed the base language hypothesis only in part. In fact, it is becoming increasingly clear that more than one language can become learners' preferred source of information at any one time, often leading to forms of combined CLI. Multilinguals can clearly draw upon a vast amount of linguistic information that is simply not available to the L2 learner, and the exclusive reliance on one source language is likely to decrease as more languages are added to the mind. Nonetheless, relatedness and formal similarities remain important triggers of CLI.

Relatedness is here defined on the basis of genetic affiliation, whereby languages are said to be related or close to one other when they belong to the same family (e.g. Indo-European) or the same subgroup of a family (e.g. Romance or Germanic subgroups within the Indo-European family). Formal similarity instead explicitly identifies the similarity between specific features or components of languages, ranging from their grammatical structures to their lexicons, phonetic features, graphic forms and so forth. Two unrelated languages can consequently be formally similar with respect to some features or components. The usefulness of this distinction will become clear as we examine the evidence of language distance and CLI available in the literature. We can, however, start to emphasise this distinction by mentioning Ringbom's (2003) most interesting paper 'If you know Finnish as L2, there will be no major problem learning Swahili'. In this paper, Ringbom explains that, even though there is no genetic relationship between Swahili, a Bantu language, and Finnish, a Finno-Ugric language, there are a number of formal similarities between these two languages that a learner can easily identify. Finnish and Swahili are both agglutinative languages, for instance, they display extensive morphemic and morpho-phonemic variation, and are both vowel-dominant. In addition, since many

Swahili words have been borrowed from English, open-minded learners with knowledge of English can easily find some familiar words. Some of these words are, for instance, tikiti (English: ticket), keki (English: cake, Finnish: kakku), baisikeli (English: bycicle), or sukari (English: sugar, Finnish: sokeri). Ringbom (2003) also correctly notes the difference between similarity perceived, and similarity assumed. In comprehension, he says, similarities between languages or their components are perceived, while in production similarities are assumed.

Let us now move on to examine the empirical evidence on language distance in three contexts: (1) when learners have knowledge of related and unrelated languages; (2) when learners have knowledge of languages that belong to the same language family, but not the same subgroup within the family; (3) when learners have knowledge of languages that belong to the same family, and to the same subgroup within the family.

With respect to having knowledge of related and unrelated languages, several studies have compared Indo-European with non-Indo-European languages. With regard to African languages, Ahukanna *et al.* (1981) found that Igbo L1 informants relied extensively on the English L2 during the acquisition of the French L3. Since English and French belong to the same Indo-European family while Igbo does not, it was clear that learners relied on the language closest to the target language for information. Similarly, Sikogukira (1993) found that Kirundi L1 speakers were more influenced by their French L2 when acquiring English as a non-native language.

One unusual case with respect to genetic relationship is that of Basque, as the origin of Basque remains unknown to date. Nonetheless, the data involving Basque is in line with the findings just mentioned. In a study with Spanish L1 speakers who had prior knowledge of Basque, Cenoz (2001) found that these learners relied more extensively on Spanish than Basque when learning English as a third language. Spanish and English belong to the same Indo-European family while Basque does not. With respect to Asian languages, Fouser (2001) reports on two English L1 informants influenced by their prior knowledge of Japanese L2 in the acquisition of Korean as an L3 or L5. The author explains that Japanese and Korean are commonly believed to be related to one another, even though their relationship is still a matter of debate in the field (Shibatani, 1990). Japanese is nonetheless closer to Korean than the informants' English L1 would be. Ringbom (1987) also mentions the work of Uljin *et al.* (1981), who showed that Vietnamese immigrants to the United States were helped by their knowledge of French in the acquisition of English as a non-native language. Ringbom (1987) also discusses how his English L3 learners were generally more influenced by Swedish than Finnish, regardless of whether Swedish was the L1 or the L2. Swedish and English are Germanic languages, while Finnish is a Finno-Ugric language.

Finding evidence in favour of language closeness is relatively easy and straightforward whenever speakers are familiar with a combination of related and unrelated languages and only two of these (the source and the target) are related to one another. These are the cases listed above. The question becomes more complex and challenging whenever learners are familiar with languages that belong to the same language family, but not to the same subgroup within the family. In this case, the evidence shows the following two general tendencies. First, learners continue to rely on the languages more closely related to the target, irrespective of whether these are first or non-native languages. Second, learners no longer elect one language as the preferred source of information and may rely on more than one language at the same time. With respect to the first tendency, several studies can be mentioned. Chandrasekhar (1978), for instance, found that her Hindi L1 informants relied on their knowledge of English as an L2 when acquiring German as an L3. Similarly, Ecke (2001) showed that Spanish L1 speakers were more influenced by their knowledge of English as an L2 while in tip-of-the-tongue (TOT) states in the German L3. Singh and Carroll (1979) also showed that Hindi L1 learners of French were most influenced by their prior knowledge of the English L2 than those learners whose native language was a European one (French or German). With respect to relying on more than one source of information, Bouvy (2000) discusses how some of her French L1 learners of English relied on their prior knowledge of two related languages (Dutch and German) rather than on their knowledge of Spanish.

This takes us to the most challenging issue of all, which is how to predict multilinguals' behaviour when several languages that belong to the same family, and to the same subgroup within the family, are in the mind. Let us imagine the case of a speaker familiar with five Romance languages in the process of learning the sixth Romance language. With this language background, it would be very hard to predict which of the languages already in the mind is most likely to become the learner's preferred source of information during the acquisition process. In order to offer a useful prediction, other factors would necessarily need to be examined. Williams and Hammarberg (1998) propose to use typology as well as three other additional factors as predictive tools. The other three factors are proficiency level in each language, recency of use of all languages, and L2 status. It may be recalled that the main supplier is assumed to be the language that scores the highest on these four conditions.

While Williams and Hammarberg's (1998) proposal has proven useful and correct with some language combinations, some empirical data also suggests that other factors are likely to be involved. De Angelis (1999), for instance, examined the Italian oral production of a French-Canadian L1 speaker with prior knowledge of Spanish as a second language. French was expected to emerge as the main source language since the informant had not used her Spanish for the previous 30 years and claimed not to be fluent in this language. According to Williams and Hammarberg's model, French scored the highest on the four conditioning factors outlined. French, however, did not turn out to be the speaker's preferred source of information; in fact the learner did not rely on her French L1 at all, while she showed a clear reliance on her little and rusty knowledge of Spanish as a second language. Since Spanish, French and Italian are all Romance languages, it is somewhat peculiar that a rusty L2 (Spanish) not spoken for thirty years would override the French native language and become the primary source of information. Clearly some other factors must have influenced the speaker's decision.

De Angelis (2005b) accounts for this unusual data by proposing the existence of two interacting constraints which concur in blocking native language influence in favour of non-native language influence. These two constraints are perception of correctness and association of foreignness. In brief, perception of correctness predicts that multilinguals resist incorporating L1 information into the target language as L1 information is perceived to be incorrect from the start, and this results in an increased acceptance level for non-native words into the target language. Association of foreignness refers to the cognitive association that learners establish between non-native languages, which are assigned the common status of 'foreign languages'. Whenever several languages related to each other are in the mind, this cognitive association favours the use of non-native language words over the use of native ones as foreign languages are generally perceived to be closer to each other than to the native language. Association of foreignness thus results in an increased acceptance level for non-native information into the target language.

A similar proposal with respect to foreignness which precedes De Angelis (2005b) is found in Williams and Hammarberg (1998). The English L1 speaker in this study, who was also the first author, relied more extensively on her German L2 than on her English L1 when acquiring Swedish as an additional language. Given the same condition of relatedness, the authors asked the question of why the German L2 would take precedence over the English L1. They argued that the speakers' behaviour was the result of a deliberate strategy. The learner (Williams) said that she did not want to sound like a native speaker of English so she refrained from integrating L1 elements into the Swedish target language. She also reported relying on a foreign language because it sounded more foreign to her, hence closer to the Swedish target language. This explanation differs from the claim found in De Angelis (2005b) who argues that association of foreignness is a cognitive constraint and not a deliberate strategy a learner can control.

The cognitive association between foreign languages is further noted in Aronin and Toubkin (2002), Cohen (1995), De Angelis and Selinker (2001), Rivers (1979), Schmidt and Frota (1986) and Selinker and Baumgartner-Cohen (1995). Cohen (1995: 102), for instance, reports some of the comments of an English L1 trilingual who wrote:

> I studied Spanish in Sweden as an exchange student. A question would be posed in Swedish with the goal of a reply in Spanish, but in my head it went Swedish English Swedish, as I were speaking 'foreign' – that is, any language other than English was 'foreign'. It was very confusing for the instructor, and I often wouldn't know which language I had produced in.

Cohen (1995) explains this behaviour by saying that the learner's mind 'would go into a "foreign language" mode in what would appear the dominant foreign language rather than the target one'(Cohen 1995: 102). Along the same line, Schmidt and Frota (1986: 255) write:

> I am beginning to wonder if I have English stored in one part of my brain and Arabic in another. If so, I am putting Portuguese where Arabic is. Or maybe I've got a translate-to-foreign language program [. . .] This morning in class I said *yimkin* [Arabic, perhaps] without realizing that it wasn't Portuguese until L looked at me and signalled noncomprehension.

In contrast with all the studies reported so far is the evidence that some multilinguals rely on distant languages for information, even when they have knowledge of languages closely related to the target language (Rivers, 1979; Schmidt and Frota, 1986; Selinker and Baumgartner-Cohen, 1995). These reports are admittedly few in number and are mostly found in the form of diary studies. Nonetheless, the evidence they provide must be accounted for, above all because they describe a type of behaviour which does not confirm the base language hypothesis (Chandrasekhar, 1978) that so many other studies seem to support.

Rivers (1979) discusses the case of an English L1 learner of Spanish with good prior knowledge of French and a little knowledge of German and Italian. Given this language combination, one would predict a strong reliance on French and possibly Italian during the acquisition process, which is a reliance the author indeed reports. However, the learner was also found to be influenced by her knowledge of German to a great extent, a non-native language she had not used for a long time and in which she claimed to have very little fluency. Similarly, Schmidt and Frota (1986) discuss the case of an English L1 learner of Portuguese during a trip to Brazil. The learner had an interesting and varied language background. He was a fluent speaker of Arabic with some knowledge of French (three years in high school), some knowledge of German (one semester of study) and some tourist survival knowledge of Dutch, Italian, Greek, Hebrew and Farsi. With this language combination, the most likely candidates as source languages are the English L1 or the French L2. As was the case in the previous study, some influence from these languages was reported, but in the early stages of acquisition the learner was also found to be influenced by his knowledge of Arabic to a large extent. Arabic was the learner's most fluent foreign language but had not been spoken for a very long time. Selinker and Baumgartner-Cohen (1995) also found some influence from French and Hebrew on the German speech of one of the authors (Selinker), a native speaker of English.

While these studies suggest that some instances of crosslinguistic influence can also occur from languages that are typologically more distant from the target language, a closer look at the type of information that is transferred shows that learners tend to draw upon those elements of the source language that are phonetically similar, hence formally similar, to those in the target language. This is not an unfailing rule, but a definite tendency, which additionally entails that the learner must be somewhat familiar with the target form in order to transfer. To mention a few examples, in a discussion on the pronunciation of the number *setenta* (seventy) in Portuguese, Schmidt and Frota (1986) claim that the learner was incorrectly pronouncing this word as 'sittenta' due to the influence of the Arabic word *sitta*, which means six in English. Similarly, Rivers (1979) comments on the use of the German *sehr gut* with the Spanish maid, an expression phonetically and structurally similar to the English *very good*. Selinker and Baumgartner-Cohen (1995) note the replacement of the target German *du hast* with the French *tu as* in the sentence *tu as mein fax bekommen* (Did you get my fax)? On the basis of this type of evidence – and more examples can be found in the actual articles – CLI from distant languages seems to occur whenever a condition of phonetic similarity is met. Often the items involved also belong to the same language class and the speaker has some knowledge of the target form or expression.

One other factor which has been argued to trigger instances of CLI from distant languages is source language proficiency. Schmidt and Frota (1986) note the influence of Arabic on Portuguese word order and on the rate of use of indefinite articles. It may be recalled that the subject in question was a fluent speaker of Arabic as a non-native language. Schmidt and Frota maintain that for CLI to occur at the level of sentence structure, the speaker must be highly fluent in the source language. Similarly, Ringbom (2001) claims that transfer of meaning can only occur from the L1 or from non-native languages the speaker knows well. This is additionally confirmed in Alcantarini (2005), who examined learners of English as an L3 with different L1s. These learners were living and studying in Italy at the time the data was collected, and had good knowledge of Italian. Their production showed clear influence from the Italian non-native language when coining new terms in the English target language. For instance, they used the word *can* meaning to say *dog* (Italian for dog: cane), they used the word *rest* meaning to say *to stay/remain* (Italian to stay/remain: restare); or they used the expression *was senting* meaning to say *was hearing* (Italian: stava sentendo). As previously noted, phonetic similarity between the source and the target seems to ease the path of non-native language influence on the target language.

At the beginning of this section I emphasized the difference between formal similarity and perceived language distance as I believe the first is suitable to explain individual instances of transfer like the ones we have just seen, and the other is more suitable to explain learners' general tendency to rely on one, or sometimes more than one, of their languages for information.

As we have seen, languages that are perceived to be close to the target language, or closer to it with respect to other languages also in the mind, are generally favoured as sources of information and they also seem to have a general facilitative effect on learning processes. In contrast, formal similarity, and phonetic similarity in particular, seems to have a major role in triggering individual instances in CLI from close as well as distant language. Most scholars (Cenoz, 2003b; De Angelis, 2005a, 2005b; De Angelis and Selinker, 2001; Dewaele, 1998; Ecke, 2001; Herwig, 2001; Möhle, 1989; Wei, 2003a, 2003b; Williams and Hammarberg, 1998) explain the latter phenomenon using the notion of activation, which describes a process by which a language, or some elements of a language, is stimulated and accessed during the execution of task.

The meaning of activation and how it operates varies substantially depending on the framework used (for an overview, see Chapter 3). With reference to the phonetic similarity so frequently observed between source and target items, the activation explanation essentially proposes that, during on-line processing, activation can spread from a target word or its components to phonologically/phonetically and sometimes semantically similar non-target words and their components. These words or components can belong to the target language or to another language in the mind. Non-native language influence is thus argued to be the result of semantic or phonetic/phonological activation across languages.

## Proficiency in the Target Language and Proficiency in the Source Language

In CLI literature the proficiency factor is discussed in relation to proficiency level in the target language, and proficiency level in the source language. With respect to proficiency level in the target language, most researchers maintain that CLI is more likely to occur at the early stages of acquisition, when learners' knowledge of the target language is still weak and fragmentary and the need to fill knowledge gaps in the target language is more pressing (Navés *et al.*, 2005; Odlin, 1989; Ringbom, 1986; Sikogukira 1993; Singleton 1987; Taylor, 1975; Williams and Hammarberg, 1998). This, nonetheless, does not mean that transfer does not occur at more advanced stages of acquisition.

Odlin (1989) expresses some words of caution with respect to associating transfer and proficiency level in the target language. He argues that while some types of transfer indeed occur at the early stages of acquisition, some others do not. For instance, the transfer of resumptive pronouns in relative clauses requires that a learner is familiar with relative clauses, and therefore that he or she has an advanced knowledge of the target language. Odlin (1989) additionally notes that, at the early stages of acquisition, transfer is often negative as it is the result of a general strategy to fill knowledge gaps in the target language. In comprehension, on the other hand, the effects of positive transfer are most typically found at the advanced stages of acquisition, when learners are more likely to benefit from their knowledge of other languages, and of cognate vocabulary in particular. Clearly, the types of transfer that can occur at early or advanced stages of acquisition are likely to differ as learners' needs are different and their underlying competence is different. Transfer cannot then be safely assumed to decline as proficiency in the target language grows, not at least until an individual has reached a very high level of proficiency and automaticity in the target language.

With respect to proficiency level of the source language, we have very limited understanding of how it affects the CLI process because there are virtually no experimental studies that analyse proficiency level in the source language as a central variable. Some data relevant to a discussion on proficiency level can however be inferred, as most studies provide details of learners' proficiency levels in the non-native languages.

From a methodological perspective, information on proficiency level in previously acquired non-native languages is central to be able to establish a distinction between the L2 learner and the multilingual learner, and consequently between Second Language Acquisition and Third or Additional Language Acquisition. In the previous chapter I raised the question of how learners can be classified effectively using language background information. The difficulty relates to whether learners with little knowledge of a non-native language – for example one or two years of formal instruction – should be classified as L2 learners or as multilingual learners, and consequently pooled with L2 learners in experimental research. In order to answer this question, we first need to address the question of threshold levels, in other words how proficient learners need to be before their prior knowledge begins to affect the production and development of a target language to a significant extent.

So far, transfer has been shown to equally occur from non-native languages a speaker knows well (Ahukanna *et al.*, 1981; Chandrasekhar, 1978, Clyne, 1997; Clyne and Cassia, 1999; Ringbom, 1987; Schmidt and Frota, 1986; Singleton, 1987; Williams and Hammarberg, 1998) and from non-native languages the speaker does not know well (De Angelis 1999, 2005a, 2005b; Rivers, 1979; Selinker and Baumgartner-Cohen, 1995; Vildomec, 1963). This then suggests that proficiency threshold levels are relatively low, i.e. one or two years of formal instruction are sufficient to affect target language production and development in some meaningful ways.

Ringbom (1987) claims that proficiency in the source languages determines the type of transfer that is likely to occur in the target language. He believes that transfer of form is a relatively superficial type of transfer which can equally concern the L1 or the L2 since proficiency in the non-native language does not need to be very high for this type of transfer to occur. In contrast, he maintains transfer of meaning can only take place from languages the speaker knows well, therefore from the L1 or from an L2 in which the speaker is highly fluent. From these premises, evidence of transfer from languages a speaker does not know well which go beyond transfer of form would provide further support for the view that L2 learners must be distinguished from multilingual learners, regardless of proficiency attained in the prior non-native languages.

A clear example of learners being influenced to a significant extent by a language they did not know well is reported in De Angelis (2005a). She carried out a within-group comparison with two groups of learners with the same native language (English L1 or Spanish L1), the same target language (Italian L3 or L4) and different non-native languages. Those in the English L1 group had prior knowledge of French or Spanish; those in the Spanish L1 group had prior knowledge of English, or of English and French. All subjects were asked to read a text in their respective native languages and provide a written summary in the Italian target language. The summaries of learners with and without prior knowledge of French were compared, and some significant differences were found with respect to the rate of subject insertion and omission. Those who had studied French prior to taking up the study of Italian used overt subjects significantly more than those who had no prior knowledge of French. Of most relevance to this discussion is the fact that learners' proficiency level in the French non-native language was extremely low. None of the Spanish L1 speakers with knowledge of French had formally studied French for more than 1.5 years. Within the English L1 group, none of the participants who had prior knowledge of French was able to translate more than ten words into basic French in a 30-item translation task.

As discussed in Chapter 1, evidence of this kind raises considerable concern about the widespread assumption in SLA research that the non-native languages a speaker does not know well can be safely ignored in research. The evidence also leads us to wonder how many of the SLA studies currently available have in fact followed proper subject selection procedures providing unbiased results.

## Recency of Use

Discussions on multilingualism and the recency factor appeared as early as in the 1960s. Vildomec (1963) in particular was the first to note that non-native language influence is more likely to occur from 'vivid' languages rather than from languages gone unused for a long time.

The notion of recency of use or of a recency effect during the acquisition process refers to how recently a language was last used. Some assume that recent use facilitates the occurrence of some kinds of influences due to easier access to linguistic information stored in the mind (cf. Poulisse, 1997; Poulisse and Bongaerts, 1994). Among those who believe that a language recently used is likely to influence target language production are Williams and Hammarberg (1998), who list recency of use among the four factors likely to determine whether a language will take on the main supplier role during the production process. The other three factors are typology, proficiency and L1/L2 status. Shanon (1991) goes even further proposing the existence of a last language or recency effect, according to which learners rely upon the language that was learned last. This prediction, however, does not find much confirmation in the literature. There are a number of studies that show instances of transfer from languages which were not learned last, and that had even gone unused for decades (De Angelis, 1999; De Angelis and Selinker, 2001; Rivers, 1979). Schmidt and Frota (1986) further associate the notion of recency of use with proficiency level and specifically claim that their subject – an English L1 learner of Portuguese – was most influenced by his most fluent non-native language (Arabic), and not by the least fluent but most recent one.

Sometimes it is learners themselves who believe that the languages they have not used for a long time will not influence them in the production of a target language – a belief which we now know to be incorrect. Rivers (1979), for instance, comments on her reliance on German saying it is 'ridiculous since I am so unfluent in German and rarely, rarely use it '(Rivers, 1979: 70). Möhle (1989), who interviewed her German L1 learners of Spanish as an L3 or L4 after finding traces of French in their speech, reports on how learners claimed they did not expect any influence from French because they had not used it for several years. Möhle (1989), however, found ample evidence of French influence in learner's Spanish, ranging from lexical choices to idiomatic expression and surface syntactic structures. Herwig (2001) also reports that one of the participants to her study, an Irish L1 learner of German, claimed some difficulty in controlling the influence from one of her non-native languages (Dutch). Interestingly, the subject's knowledge of Dutch was quite weak in comparison to her knowledge of other languages, and Dutch had not been used recently.

While these studies suggest that languages not used for a while can still influence a target language, there is also evidence that significant differences can arise in performance depending on whether learners have active or passive knowledge of their languages. Mägiste (1984, 1986) is typically associated with this claim. Mägiste's work does not specifically focus on crosslinguistic influence phenomena, it nonetheless provides valuable information on prior knowledge in general. Using a nationwide investigation conducted by Balke-Aurell and Lindblad in 1982 in Sweden, she compared the English language proficiency of immigrant students (N = 2,736) with that of monolingual Swedish students (N = 67,162) and examined test results in word comprehension, reading and listening comprehension and grammar. Results initially indicated that bilinguals do not perform differently from monolinguals, but some difference emerged when the bilingual immigrants of Finnish L1 were divided into two groups: those who used Swedish at home and had only passive knowledge of their first language, and those who actively used their first language at home. Bilinguals with passive knowledge of the Finnish L1 were found to perform better than Swedish monolingual students, but bilinguals who actively use their L1 did not perform better than monolinguals. Mägiste thus suggested that passive bilingualism facilitates third language learning, while active bilingualism might delay the acquisition process.

## Length of Residence and Exposure to a Non-native Language Environment

Vildomec (1963) believed that a long period of residence in a non-native language environment could influence the amount and type of influence on a third or additional language. His claim was further explored in several other studies, and more evidence in its support is now available.

Stedje (1977, as reported in Williams and Hammarberg, 1998) examined the German production of Finnish L1 learners of German during a period of residence in Sweden, and compared it to the German production of Finnish L1 learners who spent only a short period of time in Sweden. She found extensive Swedish influence in the production of those who had spent considerably more time in Sweden, concluding that these learners' production was influenced by the longer exposure to the Swedish environment.

Fouser (2001) examined two English L1 learners of Korean as a third or fifth language who had lived in Japan for a long time prior to taking up the study of Korean. Both learners had acquired Japanese as a non-native language and both were more fluent in Japanese than in Korean. Fouser (2001) raises several points of discussion, including whether the period of residence in Korea was having any impact on these learners' Japanese. One subject reported frequent unintentional switching to Korean while speaking Japanese, and the other reported often thinking in Japanese while speaking Korean.

With reference to Elwert's (1973) work, Hoffmann (2001) discusses how the psychological attachment individuals develop with each of their languages has the potential to affect language maintenance. Elwert remained deeply affected by a change of residence from Italy to Germany, which he claims affected his ability to maintain the three languages he was familiar with at the time of his departure (German, Italian and English). Elwert had been raised in Italy by an English mother and a German father, and had moved to Germany with his parents at the age of nine. Hoffman points out that trilinguals assign a relative importance to the languages they speak at any given time, and a gradual loss of dominance can arise for the

language(s) used the least, presumably because they become less important for the individual. Elwert identifies time and place in particular as
decisive for the maintenance of both fluency and dominance. He notes that
the most dominant language was for him the language of his immediate
environment, while for abstract thinking dominance seemed to be
determined by factors such as 'where he was, who he was with and what
he was thinking of' (Hoffmann 2001: 4).

This leads us to consider one other aspect associated with exposure to a
non-native language environment. As we have seen, exposure to a non-
native language environment may have an immediate effect, as was the
case for Stedje's (1977) learners. On the other hand, exposure can also
influence the language of thought at a later time. Cohen (1995) explains that
memory of a non-native language can be triggered by factors such as when
the language was spoken, with whom, and in what situation. He gives
the example of an English L1 trilingual who stated (Cohen, 1995: 102):
'sometimes when something triggers a memory of being abroad where I
spoke an L2 (i.e. Guatemala, Poland, etc.), I think in the language I used at
the time, especially if the memory involves conversations or encounters
with native speaker of those places.' Similarly, an English L1 quadrilingual
claimed the following: 'I think in Hebrew, French or German when I'm
thinking about people who speak those languages or situations in which I
used those languages' (ibid.).

During a period of residence in a non-native language environment,
many personal experiences are bound to be memorized, but when learners
leave the non-native language environment, they may face some difficulty
in recalling those experiences if in the meantime fluency in the non-native
language has decreased. This is the experience of an English L1 learner of
Spanish, who had lived in Italy prior to moving to Spain. The learner makes
several interesting remarks about his learning experience (De Angelis,
2005b). For example, he explains how sometimes he would recall conversations with foreign friends, but when the friend was Italian, he found
remembering was very difficult as his Italian was no longer as strong as it
used to be. Not knowing which language to use, he writes 'I can't talk in
English to them so sometimes the conversation proceeds in Spanish. Since
I've been trying to get my Italian back I have stopped doing this as I think
it important to separate the two different worlds. (It also feels unpleasant
to talk in Spanish.)' (De Angelis, 2005b).

## Order of Acquisition

Order of acquisition has been argued to be connected to the type of
associations that can be established between two or more languages in the

mind, and consequently the amount of crosslinguistic influence that can occur. The best-known study on order of acquisition was carried out by Dewaele (1998), who examined 218 lexical inventions in the French oral production of 39 Dutch L1 speakers with English as an L2 or an L3. The term lexical invention refers to items which are 'morpho-phonologically adapted to the target language but which are never used by native speakers' (Dewaele 1998: 475).

In this study, 32 participants had knowledge of French as a second language and English as a third language, while seven participants had French as a third language and English as a second language. Dewaele categorised learners' lexical inventions according to intralingual and interlingual sources and generally argued that the items listed under intralingual sources were the result of slips of the tongue or of strategies such as overgeneralization and simplification, while the items listed under interlingual sources were the result of activation of a non-target lemma, resulting in non-target information being passed on to the target form. Following this initial categorization, Dewaele used a chi-square test of interaction to associate the type and amount of lexical inventions with order of acquisition. French L2 and L3 speakers were found to differ significantly in the amount of lexical inventions produced (DF = 6, Chi = 20.1; p = 0.002). French L2 speakers were also found to rely more extensively on intralingual strategies and French L3 speakers on interlingual strategies. Dewaele then looked at the intralingual sources and found that speakers of French as an L2 were more reliant on their Dutch L1 (15.2% versus 9.2% for the French L3 group), while speakers of French as an L3 were more reliant on their English L2 (21.8% versus 6.9% for the French L2 group). Since these speakers had the same language combination, Dewaele concluded that the order in which a language is acquired can determine the type and amount of CLI that occurs in the target language.

## Formality of Context

As all teachers are aware, formal situations such as tests or class presentations generate a great deal of performance anxiety in students, even more so when these are to be carried out in a non-native language. As Hamers and Blanc (1989) have discussed, the stressful situations that can negatively impact bilingual behaviour are several, the most common being environmental noise and mental tiredness. To these we can add peer pressure and fear of failure, which can be more commonly associated with the classroom environment. With respect to language learning, while the stress of a formal situation is known to generate performance anxiety, a healthy dose of anxiety can also improve students' performance, and by healthy dose of anxiety I mean students being in performance mode during a test or class presentation.

So far, only one study has examined how the formality of context affects multilinguals' performance. The study was conducted by Dewaele (2001), who compared students' performance in formal and informal situations. He wanted to assess whether the formality of the situation led to more effective monitoring of the speech output. He examined the proportion of mixed utterances produced in formal and informal contexts in the French oral production of 25 speakers of Dutch L1 and English L2 or L3. With a series of t-tests he showed morpholexical errors to be more frequent in French L3 speakers, regardless of the condition of formality in which they were tested. Further analysis, however, showed a significant difference ($t = 3.773$, $df = 24$, $p < 0.001$) in the proportion of mixed utterances in the informal situation (Mean = 9%, S.D. = 8.8) and the formal situation (Mean = 3%, S.D. = 3.9). In other words, students in the formal situation produced less mixed utterances in the French non-native language than those learners who were interviewed informally, presumably because of increased monitoring activity during the formal situation.

# Chapter 3

# *What Can be Transferred from One or More Non-native Language to Another*

In the previous chapter we examined the factors that influence the amount and type of transfer in third or additional language production. In this chapter we shift the focus to the type of linguistic information that can be transferred from one or more non-native language to another, with special reference to lexis, phonetics and phonology, morphology and syntax.

## Lexis

Non-native linguistic influence is particularly visible in the area of lexis, where traces of non-target information are mostly overt and therefore easily recognizable. One of the most comprehensive studies on non-native linguistic influence and lexical choices was conducted by Ringbom (1987) in Finland, a country with two official languages: Finnish, a Finno-Ugric language, and Swedish, a Germanic language. Finland is widely considered an ideal location for research on non-native language influence due to the sociocultural and educational homogeneity of its people and the language combination that it offers. According to a 1982 survey, 93.3% of the population was estimated to be of Finnish L1 while only 6.3% was estimated to be of Swedish L1. Swedish L1 speakers are generally competent speakers of Finnish as an L2, and Finnish L1 speakers are formally taught Swedish in school (Ringbom, 1987). Even though several years have gone by, Finland has maintained a similar proportion of Swedish-speaking Finns in the country.

Ringbom (1987) examined about 11,000 essays written in English (L3) by Finnish students of Finnish L1 and of Swedish L1 enrolled in an English national exam. He identified several instances of non-native linguistic influence which he broadly categorized as instances of borrowing or instances of lexical transfer (see Table 3.1). Ringbom explains that borrowing and lexical transfer are not clear-cut categories, 'but [are] rather

**Table 3.1** Overt crosslinguistic lexical influence in production (modified from Figure 12, Ringbom, 1987: 117)

| *Lexical transfer* | |
|---|---|
| Loan translations: | Semantic properties of one item transferred in a combination of lexical items. E.g. *'child wagon'* for *'pram'* (Swedish *barnvagn*) |
| Semantic extension: | Semantic properties extended to L2-word. E.g. 'He bit himself in the *language*' (Finnish *kieli* = both 'tongue' and 'language') |
| Cognates (as seen in false friends): | Formal crosslinguistic similarity between items with varying systematic relationships: (a) wholly different meaning: 'at the time he works in a *fabric*' (Swedish *fabrik* = 'factory'); (b) Similar, but in no context-identical meaning: 'The next day we *grounded* a club' (Swedish *grunda* = 'found'); (c) In some, but not all context-identical or near-identical meaning: ' The *hound* is the best friend of man' (Swedish *hund* = 'dog', occasionally also 'hound') |
| *Borrowings* | |
| Hybrids, blends and relexifications: | Morphological or phonological modification of item according to L2-norms. E.g. 'In the morning I was tired and in the evening I was *piggy*' (Swedish *pigg* ='refreshed'); |
| Complete language shifts: | No modification of item according to L2-norm. E.g. 'I'm usually very *pigg* after the diet' (Swedish *pigg* = 'refreshed') |

a continuum, since the learner rarely relies on form alone or on meaning alone. The distinction rather establishes which of the two is the dominant factor in individual instances' (Ringbom 1986: 158).

Ringbom's (1987) distinction between form and meaning can help us identify the type of information that can be transferred from a native and a non-native language. We already know that semantic transfer is possible from an L1 to an L2 (cf. Odlin, 1989), but the same is not necessarily true with respect to non-native languages. Ringbom (1987, 2001) believes that transfer of meaning can only occur from languages the speaker knows well. When no transfer of meaning is involved, transfer becomes a more superficial phenomenon and learners' errors are best viewed as forms of borrowing. In the essays he analysed, Finnish L1 speakers were found to draw extensively on the Swedish L2, but their errors hardly ever involved transfer of meaning and were principally categorized as forms of borrowing. Conversely, Swedish L1 speakers did not seem to rely as much on their Finnish L2 and the Swedish L1 remained their preferred source of lexical information. Most importantly, transfer of meaning occurred only from the Swedish L1. This comparison led Ringbom (1987) to argue that transfer of meaning is mainly restricted to the most fluent language, hence the L1 or the non-native languages the speaker knows well.

The linguistic distance between Finnish and Swedish is clearly a major factor involved in the instances of CLI that Ringbom (1987) has identified. It is in fact the language that bears the closest relationship to the target language which becomes the preferred source of non-target lexical information, particularly when the language involved is the speaker's native language (Swedish L1). When Swedish is the second language, learners appear to be more 'selective' in the choices, in that the influence of Swedish is mostly limited to false friends and borrowings.

Ringbom's (1987, 2001) hypothesis that transfer of meaning is restricted to the L1 and the non-native languages a speaker knows well finds some confirmation in the literature (Chandrasekhar, 1978; Clyne, 1997; Clyne and Cassia, 1999; Möhle, 1989; Schmidt and Frota, 1986; Singleton, 1987; Wei, 2003a). Wei (2003a), for instance, discusses some overt instances of semantic transfer from Japanese, a non-native language his Chinese L1 informant knew quite well. He examined the informant's English production and argued that some semantic patterns found in the English L3 were the result of Japanese influence, as in 'when I'm sick, when I've cold I eat medicine, cold medicine' (Wei, 2003a: 65), where the word 'eat' is presumably taken from Japanese. Wei, however, does not specify how the same sentence would be expressed in Chinese, the subject's L1.

Other interesting examples are described in Möhle (1989). The author describes the production of German L1 speakers who used one of their non-native languages (French) to invent new terms in the target language (Spanish). These learners did not have advanced knowledge of French and, as predicted, mostly produced false friends or borrowings. The following are some of the words they created: *remarcar (French: remarque, English: to remark); *recoltar, *recolta (French: récolte, English: act of picking or crop); *groso (French: gros, English: big). Möhle (1989) also notes the influence of the French L2 in some phrases, as in *no hace atención* instead of *no presta attention* for 'to pay attention'. Hace (to do) in this case is argued to be modelled upon the French verb 'faire' (to do).

More of a puzzling issue relates to how learners make use of content and function words from their non-native languages. Some studies have suggested that transfer phenomena can vary depending on the semantic weight of the words concerned. More specifically, researchers have found that content words (nouns, verbs, numerals, adjectives and most adverbs) and function words (prepositions, determiners, conjunctions and pronouns) from the L1 and the non-native languages are not equally relied upon during the production process.

Garrett (1975) first noted that the speech errors of monolingual speakers hardly ever involved function words. The phenomenon was later confirmed by other researchers also working in the field of speech processing (see discussion in Dell, 1995). The finding that function words appeared to be invulnerable to speech errors raised the question of whether the mind processes content and function words in the same way or if different mechanisms underlie the selection of these elements of speech. Bock notes that the question generated a considerable debate in the literature, with some authors arguing that content and function words are retrieved in a similar manner (Stemberg, 1984) and others (Garrett, 1982) arguing that function words 'are specified in a manner that, in effect, bypasses the need for lexical retrieval.' (Bock, 1995: 187)

From a multilingual perspective, the concern relates not only to how content and function words are processed in the mind, but also to how they are processed in different languages. In L2 speech production research, the use of L1 content or function words is generally viewed as a form of borrowing, the assumption being that the second language system is not as highly developed and automatised as the native language one, so learners resort to L1 content and function words as a compensatory mechanism (Poulisse, 1997; Poulisse and Bongaerts, 1994).

In a study with 45 Dutch learners of English as a second language, Poulisse and Bongaerts (1994) examined the rate of use of L1 content and function words in oral speech. They examined 771 unintentional language switches, divided into non-adapted language switches and morphologically or phonologically adapted language switches. The distinction between these two types of switches was based on 'hesitation phenomena and intonation' (Poulisse and Bongaerts 1994: 43). The items pronounced without hesitation and without a strong intonation were regarded as unintentional language switches. The study found that Dutch learners of English in grade 11 and in grade 9 used more L1 function words than L1 content words in their L2 speech.

Poulisse and Bongaerts (1994) accounted for these results by proposing that in L2 production L1 function words are more likely to be used than content words because function words occur more frequently in speech and are therefore accessed more easily. The authors base their argument on the word-frequency effect, which is a well-known phenomenon in the psycholinguistic literature. According to the word-frequency effect, it is easier to access a word which is used frequently such as 'table', for instance, than a word used less frequently such as 'tank' (see Levelt and Meyer, 2000; Levelt *et al.*, 1999). Poulisse and Bongaerts also elaborate on Giesbers' (1989) claim that content words carry more meaning than function words do. Learners devote more attention to the most meaningful parts of speech, hence content words are more likely to be selected correctly in L2 speech.

When the languages are more than two, it seems that function words are no longer drawn from the L1, but are instead drawn from one of the speakers' non-native languages. Vildomec (1963) initially claimed that multilinguals tend to use words from their non-native languages even when the source and the target items are dissimilar in sound. Several other authors have examined this claim reaching very similar conclusions. Stedje (1977, as reported in Williams and Hammarberg 1998), for instance, claimed that her 55 Finnish L1 learners of German as an L3 with prior knowledge of Swedish as an L2 preferred to use content words from the Swedish non-native language rather than the Finnish native language. As was the case with Ringbom's (1987) work, relatedness may have been the key discriminating factor here.

Ringbom (1987) found complete shifts from the Finnish L1 to be rare for both content and function words. With respect to function words, in a total of 11,000 English L3 essays he found only five function words from the Finnish L1, and three of these words consisted of the Finnish conjunction *ja* (and), which was used exclusively between proper names. Ringbom traced many of learners' errors to the Swedish L2, and function words made up 18% of the total number identified. Among these errors, learners produced 13 instances of the word *fast* (although), 10 instances of *men* (but) and 8 instances of *och* (and). Ringbom (1987) explains this data by drawing a distinction between knowledge and control, claiming that 'with function words (. . .) the attention given to control procedures tends to slacken, since the learner gives only peripheral attention to them, normally focusing on those other words in his utterance which are communicatively the weightiest' (Ringbom, 1987: 128). With respect to the words *fast* and *men*, he also argues that the actual existence of these words in English may have influenced learners' production, even if these words have an entirely different meaning in Swedish and in English.

Williams and Hammarberg (1998) also examined the use of content and function words in L3 oral speech. They examined the Swedish production of an English L1 speaker with fluent German as an L2 and categorized the data according to a pragmatic-based distinction between words with an intended pragmatic purpose, and words without any intended purpose, accordingly labelled as WIPP switches (Without an Identified Pragmatic Purpose). The following is an example of WIPP switch where the speaker uses the German preposition *mit*: 'en tjuv % <*mit*>/ med en nyckel; GLOSS: a thief % <with>/ with a key' (Williams and Hammarberg 1998: 308; italics in the original).

Williams and Hammarberg (1998) found that 92% of the WIPP switches were from the German L2, 4% were from the English L1, and 4% were from other L2s. In the presence of three related languages, the learner then favoured the German L2 over the English L1 for function words.

While multilinguals have been found to be influenced by function words from non-native languages, there is also evidence that L3 production is influenced by L1 prepositions. Jarvis and Odlin (2000), for instance, compared Finnish L1 speaker with English and Swedish as non-native languages with Swedish L1 speakers with English and Finnish as non-native languages and found that these learners were indeed influenced by their respective native languages in the use of prepositions in the third language.

A more recent study claims that not all function words are perceived as equally transferable to the target language. De Angelis (2005a) gave a summary task to two groups of learners with English or Spanish as their native language, the same target language (Italian L3 or L4), and different non-native languages. Among the English L1 speakers, some had French and some had Spanish as their L2. Most of the non-target function words these learners used were from the French L2 (90.91%) or the Spanish L2 (81.40%) respectively. Among the Spanish L1 speakers, some had English as their L2, and some had English and French as non-native languages. The non-target function words these learners used were from the Spanish L1 (97.06%) when no French was known, but were from both the Spanish L1 (36.67%) and the French L2 (60%) when French was known. Of interest is the type of function words used from the French L2. In both groups, learners used several instances of the French subject pronoun *il* (he), more specifically 7 out of 10 (English L1 group) and 12 out of 18 (Spanish L1 group). This result then raised the question of whether the frequent use of the French subject pronoun *il* was a chance occurrence or a surface manifestation of CLI. The rate of subject insertion and omission was thus analysed using a one-way ANOVA. The 17 English L1 speakers with French as an L2 used significantly more subject insertion (Mean = 78.36%, SD = 28.32) than the 37 English L1 speakers with Spanish as an L2 (Mean = 36.55%, SD = 37.58). Similarly, the 45 Spanish L1 speakers with English as an L2 used significantly less subject insertion (Mean = 30.95%, SD = 26.32) than the 9 Spanish L1 speakers with English and French as non-native languages (Mean = 57.83%, SD = 39.70). These results then led the author to conclude that the use of French function word *il* was the surface manifestation of CLI rather than a chance occurrence.

With respect to integrating function words into written or oral production, these results also suggest that function words are not perceived as being equally transferable by the learner and therefore that the general claim that function words tend to be drawn from non-native languages is not entirely tenable. Function words are indeed drawn from non-native languages but, as far as we can see, this applies to some type of function words (e.g. pronouns) and not others. Further research would need to use different language combinations and clarify the extent to which other types of function words, such as determiners, prepositions and conjunctions, are also used in third or additional language production.

Let us now turn to a study (Odlin and Jarvis, 2004) that focused on whether learners with knowledge of Swedish as an L1 or as an L2 display any differences in their use of Swedish as a source language. The authors examined the written production of 140 Finnish L1 speakers and 70 Swedish L1 speakers, all learners of English as a non-native language. Thirty-five of the Finnish L1 speakers had no knowledge of Swedish as an L2, while the remaining participants had studied Swedish from 1 to 7 years. The 70 Swedish subjects had formally studied Finnish as an L2 for a period that ranged from 5 to 7 years. In addition to these two main groups, three control groups were also used, consisting of 66 Finnish L1 speakers, 44 Swedish L1 and 66 English L1 speakers.

Odlin and Jarvis (2004) showed their participants a silent Charlie Chaplin movie and asked them to provide a written summary of what they saw. They then proceeded to analyse learners' use of four English lexical items: *instead, for, some* and *what*. These four items were chosen because of their cognate status in English.

*Instead*, and *instead of* are similar to the Swedish expressions *i stället* and *i stället för*, while the equivalent expression in Finnish are the adverb *sen sijaan* and the postposition *sijaan/sijasta*, both more distant from English. Odlin and Jarvis first asked whether learners with knowledge of Swedish would readily identify the similarity between the Swedish and the English forms, and second whether Swedish L1 speakers made a different use of Swedish than those who had knowledge of Swedish as a second language. Results indicated some differences in behaviour between the Finns and the Swedes. Only 1 (0.7%) out of 140 Finnish L1 speakers made use of the word *instead* in English, while 18 (25.7%) out of 70 Swedish L1 speakers used the word *instead* in their writing. The same pattern of use was found in the writings of the Swedish and Finnish control groups. The Finns never used *sen sijaan* or *sijaan/sijasta*, while the Swedes used *i stället* and *i stället för* 18 times. In the use of *instead* then, Swedish as an L1 seems to inform learners' decisions more markedly than Swedish as an L2.

The English preposition *for* is similar in form and function to the Swedish preposition *för*. There are several equivalents of *for* in Finnish. The authors do not list them all but discuss some of their properties throughout the article. They generally argue that Finns and Swedes show some differences in their use of *for* in that Finns seem to be more prone to overgeneralize and use the preposition with verbs of saying such as *say for* and *ask for*. Eight cases of overgeneralizations of this kind were found.

For the English word *what*, distance is generally argued to influence learners' decisions as in the other examples above. The other interesting example concerns the use of the word *some*. In Swedish, *som* is a relative pronoun, while in English *some* is a determiner or an indefinite pronoun. This is a case in which the spelling and pronunciation in Swedish and English are similar, but the function is not. Jarvis and Odlin found three instances where the Swedes used the word *some* in English with the relative pronoun function, and two of these instances were produced by the same person. By contrast, Finns never used the word *some* as a relative pronoun in English. In terms of non-native linguistic influence, then, what we see once again is that learners make a different use of the Swedish L1 and the Swedish L2. It must be noted, however, that in most cases the data available is so little that conclusions are difficult to reach. In the last example, for instance, the authors found only three instances of *some* as a relative pronoun, two of which were produced by the same individual.

In a totally unrelated study, Gibson and Hufeisen (2003) also comment on the Swedish word *som*. In this study, the authors examined whether learners of German (GFL group) and learners of English as a non-native language (EFL group) would be able to take advantage of the number of cognate relations that exist between Swedish, German and English and translate a short Swedish text into their respective foreign languages. None of the participants had been previously exposed to Swedish. The authors found several differences in learners' accuracy rates, and similarly to Odlin and Jarvis (2004), they also singled out the Swedish word *som*. Learners of both groups found *som* to be one of the most difficult words to translate, with a reported error rate of 69% for the GFL group, and of 80% for the EFL group. Gibson and Hufeisen's learners did not easily identify the Swedish word *som* with an English relative pronoun and when they did so, they seemed to be helped by the context in which the word was used.

Before I conclude this section on CLI and lexis, I would also like to mention some instances of combined CLI. It may be recalled that combined CLI is a type of transfer that occurs when two or more languages interact with one another and concur in influencing the target language, or whenever one language influences another, and the already influenced language in turn influences another language in the process of being acquired.

As is usually the case, Vildomec was the first to note that: 'if two or more tongues which a subject has mastered are similar (both linguistically and psychologically) they may "co-operate" in interfering with other tongues' (1963: 212). Several decades have gone by since this remark, yet combined CLI has remained one of the least investigated forms of influence on the target language to the present day. The small amount of evidence that is indeed available amounts to brief descriptions and remarks (Chamot, 1973; Chandrasekhar, 1978; Clyne, 1997; Clyne and Cassia, 1999; De Angelis, 2005c; Dewaele, 1998; Möhle, 1989; Odlin and Jarvis, 2004; Ringbom, 1987). This said, so little research is available that other manifestations of combined CLI will no doubt be identified in the future.

Among the first to discuss instances of combined CLI was Chandrasekhar (1978), who found some cases of it in the German L3 production of a Hindi L1 speaker with prior knowledge of English. He claimed that the learner's source language included information from two languages, the Hindi L1 and the English L2 combined, as the following statement indicates:

> the mother tongue (Hindi) construction has influenced the English of the learner, and it is this Hindi-influenced English which forms the base language when German is being learned: *Ich treffe mit meinem Bruder* instead of **Ich treffe meinen Bruder.** The erroneous German construction is the result of the wrong English of the learner *I meet with my brother*, the *with my brother* here being the equivalent of Hindi bhai se. (Chandrasekhar 1978: 64, italic and bold in the original)

More recently, Clyne (1997) noted that formal similarity between two languages can have a reinforcement effect leading to a lexical substitution in production (see also discussion in De Angelis, 2005c). He accordingly proposed that 'if two languages share a feature, the informants tend to extend it to the third language (Clyne 1997: 110–111). He gives the example of an Italian/Spanish/English trilingual who produced the following sentence in Italian: 'ecco diceva che no che c/'affettava un po' alla scuola il bambino allora piu' per questo (English: here (the teacher) said that it affected him a little at school – more for that reason). Clyne argues that the word 'affettava' is the result of the influence of Spanish 'afectar' and English 'affect'. Similarity, in this case, is implied to lead to the persistence of interlanguage-based lexicon in speech.

Some more evidence of combined CLI is mentioned in Möhle (1989), who examined German L1 learners of Spanish with prior knowledge of French. As may be expected, the author noted extensive interaction between French and Spanish. She also found several words that appeared to be the result of combined influences. For example, the use of the word *emplear* instead of *llenar* (to fill) in Spanish, which is argued to be the result of the combined influence of French *remplir*, Latin *plenus*, and of course Spanish *emplear*, a word that means to employ rather than to fill.

## Phonetics and Phonology

Foreign language speakers typically retain some phonetic features of their native language when speaking in the target language. This gives that special accent to someone's speech which can often reveal the person's place of origin and language background. Non-native languages are not usually regarded as significant sources of influence on the target language, but some forms of influence are however possible (Chamot, 1973; Hammarberg, 2001; Hammarberg and Hammarberg, 1993; Rivers, 1979), as this section will discuss.

Hammarberg and Hammarberg (1993) provide a detailed account of non-native phonetic influence on the acquisition of Swedish as a third language. Their subject – an English L1 speaker with excellent knowledge of German as an L2 – was asked to complete a story narration task in the Swedish target language. Two samples of the subject's Swedish speech were tape-recorded and played back to Swedish native speakers on two separate occasions. The first recording was made soon after the subject had moved to Sweden, and the second about a year later. The Swedish native speakers were not told they would be hearing speech from the same person, they were simply instructed to listen to the recordings and identify the speakers' native language. Results were quite clear with respect to non-native phonetic influence. The speaker of the first recording was judged to be a native speaker of German, when German was in fact the subject's second language, while the speaker of the second recording was mostly judged to be a native speaker of English, which was indeed correct. Box 3.1 shows some of the sound segments from the English L1 (E) and the German L2 (G) observed in the first and the second recordings (Hammarberg and Hammarberg, 1993: 63):

## Box 3.1

First recording:

| G | German labial (u: ]) | huset |
|---|---|---|
| G/E | Very lax short /i/ | vill, till |
| G | Less retracted long /a: / | ha, ja |
| G | Voiced intervocalic /s/ ([z]) | huset, läser |
| G | Postvocalic /r/; uvular approximant or vocalized (Prevocalic /r/ is an apical trill or weak approximant) | är, tar, går, framför, springer, läser |
| G | Syllabic nasal | hunden, tidningen |

Second recording:

| G/E | Very lax short /i/ | finns, till |
|---|---|---|
| E | Occasional reduction of unstressed vowel to shwa | kastar, fortfarande |
| E | Retracted, alveolar /t,d/ | till, lite, sista, ett, de, bilden |
| E | Slightly velarized /l/ | till, bilden, själv |
| non-G | No longer [z] for /s/ | läsa, huset |
| E | Postvocalic /r/: a somewhat too prominent apical approximant, like the type used pre-vocalically | här, ser, sitter, framför |

The same subject was also asked to read two short texts from a Swedish language textbook and carry out two tasks. The first was to listen to a native speaker read a Swedish text and then read the same text aloud (read-after-me condition). The second was to read the text without listening to a native speaker first (read-on-your-own condition). Results showed that the subject displayed a more pronounced German accent in the second condition. Box 3.2 shows the German settings that were observed (ibid.):

**Box 3.2**

| Long /a: / | Relatively fronted quality, like German [a: ]: laga, mat |
|---|---|
| /r/ | Uvular/vocalized throughout: rum, draperi, dörren, värd, mattor, framför etc. |
| Prevocalic /s/ | [z]: sätt, säng, sängen, [s]: sang, så |
| Syllable-final obstruents | Devoiced: bord, värd, bred, tavlor |

Hammarberg and Hammarberg (1993) make several remarks as to why an English L1 speaker would rely so extensively on the phonetic settings of the German second language while producing speech in the Swedish target language. While they argue that the German L2 appears to be a stronger influence in the early stages of acquisition, they also note that the reliance on the English L1 or the German L2 seems to be triggered by different needs. They believe that the reliance on the L1 'is a basic *constraint* in language learning and tends to be persistent, whereas the reliance on L2 is a *coping strategy* which the learner resorts to at an initial stage when the phonetic form of L3 is too unfamiliar to master, and abandons when proficiency in L3 increases' (Hammarberg and Hammarberg, 1993: 65; italics as in original).

The authors additionally suggest that, in some cases, the German articulatory settings turned out to be of great help to the learner because they allowed her to avoid unwanted L1 phonetic features such as diphthongal vowel qualities in her speech. The speaker clearly claimed consciously suppressing the English L1 phonetic settings in favour of the German ones because she did not want to sound like an English native speaker when speaking Swedish.

While a speaker can consciously decide to select some phonetic features at will, Hammarberg and Hammarberg (1993) also maintain that the subject's reliance on the German phonetic settings was partly due to the complexity of the task she was given. In fact, she showed a strong German accent when doing the most complex reading task, which is when she was asked to read a Swedish text without being able to hear the same text read by a native speaker first.

Some evidence of non-native phonetic influence can also be found in Rivers' (1979) diary of a sixth-language learner. The informant is an English L1 learner of Spanish as a non-native language, with good knowledge of

French and very little knowledge of German and Italian. Rivers provides a fairly detailed report of various types of influences, including phonetic influences. Given the combination of languages, it is perhaps not surprising that language distance plays a crucial role in instances of CLI and therefore that the Romance languages (French and Italian) surface more strongly in pronunciation. Rivers discusses the use of French vowels and consonants as well as French stress patterns. For instance, French /y/ is often used instead of /u/, and a French stress is placed on the words' last syllables, as in *habló* instead of *háblo*. Also, she reports on the occasional use of the French uvular /r/. Perhaps more of a surprise is the influence from Italian, a language the learner believed mostly forgotten. The Italian influence seems, however, confined to the pronunciation of words that are phonetically similar in the two languages, such as Italian *cento* for *chiento*, or Italian *buon giorno* for *buenos días* (Rivers 1979: 70). As noted in the section on language distance, phonetic resemblance seems to facilitate instances of transfer from native as well as non-native languages, and from distant as well as close languages.

Chamot (1973) also discusses some evidence of phonetic influences on the target language. Her evidence is from a French-Spanish bilingual boy who was raised speaking two languages: French at home and Spanish at school. The boy had moved to the United States with his family at the age of ten and had been learning English since. French and Spanish were maintained as his home languages. The child was tape-recorded twice a month for nine consecutive months for approximately 15 to 30 minutes at dinner time. Chamot focused on various aspects of acquisition, including the child's difficulties at mastering phonetic features that were either absent or present in the two languages he knew, French and Spanish. One of the problems she identifies, and that she defines as a case of 'double interference', is the child's difficulty in acquiring vowels that are nearly-identical in French and in Spanish, but are different in English. For example, the child often replaced the English vowels /iy/ /ɛ/, /ow/ and /vw/ with the cardinal vowels /i/, /e/, /o/ and /u/, which are all very similar in Spanish and French. The prior knowledge of two languages which share some phonetic features with one another then seems to influence the acquisition of the third language. Would the same have occurred had the child been familiar with either Spanish or French but not both? The instances of 'double interference' Chamot (1973) describes are a form of combined CLI, whereby two languages interact with one another and concur in influencing a target language. In this case, the presence of similar features in Spanish and French seems to have had a negative impact on the acquisition process, reinforcing the use of the source pattern while delaying the acquisition of the new one.

Singh and Carroll (1979) also examined learners of different language backgrounds finding some evidence of non-native transfer. The authors observed that those learners whose mother tongue was a non-European language, but who had prior knowledge of English, produced French L3 speech that seemed 'suspiciously anglophonic' (Singh and Carroll, 1979: 58). For example, a Turkish L1 speaker was found to use /w/ for French /v/. Since Turkish does not have the phoneme /w/, but has the phoneme /v/, the authors argue that the informant must have overgeneralized the difference between /w/ and /v/ in English, creating an indirect form of phonetic influence from English to the French L3. The assumption here is that when the informant initially learned English, he first used his knowledge of Turkish /v/ and then learned the allophonic distinction between English /w/ and /v/, which was subsequently extended to French. Among the explanations Singh and Carroll provide is the suggestion that these informants were 'working with an extended notion of cognates across European language boundaries' (Singh and Carroll, 1979: 58).

## Morphology

In the CLI literature we find widespread scepticism about the transferability of bound morphology, and of inflectional morphology in particular. The evidence of inflectional and derivation morphological transfer from the L1 or the non-native language is most certainly quite sparse, but the growing empirical record is beginning to show that bound morphology does not seem as immune to transfer as is traditionally thought.

Long ago, Weinreich (1953: 44) pointed out that:

> a statement of the form 'Morphologies can(not) be mixed' is premature at the present state of our knowledge. The transfer of a full grammatical paradigm, with its formant morphemes, from one language into another has apparently never been recorded. But the transfer of individual morphemes of all types is definitely possible under certain favourable structural conditions, such as a preexisting similarity in patterns or the relatively unbound and invariant form of the morpheme.

More than fifty years later, stating that bound morphology does not transfer continues to be premature, especially as we now have more evidence that certain types of bound morphemes can transfer under certain conditions.

Weinreich suggests that:

> it stands very much to reason that the transfer of morphemes is
> facilitated between highly congruent structures; for a highly bound
> morpheme is so dependent on its grammatical function (as opposed to
> its designative value) that it is useless in an alien system unless there is
> a ready function for it. (Weinreich, 1953: 33)

Weinreich's idea that transfer 'is facilitated under congruent structures'
raises some concerns as to how this statement should be interpreted. First,
as Odlin (1989) pointed out, it is problematic to establish what the necessary
degree of congruence should be for transfer to take place. Second, the notion
of congruence is vague, as it can be taken to refer to phonological patterns,
semantics, grammatical functions and so on.

Weinreich (1953) reports only a few cases of morphological transfer, but
in reading his work we can understand that he was not entirely sceptical
about this type of transfer, even coming to argue that highly bound
morphemes may be subject to transfer. For example, he writes:

> 'Almost equally favourable conditions characterize the Romansch-
> Schwyzertütsch, where a case bordering on bound-morpheme transfer
> has occurred. Bilingual children have been replacing the Romansh
> feminine indefinite article *in*, an alternant of *ina* used before vowels, by
> *ina-n* (*ina-n-ura* 'an hour' for *in'ura*) on the model of Schwyzertütsch,
> where, just as in English, the article *a* has an extended alternant, an,
> before vowels (a p$^f$ luag 'a plough', an ap$^f$ al 'an apple'). (Weinreich
> 1953: 32)

Odlin (1989) discusses the fact that morphological transfer is possible
but quite rare, and emphasizes that only a few cases are reported in the
literature. He mentions evidence from Fantini (1985), for instance, who
showed that pluralization rules of one language can be employed in the
production of another, as in the sentence *too manys cars* produced by a
Spanish-English bilingual child. In Spanish, nouns and adjectives agree
in number and gender, while in English they do not. The pluralization of
the English adjective *many* is taken as evidence of transfer of adjective
pluralization from Spanish into English.

Evidence that morphological knowledge is exploited in the acquisition
of a second language is also presented in Orr (1987), who found that
speakers of Ngoni were clearly advantaged in the learning of prefixation
of Chichewa, another Bantu langauge, when compared with L1 speakers of
Gujarati, a language that does not make use of the same complex prefixation
system (see discussion in Jarvis and Odlin, 2000)

Examples of morphological transfer from non-native languages are reported in Bouvy (2000), Clyne and Cassia (1999), De Angelis and Selinker (2001), Hammarberg (2001) and Jarvis and Odlin (2000). Let us examine some of these examples focusing on inflectional morphology, since this is the most debated type of transfer of all.

Bouvy (2000) gives some example of morpho-semantic code-mixing between two non-native languages, Dutch and English. She found cases in which Dutch pluralization rules and suffixes were being applied to English words, as in *help-t* for *helped*, where *-t* is a Dutch suffix; *product-en* and *good-eren* for the word *goods*, *-en* and *-eren* being Dutch inflectional suffixes.

Hammarberg (2001) also offers some clear examples of transfer of inflectional morphemes. One of these involves the use of a German infinitive ending. The subject was trying to say 'to camp' but used the word *tälten* in Swedish instead of using the correct form *tälta*. The influence in this case is argued to be from the German verb *zelten*. Most interesting is the sudden presence of the Italian verb morphology in the subject's Swedish speech. The subject was an English L1 speaker with good knowledge of German and very little knowledge of Italian. She produced sentences using the Italian first conjugation infinite ending *-are*, as in *skrivare* (target form: att skriva; English: to write) or *lärare* (target form: att lära; English: to teach).

Some other convincing evidence of morphological transfer can be found in Jarvis and Odlin (2000), who compared the type and frequency of spatial expressions used by 140 Finnish L1 speakers and 70 Swedish L1 speakers, all learners of English as a second language. Finnish marks spatial relationship by agglutinative postverbal morphology, while Swedish marks spatial relations by way of preverbal prepositions, therefore by the use of free morphology as in English. The authors asked participants to describe a silent film and then examined how they used spatial prepositions after English verbs such as 'sit', 'take' and 'put'. They found a clear difference in terms of the prepositions that were favoured depending on the participants' L1 background. Finns, for instance, displayed a marked tendency to use the expression 'sit *on* the grass', while Swedes favoured 'sit *in* the grass'. The same preference is reflected in the results obtained from the control groups. Finnish L1 speakers used 27 instances of *-lle/-lla* (on) and never used the bound morpheme *-ssa/-Vn* (in). Swedish L1 speakers used 11 instances of *i* (in) and 5 of *på* (on). The overall results, the authors claim:

> indicate that the bound agglutinative morphology of the Finnish spatial system and the free prepositional morphology of Swedish constrain the type of options that learners pursue in their L2 English spatial reference. Whether the information is coded as a preposition, postposition, inflectional morpheme, the native language can inform the semantic choices learners make. (Jarvis and Odlin, 2000: 553)

Jarvis and Odlin's (2000) results illustrate with clarity the existence of morphological transfer between a native and a non-native language. An issue the authors do not directly address, but that would have been important to address, relates to the role of learners' prior linguistic knowledge since Finnish and Swedish L1 speakers also have knowledge of Swedish and Finnish as non-native languages. This is to say that in order to obtain a clear picture of the transferability of bound morphology with these speakers, it would have been important to evaluate how the same participants would have expressed spatial relations in their respective non-native languages as well. Nonetheless, the authors have provided us with some very convincing data on the transferability of bound-morphology.

## Syntax

Research on the acquisition of third or additional languages from a generative perspective is scarce, but the few studies that have been published all overwhelmingly point to a difference between L2 and L3 acquisition.

One of the first to investigate multilingualism from a generative perspective was Zobl (1992), who tested whether prior linguistic knowledge leads to the creation of more or less conservative grammars in multilinguals, following the assumption that a preference for wide grammars suggests that hypotheses are being overgeneralized resulting in higher acceptance scores with respect to marked as well as ungrammatical sentences. Accordingly, Zobl (1992) investigated the hypotheses that 'in judgements of grammaticality, Mls will more often than Uls accept sentences whose generation presupposes a more marked grammar. Similarly they will more often accept sentences which presuppose a grammar that overgenerates' (Zobl, 1992: 179). Let us clarify this point with an actual example (adjacency of verbs and objects) and examine the acceptability scores that Zobl obtained.

With respect to adjacency of verbs and objects, Zobl explains that a grammar which allows V NP and NP in contiguity is more conservative than a grammar which allows the introduction of elements such as adverbs and prepositions in the sequence, as in the following three sentences (Zobl 1992: 183): '1) *A waitress brought the customer quickly a menu, 2) *Did the teacher explain patiently the answer?, 3) *The girl was sending to her boyfriend a letter.' In (1) and (2), the adverbs 'quickly' and 'patiently' are introduced, while in (3) the Prepositional Phrase (PP) 'to her boyfriend' is introduced. Zobl's results for this instance, and more broadly for the entire study, turned out not to be statistically significant, he nonetheless notes the presence of a wide margin of difference between the scores of two groups, which understandably casts some doubts as to whether a complete rejection of the null hypothesis is appropriate. For instance, with respect to the first sentence (V NP Adv. NP), the margin of difference in question is 19.2%; for the second sentence is 10.0%, and for the third sentence is 5.5%. In addition to adjacency of verbs and objects, Zobl also tested the two groups of participants on several other structures, finding an overall ratio of wider to narrower grammars of 2: 1 in favour of multilinguals which, he argues, provides some tentative support for the hypothesis originally outlined. Multilinguals, in a few words, seem to create less conservative hence more powerful grammars than monolinguals do.

Klein (1995) also asked whether multilinguals are in any way different from monolinguals with respect to language acquisition. She compared a group of 17 learners of English as an L2 with a group of 15 multilinguals of different language backgrounds, all learners of English as an L3 or L4. She also used 15 English L1 speakers as a control group. The investigation focused on the acquisition of English verbs and their prepositional complements, and on the acquisition of preposition stranding. Let's examine the case of preposition stranding.

In brief, when a wh-element in a question involves a PP, English has two options. The first is that the PP is extracted and fronted, creating what is called pied-piping, as in ([For whom$_i$] are the girls waiting [$_{pp}$ t$_i$]). The second, known as preposition stranding, entails that it is only the object that is extracted, as in ([Who$_i$] are the girls waiting [$_{pp}$ for [t$_i$]])

All the participants to Klein's study were familiar with languages that constructed wh- questions via wh-movement, but none of them allowed preposition stranding. Learners in each group then had an equal chance of acquiring preposition stranding in English. Using grammaticality judgements and corrections tasks, Klein (1995) tested a number of verbs with prepositions like *wait for, work for, play with, dance with, talk about, worry about*. Participants were given 18 sentences containing verbs with their prepositions omitted, like 'The young girl waited the school bus yesterday' or 'which bus did the young girl wait yesterday?'

Klein (1995) had hypothesized that multilinguals would show an advantage over monolinguals in the acquisition of preposition stranding, a hypothesis which the results of the study indeed confirmed. Klein explains that 'because none of the learners' prior languages exhibit preposition stranding, former parameter settings could not have been the cause for this increased rate of acquisition among the Mls' (Klein, 1995: 450–1). Accordingly, she maintains that all the added qualities previous studies had already observed in multilinguals, such as better metalinguistic skills

(Thomas, 1988, 1992) or less conservative learning processes (Zobl, 1992), contribute to triggering the settings of UG parameters in multilingual speakers. (Klein, 1995: 420)

More directly associated with the study of CLI and multilingualism is the debate on the L2 initial state, which has been extended to L3 acquisition. Before reviewing the study itself (Leung, 2005), some background information on what this debate entails may be helpful.

The task of defining the L2 initial state, which is commonly understood to be the grammar at the beginning of the acquisition of a second language, has attracted much attention in the literature as it is essential to explain what subsequent grammars start *from* (see Schwartz and Eubank, 1996). With respect to L1 transfer, two influential hypotheses can be mentioned: the 'Minimal Trees' hypothesis (Vainikka and Young-Scholten, 1996) and the 'Full Transfer/Full Access' hypothesis (Schwartz and Sprouse, 1996). These two hypotheses of L2 syntactic development differ in their assumptions of how grammars are built and in what they believe the L2 initial state contains.

Hawkins (2001) presents two major views of how grammars are built: the lexical array and the structural template views. According to a structural template view 'the syntactic module constructs phrase markers independently of the lexicon, into which lexical items are subsequently inserted. In other words, the syntax provides a "structural template" and then fills it with morphemes drawn from the lexicon' (Hawkins 2001: 330, inverted commas in the original). According to the lexical array view based on Chomsky (1995), 'the syntax does not construct structural templates independently of the lexicon. Instead, the lexicon selects arrays of lexical items directly from the lexicon and "merges" them into an initial phrase marker' (ibid.).

The Minimal Trees hypothesis and the Full Transfer/Full Access hypothesis differ in their view of the relationship between the syntax and the lexicon and therefore differ in how they assume L2 grammar development takes place. The first hypothesis subscribes to the lexical array view, the second to the structural template view (Hawkins, 2001).

These two hypotheses also substantially differ in what they believe the L2 initial state may contain. The Minimal Trees hypothesis makes use of the distinction between lexical and functional categories and claims that only the L1 properties of lexical categories (N, V, P and A) initially transfer. The L1 properties of functional categories such as IP or CP do not. These develop later in the acquisition process through exposure to input. In assonance with the lexical array view, functional categories are constructed only after the acquisition of morphemes belonging to IP or CP, but they are not initially present in the L2 initial state. The 'Full Transfer/Full Access' hypothesis instead proposes that learners have full access to both lexical and functional categories which, in agreement with a structural template view, are already present at the initial stage of L2 acquisition. The hypothesis thus claims that the L2 initial state includes all the grammatical representations determined by the L1, the only exception being the surface realization of bound morphology. Learners subsequently restructure their grammar upon exposure to the L2 input. According to this hypothesis then 'the initial state of L2 acquisition is the final state of L1 acquisition (excluding the phonetic matrices of lexical/morphological items) (Schwartz and Sprouse, 1996: 41).

The two hypotheses attempt to capture L1 transfer by latching on to a constant, i.e. the L2 input, which is viewed as the trigger of syntactic development. Vainikka and Young-Scholten (1996: 7) argue that 'the development of functional projections is driven solely by the interaction of X'-Theory with the target-language input'. Schwartz and Sprouse (1996: 41).instead argue that 'the initial state of the L2 system will have to change in light of TL input that cannot be generated by this grammar'; that is, failure to assign a representation to input data will force some sort of restructuring of the system ('grammar').

As anticipated, Leung (2005) extended the above arguments about the L2 initial state, and the theoretical developments that followed, to the acquisition of a third language. Aiming to compare the L2 with the L3 initial state, Leung (2005) tested two groups of French learners. One group (the L3 group) was formed by L1 speakers of Cantonese with prior knowledge of English, and another group (the L2 group) was formed by L1 speakers of Vietnamese with no knowledge of English. These subjects were tested on the following grammatical properties: Determiner (D), Number (Num), the feature strength of Num, and the formal feature [± definite]. The results obtained were then discussed within two currently competing models of acquisition: the Failed Functional Features Hypothesis (FFFH) and the Full Transfer Full Access Hypothesis (FTFA) reviewed above.

Leung explains that, with respect to L2 acquisition, the FFFH essentially claims that all those properties such as functional categories, formal features and feature strength which are not instantiated in the L1 grammar will not be acquired in the second language. The implication for L3 acquisition is that the same properties will not be acquired in the L3 either. In contrast, the FTFA, assumes that all properties, functional and lexical, will transfer. An important distinction Leung makes is that the FFFH entails the existence of failure due to the L1, while for the FTFA there are no failures. In fact, he says, in L3 acquisition 'whether there is transfer from the L1 or the L2 initial state, parameterized properties are in principle always attainable' (Leung, 2005: 41).

Focusing on the grammatical properties listed earlier (Determiner (D), Number (Num), the feature strength of Num, and the formal feature [± definite]), Leung carried out two experiments using a wide range of oral and written tasks, and overall results provided support for 'the full transfer of L1 in the L2 initial state and partial transfer of L2 in the L3 initial state' (Leung, 2005: 39). Leung also notes that learners in the L3 groups performed significantly better than learners in the L2 group. This, he argues, is not consistent with either the FFFH or the FTFA hypotheses and clearly point to the fact that L3 acquisition is not just an extension of L2 acquisition. In L2 acquisition, transfer can only come from the L1, while in L3 acquisition, the sources of transfer can be both the L1 and the L2.

Another valuable contribution which highlights the difference between L2 and L3 acquisition can be found in Flynn *et al.* (2004). The authors propose a Cumulative-Enhancement Model for Language Acquisition, which essentially entails that the learning process is cumulative and therefore that all the languages a speaker is familiar with can potentially influence the development of the target language. The influence is therefore no longer a prerogative of the L1, which is in fact argued not to have a privileged status in L3 acquisition.

The proposals stem from a series of studies on relative clauses with adults and children (Flynn 1983, 1987; Flynn and Lust, 1981) and the comparison of results for L1, L2 and L3 acquisition. With respect to the study on L1 acquisition, Flynn and Lust (1981) compared English L1 children's developmental patterns of three types of relative clauses: (1) lexically headed, head with semantic content (Big Bird pushes the balloon [which bumps Ernie]); (2) lexically headed, head with no semantic content (Ernie pushes the thing [which touches Big Bird]); and (3) free relative (Cookie Monster hits [what pushes Big Bird]). Using an elicited imitation method, the author found that free relative clause structures were significantly more productive than the other two types of clause structures. This means that children who were asked to imitate these structures, correctly imitated the free relative clause structures more often than the remaining two other structures. The authors concluded in favour of the primacy of free relative structures with respect to the development of subordination in L1 acquisition.

The same types of structures were then tested with adult L2 learners of English with different L1s (Spanish and Japanese). These two native languages were chosen because of the structural contrast they offer. Spanish, like English, is a head-initial, right-branching language, while

Japanese is a head-final, left-branching language. Using elicited imitation, findings indicated that the free relative clause structure appears before the lexically headed structures in the production of Japanese L1 speakers but not in the production of Spanish L1 speakers. The authors explain these results with the argument that Japanese L1 speakers, as well as the monolingual English children, had no prior experience with head-initial, right-branching languages, so they all had to set the correct parametric value for the English L1 or L2. More specifically, they claim that the results indicate that 'both "determining" and experience with the consequences of the parametric value of this grammatical principle is necessary in acquisition in terms of the development of a language-specific grammar' (Flynn *et al.*, 2004: 8).

Moving on to L3 acquisition, Flynn *et al.* (2004) matched the design of this study with the design used in the previous two studies just reported, hence three types of relative clause structures were tested: (1) lexical head with semantic content (The owner questioned the businessman [who greeted the worker]); (2) lexical head with no semantic content (The janitor criticized the person [who called the lawyer]); and (3) free relative (The professor introduced [whoever greeted]). A total of 33 Kazakh L1 adults and 30 children at three proficiency levels were tested. Proficiency was assessed with the Michigan Test and learners' proficiency was accordingly classified as High, Medium or Low.

A major strength of this research design lies in the choice of languages. Kazakh is a Turkish language with a head-final, left-branching structure like Japanese, while Russian is a Slavic language with a head-initial, right-branching structure like English. It follows that, if learners draw on their prior knowledge with respect to relative clause structures in the English L3, evidence of use of a right-branching language would suggest the influence of the Russian L2, which in turn would provide support for a Cumulative-Enhancement Model of Acquisition. Results showed similar acquisition patterns for the Kazakh L1 speakers and the Spanish L1 speakers of the second study which, according to the authors, indicates that 'prior CP development can influence development of CP structure in subsequent language acquisition' (Flynn, *et al.*, 2004: 13). Results obtained from children, however, showed something unexpected, in that their behaviour seemed more in line with the results obtained from English L1 children and Japanese L1 speakers. In the search for an explanation, the authors looked more closely at the time of acquisition, noting that some of the children were learning Kazakh and Russian simultaneously as L1s. They thus postulated a possible difference associated with when the L2 is acquired, that is if the acquisition of the L1 and the L2 is simultaneous or near-simultaneous, or if it is sequential. They accordingly argued that 'when the L2 is still "in progress", its influence on L3 acquisition in not the same as it is when L2 and L3 are sequential.' (Flynn *et al.*, 2004: 14).

By showing that previously constructed grammars are relied upon during the acquisition process, Flynn *et al.* (2004) provide a highly valuable contribution to the field, as they show that previously known non-native languages can indeed influence target language development to a significant extent, even when proficiency in the second language is low or intermediate. Moreover, the authors highlight the possible difference between simultaneous and sequential acquisition. Given their results, the observation looks very promising for future progress and seems to warrant further investigation.

# Chapter 4
# *Multilingual Speech Production*

The primary objective of this chapter will be to examine the few models of multilingual speech production that are currently available. Since most of these models are based on proposals originally made in relation to monolingual and bilingual speakers, I shall first summarize two key models of monolingual speech production (Dell, 1986 and Levelt, 1989) before proceeding to examine those models of bilingual speech production which are argued to account for multilingual production as well.

## Two Influential Monolingual Speech Production Models: Dell (1986) and Levelt (1989)

Among the most influential models of monolingual speech production are those proposed by Dell (1986) and Levelt (1989). These two models substantially differ in their assumptions of how feedback between levels of encoding operates, and in their views of how the speech production process takes place.

From an interactionist perspective, Dell (1986) believes that encoding occurs by way of activation spreading from node to node between levels of encoding. Activation is the driving force behind the production process, and the various levels of encoding interact with one another passing on feedback in two directions: from higher to lower levels of encoding (feedforward), and from lower to higher levels of encoding (feedback). In contrast, Levelt (1989) maintains that processing is strictly modular and no feedback between levels occurs. Due to this inflexibility with respect to the flow of information, models of this kind are sometimes called feedforward models, in that they only allow input to be passed on to the level of encoding that is next in line.

Dell's (1986) model is based on the principle of spreading activation, which is a retrieval mechanism by which speakers are able to select the relevant information during the entire speech production process, from message conceptualization to the articulation of speech. If we take picture naming as an example, spreading activation would work as follows. In order to name a picture (e.g. strawberry), the speaker needs to access the relevant conceptual representation for strawberry. While the speaker is in the process of accessing this conceptual representation, other semantically-related conceptual representations become activated as well (e.g. banana, kiwi or blueberry) resulting in multiple representations being activated at the same time. Each activated conceptual representation spreads activation to the relevant lexical node, and the activated lexical node spreads activation to the corresponding phonological segments which in turn lead to the phonetic realization of the target word into speech.

The presumed activation of multiple representations entails the existence of a selection mechanism that allows the speaker to choose only the intended representation, or the speakers would inevitably produce mixed speech containing target and non-target words. This selection mechanism is believed to be dependent upon the level of activation raised for each lexical node. Specifically, Dell (1986) explains that spreading activation involves three core components – spreading, summation and decay. He describes the role of these components as follows:

> when a node has an activation level greater than zero, it sends some proportion of its activation level to all nodes connected to it (spreading). This proportion is not necessarily the same for each connection. When the activation that is sent out reaches its destination node, it adds to that node's current activation level (summation). For the sake of simplicity I assume no thresholds, saturation points, or other nonlinearities in the spreading process. It is necessary, however, to include a passive decay of activation over time to keep levels down. Specifically activation is assumed to decay exponentially toward zero. (Dell, 1986: 287)

On the basis of these assumptions, Dell (1986) proposes that activation spreads from node to node between three different levels of encoding – the syntactic, morphological and phonological levels. At each of these levels, encoding occurs by way of production rules which generate frames with slots, and each slot is filled with a specific unit, which can be a word (syntactic level), a morpheme (morpheme level) or a phoneme (phonological level). A node is selected when its activation level is higher than that of other nodes, and once a node is activated, activation spreads to the nodes at the lower levels of encoding. This process continues until all the information necessary to produce the intended output has been encoded (see also Dell *et al.*, 1993)

In contrast with Dell's views is the second model of monolingual speech production proposed by Levelt (1989). Levelt maintains that a verbal message is processed in four separate stages. The initial conceptualization occurs during the first stage, called message generation. The second and the third stage, respectively called grammatical encoding and phonological encoding, are concerned with selecting semantic, syntactic, morphological and phonological information. The fourth and last stage, articulation, is where the message is realized into overt speech.

Levelt (1989) believes that each of these stages is completed in three distinct processing components: the conceptualiser, the formulator and the articulator (see Figure 4.1). Central to the model is the idea that processing in each component is incremental and parallel. It is incremental because each component starts working as soon as input is received, so the output

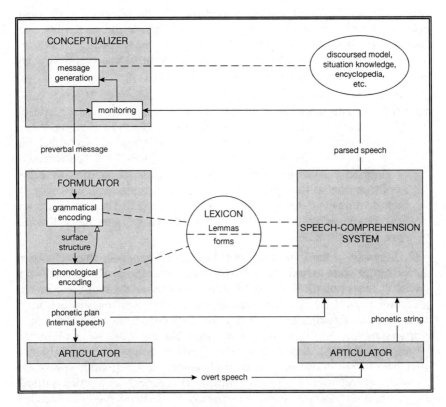

**Figure 4.1** Levelt's speech production model (Levelt, 1989)

of one component becomes the input of the next component, and it is parallel because each component is processing speech independently of what other components are processing at the same time.

*Conceptualizer*: Message generation occurs in the first processing component, the conceptualizer, where the speaker has access to a wide range of information via a knowledge store which is believed to contain the discourse model as well as situational and encyclopedic knowledge. The message generated at this point is called preverbal because, as the label indicates, it is still non-linguistic. Levelt believes this preverbal message is elaborated in two different stages, which he calls macro-planning and micro-planning. What the speaker intends to say, i.e. the communicative intention, is initially specified at the macro-planning stage, and then a set of information is assigned during micro-planning. The information assigned at this second stage is not used immediately within this first component, but will be used in the next processing component, the formulator, where it will be matched with the information already attached to the entries in the lexicon.

*Formulator*: When the preverbal message is ready, it is passed on to the next component, the formulator, where it is converted into meaning. The conversion occurs by activating semantic, syntactic, morphological and phonological information contained in the lexicon, a process which involves the retrieval of information at the lemma and the lexeme levels. Semantic and syntactic information is specified at the lemma level while phonological and morphological information is specified at the lexeme level. Lemma activation is argued to be the first to occur.

*Articulator*: When the output of the formulator (phonetic plan) is ready, it is passed on to the articulator where it is converted into overt speech. Here the phonetic plan (internal speech) is further checked via the speech-comprehension system so that any errors can be detected and rectified before overt speech is produced.

## Bilingual and Multilingual Speech Production

The psycholinguistic process that underlies the production of speech in multilinguals is perhaps one of the least studied areas of inquiry in the field of multilingualism. As anticipated at the beginning of the chapter, all models of multilingual speech production are essentially extended or revised versions of models of bilingual speech production. In actual fact, it is more accurate to say there are no models specifically formulated to account for multilingual speech production, there are only models of bilingual speech production which are argued to account for multilingual production as well.

The practice of using a model devised for one type of speaker (the bilingual) to account for another type of speaker (the multilingual) does not come without its problems. First, models of bilingual and multilingual speech production must be able to account for different amounts of knowledge in the mind. Multilinguals clearly have more knowledge that can be selected during the speaking process, and this additional knowledge is likely to generate an increase in the type and amount of crosslinguistic associations and interactions that take place in the mind. Since current multilingual speech production models do not systematically acknowledge the distinction between bilingual and multilingual speakers, they do not attempt to account for this presumed additional activity and, more broadly, for the presence of additional knowledge in the mind. Second, the almost exclusive focus on bilinguals leads to proposals which seem feasible for bilinguals but turn out to be unfeasible, or at least of difficult application, for multilinguals. We will see some of these proposals later on in the chapter. Third, accepting that models of bilingual speech production can predict how multilinguals also produce speech perpetuate the practice of developing theory by relying on empirical evidence from bilingual rather than multilingual speakers. As a result, phenomena specific to multilingualism continues not to be properly examined and accounted for.

Models of speech production generally seek to provide a step-by-step explanation as to how linguistic knowledge is used. To describe the speaking process, a model must be able to satisfy two core requirements: (1) it must be able to specify how the production system works; and (2) it must be able to define what knowledge speakers possess (Bock, 1995). Most models of speech production focus on the first requirement and therefore predict the path of production from conception to articulation. The second requirement is instead far more difficult to satisfy because of the individual variation of non-native knowledge in the mind.

Any model of multilingual speech production must meet the general condition of comparability, i.e. it must explain how the speech of any multilingual speaker is produced, regardless of differences in the proficiency levels attained in the various languages. In order to meet this condition and bypass the variability problem, researchers widely adopt the working assumption that all knowledge in the mind is native-like or, with respect to non-native knowledge, an incomplete version of it (see discussions in Poulisse, 1997; Poulisse and Bongaerts, 1994; Poulisse, 1999; Green, 1986; Wei, 2003a, 2003b). This implies that non-native speech is viewed as an imperfect product at all times (because it is incomplete), and instances of borrowing or crosslinguistic influence are errors that result from a production system not functioning properly, or from lack of knowledge in the target language.

The assumption that all knowledge is native-like is a useful stance that allows researchers to identify and control what knowledge speakers possess and therefore satisfy the second of Bock's (1995) requirements. Following the rationale of this assumption, an infinite number of languages can be added to the mind, and the need to define their content is by implication effectively bypassed. Moreover, the assumption is useful to avoid dealing with issues of individual variation and changes in proficiency over time. From a language acquisition perspective, however, there is one essential problem with this assumption. It conflicts with the widely held view that a non-native language is a language with its own internal coherence governed by its own internal rules, hence not an incomplete or defective product in any way.

If we accept the hypothesis that non-native knowledge is incomplete, it would be counterintuitive to presume that two different speakers would have the same incomplete knowledge in their mind and end up producing the same item. Let us clarify with an example. De Angelis (2005b) comments on the production of a non-existent Italian word – *abbastante* – which is a combination of an Italian prefix (ab-), a Spanish or Italian stem (-basta-) and a Spanish suffix (-ante). The Italian target word in question was *abbastanza* (enough). The incorrect word *abbastante* was produced by two different speakers of different language backgrounds. One was a French-Canadian L1 speaker with prior knowledge of Spanish and English; the other was an English L1 speaker with prior knowledge of Spanish. Since the word *abbastante* does not exist in the Italian target language, one would have to wonder whether it is truly feasible that two different speakers, with different language backgrounds, might produce the same non-existent word by accessing the same wrong lemmas during the production process. While such coincidences may be possible, one can also explore the possibility that linguistic knowledge belonging to different languages is associated and organized according to features of similarity which ease the path of lexical retrieval in production.

When these two multilingual speakers first stored the components of the Italian target word *abbastanza*, what kind of associations did they establish between the morphological and phonological components of this word and the linguistic knowledge that was already in their mind? Did these associations in any way facilitate the selection and retrieval of the same non-target elements during the production process? We already know the mind to be equipped with the capability of comparing incoming input with existing knowledge and establishing associations based on the formal characteristics of the input. How does this process work when someone has knowledge of several languages in the mind? Research on speech production has hardly focused on how multilinguals may store, select and retrieve linguistic information. There are, however, some theoretical frameworks that seem promising, for instance those that utilize the principle of activation to explain the production process.

The concept of activation has already been mentioned in relation to Dell's (1986) model of monolingual speech production. I now return to this concept as it is also widely employed in models of multilingual speech production. In linguistics, activation describes a process by which an entire language – or some elements of it – are stimulated and accessed during the execution of a receptive or productive task. Activation can then assume a very general meaning, as in the activation of an entire language, or a very specific meaning, as in the activation of a lemma or a morphosyntactic node. Harley (1995: 23) says that activation 'can be thought of as a property like heat', which spreads and expands from node to node within the confine of a neural network.

The idea of activation is mostly associated with connectionism or parallel-distributed processing, even though the notion was used in the literature well before connectionist approaches came into existence (Mitchell and Myles, 1998; Singleton, 1999). The connectionist approach is based on the assumption that the mind or brain processes linguistic information through a complex network of interconnected nodes. Parallel-distributed processing more specifically refers to the claim that information is processed in parallel at different levels. According to connectionism, the mind creates links or connections between information nodes, and the creation of new links when new input is received implies that the network becomes progressively larger and more complex. Links can, however, become progressively weaker if they are not activated with some frequency. Mitchell and Myles (1998) explain that from this perspective, learning is viewed as a process by which links are either strengthened through activation, or weakened by lack of activation. The development as well as the maintenance of the network is thus dependent upon the repeated activation of the associative links.

The arguments connectionists put forward reflect the belief that learning processes must be uncovered from within the brain structure itself. Mitchell and Myles (1998: 84) point out that one of the distinctive features of connectionism lies precisely in its attempt to establish a link between language, neurology and neurobiology. The authors also express some words of caution about relying on connectionist approaches to explain L2 learning. They maintain that connectionism is too far removed from real

L2 learning situations to be able to offer adequate explanations because it is too reliant on controlled laboratory research and mostly use artificial data.

Dijkstra and van Hell (2003) also comment on the meaning of activation with reference to how the notion is used to refer to an entire language. They specifically ask what the word 'active' means, and argue that if we say that a language is active, we also imply that the words of that language are active without being used. The observation is insightful but also reflects a word recognition perspective, whereby activation entails that frequency or recency of use determine the word's level of activation and therefore the possibility that the information is selected and retrieved. The models we will see in this chapter do not adhere to the same premise and utilize the notion of activation in a much broader sense.

One further issue of concern relates to the sources of data bilingual and multilingual speech production models are based upon. Bilingual speech production models are empirically based on evidence from healthy bilingual individuals or from aphasic patients. With respect to the latter, evidence is mostly about patterns of language recovery following injury and the subsequent ability or inability to perform certain tasks such as speaking, translating or comprehending speech in the two languages. Bilingual speech production models additionally make use of evidence of code-switching, borrowing or crosslinguistic influence. With respect to multilinguals, since there are only a handful of studies that specifically examine theories of (bilingual) speech production with multilingual subjects, it is difficult to assess how the multilingual production system may work and whether the various proposals advanced are accurate and feasible. Evidence from bilinguals is usually assumed to be representative of multilingual behaviour as well, even though there is no clear evidence that the assumption is warranted. De Bot (2002: 288) points out that a 'model should be able to explain not just the typical but also the atypical, which is often most revealing.' This seems particularly true with regards to multilinguals who may well be producing a sentence mixing three or four languages at a time. While these instances cannot be truly classified as being 'unusual', they form combinations that bilingual production models do not consider and, consequently, do not explain.

In the following sections, I shall focus the discussion on three major models of multilingual speech production (de Bot, 1992; Green, 1986; Grosjean, 1992). These models address issues related to the architecture of the production system, for instance how many separate levels of processing can be distinguished, and issues related to how information is passed on between the various levels of representation.

## Green (1986)

Focusing on issues of control, activation and resources, Green (1986) proposed a speaking model which, he argues, can accommodate the speech production of healthy as well as brain-damaged individuals. Green makes a point of including evidence from brain-damaged patients in his discussions, as he believes this type of evidence shows more than any other type that languages can be selectively impaired and selectively recovered. For instance, he discusses the case of 48-year-old French nun who spoke fluent French and Arabic before suffering a moped accident. After the injury, the nun displayed very peculiar language recovery patterns. She shifted from being able to speak French or Arabic, to not being able to speak these languages at all – a pattern of recovery known as 'alternate antagonism'. These languages did not appear and disappear in their entirety. One day she could not speak French, but could speak Arabic and name objects in Arabic; the following day she could speak French but could no longer speak fluent Arabic. At the same time, the nun was also showing evidence of a phenomenon known as 'paradoxical translation'. On the day she could speak fluent Arabic, she could translate from Arabic into French, even though she could not produce spontaneous speech in French, but on the day she could speak French but had poor Arabic, she could translate from French into Arabic, but not from Arabic into French. Phenomena of alternate antagonism and paradoxical translation are taken to be evidence of functional separation of these languages. Green (1986) also takes into account the work of Albert and Obler (1978) who wrote one of the most comprehensive reports on recovery patterns in bilingual and polyglot aphasic patients to date. Albert and Obler offer additional evidence of separation with regard to the comprehension and the production system. Specifically, Green refers to the the case of a brain-damaged individual who could either understand speech but not produce it, or could produce it with extreme difficulty.

Green (1986) introduces all these cases with a theoretical argument in mind. He believes the ways aphasic patients behave essentially indicate an underlying problem associated with the control of 'intact language systems' (Green, 1986: 210). He believes languages cannot be lost following injury, they simply become less accessible during the production or comprehension process. The two key words of Green's claim are 'control' and 'intact systems'. If evidence from aphasic patients reflects poor control of an intact system, as he maintains, it follows that the errors found in the speech of healthy individuals also result from a lack of control of an intact system. Green, in fact, defines as errors blends such as 'strying', a mixture of 'trying' and 'striving', or words such as 'springling', a blend of English *spring* and German *Frühling*. But are these truly errors?

Green's model is constructed around the notion of intact systems and any deviation from the norm is viewed as an error and a failure to exercise control over the system. He does not define what an intact system is, but from what he writes we can infer an intact system is a system which contains native-like knowledge. As discussed earlier in the chapter, assuming that language knowledge is native-like is a common (and convenient) approach in bilingual speech production which allows one to predict the path of production without having to define the type of knowledge that is in the mind. A trilingual would simply have three intact (native-like) systems, a quadrilingual four intact systems and so forth. From this perspective, any language in the mind is an intact system, so any system can be essentially added bypassing the need to define its content. It is from these premises that Green extends his model to multilingual speakers.

In order to explain how control is executed, Greens' (1986) combines the notion of activation with that of inhibition, proposing that activation and inhibition operate concurrently during the production process. The selection of a target item takes place by the activation of the item itself and the simultaneous inhibition of all its competitors. Inhibition occurs by raising the activation level of all potential competitors, which reduces the possibility that the incorrect item will be selected in place of the target one.

The speaker controls the activation and inhibition process by using a certain amount of resources, which are constantly replenished by a 'resource generator'. Resources are argued to be the fuel or energy of the production system, but since only a limited amount of resources can be used at any given time, there are situations in which the speaker will not have sufficient resources to control the system, for instance when the speaker is tired or distracted. Second language learners in particular need a lot of energy to control the system because their L2 system is not as automatized as the L1 system. When the speaker does not have sufficient resources to use, the type of errors described earlier (strying, and springling) can arise in production.

A proposal based on the use of a certain amount of resources to control the speech output is problematic for multilinguals, as the hypothesized increase in number of languages entails the use of supplementary control and therefore of additional resources. Green solves the problem by stating that there is a limit to the number of languages that can be activated at any one time, hence by implication the need for supplementary control is automatically reduced.

With respect to how a speaker effectively controls multiple languages in the mind, Green (1986) proposes that languages can be activated to various degrees and are always in one of the following three states. They can be 'selected, (and hence controlling speech output), active, (i.e., playing a role in ongoing processing), and dormant, (i.e., residing in long-term memory but exerting non effects on ongoing processing).' (Green 1986: 215). Frequency of use determines whether a language is in an active or a dormant state. The languages used more frequently can remain active in the background during online processing and the parallel activity that occurs can result in some form of influence on the target language. Languages which are not used for a long time are instead in a dormant state and do not influence ongoing processing directly. Speakers also select the language they want to speak by way of 'tags', which are attached to words, structures, or even registers within one language. Since a person can switch from speaking to translating, Green also postulates the existence of a 'specifier', whose function is precisely to specify the type of control needed in order to execute a given task.

Green's proposal is useful to explain the interaction between more than two languages in a general sense, but the proposal is also based on assumptions that raise a number of concerns. A first concern already outlined is that the model is based on the notion of intact systems, and this notion introduces a clear monolingual bias in research that several scholars have already argued against (see Chapter 1). Second, the argument that languages become active or dormant depending on frequency of use can be partly questioned as there is evidence in the literature that crosslinguistic influence can also occur from languages a speaker has not used for a long time (see Chapter 2). Besides frequency or recency of use, crosslinguistic influence is also known to be influenced by a long list of other factors, for example proficiency, L2 status or typology, and these are not taken into account in a clear way. Finally, the question of how many parallel plans a multilingual speaker can formulate at any one time remains far from settled. While it is proposed that there may be a limit as to the number of languages that can be activated at any one time, Green does not define what these limits may be or how they would operate. In a later article, Green (1998a; 1998b) talks about the role of activation and inhibition further. He does not, however, substantially elaborate on the issues of direct relevance to multilingual speech production just mentioned.

A study that uses Green (1998a, b) as a main framework of discussion is Festman (2004), who applies Green's inhibitory control model to trilingual processing arguing that proficiency in the target language can affect the lexical retrieval process and the ability to inhibit potential competitors. To test the hypothesis, Festman gave a production task to ten trilinguals (German, English and French) and found that processing difficulties varied according to proficiency in the target language. She accordingly claimed that speakers can execute better control in the stronger languages, while in the case of weaker languages more cases of interference are likely to arise.

## De Bot (1992)

De Bot (1992) proposed a model of bilingual and multilingual speech production based on Levelt (1989). The model accounts for the speech of healthy individuals and is not specifically concerned with language disorders, language learning processes or language skills other than speaking.

De Bot justifies the initial adaptation (from a monolingual to a bilingual version) by emphasizing that Levelt's model (1989) is based on 'several decades of psycholinguistic research and is based on a wealth of empirical data, obtained through experimental research and the observation of speech errors' (de Bot 1992: 2). Accordingly, he maintains that the bilingual version of the model only needs some minor modifications to work effectively. De Bot, however, also extends his model to multilingual speakers, which means that he effectively accounts for multilingual speech production using a framework empirically based on monolingual data. In spite of the huge leap, de Bot's (1992) model remains one of the most comprehensive and detailed proposals available to us today.

Trying to understand and predict multilinguals' speech processes by relying on what we know about bilingualism is not always the most productive approach, as this stance inevitably holds us back in the identification of principles and constraints that may govern the mind's operations. For instance, let us consider a speaker of ten languages. We know that our hypothetical speaker has a lot more information stored in the mind than a bilingual person, and that this knowledge is stored, selected and retrieved at the various levels of conceptualization, formulation and articulation. All this additional knowledge the bilingual does not have is likely to be managed according to principles which bilinguals may never need to use and rely upon during the production process simply because they have a lesser amount of information to deal with. I will return to illustrate this point later in this section when discussing de Bot's position on the number of speech plans a speaker can generate during the production process.

De Bot (1992) believes a model of bilingual production should satisfy five conditions: (1) it should be able to account for the speakers' ability to use languages separately or mix them during speech, as is the case with code-switching; (2) it should be able to account for instances of crosslinguistic influence; (3) it should not be concerned with the speed of production as the use of several languages should not slow down the entire production process; (4) it should be able to account for the different levels of proficiency of the bilinguals' languages; and (5) it 'should be able to cope with a potentially unlimited number of languages, and must be able to represent interactions between these different languages' (de Bot 1992: 6). In order to satisfy these requirements, de Bot proposes the following changes to Levelt's (1989) original model.

*Conceptualizer*: Levelt (1989) assumes the activities of the conceptualizer to be language-specific while De Bot believes that only the microplanning stage is language-specific. De Bot's rationale is born out of two considerations: Levelt's discussion on registers, and the knowledge of how concepts are lexicalized in different languages. With respect to Levelt's discussions on registers, Levelt proposes that information on language registers are added to the preverbal message in the conceptualizer, as it is at this stage that the speaker has access to this type of information through the knowledge store. De Bot agrees with this principle and extends it to the bilingual version. De Bot additionally takes into consideration the difference in the way concepts are lexicalized in different languages and argues that language-specific information must necessarily be added to the preverbal message in the conceptualizer. He gives the example of spatial reference in Spanish and English. In Spanish, special reference is expressed as being proximal, median and distal (aquí/ahí/allí) whereas in English only two options are available, i.e. the proximal and distal distinction (here/there). Since this difference entails that the preverbal message must contain some information which allows the speaker to make the distinction early on in the process, decisions must be made during the microplanning phase, when the speaker has access to information such as discourse model, situational knowledge and so forth. The macroplanning stage is argued to be too basic to be language specific as at this stage it is only the communicative intention/goal that is specified, and bilingual speakers do not yet have sufficient information to allow them to specify which language they are going to speak.

From a feedback perspective, one interesting point de Bot raises relates to the ability of non-balanced bilinguals to predict potential lexical problems during the production process. Let us imagine a speaker who needs to express the concept of 'castle' but does not have the lexical information that corresponds to this concept. In the absence of the necessary knowledge, the speaker may resort to paraphrasing or may decide to use other strategies to solve the communication difficulty. De Bot (1992) does not provide a solution for this problem, but he points out that bilinguals must already know at the conceptual level that a word cannot be realized later on in the production process. This observation, however, raises the additional question of how this can be achieved within an incremental process which does not allow a lower level of processing to pass feedback on to a higher level.

*Formulator*: De Bot (1992) initially proposes two scenarios. The first proposes the existence of one common lexicon for both languages where information is distinguished through a labelling system. The second proposes there are entirely separate formulators and lexicons for each of the speakers' languages. De Bot then goes on to offer a solution somewhat in the middle of these two extremes, i.e. that some elements of the two languages are stored together and some others are stored separately, depending on factors such as linguistic distance and proficiency level. This, he maintains, 'places languages along a continuum based on formal characteristics such as the number of cognates in languages or sets of shared syntactic characteristics' (de Bot 1992: 9). In accordance with Green's (1986) proposal that two languages can be processed in parallel to one another until they reach the articulatory stage, de Bot (1992) then proceeds to argue that the formulator has different processing components for each language which produce different speech plans, one for each language. The two speech plans can account for some of the differences that exist between different languages, for instance agglutinative languages such as Turkish and Finnish, and an inflectional language like English. Agglutinative languages have morphological characteristics which increase lexical productivity and form words by combining morphemes together. The encoding process necessary to form speech in these languages is by necessity different from the encoding process for inflectional languages. With respect to the organization of the mental lexicon, de Bot (1992) adopts Paradis's (1987) Subset Hypothesis and argues for the existence of one large lexicon which contains language-specific subsets that can be activated independently.

Since de Bot (1992) specifically claims that one of the requirements of a bilingual production model is that it should be able to account for an unlimited number of languages, one has to wonder how many parallel speech plans a multilingual will actually be able to produce, or be constrained to produce, during the speaking process. If we imagine our hypothetical speaker of ten languages again, the options would be that ten speech plans are produced, or that only two or three speech plans are produced. Since the first seems too illogical to be feasible, we can only assume the second to be possible. This last possibility, however, entails the presence of a mechanism that allows the speaker to select some language-specific speech plans but not others, and also entails the existence of some principles that guide the speaker to select the relevant speech plans. De Bot's does not postulate the existence of such a mechanism hence does not elaborate on these issues.

A proposal that partly deals with this hypothesized mechanism is discussed in Williams and Hammarberg (1998). In line with de Bot (1992), the authors also believe that more than one speech plan can be produced, and attempt to identify the factors that may guide the selection process. They believe one of the speaker's languages is selected as a main supplier of information during production. This language is selected through a competition process that involves four conditioning factors: linguistic distance and proficiency, which de Bot (1992) also mentions, and recency of use and L2 status. The language that scores the highest on these four factors in relation to the target language is the language that is most likely to be assigned the function of main supplier during production.

Poulisse and Bongaerts (1994) further note that de Bot's (1992) two speech plans proposal is in contradiction with the statement that the preverbal message contains language-specific information. If language-specific information is specified in the preverbal message, why would a speaker need to produce two speech plans? Poulisse and Bongaerts offer an alternative proposal, which they believe is more economical and efficient. The proposal entails that the language membership information added to the preverbal message is attached in the form of a language feature. This feature is subsequently used to find the lemmas tagged for language in the mental lexicon. The process is illustrated in more detail in the section on language choice in this chapter.

*Articulator*: The idea of separate formulators for each language is abandoned at the phonological encoding stage. Levelt (1989) believes that speakers store a large number of syllables and articulatory patterns, and that the units of speech planning are syllables rather than sounds. The phonetic plan is argued to consist of strings of such syllables. De Bot (1992) proposes that bilinguals have a common store for the syllables of both languages, and patterns are stored only once if they are identical in the two languages, or individually if no matching pattern is present. The idea that syllables belonging to different languages are all grouped in a common store raises some questions with respect to the language selection mechanisms involved for storage and retrieval. De Bot's suggestion entails the existence of a mechanism that allows L2 patterns or norms to be added to the existing ones already in the syllable store. In order to add the information, or not add it if already present, some language-specific labelling mechanism must necessarily be in place or the learner would not be able to match incoming information with the syllables and their articulatory patterns already in the mind. Once stored, the information must also be retrieved and learners would need to distinguish what information applies to which language by way of some language-specific mechanism. There is also the added question of why the articulator would receive a language-specific plan from the formulator, and then match it with information that is presumably not labelled for language.

De Bot explains that speakers have all sounds and patterns in the mind, but he is quite unclear as to how these sounds are distinguished during the production process. He believes learners start off by applying L1 norms to L2 sounds until their proficiency in the second language allows them to become independent of the L1, and argues that this mechanism explains the widely attested phenomena of phonological crosslinguistic influence from an L1 to an L2. De Bot does not go on to explain what would happen when more than two languages are in the mind. On the whole, his proposal seems logical when information from two languages is concerned, but the same explanation seems far less able to account for phonological influence from non-native languages, for instance, or cases of combined CLI. If we hypothesize that learners start off with all the knowledge they have, that is L1 and the non-native norms, then it is hard to explain how a multilingual can be influenced by only some of the information contained in the common store, for instance the L2, and not the L1, if the information at this level is not language-specific.

### Grosjean (1992)

Grosjean (1992, 1997, 1998, 2001, 2004) proposes that the speech of bilinguals (and multilinguals) is regulated by different modes in which the speaker can be set during speaking. He explains his Language Mode Hypothesis and the factors that influence the speech output as follows:

> A mode is a state of activation of the bilinguals' languages and language processing mechanisms. This state is controlled by such variables as who the bilingual is speaking or listening to, the situation, the topic, the purpose of the interaction, and so on. At one end of the continuum, bilinguals are in a totally monolingual language mode in that they are interacting only with (or listening to) monolinguals of one – or the other – of the languages they know. One language is active and the other is

deactivated. At the other end of the continuum, bilinguals find themselves in a bilingual language mode in that they are communicating
with (or listening to) bilinguals who share their two (or more) languages
and where language mixing may take place (i.e. code-switching and
borrowing). In this case, both languages are active but the one that is
used as the main language of processing (the base of the matrix
language) is more active than the other. These are end points, and
bilinguals also find themselves at intermediary points depending on
the factors mentioned above. (Grosjean 1998: 136)

In support of this proposal, Grosjean (2001) mentions evidence from
studies conducted with healthy adults or children and aphasic patients.

With respect to multilingualism, Grosjean (2001) claims that the language
mode hypothesis can be applied to speakers of several languages as well,
as languages can be activated to varying degrees during the speaking
process and influence the target language output. The hypothesis has not
been widely tested with multilinguals and its validity remains to be
empirically assessed. There are, however, a few studies which offer some
useful feedback in this regard.

One of these studies was conducted by Cenoz (2003b). The author
examined the speech production of 18 children of Spanish (L1), Basque (L2)
and English (L3). All these children were learners of English as a non-native
language and were enrolled in a Basque-speaking school. Most importantly
for the present discussion, all children were aware of interacting with an
interlocutor who could speak both Basque and Spanish. According to
Grosjean, the awareness of the interlocutor's bilingualism should have set
these children in a bilingual mode from the start. Cenoz (2003b) indeed
found that both Spanish and Basque were relied upon in production, but
rather differently, however, depending on learners' communicative needs.
Spanish was mostly used for what Cenoz called 'transfer lapses', which
include borrowings, words morphologically or phonologically adapted to
the target language, and any other form that did not carry any noticeable
hesitation or marked intonation. Basque was instead mostly used to ask
for help when children did not know a word they wanted to use. Cenoz
(2003b) traced 19% of the transfer lapses to Basque, and 78.6% to Spanish.
In contrast, Basque was identified as the main source language for
interactional strategies in 89% of the cases, while Spanish was used only
2.6% of the time. With respect to Grosjean's model, these results indicate a
clear difference in learners' reliance on Basque or Spanish which depends
on pragmatic function rather than the external factors Grosjean postulates,
i.e. the interlocutors' knowledge of Spanish and Basque. Assuming that

both Basque and Spanish were activated in the background during production, we should not find a major difference in the way these languages were used. One could argue that the language mode hypothesis accounts for interactional strategies only, but Grosjean's (1992) proposal specifically includes instances of borrowings and morphologically or phonologically adapted words as well (Grosjean, 1992: 59), a claim which the results reported in Cenoz (2003b) do not seem to support.

Grosjean (1992) briefly touches upon crosslinguistic influence in his writing, saying that some of the evidence in the literature could be explained by the presence of a bilingual interlocutor. He specifically states that 'what might appear to be an interference could also be a guest element or structure produced by the speaker who is aware that his or her interlocutor can understand mixed language' (Grosjean, 2001: 14). This and other statements Grosjean makes suggest that he is referring to overt influences of crosslinguistic influence rather than to the range of possible manifestations of CLI. As Jarvis has pointed out, CLI is often understood as a 'you-know-it-when-you-see-it phenomenon' (Jarvis, 2000: 246), while transfer can also be covert (Schachter, 1974) and sometimes 'does not involve the outright transfer of elements at all' (Weinreich 1953: 7). As we have seen in the previous chapter, there are strong constraints on what information can and cannot be transferred from one language to another, and the external factors Grosjean has proposed can perhaps account for some isolated instances of transfer, but not for most of the evidence that has been gathered in the field to date.

To my knowledge, only two studies (Dewaele, 2001; Dijkstra and van Hell, 2003) specifically tested the language mode hypothesis with multilingual speakers. Dewaele (2001) tested whether multilingual learners of French are closer to the monolingual or the bilingual end of the language mode continuum when interviewed in formal and informal situations. With a series of t-tests, he measured the proportion of mixed utterances in the French L2 or L3 speech of Dutch L1 speakers with prior knowledge of English as an L2 or as an L3. In terms of frequency of occurrence, he found morpholexical errors to be produced more frequently by those with French as an L3, regardless of the formality of the situation. Upon analysing the data further, he however found a significant difference (t = 3.773, df = 24, p < 0.001) in the proportion of mixed utterances in the informal (Mean = 9%, S.D. = 8.8) and in the formal situation (Mean = 3%, S.D. = 3.9). With respect to the language mode hypothesis, Dewaele argues that his results provide further support for Grosjean's (1992) proposal as they indicate the effect of the situation on the speech output. Speakers interviewed in an informal situation are closer to the bilingual end of the language mode continuum, while those interviewed in a formal situation monitor their speech more carefully and are closer to the monolingual end of the continuum.

Dewaele (2001) also proceeds to explain the process that underlies speakers' selections in production. He argues that when speakers are in a monolingual mode, the selection of non-target linguistic forms is the least preferred option, but when speakers are in a bilingual mode the opposite occurs, that is the speaker is more likely to choose to code-switch and therefore include non-target forms into speech. But how does this occur? Dewaele proposes that speakers make use of a set of production rules during speaking, which are hierarchically organized. Whenever 'the production rule at the top produces no satisfactory result, the speaker will opt for an alternative one lower in the hierarchy and repeat this if necessary' (Dewaele 2001: 85) This process, he argues, entails that 'the difference between the multilingual and monolingual modes would [. . .] be the explicit interdiction in the latter case to select a lemma with the wrong language-tag' (ibid.).

The second study that specifically focused on the language mode hypothesis was conducted by Dijkstra and van Hell (2003). The authors tested the language mode hypothesis with trilingual subjects of Dutch L1, English L2 and French L3. To ensure that no participants would be set in a bilingual mode throughout the experiment, the authors did not notify participants that the study intended to examine their foreign language knowledge. The objective was to show that a language can be activated in the background even if the speaker is intentionally set in a monolingual mode. To this end, the authors examined whether participants set in a monolingual mode would process cognate words differently from non-cognate words, as evidence of parallel activation would indicate that languages are activated in parallel regardless of mode. They indeed found that cognate words activate parallel linguistic information in other languages even if the speaker is intentionally set in a monolingual mode. They argued that the finding does not provide support for Grosjean's language mode hypothesis and in fact suggests that the 'multilingual's processing system is strongly non-selective with respect to language' (Dijkstra and van Hell, 2003). It must be noted, however, that Grosjean (1992) partly accounts for this type of evidence in his writing, saying that a speaker in a monolingual mode can still have some 'residual activation' in the background as 'bilinguals rarely deactivate the other language totally' (Grosjean, 1992: 59).

Clearly, the language mode hypothesis still needs to be examined more systematically with multilingual speakers. The evidence we have to date is too sparse for us to be able to draw firm conclusions on the effectiveness of Grosjean's proposal and the extent to which it can help us explain multilingual production phenomena. The line of research seems nonetheless promising and worth pursuing further.

## Language Choice

How do multilinguals select and retrieve language-specific information during the production process? And when do they commit to speaking one of their languages?

Language-specific information is widely believed to be retrieved by way of language tags, which are labels attached to each entry in the lexicon that specify language membership information. Given the important role of tags in the production process, it is somewhat surprising that the tags' properties, roles and functions are hardly ever a topic of debate in the literature. Very little is in fact known about the way tags operate or even come into existence.

Several scholars use the notion of language tags to explain how the intended language is selected during the speech production process, or how the selection of the wrong tag can lead to errors in production. Green (1986), for instance, believes that language tags are used to activate or deactivate the speaker's languages at any one time. Poulisse and Bongaerts (1994) believe that language choice initially occurs at the conceptualization stage, and therefore that language-specific information is first attached to the preverbal message. As Figure 4.2 illustrates, the information specified at the conceptualization stage defines semantic features (+human, +male, –adult) as well as language membership (+English). All this information is used to activate the lemma that corresponds to the specified meaning and the specified language. Sometimes errors can occur, and these errors can concern semantic features or language membership. For example, when all the features of the target word are selected, with the exception of one, the error is likely to be semantically related. If instead the error involves a substitution from another language, it is the information on language membership that is matched incorrectly at the lemma level.

Poulisse and Bongaerts believe in the existence of a large multilingual lexical network. This position by necessity entails that language tags must be part of the network or the speaker would be unable to identify what information belongs to which language during the speech production process. From these premises, Poulisse and Bongaerts (1994) propose that L2 lexical items contain the specification [+L2] and that lemma selection occurs by way of activation spreading to the relevant node. They explain

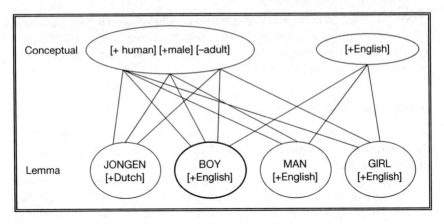

**Figure 4.2** The selection of an L2 lemma through spreading activation

that the specification [+L2] allows learners to establish a distinction between the lexical items of two different languages because, as a result of the tag guiding the process, the 'L2 lexical items [. . .] receive more activation than the corresponding L1 lexical item' (Poulisse and Bongaerts 1994: 42). Poulisse and Bongaerts (1994) additionally argue in favour of de Bot's (1992) suggestion that sounds and articulatory patterns are contained in one single store. They believe that this would explain why a bilingual can pronounce Dutch words such as *stuk* (piece) and *rok* (skirt) using English phonemes (Poulisse, 1999) instead of Dutch phonemes.

De Bot and Schreuder (1993) also believe that language information is specified at the conceptualization stage, but suggest that language membership is not associated with tags but with cues of different strength values. They argue that this solution can explain a range of phenomena, including why immigrants that often switch from one language to another produce speech that carries non-target information. Cues may be weak, they say, and therefore easier to ignore during the production process.

Costa (2004) also maintains that the language in which the message is going to be produced is specified in the preverbal message. He argues that this is the only possible explanation because it is at this stage that the speaker has access to language-sensitive information such as the context of the conversation, who the interlocutor is, the topic of discussion and so forth. This position entails that language choice occurs at the conceptualization level before any lexical access activity is initiated.

With respect to accessing the correct language-specific item later on in the production process, Costa (2004) presents two possible scenarios. The first would have activation spread from the conceptual to the lexical system, activating only the words of the target language; the second would have activation spread from the conceptual to the lexical system, activating words in both languages. This second option, which Costa indicates as the most likely as it finds empirical support in the speech production literature, in turn raises the question of how the correct target words are selected, and the extent to which the activation of non-target information will affect the overall selection process.

Costa (2004) explains that two main proposals can be distinguished in this regard. The first predicts that the non-target words will be suppressed via a mechanism of inhibition (Green, 1986, 1998a, b). The second, which the author defends in his own work (Costa and Caramazza 1999; Costa *et al.* 2000), 'assumes the existence of a suppression mechanism that considers only the level of activation of the lexical nodes belonging to the response language, neglecting the activation of the words belonging to the non-response language' (Costa, 2004: 207). In brief, these two proposals essentially view lexical access as either occurring by inhibiting potential competitors in the lexical system, or by neglecting the potential competitors altogether. What seems logical to assume is that in order to carry out the process just described some language-specific marker must necessarily be attached to the relevant information in the lexicon. The question of how language choice occurs remains nonetheless open.

Li (1998) explicitly questions the role and even the existence of language tags, but he seems to be a fairly isolated voice in this regard. He points out that if tags indeed guide the production process, they are likely to play a central role in the production process. There is, however:

> overwhelming empirical evidence for the existence of both priming and interference effects in a variety of inter-lingual experimental tasks. Thus it is difficult to see that the language tags can play a significant role in differentiating the two lexicons, or that language tags can be easily identified, or that even there are language tags. (Li, 1998: 93)

One other question can be raised in relation to the properties of language tags over time, as some evidence in the literature indicates that language membership information is not as stable as may be assumed. De Angelis (2005b) discusses several instances of CLI where learners do not seem to be aware of producing non-target words in their speech. For example, a French-Canadian learner of Italian with prior knowledge of Spanish introduced the Spanish word 'mesa' (English: table) in her Italian speech in place of the Italian target word 'tavolo'. De Angelis argues that researchers would normally classify this instance as a form of borrowing necessary in order to compensate for lack of knowledge in the target language, but that this may not be a form of borrowing for the learner. Further testing showed that the learner believed the word 'mesa' to be an Italian word, and not a Spanish one, which means that from her point of view there was nothing that needed compensating as the word was already an entry in her Italian lexicon. With respect to the retrieval process, we can then ask how this specific word was retrieved if the (original) language tag was supposedly Spanish.

De Angelis (2005b) believes a word can be initially stored as belonging to one language, and can then be later associated with another language. She labels this phenomenon 'system shift', which defines a shift in lexical knowledge from a source to a guest system. She points out that, while it is reasonable that language membership information is used at some point during the production process, we do not know how language tags are attached to the entries in the lexicon during the acquisition process, if tags can weaken or change over time, or if language dominance and proficiency can affect their status.

De Angelis (2005b) further discusses the issue presenting the case of an English L1 learner of Spanish with prior knowledge of Italian. The speaker claimed to be familiar with words such as *dinero* (Spanish) and *soldi* (Italian), both meaning 'money' in English, but to be unable to say which word belonged to which language. A similar case is reported in Bardel and Lindqvist (2006). One of their participants provided the following: 'I think that I mix up Spanish and Italian sometimes, become unsure whether a word is Spanish although I think it is Italian [. . .] When I said *ahora* I was really unsure whether it was Italian or Spanish.'

With reference to the first example – but the comment applies to the Bardel and Lindqvist example as well – De Angelis notes that:

> if language tags or cues are essential features of the selection process and are added to the preverbal message, one has to wonder what language tag or cue may have been added to this speaker's preverbal message since he seems to be able to fully retrieve both words without being fully aware of language membership. (De Angelis, 2005b: 13)

She then proposes that language tags or cues may have different strength values at different stages of the acquisition process, and strengths may vary depending on changes in language proficiency over time.

This takes us to the next chapter on the multilingual lexicon, which examines what is now known about the way information is stored, associated, organized and retrieved in the multilingual mind.

# Chapter 5
## *The Multilingual Lexicon*

In the previous chapter I reviewed existing models of multilingual speech production focusing on how multilinguals produce overt speech in one language and at the same time control the additional knowledge that is also in the mind. Discussions focused on the various stages of processing and the selection and retrieval mechanisms that guide the overall production process. In this chapter the focus is shifted to the multilingual lexicon and what we know about the way multilinguals organize, store and associate linguistic knowledge in the mind.

As was the case with models on multilingual speech production, models of lexical representation that specifically focus on the multilingual lexicon and its processing operations are mostly extended versions of models of bilingual lexical representation. As noted in the previous chapter, adaptations of this kind generate advantages as well as disadvantages. On the one hand, hypotheses of bilingual lexical representation are based on a wealth of empirical data and therefore provide a firm base on which theoretical extensions can be made. On the other, a sound empirical base about the bilingual lexicon cannot adequately inform hypotheses about multilingual lexical organization as questions of direct relevance to multilingualism have not been specifically addressed. In this chapter we will see that only a few studies have addressed questions of direct relevance to multilingualism, and all of these are based on previous research on bilingual memory and bilingual lexical representation. Some review of research on bilingualism is therefore essential to understand the type of questions which have been raised about the multilingual lexicon over time.

The chapter is organized in five sections. The first provides an overview of research on bilingual and multilingual memory and discusses some implications and areas of future research of relevance to multilingualism. The second examines research on the relationship between proficiency level and lexico-semantic organization. The third introduces issues associated with storage capacity and the amount of information that is held in the mind. The fourth examines the evidence available in support of the separation or the integration hypotheses. The fifth and last section discusses the notion of activation and its role in language processing.

## From Bilingual to Multilingual Memory

Bilingual memory research has been mostly concerned with defining how the bilinguals' languages are stored in the mind and the relationship between the lexicon of the first and the second language (for a review, see Heredia and Brown, 2004). This section examines the major developments in bilingual memory research that most influenced work on multilingualism lexical organization, beginning with Weinreich's (1953) influential proposal on bilingualism.

Based on the Saussurian distinction between the signifier and the signified, which refer to the concept and the expression of a word respectively, Weinreich (1953) proposed that the relationship between the bilinguals' languages can vary according to how word meanings and word expressions are linked to each other. The bilinguals' languages can establish a coordinate, compound or subordinate relationship with one another. In coordinate bilingualism, signified and signifier are kept separate so two expressions are linked to two separate concepts. In compound bilingualism, two expressions are merged and linked to a single concept. In subordinate bilingualism one language is subordinate to the other, which results in one language being dominant over the other. The expression of the less dominant language is linked to its corresponding concept via the most dominant language, which is usually the bilinguals' first language. According to Weinreich (1953), these types of associations are not to be regarded as mutually exclusive since different types of bilingualism may coexist within an individual. Some words may form a compound relation with one other, while others may establish a coordinate or subordinate relationship.

While Weinreich's (1953) proposal is specifically concerned with bilingualism, traces of the coordinate, compound and subordinate distinction can be found in most of the proposals about bilingualism and multilingualism that followed. In fact, Weinreich's distinction is the antecedent to what later models called lexical and conceptual levels of representation (Kroll, 1993; Kroll and Sholl, 1992; Kroll and Stewart, 1994) and to the word association, concept mediation and intermediate hypotheses (Potter *et al.*, 1984).

Singleton (2003) notes how Weinreich (1953) did not provide any information about the type of relationship that languages already in the mind may come to establish with languages that are acquired at a later stage. He considers the hypothetical case of a co-ordinate bilingual learning a third language and asks: If the new language initially develops a subordinate relationship with one of the existing languages, which language would it be subordinate to? He then outlines the following two possibilities. The first is that the closest languages develop a coordinate relationship with one another, and the second that the lexicon of the new language develops variable interconnections of different strengths with the existing lexicons, which is the position Singleton seems to favour.

Later in this section I will discuss how recent research on bilingual memory has indeed come to highlight that the interconnections between the words of two languages may vary in degrees of strength. Before moving on to examine these studies in more detail, I would like to briefly outline some of the major developments in bilingual memory research, as these developments are fundamental to understanding the frameworks now used in more recent work on the multilingual lexicon.

During the early stages of bilingual memory research, scholars were largely concerned with issues of lexical storage, mostly in relation to whether linguistic information of two different languages is stored in a single memory store (interdependence hypothesis), or in separate memory stores for each language (independence hypothesis). The issue of language storage was initially investigated by way of experimental paradigms that involved word association, word recognition and recall tasks. These research techniques were later argued to cause inaccurate and contradictory findings, and were replaced with experimental paradigms which involved more reliable techniques such as, for instance, reaction times experiments (French and Jacquet, 2004).

By the mid-1980s, the data on bilingual memory storage had already begun to appear rather mixed as researchers had been finding evidence in support of language specific memory stores (e.g. Scarborough *et al.*, 1984) as well as single memory stores (e.g. Mägiste, 1979). Mixed results are usually suggestive that both of the hypotheses examined are to some extent correct, which is the conclusion that scholars in the field eventually reached. Several questions helped researchers reach this intermediate position, starting from how concepts and lexical forms are associated in the mind during the language acquisition process, to whether the associations developed in early acquisition may change over time as proficiency in the second language develops.

Based on the assumption that concepts and lexical forms have distinct representations in the mind, as Weinreich (1953) had suggested, three main hypotheses were explored. The first, known as the word association hypothesis, predicted that the words of a first and a second language are associated by way of a direct connection with each other. The second, known as the concept mediation hypothesis, predicted that the words of the second language are associated to the words of the first language by way of a common conceptual store. The third, known as the developmental or intermediate hypothesis, hypothesizes a shift from word association to concept mediation as fluency in the second language develops. Within this third hypothesis, word association is believed to be the type of association typically established in early acquisition which gradually evolves into concept mediation as proficiency in the second language progressively develops (see also review in Kroll, 1993).

The word association and the concept mediation hypotheses were initially proposed by Potter *et al.* (1984), even though Weinreich's (1953) work was clearly the primary inspiration of this proposal. The word association and the concept mediation hypotheses predicted different reaction times for the completion of picture naming and translation tasks as picture naming requires access to the conceptual store, while translating requires access to the conceptual store only in the case in which the concept mediation hypothesis were correct. Similar reaction times in the two tasks would indicate that the conceptual store was accessed during the execution of these tasks, while longer reaction times in picture naming would provide evidence in support of the word association hypothesis. On the basis of these assumptions, Potter *et al.* (1984) asked the participants in their study to complete picture naming and translation tasks and compared the reaction times obtained for both tasks. Results provided clear support for the concept mediation hypothesis, and were also argued to support a hierarchical structure of representation for form and meaning, where word forms are represented independently in each language and word meanings are represented in a single conceptual system. In other words, both word association and concept mediation were argued to be partly accurate hypotheses, the former for word forms, and the latter for word meanings.

Later studies then asked whether subjects at different proficiency levels in the second language also display a conceptually mediated structural organization. Chen and Leung (1989) and Kroll and Curley (1988), for instance, compared the performance of subjects at different proficiency levels and indeed showed that changes in proficiency level affect lexical organization, as the developmental or intermediate hypothesis would predict.

Evidence that proficiency level affects lexical organization in bilingual memory allows us to raise a number of questions about the multilingual lexicon as well. Frequency of use is widely acknowledged to affect proficiency level in a non-native language, and when individuals are familiar with several languages, only some of these languages are likely to be used on a daily basis. As is well known, lack of use can cause a rapid decrease in proficiency level, but the level reached can also be maintained or even increased if the language is studied further or kept active. What is the effect of these 'fluctuating' proficiency levels over multilingual lexical organization? To what extent do changes in proficiency level affect multilingual lexical organization? And what changes in terms of structural organization can feasibly be predicted for multilingual speakers who have used their languages variably over time? Some of these questions are partly addressed in a study with multilingual subjects (de Groot and Hoecks, 1995) reviewed later on in this section.

Returning to the distinction between lexical and conceptual representation, a clear attempt to deal with the hypothesized shift is the revised hierarchical model that Kroll and Stewart (1994) have proposed. A shift from lexical to conceptual representation entails that the L2 words, which are initially linked to L1 words via lexical links, develop direct conceptual links. The original lexical links, however, do not disappear in their entirety, and continue to influence how the L1 and L2 remain connected, and the presence of these former lexical links causes the connection between the L1 and L2 to be stronger than the connection between the L2 and the L1. This is the hypothesis that Kroll and Stewart have tested in a study involving three separate experiments. The study used a variety of tasks and materials, from picture naming and bilingual translations, to randomized and semantically categorized word lists. The overall objective of this study was to compare the speed of translation in two opposite directions: from the L1 to the L2, and from the L2 to the L1. As predicted, translating from the L1 and into the L1 was found not to occur at equal speed. More specifically it was found that translating from the L1 into the L2 is much faster than translating from the L2 into the L1. On the basis of these results, the authors argued that the interconnections between the two languages do not seem to be equally strong, and also that translating from the L1 into the L2 is conceptually mediated while from the L2 into the L1 is lexically meditated (see also Sholl *et al.*, 1995). The revised hierarchical model they proposed was aimed to account for these observed asymmetries (see Figure 5.1) (see also Dufour and Kroll, 1995; Kroll, 1993).

To my knowledge, Kroll and Stewart's (1994) model has not been specifically extended to multilingual speakers. Given what we know about

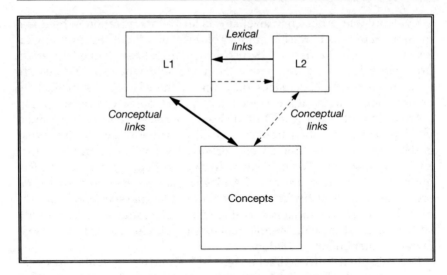

**Figure 5.1** Revised hierarchical model of lexical and conceptual representation in bilingual memory

multilingualism today, one can easily foresee the potential to test this model with multilingual speakers. For instance, if translating from the L1 into the L2 is conceptually mediated while translating from the L2 into the L1 is lexically mediated, would translating from an L2 into L3 be lexically mediated as well? And would the type of mediation change as proficiency in the non-native languages increase or decrease over time? How would speed of translation be affected by factors such as typological closeness and language similarity, which are already known to ease the path of crosslinguistic influence between non-native languages? As an example we consider the hypothetical case of a trilingual speaker with German as mother tongue and Spanish and Italian as non-native languages. One could formulate the hypothesis that, by virtue of the similarity between the two Romance languages, translating from and to the non-native languages may be faster than translating from and to the native and a non-native language. I clearly cannot provide any informed answers without empirical data at hand; this is just an example meant to illustrate how the complex make-up of multilinguals' linguistic backgrounds may provide some valuable input about the dynamic interplay that govern the interactions between the lexicons of several different languages.

## Proficiency and Lexico-semantic Organization

De Groot (1993) proposed a developmental perspective based on the distinction between abstract and concrete words, which were argued to develop connections of different strengths in the bilingual lexicon. The underlying assumption is that concrete words across languages share a common node in memory while abstract words have language-specific conceptual representations (see also Van Hell and de Groot, 1998). The hypothesis was extended to multilinguals and tested with two sets of unbalanced trilinguals (Dutch-English-French). De Groot and Hoecks (1995) hypothesized that the lexical structure between the native language (Dutch) and a weak foreign language (French) would be of a word association type, while the lexical structure between the native language and a strong foreign language (English) would be of a concept mediation type.

De Groot and Hoecks (1995) conducted two separate experiments with two types of translation tasks which they called 'translation production' and 'translation recognition'. In the translation production task, participants were asked to translate 40 Dutch words, 20 concrete and 20 abstract, into both of their foreign languages (French and English). In the translation recognition task, participants were given 80 word pairs, i.e. the Dutch word and its equivalent translation either in French or in English, and were asked to judge whether the words given were correct or incorrect translations. With respect to the concrete and abstract distinction mentioned earlier, the study predicted that if the organisation of the participants' languages was of a concept-mediation type, results would show a difference in the translation of concrete and abstract words into both languages, a prediction which was indeed confirmed. A concreteness effect was identified with respect to the translation from the L1 to the strongest non-native language, which indicated an underlying concept mediation structural organization as predicted. In contrast, no concreteness effect was identified in the translation from the L1 to the weakest non-native language, which was argued to reflect a word association type of structure. Since similar conclusions were also reached with the data from the translation recognition task, the authors generally argued that the results of their study indicate a clear association between non-native language proficiency and lexico-semantic organization. The authors, nonetheless, emphasize that the concept mediation and word association structures can sometimes coexist within the same individual, a remark which reminds us of Weinreich's (1953) claim that different types of bilingualism can coexist within the same person. Clearly, a lexical structure does not change overnight but does so progressively over time. De Groot and Hoecks note that:

one should not construe these processes of learning and forgetting as the actual replacement of one type of memory by another, but as the strengthening and weakening of connections between memory units. Links that are not used for some time become dormant, to be revived again under the appropriate circumstances. (1995: 717–718)

De Groot and Hoecks (1995) also believe that frequency of use can affect lexical organization in the opposite direction. They note that while their participants had studied French for six years, they had not used the language for months prior to being tested, and this period of time may have been sufficient to cause a reversal from a concept mediation to a word association type of structure in their lexicons. The question was therefore raised of whether it is at all possible that an individual's lexical organisation can revert to a word association type of structure once the language is unused for some time. The authors consider a number of studies which provide evidence in favour of a concept-mediated lexical structure after a short period of instruction and argue that the participants to these studies were probably using, or had recently used, the second language at the time they were being tested. In contrast, the authors' participants did not show a concept-mediated type of structure because, as mentioned, had not used French for several months.

To go over the main points of these views on proficiency and lexical organization, proficiency in the non-native language seems to determine lexico-semantic organization in at least two ways. First, words in the second language seem to develop a word association type of structure in early acquisition, which turns into a concept mediation structure as proficiency in the second language develops. Since the word association structure refers to associations between words of the first and the second language, one has to raise the additional question of what type of connection may link the words of a second and a third language, or a third and a fifth language. The word association hypothesis does not specifically contemplate the existence of a direct connection between non-native languages. Second, when proficiency in a non-native language decreases, a concept mediation structure may revert to a word association structure which is more typical of early acquisition.

Abunuwara (1992) looked more closely at the relationship between a second and a third language, asking whether there is any difference in the relationship between the native language and a weak or strong foreign language, and between two non-native languages. With a within-subject design, Abunuwara measured interference effects among Arabic L1 speakers with Hebrew and English as second and third languages. A

Trilingual Stroop colour-naming test, a trilingual picture-naming task and a translation task were used. The relationship between the two non-native languages was found to be independent, the relationship between the Arabic L1 and the weakest non-native language was found to be interdependent, and the relationship between the Arabic L1 and the strongest non-native language was found to be intermediate. These results then highlight once again a proficiency-related effect, which provides further support for the hypothesis that multilinguals' lexical organisation can change over time, and that language proficiency is a key factor in generating such change.

A further question is whether the relationship between two or more non-native languages can also change over time. To the best of my knowledge, no studies have examined this question so far. Technically, the relationship between non-native languages could (1) maintain an independent relationship; (2) develop an intermediate relationship over time as proficiency in one or in both non-native languages grows; (3) ultimately develop an interdependent relationship; or (4) develop different types of relations in different linguistic subsystems. From a crosslinguistic influence perspective, we have little understanding of how lexico-semantic organization may be related to the ease or difficulty of selecting non-target lexical information during the production process. It seems logical to assume that the stronger the association between memory stores, the higher the chance of non-native lexical influence to occur as its path may be consequently eased. However, if lexico-semantic organisation between non-native languages is indeed found to develop into an interdependent relation, this will raise the question as to why a stronger connection between memory stores does not ease the path of non-native language influence. On the basis of our current knowledge, interlanguage proficiency seems to be negatively correlated with non-native language influence, a phenomenon which seems counterintuitive when viewed within a lexico-semantic organisation framework.

## Storage Capacity and Processing Load

Two other questions of relevance to multilingualism relate to whether an increase in processing load can worsen an individual's performance in the target language, and whether a large amount of linguistic information stored in the mind can slow down production or comprehension processes to a significant extent. Festman (2004) examined the first question with 17 trilingual subjects (German, English and French) who were asked to name pictures in the three languages in two different conditions – single language and mixed blocks. She measured the speed and accuracy of retrieval in each language in both conditions and found that the frequent switching of languages in the mixed blocks condition affected speakers' control in several ways: lexical retrieval was slowed down, the error rate increased and performance was less accurate.

With regard to the second question, several researchers have discussed the possible relationship between storage capacity and comprehension or production processes. Mägiste (1979) raised the issue of quantity of storage in relation to possible interference effects, arguing that 'the greater the amount of verbal storage that an individual has for a given concept, the greater will be the interference provided that the stored verbal material is actively used by the individual' (Mägiste 1979: 87). Tulving and Colotla (1970) instead associate the storage of language tags (language membership) with slower production processes. They argue that psychology research has already shown that the act of remembering additional information during a recall task reduces someone's ability to recall information. An individual who is asked to remember additional information such as language membership is therefore more likely to be slowed down by the additional information to be remembered.

A more recent study (Schönpflug, 2003) provides some support for these early claims, in that the amount of information stored in the mind seems to affect an individual's ability to complete word fragment tasks. The author hypothesized that speakers with a high level of competence in a non-native language would display later uniqueness point in the completion of word fragment tasks than those with a lower level of competence. Uniqueness point refers to the number of letters that an individual needs to see in order to identify a target word. For instance, in order to identify the word 'banana', one may need to see 'ba' or 'ban' or 'bana' and so forth. According to decision theory, later uniqueness point occurs because a large number of alternatives slow down the decision-making process. This hypothesis was tested with 21 Polish L1 speakers with knowledge of German as an L2 and English as an L3. Results supported the hypothesis formulated showing that those with a higher level of competence require more information to complete a word fragment than those with a lower level of competence.

One factor which does not seem to affect uniqueness points (Schönpflug, 2003) but that nonetheless seems to affect performance on other types of tasks is passive or active knowledge of a non-native language. Mägiste (1984, 1986) compared the performance of Swedish monolingual students (N = 67,162) in English grammar, word comprehension, reading and listening, with the performance of Finnish-Swedish bilingual immigrant students (N = 2,376). Initial results did not identify any major difference between bilinguals' and monolinguals' performance. When, however,

Mägiste subdivided the informants into two different groups – those who used Swedish at home and had only passive knowledge of their first language, and those who actively used their first language at home – some clear differences were identified. Bilinguals with passive knowledge of the Finnish L1 were found to perform significantly better than Swedish monolingual students, but bilinguals who actively used the L1 were found not to perform significantly better than monolinguals. On the basis of these results, Mägiste (1984, 1986) then argued that passive bilingualism facilitates third language learning while active bilingualism slows down the acquisition process. With reference to storage capacity, these results also seem to provide additional support to the idea that linguistic information must be actively used in order to affect production processes in some meaningful ways.

## Separation or Integration of Knowledge in the Multilingual Lexicon

In the previous sections I discussed the issue of storage by focusing on the relationship between words in different languages. I examined the distinction between the representation of form and meaning in the mind, and how word forms and word meaning are believed to be connected to each other across languages at a single point in time. In this section I consider the issue of storage more broadly, focusing on the separation/integration debate, which relates to the degree to which linguistic knowledge is integrated into a single lexicon, or separated into two or more lexicons in the mind.

An integrated lexicon is a lexicon which contains linguistic information from all the languages known to the speaker. Information from additional languages is assumed to be added to the existing entries so the lexicon grows in size as new information is added. In this large integrated lexicon, the speaker is able to discriminate between languages by way of language tags or nodes that hold information on language membership, and the use of language tags vary depending on whether the speaker is engaged in production or comprehension processes. The opposing view holds that speakers have several discrete separate lexicons for each of their languages. Since linguistic information is already assumed to be divided according to language membership, language tags are not believed to have such a central function in guiding the comprehension or production process.

The studies reviewed in this section will show that researchers have found evidence of separation as well as integration, and therefore that a rigid either-or position cannot adequately explain the structure of the multilingual lexicon. Singleton (2003) notes that most of the scholars who support the integration position do so on the basis of evidence of strong cross-lexical connectivity between languages rather than evidence of complete integration. Likewise, one generally finds that separation is not typically discussed in terms of an either-or distinction, as may have been the case in the early literature on bilingualism.

Recent proposals seem to point to separation of functions rather than to the complete separation of information in the mind. Paradis (1997) for instance, argues in favour of modularity and claims that while languages are neurofunctionally independent they are not anatomically separate. In an article on the previous 20 years of research in cognitive neuropsychology, Caramazza and Coltheart review the evidence from brain damaged patients and conclude that 'it is because cognitive systems are composed of relatively autonomous processing components that "local" brain damage can result in dissociation of functions' (Caramazza and Coltheart, 2006: 7, inverted commas in the original). As we shall see, brain damage is included among the most important form of evidence of separation that we have today.

The separation/integration debate has been traditionally associated with the bilingual lexicon and it is only in recent years that the debate was extended to the multilingual lexicon as well. From a purely multilingual perspective, if we wish to understand how the multilingual lexicon is organized and we want to isolate its various functions, it is crucial that we are able to examine research carried out with multilinguals. At present the empirical evidence with multilingual speakers is scarce, and the few studies that are indeed available hardly ever go beyond trilingualism. We therefore have very little information on an entire range of properties of the multilingual lexicon. Part of the problem is that multilinguals are too often conceived as bilinguals with additional languages rather than as speakers of several languages. As pointed out in the discussion on the bilingual bias in multilingualism research (see Chapter 1), the way we conceptualize multilinguals can greatly influence the questions we ask and the explanations we offer.

In Chapter 1 I introduced the case of Harold Williams, the multilingual speaker who allegedly spoke 58 languages in his life. I would like to return to reconsider this case from a separation/integration perspective as I believe it can help us see how important and helpful it is to conceive multilinguals as speakers of several languages in their own right. Let us first consider the separation position, which predicts that speakers have several discrete separate lexicons for each of their languages. The proposal seems perfectly logical for a bilingual or a trilingual person, and we can easily imagine the existence of two or three separate lexicons or two or three sets of language-specific lexica in the mind. The total separation position does not however seem a feasible proposal for Harold Williams' lexicon, as it seems improbable that 58 separate lexicons would coexist in a single mind. Moreover, if some of these languages were agglutinative languages like Turkish, with a large number of languages the number of possible morphological combinations in memory would be simply immense. If we think of the amount of knowledge that must be stored, it seems more reasonable to presume that the mind is equipped with some sort of mechanism that allows the speaker not to duplicate linguistic information in memory. From an integration perspective, on the other hand, Harold Williams would have such a large lexicon in his mind that we have to ask whether language tags alone would be able to separate information efficiently and at the speed with which speech is decoded and encoded in healthy individuals. Also, it does not seem reasonable and economical that a word in one language should be searched in a lexicon containing information belong to 57 other languages.

As anticipated, a review of the evidence of separation and integration for the multilingual lexicon shows that we do not have unambiguous data in favour of either position. We have some evidence in favour of integration and some evidence in favour of separation, and mixed evidence is suggestive that both hypotheses are to some extent correct and therefore that the lexicon may be partly integrated and partly separated. But let us examine the evidence more closely.

The evidence in support of the separation hypothesis is quite abundant in the literature, starting from the wealth of data on selected recovery patterns in aphasic patients. Albert and Obler (1978) completed an extensive review of the recovery patterns of bilingual and multilingual aphasic patients and discussed the case of several individuals who recovered their languages selectively following neurological damage. The fact that languages can be recovered selectively generally indicates that they are not 'held' or organized in an integrated fashion, or neurological damage would lead to the loss of all the languages previously spoken, or maybe to the loss of a specific language function for all the languages known to the speaker. Instead, multilingual aphasic patients seem to be able to recover some languages but not others in a selective manner.

Paradis (1997) argues in favour of neurophysiological modularity, whereby a module is conceived as being an internal structure which can either feed another module, or function in parallel to another module. The module itself is autonomous and independent and this accounts for evidence of selective impairment. He maintains that:

> this does not imply that the language systems are neuroanatomically
> separated, at least not at the gross anatomical level, but the well-
> documented double dissociations between the languages of polyglot
> aphasics can be interpreted as evidence that each language is
> represented as an independent neurofunctional system. (Paradis
> 1997: 332)

He further argues that the same would apply to monolinguals who manage
several sociolinguistic registers.

A fascinating part of Albert and Obler's (1978) review relates to the
comparison they make between the recovery patterns of bilingual and
multilingual aphasic patients. They comment on some essential differences
between the two speaker groups. Polyglot aphasic patients, for instance,
seem to display regression and nonparallel recovery patterns more
frequently than their bilingual counterpart, whereby regression defines the
process by which one language improves as another one deteriorates, and
nonparallel recovery refers to the selective recovery of previously spoken
languages. The authors also note that multilinguals are more likely to follow
Pitre's rule than Ribot's rule. Pitre's rule predicts that the language used
more frequently prior to the injury will be the first to be recovered, while
Ribot's rule predicts that the language which was acquired first is the first
one that will be recovered.

Perhaps even more revealing is the clinical evidence of separation from
invasive brain procedures. Some patients were asked to name objects while
undergoing electrical stimulation of the cortex and the stimulation of
different cortical areas led to different types of interferences (for a review
of these studies, see Zatorre, 1989). In some cases, the stimulation of
one area interfered with the ability to name in both languages, while in
other cases the stimulation of another area interfered with the ability to
name in only one of the patient's languages. This second instance is clearly
suggestive that the bilinguals' languages are not organized in the same
manner. Moreover, second languages were found to be represented more
widely within the brain than the native language, which further supports
the idea of separation or at least of a different organization.

In the literature there are also discussions of healthy multilinguals who
experienced some temporary comprehension difficulties when expecting to
hear speech in a different language (see Singleton, 2003). Comprehension
appears to be blocked by the speaker's expectation, a phenomenon which
would suggest that we can tune in to one specific language while simultaneously blocking all other languages in the mind.

Singleton (1999) also discusses the process by which an individual identifies the morphological structure of unfamiliar words. Multilinguals identify the morphological structure of an unfamiliar word by referring to the phonological elements of familiar words and using the information to analogyze. He gives the example of the French word *brocanteur* (second-hand art dealer). A speaker who encounters the word and does not know what it means, identifies *-eur* (/œR/) as an end morpheme by referring to other French words which have the same morpheme, such as *vendeur* (salesman) or *serveur* (waiter). Singleton argues that since a syllable like *-eur* /œR/ is only possible in some languages but not others, the speaker must conduct a search within a language-specific lexicon rather than a unified one. A similar position is taken by Ecke (2001) in his work on TOT (tip-of-the-tongue) states with multilingual learners of German. He found that the L3, the target language itself, was the most frequent source of lexical influence for the learners he examined. This concerned the associations made in TOT states (75% of the time) as well as wrong responses (95% of the time). Ecke argues that these result indicate that speakers in TOT states search interlingually first, and an interlingual search necessarily implies the existence of a language-specific lexicon in the mind rather than a unified one that contains information from all languages.

Additional evidence in support of the separation hypothesis comes from research on crosslinguistic influence. Crosslinguistic influence has been shown to occur at all levels, in an overt or covert form (see Odlin, 1989). The manifestation of crosslinguistic influence does not seem to be compatible with the idea of a totally integrated lexicon since the lexicon of one language cannot easily influence the lexicon of another if the two lexicons coexist in an integrated manner. The fact that languages can influence one another so pervasively and as frequently as reported in the literature implies a certain degree of separation between them which allows for the selection of language-specific information during online processing. Singleton (2003) correctly notes that the notion of psychotypology (Kellerman, 1977, 1979, 1983) in particular 'runs counter to the notion of straightforward total integration within the mental lexicon, because, precisely, it implies a degree of selectivity in relation to consultation of the languages represented.' (Singleton, 2003: 169).

Some interesting evidence of deliberate crosslinguistic consultation can be found in Herwig's (2001) work on multilingual lexical processing. She examined the production of four multilingual speakers, one native Norwegian, and three English native speakers, all students of Germanic languages (Dutch, German and Swedish). Two of these students had good knowledge of German, advanced knowledge of Dutch, and basic knowledge of Swedish. The other two students were described as being fluent in two foreign languages, with a good knowledge of the third one. Herwig asked these participants to describe a picture story in their mother tongue and then translate the same story into their respective second languages. A think-aloud procedure was also used during the translation task to identify the path of lexical associations. Among the most interesting results are these associative chains she identifies, which 'reveal that lexical selection in situations of non-accessibility of an item in demand involves both automatic and deliberate consultation of several languages' (Herwig, 2001: 128).

She argues that some of the associative chains indicate activation spreading at the semantic level, as well as crosslinguistic consultation. For instance, one of her subjects (English L1) was trying to translate the English word 'comb' into German and produced the following chain of words in German (G), English (E) and Dutch (D): *komen (G) – brush (E) – bürsten (G) – brush (E) – saubermachen (G) – clean (E) – tidy (E) – opruimen (D). Herwig argues that the semantic environment of the English word 'comb' includes words such as 'brush', 'clean' and 'tidy', and their translations in Dutch and German. Similarly, another subject (English L1) was trying to translate the expression 'he colours' into Dutch and produced the following expressions: to place (E) – stellen (G) – hij stellt (G_D) – place (E) – put (E) – stellen (G) – draw (E) – mark (E) – create (E) – scheppen (E) – hij schept (E_D). As in the previous example, Herwig argues that the words 'to place', 'put', 'mark' and 'create' all belong to the semantic space of 'to colour'.

In the literature we also find evidence in support of the view that the lexicons of two or more languages are represented in an integrated manner. One of the best known supporters of this position is Cook (1991) with his notion of multicompetence. To contrast the notion of monocompetence, Cook coined the term multicompentence to describe 'the compound state of a mind with two grammars' (Cook, 1991: 112). Believing that the mind of an L2 speaker is different from the mind of an L1 speaker, Cook raised a number of questions, including whether the bilingual's languages form two separate systems or only one system. Evidence that 'the two dictionaries are combined or that they depend on a language-neutral system' (Cook 1992: 567), would provide support for the notion of multicompetence he proposed.

Cook's proposal is based on several studies such as Caramazza and Brones (1979), who showed that the reaction times to a word in one language depends on the frequency of cognates in the other language, or Cristoffanini *et al.* (1986), who showed that morphological similarity between two languages affect translation performance. With respect to the processing of interlingual homographs, the work of Beauvillain and Grainger (1987) showed that bilinguals can access meaning in both languages. In addition to this type of evidence, Cook also points out that phenomena like 'codeswitching would be impossible if the languages were not intimately related rather than two compartmentalized systems' (Cook, 1992: 570). All the evidence in support of the multicompetence hypothesis that Cook cites surely shows a strong interrelationship between the lexicons of the bilinguals' languages, but can this be argued to reflect total integration?

Cook himself is critical in this regard, mostly because he does not agree with the way the lexicon is generally conceived. He says that the literature views the lexicon as a list of words to which meaning is attached rather than as lexical entries with 'syntactic and semantic subcategorizion, lexical systems and relationships between words, componential analysis, or prototype theory, and so on' (Cook, 1992: 569). Even though some empirical evidence in support of the notion of multicompetence is available, he argues that the restricted view of what the lexicon is substantially weakens the overall support for the notion he has proposed.

Further evidence in support of the view that the lexicons of two or more languages are represented in an integrated manner comes from word recognition research on selective versus non-selective lexical access. Kroll and Dijkstra (2000) express some words of caution with respect to making categorical association between representation and manner of access. Specifically they state that 'it is not logically necessary to identify selective access with segregated lexical representations and nonselective access with an integrated lexicon; the form of representation and the manner of access can be treated as independent dimension' (Kroll and Dijkstra, 2000: 301). Nonetheless, much of the work reviewed below advances some claims with respect to the relationship between representation and access.

In brief, the selective lexical access view holds that words can be accessed individually within a language-specific lexical network and that the correct language is selected by way of an 'input switch' which guides the selection process (Dijkstra, 2003). The opposing view holds that words from different languages are activated in parallel until a certain point in the selection process, as I will now explain.

Dijkstra (2003) argues that several studies already provide support for the non-selective access position. He mantains that if parallel activation across languages occurs, reaction times (RTs) for interlingual homographs, i.e. words that share the same orthographic form across languages but do not share the same meaning, would be slower than RTs for monolingual items. An example of an interlingual homograph is the word *burro* which means 'donkey' in Spanish, and 'butter' in Italian.

Van Hell and Dijkstra (2002) conducted three experiments with Dutch L1 speakers who had knowledge of English as an L2 and of French as an L3. Subjects were asked to complete a Dutch word association task (Experiment 1) and a lexical decision task (Experiment 2 and Experiment 3). In these experiments, the authors used a list of Dutch words which were either distinctively Dutch, i.e. noncognates with respect to the other two languages, or had a cognate relationship with words in the English L2 or the French L3. In Experiments 1 and 2, the association times for cognate words were found to be slightly shorter than those for noncognates, but only in the case of Dutch-English cognates. Van Hell and Dijkstra (2002) explained this result by saying that the reduced mean association times for cognate words would indicate that cognate words are activated in parallel to one another and therefore that prior knowledge affects lexical processing in the L1 even if the speaker is not aware of it. The difference found, however, only concerned Dutch-English cognates, but not the Dutch-French cognates, and the inconsistency led the authors to investigate further. Grosjean offered a possible answer.

According to the Language Mode Hypothesis, 'if one is interested in such issues as the independence or the interdependence of the bilingual's language systems, selective versus non-selective processing, one versus two lexicons, etc., one should be careful not to activate the other language with the stimuli or the procedure used' (Grosjean, 2001: 15). Through personal communication with one of the authors (see Dijkstra, 2003), Grosjean suggested that Dutch L1 speakers are in a bilingual mode most of the time as English is heard around them on a regular basis. The same cannot however be argued for French, as French is not used or heard in Holland as often as English is, so there is no reason to suspect that a Dutch L1 speaker is often in a bilingual Dutch-French mode.

In order to clarify the issue, Van Hell and Dijkstra (2002) decided to replicate their experiment with more proficient L3 speakers hoping to find a possible proficiency threshold level effect (Experiment 3). In this third experiment, participants were asked to decide as quickly as possible whether a word presented to them on a screen was a correct Dutch word or an incorrect one. Accordingly, they were instructed to press a 'yes' or a 'no' button to record their answers. This time, the mean association times for cognate words were shorter for Dutch and English cognates (489 ms for cognates versus 541 ms for noncognates) and was also shorter for Dutch and French cognates (520 ms for cognates versus 541 ms for noncognates). Van Hell and Dijkstra (2002) then advanced the claim that lexical access seems to be 'profoundly nonselective with respect to language' (2002: 786).

While Van Hell and Dijkstra's (2002) study shows clear evidence of foreign language influence on L1 word recognition, two concerns about the study can be raised. The first relates to how the participants' proficiency level in French was assessed, and the second to how recently the participants to the third experiment had used the French non-native language. With respect to proficiency level, Van Hell and Dijkstra (2002) used a lexical decision task containing 50 words and 40 pseudowords in the three languages. The difficulty of these words cannot be examined as the proficiency test is not included in the article. We know, however, that participants of Experiments 1 and 2 had studied French in secondary school for six years – a period of time which presumably allows a person to learn a fair amount of words. Nonetheless, in the study no significant differences between cognate and noncognate words were found. In Experiment 3, the authors tested 21 Dutch-English-French trilinguals recruited from the Department of French. From this information we infer that these participants were studying French language or literature around the time they were being tested. This raises the possibility that recency of use may have facilitated the activation of French words and therefore that these participants were not in a monolingual mode as Van Hell and Dijkstra claim.

As a major advocate of the non-selective access position, Dijkstra (2003) explains the word recognition process with the Multilingual Interactive Activation (MIA) model (see Figure 5.2). The MIA is a model of multilingual word recognition which assumes the existence of an integrated lexicon as well as parallel access and activation across languages. The MIA model is an extension of the Bilingual Interactive Activation model (BIA) (Dijkstra and Van Heuven, 1998), which in turn is the bilingual version of the Interactive Activation Model (IA) originally proposed by McClelland and Rumelhart (1981) for monolingual word recognition.

In brief, according to the IA model, monolingual visual word recognition occurs at three levels of representation which are hierarchically organized, namely the feature, letter and word levels. The BIA model variant includes a fourth level – called the language level – which contains information about language membership. According to this model, an integrated lexicon contains words from two languages (word level), and the added layer (language node level) contains language tags; the node of the language in use inhibits words of the language not in use by a mechanism of top-down inhibition (Kroll and Dijkstra, 2000). The process of visual word recognition then takes place at four distinct node levels (feature, letter, word and language node levels) and the process of selection occurs by way of activation by which competitors suppress each other out until one item reaches activation threshold. The BIA model then proposes that the lexicon is integrated up to the word level, but it is no longer integrated at the language node level (French and Jacquet, 2004).

The MIA model varies from the bilingual version in that the integrated lexicon contains words from three (or more) languages (see Figure 5.2) at the word level, and the language node level contains the language tags of all the corresponding languages.

As was the case with the bilingual version of the model, selection occurs by way of activation and inhibition of potential competitors. From this perspective, one central question relates to how many neighbouring items can simultaneously compete for selection within the lexicon. Dijkstra (2003) addressed this question by simulating the possible neighbourhood effect whenever a new word is added to the lexicon. According to the calculations he made, the presentation of a Dutch word to a Dutch-English-French trilingual with a lexicon of 2628 words of three to five letters would activate three English neighbours and two French neighbours. The calculations did not include Dutch-English, Dutch-French and French-English interlingual homographs. The numbers obtained, Dijkstra says, are only an estimate as 'the number of neighbours depends on the size of the lexicon used and on the representation of intralingual and interlingual homographs, diacritical markers, and morphologically complex words' (Dijkstra, 2003: 18).

Estimates of this kind give us some indication of the number of neighbours that could potentially receive parallel activation in a trilingual lexicon. When we think of neighbouring effects and multilingualism, however, we must also consider the case of multilinguals with knowledge of more than three languages. As is often the case with proposals about multilingualism, hypotheses that seem perfectly logical for trilinguals or quadrilinguals vacillate when applied to speakers of five or ten languages. Multilinguals with knowledge of 58 languages like Harold Williams (see Chapter 1) are the exception and not the rule, nonetheless a theory of multilingual word recognition must necessarily be able to account for cases like Williams, as well as for speakers of more than three languages in general. We do not have calculations at hand to assess the possible neighbouring effect for an integrated lexicon of 58 languages, but we can only imagine how long it may take for this particular speaker to resolve the competition between activated items, particularly if these items belong to languages typologically close to each other (see also Schönpflug, 2000, 2003).

Dijkstra (2003) discusses briefly the issue of neighbouring density and language distance. He argues that non-L1 words occupy a more distant lexical space in the lexicon and therefore that 'words from more distant languages having the same script will interfere less than words from closely

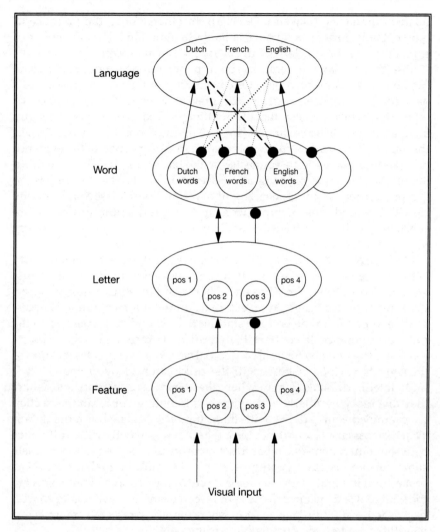

**Figure 5.2** The Trilingual Interactive Activation model. The bold arrows between word and language mode levels reflect strong activation flows during Dutch word input

related languages' (Dijkstra, 2003: 20). In other words, the presence of typologically similar languages is likely to generate a larger number of competitors within the lexicon during the retrieval process.

In sum, the following remarks about the separation/integration debate can be made. As pointed out at the beginning of the section, researchers have found evidence in support of integration as well as in support of separation, which suggests that the multilingual lexicon is likely to be partly integrated and partly separated (see also discussion in Edwards, 1994). In this regard it may be useful to note that a large proportion of the evidence of separation seems to be connected with studies on production, while a lot of the evidence of integration seems to be linked to studies on comprehension. Without meaning to oversimplify the issue and provide clear-cut boundaries, comprehension and production processes are substantially different from one another and may consequently make use of different subprocesses.

While Kroll and Dijkstra (2000) point out that the degree of similarity between the two processes is still a controversial issue in the literature, we can also say that the differences between these processes are clear. Comprehension is triggered by external stimuli and recognition is neces-sarily mapped from the bottom, starting from sound and letters up to the complete utterance. In contrast, the production process takes the opposite route. It is triggered by internal conceptual activity which guides the process through its various stages up to the production of overt speech. It is undoubtedly difficult to map where these processes overlap, and where they diverge, particularly with refence to multilingualism. In this section we examined some studies with multilingual speakers, but more data is clearly necessary to clarify the issue and assess whether the difference between comprehension and production processes may led us to formulate some further useful hypotheses about the multilingual lexicon. The separation/integration debate remains currently unsolved with respect to the bilingual lexicon after decades of research, and it is even more so with respect to the multilingual lexicon, where empirical research amounts to a handful of studies, mostly involving trilinguals.

## Chapter 6
# Prior Language Knowledge, Cognitive Development and the Language Acquisition Process

The primary objective of this chapter will be to discuss the literature on third or additional languages that examines the question of whether the prior knowledge of two or more languages, as well as the learning experience gained in acquiring these languages, have a significant impact on cognitive development and on the language acquisition process.

It is a basic principle of human cognition that learners rely on whatever they perceive as relevant to the task at hand. In a discussion on relevance theory, Wilson and Sperber (2006: 612) explain that 'the human cognitive system has developed in such a way that our perceptual mechanisms tend automatically to pick out potentially relevant stimuli, our memory retrieval mechanisms tend automatically to activate potentially relevant assumptions, and our inferential mechanisms tend spontaneously to process them in the most productive way.' During the language acquisition process, the most relevant piece of information for the learning task is likely to be the knowledge of other languages already in the mind as well as the experience gained in acquiring such knowledge (see also Pennington, 1999; Ringbom, 1986).

Prior language knowledge and prior learning experience were not always regarded in a positive light. If we examine the literature of the past century, we find that scholars maintained very different positions about bilingualism over the course of time, and that trends of thoughts were particularly strong and influential in shaping research directions. A useful chronological dividing can be identified in 1962, when Peal and Lambert published their seminal paper on bilingualism entitled 'The Relation of Bilingualism to Intelligence'. The paper is now known for having set in motion theoretical and methodological changes much needed at that time, and for having marked the beginning of new essential developments in research, as explained in this chapter.

Without meaning to simplify the issue I am about to discuss, it can be said that most of the studies published before the 1960s typically maintain that bilingualism has detrimental effects upon linguistic and cognitive development, while those published during or after the 1960s claim that bilingualism promotes linguistic and cognitive development and positively affects the language acquisition process. These two positions are reviewed here in some detail as research on the relationship between multilingualism and cognitive development inevitably evolved out of decades of discussions on bilingualism and intelligence.

## Prior Language Knowledge: an Obstacle or an Asset? An Historical Overview

The view that bilingualism has detrimental effects on cognitive development is chiefly associated with studies conducted during the first half of the twentieth century, when many scholars held the belief that bilingualism was associated with a number of problems in individuals, ranging from speech disorders to cognitive deficits, mental confusion and even mental retardation.

Hakuta (1986) provides a fascinating account of research on bilingualism and intelligence during this time, in which he explains that researchers did not really doubt whether bilingualism was detrimental to the mind or not, they simply accepted that it was. Researchers' differences were rather linked to their views on the extent to which the language experience could modify the intelligence of an individual. Hereditarians were guided by the assumption that intelligence is innate and cannot be modified by experience, so individuals with low IQ scores were argued to be genetically inferior people. Environmentalists instead believed that having knowledge of more than one language was an impediment to cognitive development, and bilingualism was therefore at the origin of mental problems like mental confusion and mental retardation (Lee, 1996).

These early ideas about bilingualism seem odd, outdated, if not outright ridiculous to us today, but these were the views that prevailed at the time and that influenced educational practices in some meaningful ways. But where did such negative views of bilingualism come from? According to Edwards (2004), one of the possible explanations is that many of these studies were conducted in the United States at a time of great social tension between the flood of incoming immigrants from Europe and the local American population. He points to the intelligence testing movement in particular as an example of how research can be misused and twisted for the purpose of supporting racial discrimination. During the early part of the twentieth century, Americans were dominated by feelings of intolerance towards immigrants, and these feelings created a fertile ground for negative views about bilingualism to find their way into research as well as society without much questioning from those who were in the position to question. The intelligence testing movement was largely driven by political and racial motivations, and instead of testing the actual intelligence of individuals, the movement provided reasons for US officials to restrict the inflow of immigrants to the United States. Deeply flawed and culturally biased tests were devised to test the intelligence of non-native speakers of English, and immigrants inevitably emerged as the least intelligent whenever compared to English monolingual speakers. Immigrants were asked to take these tests in the English language, and this inevitably placed them at a considerable disadvantage (Baker and Jones, 1998).

Edwards (2004) illustrates these extreme views about bilingualism citing several researchers such as Goodenough (1926: 393), for instance, who maintained that 'the use of a foreign language in the home is one of the chief factors in producing mental retardation'. With a touch of irony, Edward explains that opinions of this kind easily found their way into the most respectable scientific journals of the time, and this, I may add, inevitably legitimized them and made them more acceptable within the community.

Similar comments about bilingualism are also reported by Baker and Jones (1998: 63), who write about Professor Laurie's lecture at Cambridge University in 1890. During this event, Professor Laurie candidly stated that 'intellectual growth would not be doubled by being bilingual. On the contrary, intelligence would be halved.' Along the same line are Saer's (1923) statements, who maintained that bilingualism led to lower IQ and to mental confusion in children.

In reading these comments and remarks – and many more are available in the literature – it is inevitable to wonder whether all researchers working during the first half of the twentieth century truly shared these extreme views on bilingualism, or if some of them had milder interpretations in mind but were pressured to conform to mainstream ideas. Whatever their true position may have been, time went by, and the widespread discrimination, coupled with the wealth of negative associations researchers were constantly making, inevitably led to some tangible consequences in educational practices. It didn't take too long for bilingualism to begin to be identified as the source of potential learning difficulties and mental confusion in children, so much that many educators and administrators went to considerable lengths to discourage the use of home languages among pupils, if not to repress the use of home languages altogether (Cantoni, 1997).

The history of immigration as well as the social tensions that character-ized it cannot be summarized in a few paragraphs and a brief overview cannot possibly do justice to the complexity of the issue. While there is little doubt that the overall perception of bilingualism was deeply rooted in existing social tensions and that early negative beliefs had found fertile ground in a society filled with prejudice and intolerance, other reasons may also have helped negative views of bilingualism to flourish. Several researchers have pointed to lack of rigour in research practices, for instance. Studies frequently lacked adequate controls, and it was not uncommon to find subjects of very different socioeconomic backgrounds, or of different proficiency levels, pooled together to form a supposedly homogenous group and compared with monolinguals (Baker and Jones, 1998; Barik and Swain, 1976; Diaz, 1985; Edwards, 2004). As a counterargu-ment, Cummins (1979) cautions us against the entire dismissal of the early studies on pure methodological grounds because some of the negative associations these studies established also emerged in the later research that used more rigorous research practices, such as Tsushima and Hogan (1975), who found bilinguals to have less-developed verbal skills than their monolingual counterparts, and Torrance *et al.* (1970) who found bilinguals' perform-ance on measures of fluency and flexibility to be inferior to those of monolinguals.

The shift from a negative to a positive view of bilingualism did not appear overnight. There was a period from the late 1950s to the early 1960s when the work of several researchers indicated that there were no substantial differences between the IQ scores of monolinguals and those of bilinguals. This period of time, which is usually referred to as the neutral period, had the effect of raising researchers' awareness about the methodological shortcomings of previous research (Baker and Jones, 1998). During this time of transition, Peal and Lambert (1962) published their highly influential paper 'The Relation of Bilingualism to Intelligence'.

According to Hakuta (1986), the criticism that Peal and Lambert offered with regard to subject selection procedures were very valuable in bringing about positive changes in research practices and in fact established 'a criterion for sample selection that became standard for subsequent research' (Hakuta, 1986: 34). Peal and Lambert (1962) provided some clear methodological arguments against the early studies, saying that they frequently used subjects whose socioeconomic status and type of bilingualism had not been properly controlled. Saer (1923), for instance, had reached some very negative conclusions about bilingualism and intelligence, but he had also compared children of low socioecomic status (bilinguals) with children of more privileged backgrounds (monolinguals).

Peal and Lambert's (1962) work was indeed highly influential at the time and is now regarded as one of the classic studies on bilingualism and intelligence. The study itself compared monolingual and balanced bilingual children attending school in Montreal, Canada. Children's cognitive abilities were examined with a series of verbal and non-verbal tasks, and variables such as proficiency level and socioeconomic status were properly controlled. Using 18 measures of intelligence, bilinguals' performance was found to be superior on most counts, and bilinguals were argued to be more flexible in their thinking and better at concept formation than monolinguals. Back in 1962, claims of this kind were uncommon, and in some cases probably unwelcome. Nonetheless, Peal and Lambert (1962) challenged the widespread negative associations between bilingualism and intelligence reaching some very positive results. Moreover, Peal and Lambert were not an isolated voice. Contemporary to their work is Vildomec's (1963) book on multilingualism, for instance, where the beneficial effects of bilingualism are clearly noted, and it is openly argued that 'multilingualism is not as harmful as it would appear to be' (Vildomec, 1963: 202).

Starting from the late 1960s and the early 1970s, most researchers have shared the view that bilingualism fosters cognitive development and facilitates the acquisition of subsequent languages, especially in the case of additive bilingualism (for a review, see Cenoz, 2003a). Some negative association between bilingualism and linguistic development can still be found from time to time, for instance in relation to speech disorders. Bilingualism, however, is no longer viewed as the primary cause of speech disorders as may have been the case in the early studies, but as one of the many variables that can potentially affect speech disorders, together with social status, motivation, intelligence, age and so forth (see Au-Yeung *et al.*, 2000).

In the most recent literature, the dominant belief among scholars is that bilingualism is an advantage rather than a disadvantage for individuals. Recently, bilingualism has been even argued to help our brains remain young and active during the old age (Bialystok, 2004). As we shall see in the remainder of the chapter, evidence in favour of bilingualism being an advantage for individuals is clear and abundant, but a closer look at these studies also shows that only a limited number of questions have been addressed to date. This is particularly true with respect to multilingual speakers who, as is usually the case, have been investigated to a lesser extent than monolinguals and L2 learners.

If knowledge of a second language enhances cognitive development and aids in the acquisition of languages beyond the L2, there are at least three hypotheses about multilingualism that can be formulated. First, it can be hypothesized that the acquisition of languages beyond the L2 may further enhance cognitive development and progressively facilitate the language acquisition process. That is, the more languages an individual is familiar with, the more likely it is that his or her cognitive skills will be enhanced, and that the language acquisition process will increase in speed and efficiency. The alternative hypothesis may be that additional linguistic knowledge does not make any difference at all. Bilinguals and multilinguals are better and more efficient than monolinguals, but are essentially very similar to each other in terms of cognitive development and language acquisition processes. A third hypothesis can be that additional linguistic knowledge may lead to some kind of cost for the other languages the speaker is familiar with.

These hypotheses include two core elements which must be distinguished. One is the effect of prior language knowledge and prior learning experience on the development of cognitive skills, for instance problem-solving abilities or memorization skills. The ability to solve problems or memorize information does not necessarily imply that the acquisition process will be affected, even though it would be a logical consequence. The other relates to the effect of prior language knowledge and prior learning experience on the acquisition process itself, i.e. whether these factors affect the overall development of target language proficiency or the development of some aspect of grammar or the lexicon of the target language.

According to Cook (1997b), researchers' own beliefs and assumptions about language and the human mind shape the way language learning is conceptualized, and therefore what we identify as an advantage or a disadvantage in research. He argues for the existence of two main positions, which he calls the monolingualist and the multilingualist positions.

In brief, monolingualists believe that it is essentially normal for humans to have knowledge of one language and the addition of other languages to the mind can generate a negative or a positive effect. The negative effect would consist in some kind of damage or loss to the individual's linguistic knowledge and to the ability to process information, while the positive effect would entail an enhancement of the individual's knowledge and of his cognitive or processing abilities. Researchers embracing a monolingualist position therefore either search for evidence of deficiency (negative effect), or for evidence of enhancement (positive effect). Evidence of deficiency and enhancement is traditionally measured in terms of speed, i.e. how fast or slow are monolinguals and bilinguals at completing cognitive and processing tasks in their languages. In contrast, multilingualists believe that the norm for humans is to have knowledge of more than one language.

From this perspective they ask whether the 'lack of' additional linguistic knowledge, i.e. of languages beyond the L1, make monolinguals more deficient in their cognitive or processing abilities than their bilingual counterpart. In essence they believe that depriving learners of additional linguistic knowledge will lessen their chances for intellectual growth, and they ask whether those who have knowledge of more than one language display some meaningful advantages in terms of cognitive development. One of the arguments is that individuals with two languages learn to see and perceive the world around them through two linguistic systems. They can encode in two languages, and they can express themselves with two languages, and this is a form of enrichment that monolinguals do not have at their disposal (Malakoff and Hakuta, 1991).

These two positions are outlined here as they can help us understand and place researchers' views and questions in their right perspective.

## Prior Language Knowledge and Foreign Language Achievement

There are two critical questions with regard to the effect of prior language knowledge on cognitive development and the language acquisition process. The first is how proficient in the non-native language one needs to be before bilingualism or multilingualism turns into an asset for the learner. The second is whether the linguistic development reached in one language can be transferred to another language and affect performance in that language. Cummins (1976, 1979) proposed two hypotheses in this regard, known as the Developmental Interdependence hypothesis and the Threshold hypothesis.

The Threshold hypothesis proposes the existence of two different threshold levels of linguistic competence. Learners must reach the first level in order to avoid the cognitive disadvantages associated with bilingualism, and must reach the second level to enjoy the benefits of improved cognitive functioning. The Developmental Interdependence hypothesis instead proposes that learners' linguistic competence in the L2 is partly dependent upon the competence already achieved in the L1, as the skills developed in the first language can be transferred and used in the second language.

In his discussion of the Threshold hypothesis, Cummins (1979) takes into account Lambert's (1975) distinction between additive and subtractive bilingualism, as well as of the concept of semilingualism credited to Hansegard (1968) and Skutnabb-Kangas and Toukomaa (1976). Substractive bilingualism and semilingualism imply that learning a second language has a cost for the other language in the mind. More specifically, subtractive bilingualism means that adding a second language causes some damage or loss to the L1. This would be the case for immigrants, for instance, who use the majority language at school at the expense of their L1, which becomes progressively weaker as a result of the L2 acquisition process. Semilingualism, instead, refers to speakers having weak knowledge of both of their languages. This is the case of children who frequently move from one country to another with their families and do not have sufficient time to develop adequate competence in their first or second language. The term semilingualism, which remains highly controversial in the literature, therefore implies low linguistic development in both of the speaker's languages. Lambert (1975) also discusses the case of additive bilingualism, when learning a second language does not imply any cost to the L1.

Cummins proposed the Developmental Interdependence hypothesis and the Threshold hypothesis to account for the cognitive advantages and disadvantages associated with having knowledge of two languages. Although Cummins did not discuss these two hypotheses in relation to multilingual speakers, others have discussed them in relation to multilinguals. Lasagabaster (2001), for instance, says that if we assume L2 competence to depend upon the competence achieved in the L1, as the Developmental Interdependence hypothesis would predict, then we may consider the possibility that multilingual learners may transfer the skills developed in the L1 or in any other language to another non-native language. In other words, if two languages can have an interdependent relationship with each other, i.e. can influence each other, the same can occur between a second and third language, or a third and a fifth language and so forth. The higher the competence attained in the previous languages, the stronger the likelihood that some influence will occur. The same holds true for the Threshold Hypothesis, perhaps not as much for the existence of the first threshold level, but most certainly for the existence of the second threshold level. When we refer to the second level, the underlying assumption is that proficiency positively correlates with intellectual development. If a certain level of competence must be achieved for learners to cognitively benefit from their bilingualism, then we may consider the possibility that those who have attained a high level of competence in three or more languages may display superior cognitive functioning than those who have not attained a similar competence.

Barik and Swain (1976) tested Cummins' threshold hypothesis in a five-year longitudinal study with children attending regular school programmes and French immersion programmes in Canada. The initial assessment involved establishing the relationship between children's IQ and the type of school programme attended. With this initial analysis the authors did not identify significant differences in terms of children's cognitive abilities. In a second stage of the study, children in the French immersion programme were divided according to their achievement scores on various tests on mental ability. This created two groups, the high French achievers and the low French achievers, which were formed as follows. Those children whose scores were found to be in the top third of the entire group were included in the high French achievers group, while the children whose scores were found to be in the bottom third were included in the low French achievers group. The authors divided participants in this manner believing that, if the threshold hypothesis were true, the relationship between French achievement scores and scores on tests of cognitive functioning would emerge. Results provided some support for the existence of a second threshold level, as high achievers were found to score significantly higher on tests of mental ability over time. Nonetheless, evidence in favour of the first threshold level did not arise as the IQ tests of pupils in the low achievers group were consistent over time, with scores of 106.7 in Kindegarten, and scores of 107.2 in the period from Grade 1 to 3. The authors argued that this data indicates no cognitive disadvantage associated with language learning in French immersion programmes.

Ample criticism of Cummins' Threshold hypothesis and some counter-evidence for it is found in Diaz (1985), who conducted a longitudinal study with 100 Spanish-English bilingual children. Diaz claims that bilingualism promotes the development of cognitive flexibility from the early stages of acquisition, and not after a threshold level has been reached as Cummins (1976, 1979) postulates. He proposes that it is the early effort put forward in acquiring a second language which promotes cognitive development in children, and not proficiency level in the second language. In Cummins' (1979) defence, his work specifies that the effect of proficiency may not arise in studies which evaluate only early grades because 'the children's interaction with the environment and, consequently, cognitive development, is less dependent on the mediation of language than at later grades' (Cummins, 1979: 230). In the same article, Diaz (1985) also raises some methodological concerns in relation to the use of the socioeconomic variable in this line of research. He takes his own data as an example. The data initially identified a positive effect between proficiency level and cognitive development, which would have provided support for the view that proficiency level positively affects cognitive development. When, however, the most fluent children in the sample were subdivided according to their socioeconomic status, results changed in some substantial ways, and the previous claim turned out to be no longer feasible.

This background literature on bilingualism offers important insights about the relationship between prior knowledge and learning processes. On the one hand, as Lasagabaster (2001) has pointed out, multilingual learners may transfer the skills developed in all of their prior languages to another non-native language and this may improve speed and rate of acquisition, and possibly affect the route of acquisition as well. On the other, the literature on bilingualism highlights a clear relationship between additive or subtractive environments and learning processes, which leads us to examine the role of these contexts more carefully when doing research with multilinguals.

Studies with multilingual learners generally establish a positive association between bilingualism and third or additional language achievement (Cenoz, 2001; Cenoz and Valencia, 1994; Lasagabaster, 2000; Sanz, 2000; Valencia and Cenoz, 1992), but several researchers have also pointed out that positive effects tend to emerge in additive learning contexts. Cenoz (2001), for instance, emphasizes that studies which involve bilingual subtractive learning environments (Jaspaert and Lemmens, 1990; Sanders and Meijers, 1995; Van Gelderen *et al.*, 2003) do not identify significant differences between bi/multilinguals and monolingual learners. Similar arguments are found in Cenoz and Hoffman (2003) and Sanz (2000).

Swain *et al.* (1990) claim that it is not bilingualism per se that has an impact on third language learning, but it is bilingual literacy. The claim stems from a study with children studying in an English/French bilingual immersion programme in Canada. Some of these children had acquired a heritage language in the home while others, in addition to having learned the heritage language in the home environment, had also acquired literacy skills by attending heritage language programs. Learners' proficiency level in French was measured with a test which included writing, reading, speaking and listening components. The authors found that bilingualism has a positive effect on third language learning, but only when coupled with the acquisition of literacy skills. They consequently claimed that bilingual literacy has a crucial role in bringing about positive effects in third language learning.

Studies with bilinguals literate in their two languages indeed seem to point to superiority in language learning (Cenoz and Valencia, 1994; Keshavarz and Astaneh, 2004; Sanz, 2000; Thomas, 1988; Valencia and Cenoz, 1992). Some of these studies offer clear evidence in support of Swain *et al.*'s (1990) claim as they directly compare learners with and without literacy, or with and without formal academic training, in the second language. Keshavarz and Astaneh (2004), for instance, compared three groups of EFL students: 30 Turkish-Persian bilinguals studying Persian academically, 30 Armenian-Persian bilinguals studying both languages academically, and 30 Persian monolinguals. Bilinguals were generally found to perform better than monolinguals on English vocabulary tests. Armenian-Persian bilinguals were also found to perform better than Turkish-Persian bilinguals on measures of vocabulary production and achievement. Likewise, Thomas (1988) compared ten monolingual (English L1) with 16 bilingual (English L1 and Spanish L2) learners of French as a second and third language respectively. Bilinguals were generally found to perform better than monolinguals on various measures of foreign languages achievement. Most importantly, bilinguals were divided according to the amount of formal instruction received in the Spanish second language, and those who had received some formal training outperformed those who had never received any training and learned the language in the home environment.

Other studies that involve bilinguals who are literate in the two languages can also be argued to provide some indirect support for Swain *et al.*'s (1990) claim. Sanz (2000), for instance, compared Spanish monolingual learners of English as a second language with Spanish-Catalan bilingual learners of English as a third language. All these participants were asked to complete a vocabulary test and a structure test in the English non-native language containing 75 questions each, and fill out a questionnaire with questions on language background, prior exposure to English, motivation and attitude. Using a hierarchical multiple regression analysis, Sanz then examined the relationship between bilingualism and foreign language achievement, and indeed found bilinguals' English language achievement to be superior to those of monolingual learners of English as a second language. As anticipated, these bilinguals were literate in the two languages. Similar results were also found in studies conducted in the Basque country (Cenoz and Valencia, 1994; Valencia and Cenoz, 1992).

While it can be said that the evidence seems to indicate that biliteracy positively affects foreign language achievement, there is also evidence that adding a third language to the curriculum can influence overall achievement in the second language. This is the claim we find in Griessler (2001), who compared three groups of German L1 students studying in three different Austrian schools. One group of students was attending classes at the LISA school (Linz International School Auhof), which is an English immersion school. The second group was attending classes at the Licée Danube (LD), where English is studied according to a traditional curriculum, and the French non-native language is introduced early on in the programme. The third group of students was attending a regular Austrian secondary school, where English is studied according to the traditional curriculum as in the previous school. The study focused on these learners' English proficiency level, which was tested with the oral narration of the picture story 'Frog, Where are You?' (Mayer, 1969). Focusing on vocabulary richness and grammatical accuracy, and verb morphology in particular, it is not surprising that Griessler found LISA students to be superior on all measures of foreign language proficiency. The interesting difference emerged when she compared the performance of students of the other two groups. Licée Danube (LD) students clearly outperformed students attending the regular secondary school and since the only difference between learners in these groups was French instruction, Griessler concluded that French L3 instruction positively affects learners' proficiency in the English second language.

Evidence that instead seems to depart from the idea that literacy has a major impact on performance in a third language is discussed in Mägiste (1984, 1986), who compared the English language proficiency of bilingual immigrant students (N = 2,736) with that of monolingual Swedish students (N = 67,162) using various measures of English language proficiency. Mägiste found that bilinguals with passive knowledge of the Finnish L1 performed better than Swedish monolingual students, while bilinguals who actively used their L1 did not perform better than monolinguals. According to these results, then, differences in performance are to be attributed to whether a language is used or not, rather than to the level of literacy achieved in the second language.

## Metalinguistic Awareness and Metalinguistic Thinking

As we have seen in the previous section, among the possible explanations for bilinguals' apparent superiority in language learning are literacy in the two languages and the passive use of one of the languages. One other much accredited and debated explanation is that bilingual and multilingual speakers develop an increased awareness of language which aids them in the process of acquiring additional languages.

Metalinguistic awareness has been variably defined in the literature. Bialystok and Ryan (1985) view metalinguistic awareness as an ability that allows one to solve a range of different problems. Sagasta Errasti (2003: 28) says metalinguistic awareness involves 'greater sensitivity towards language use'. Thomas (1988: 236) defines it as 'student's conscious knowledge of the rules and forms of language', and Diaz and Klingler (1991: 173) say 'it refers to a set of abilities involving an objective awareness and control of linguistic variables, such as understanding the arbitrariness of word-referent relations and the capacity to detect and correct syntactic violations'. For the purpose of this discussion and in an effort to simplify the issue, I shall use the term metalinguistic awareness in a broad sense to refer to learners' ability to think of language and of perceiving language, including the ability to separate meanings and forms, discriminate language components, identify ambiguity and understand the use of grammatical forms and structures.

Studies that compared the metalinguistic abilities of monolinguals and bilinguals have shown that bilinguals develop a heightened awareness of the forms, meanings and rules of language (Ben-Zeev, 1977; Bialystok, 1987, 1988, 1991, 2001a, 2001b, 2004; Eviatar and Ibrahim, 2000; Galambos and Goldin-Meadow, 1990; Ianco-Worral, 1972; Ricciardelli, 1992a, 1992b; Yelland *et al.*, 1993). Research with multilinguals seems to point in the same direction. Before we examine the empirical evidence available, I would like to touch on the use of language as a medium for metalinguistic thinking and reflection.

Additional knowledge in the mind provides further metalinguistic knowledge learners can rely upon during the learning process, particularly if the additional languages are studied in formal learning contexts. Additional knowledge also provides more languages in which metalinguistic thoughts can be held. Jessner (2005) points out that within the field of multilingualism, the use that learners make of metalanguage and of metalinguistic expressions has been mostly examined from a communication strategy perspective. Zimmermann (1992), for instance, proposed a taxonomy for learners' lexical uncertainties, like asking questions (what does 'foreign word' mean?) or expressing doubts.

Cohen (1995: 103) emphasizes a distinction between thinking about language, and thinking through a language, and raises the important question of whether multilingual learners hold metalinguistic thoughts through the L1, the prior non-native languages, or the target language. He observes that in the early stages of acquisition, learners may not be able to deal with complex thoughts, and more specifically with metalinguistic thoughts, as they are too difficult to deal with at low levels of competence. We can presume that this situation may change in later stages of acquisition, when learners are more capable of articulating thoughts in their non-native languages. Cohen also maintains that multilinguals may rely on different languages for metalinguistic information, as the answers of some of the multilingual learners he surveyed would suggest:

> *Turkish-L1 trilingual*: The grammar of my L3 (English) is more similar to my L2 (German) than my L1 (Turkish). When I was learning English I was comparing it to German rather than to Turkish.

*English-L1 sextilingual*: I guess when I learned Spanish I compared verb conjugations to French, which I had studied previously, because person, tense, and gender matched better than comparing to English.
(Cohen, 1995: 104; italic in the original)

In some cases, multilinguals consciously draw upon their non-native languages to devise memorization strategies. He gives the example of some of the strategies he used while learning Hebrew. He often generated easy to remember keywords from English or Spanish. When he wanted to remember how to say the Hebrew word *arbolet* 'whirlpool', for instance, he made reference to the Spanish keyword *árbol* (tree), and at the same time created the image of a tree in a whirlpool.

Multilinguals clearly have more information that can be used to devise learning strategies as well as generate hypotheses born out of comparison across languages. Jessner (1999) discusses metalinguistic thinking involving crosslinguistic consultation with reference to data from Italian/German bilingual learners of English as a third language. These learners were asked to think aloud while completing an English academic writing task and some of the remarks they made show unambiguously that multilinguals can complete a task by thinking it through in three different languages, as the following example indicates:

> Ok, this is proved, no this is sustained, #sostenere, sustained by the theory that all our 4000–6000 languages on earth, hmm, are expected to be all the same for an external, how do you call it, *Beobachter, observer (English → Italian → English → German → English). (Jessner, 1999: 204)

Jessner (1999) reports several examples of this kind and argues that 'the search for similarities between the languages can be seen as part of the activities related to metalinguistic thinking in the learner. (Jessner, 1999: 205)'

Metalinguistic awareness is likely to be among the most important factors that contribute to increase multilinguals' ability to learn languages. This is at least what many scholars believe. Thomas (1988) was one of the first to associate metalinguistic awareness and multilingualism with the claim that learners who received formal instruction in the second language are more effective learners of a third language.

As reviewed earlier in the chapter in the discussion on literacy, Thomas (1988) examined the French proficiency of ten monolingual (English L1) and 16 bilingual (English L1 and Spanish L2) learners of French as a second and third language respectively. Some of these bilinguals had received formal instruction in the Spanish second language while others had not received any instruction at all. Bilinguals were generally found to be more accurate than monolinguals, but those who had received formal training in the second language were also found to outperform those who had never received any formal training in Spanish and used the language actively or passively in the home environment. In other words, formal instruction in the second language was found to have an impact on students' performance. Thomas concluded that the different performance in the two groups was due to bilinguals' heightened metalinguistic awareness, defined as the 'conscious knowledge of the rules and forms of language' (Thomas 1988: 236).

Fouser (2001) also calls upon the notion of metalinguistic awareness to explain the results of an introspective study of two English L1 learners of Korean as an L3 and an L5. Both learners had advanced knowledge of Japanese as a non-native language. The author explains that the genetic affiliation between Korean and Japanese has been questioned over the years, but it is mostly believed, at least intuitively, that Japanese is the closest language to Korean. The two languages are similar in their syntax and morphology, but are dissimilar in their phonology. In the early stages of acquisition, Fouser (2001) found that his two English L1 informants were drawing extensively on their knowledge of Japanese, particularly in the area of syntax, morphology and the lexicon. Most importantly, he found evidence that learners had a good understanding of their own learning processes and of the relationship between Korean and Japanese which helped them develop metalinguistic knowledge useful for the learning task.

The development and the use of metalinguistic awareness in language learning imply a degree of interaction among the learners' prior languages. This interactive aspect of knowledge is especially emphasized in Jessner (2003). She believes the multilingual mind to be a complex system governed by its own parameters, an idea based on dynamic system theory, which assumes that 'biological and many physical systems are irregular, discontinuous and inhomogenous' (Jessner, 2003: 48). Accordingly, the multilingual system is a dynamic system subject to time-related changes and constantly evolving and readjusting within its own self. Learning within this system is a non-linear process, it is reversible and dependent upon the interaction with the existing knowledge (see also Herdina and Jessner, 2000, 2002). As anticipated, Jessner (2003) emphasizes the inter-active aspect of knowledge in the mind and argues that such interactions are at the origin of the enhanced abilities and skills found in L3 learners, particularly in terms of metalinguistic awareness and metacognitive skills.

Sometimes, however, the interaction of knowledge does not seem to lead to the positive effects one would expect to find. The next section examines cases of this kind offering some alternative answers for the results.

## Prior Language Knowledge and the Lack of Significant Effects

The ability to think of language and of perceiving language to a positive effect does not seem to apply to all multilinguals. Several studies have found evidence that bilingualism positively affects linguistic development in third or additional languages, and that this occurs in different domains, such as grammar (Thomas, 1988), syntax (Flynn *et al.*, 2004; Klein, 1995; Zobl, 1992), surface structures (Fouser, 2001); writing skills (Sagasta Errasti, 2003), lexical learning (Keshavarz and Astaneh, 2004) and pragmatic competence (Safont Jordà, 2005). Some other studies, however, have also found evidence of the opposite, that is of a lack of a relationship between prior linguistic knowledge and some aspects of acquisition, more specifically the ability to discriminate phonetic contrasts (Werker, 1986) and the acquisition of prepositional verbs (Gibson *et al.*, 2001).

Gibson *et al.* (2001) examined the effect of previous linguistic knowledge on the acquisition of prepositional verbs in German as a third or additional language. Participants were 64 multilinguals who were divided into six different groups, set up according to whether the languages they were familiar with had prepositional verbs or not. All participants were given a fill-in-the-blank task which included 33 German prepositional verbs like *talk to, listen to, consist of* and so forth. Thirteen of these verbs had an equivalent preposition in English, for instance *gehören zu – belong to*, while the remaining 20 verbs did not have a direct equivalent in English, such as *sprechen über* and *talk about*. Overall results indicated that (a) prior knowledge of an L2 does not significantly affect task accuracy; (b) prior knowledge of English as an L2 does not significantly affect accuracy rates of German prepositional verbs; and (c) prior knowledge of an L1 structurally similar to the L3 does not significantly affect task accuracy. In sum, the results of the study do not support the idea that multilingualism is positively correlated with foreign language achievement and German prepositional verbs in particular.

Another study which claims that multilinguals do not have superior abilities with respect to discriminating phonetic contrast is reported in Werker (1986). Werker compared the ability of monolinguals, bilinguals, and trilinguals to perceive two place-of- articulation contrasts in a new language. One contrast was from Hindi (retroflex versus dental) and second was from the Thompson, a West Coast Indian language (glottalized velar versus glottalized uvular). Multilinguals were not found to have superior abilities in discriminating phonetic contrasts than bilinguals.

The results we find in Gibson *et al.* (2001) and Werker (1986) clearly diverge from the general claim that bi/multilinguals show some advantages in third or additional language learning. One plausible explanation for these results takes us back to consider Cummins' (1976, 1979) threshold hypothesis, according to which learners must reach a certain level of competence in order to benefit in improved cognitive functioning. It is possible that the threshold level required had not been reached. In the case of Werker's (1986) study, a methodological concern must also be raised. Werker states that his learners were divided into groups according to the number of languages they were familiar with. Seven out of the ten monolinguals, however, were described as having received some formal training in a foreign language, which means that most of these monolinguals were not true monolinguals. In Chapter 1 I discussed how even a little knowledge of a foreign language can affect learners' processes, and in this case it is quite possible that a bias was introduced due to the wrongful assumption that low proficiency in a non-native language does not lead to significant differences in performance.

The two studies just reviewed (Gibson *et al.*, 2001; Werker, 1986) are not the only ones that do not provide evidence in support of multilinguals' superiority in language learning. There are also other studies developed within an information processing framework that reach similar conclusions.

Information processing is based on the notion of controlled and automatic processing. McLaughlin and Nayak (1989: 6) distinguish these processes saying that:

> controlled processes require attention and time; they use relatively large amounts of processing energy but are easy to set up and alter. Automatic processes require little attention and occur rapidly; they use little processing energy, but have the disadvantage of being difficult to suppress or alter.

Within this framework, learning is the result of controlled processes, and the expert, i.e. more experienced, language learner is assumed to use different information processing strategies and techniques than do more novice learners (McLaughlin and Nayak 1989).

From these premises, Nation and McLaughlin (1986) assessed whether expert and novice learners adopt different strategies when learning a new language. The new language was not a real language, however, but an artificial grammar, which was taught to multilingual, bilingual and monolingual participants. Results showed that multilinguals tend to perform better than the less experienced learners, but only in the case in which learning is implicit, that is when they are not given specific instructions on how to learn the artificial language. In the case of explicit learning, that is when learners are asked to learn the rules of the artificial language, multilinguals do not seem to display superior abilities.

In a similar study, Nayak *et al.* (1990) also asked whether multilinguals' learning strategies differed from those of monolinguals. To answer the question, Nayak and his colleagues taught an artificial grammar to a total 48 participants, who were asked to complete a series of memorisation and rule discovery tasks about the artificial grammar. The following is an example of the type of rule participants were asked to learn:

Rule 1:  Every sentence must contain at least one A word.
         RUD TIZ JAX NEB    [A-D-E-C]
         *LUM TIX JAX NEB    [C-D-E-C]
         (Nayak *et al.*, 1990: 233)

The learning phase lasted about 25 minutes, after which all participants were given a syntax test and a vocabulary test that measured accuracy and speed of response. Participants were also asked to verbalize the strategies used in the learning process, and the following four main strategies were identified: (1) focus on structure; (2) focus on position; (3) use of visual cues; and (4) use of verbal cues. As in the previous study, multilinguals were found to perform better than monolinguals under some of the task conditions but, on the whole, it was concluded that multilinguals do not seem to have superior language learning abilities than monolinguals. All considered, overall results seem rather convincing, but there are also difficulties when the authors' data is closely examined.

Two main reasons of concern can be raised. The first is how participants were divided into groups, and more specifically who was included in the monolingual group. Nayak *et al.* (1990) gave their participants a seven-point self-rating proficiency scale of language proficiency, where a mark of seven indicated complete fluency, and mark of one no fluency at all. The self-rating scores were then used to assign learners to the monolingual or the multilingual group. Those included in the monolingual group were described as being 'native speakers of English, with very minimal or no proficiency (ratings of three or below) in any other natural language' (Nayak *et al.* 1990: 226). Since no distinction is made between learners with a score of three (some fluency) and learners with a score of one (no fluency), it is then reasonable to wonder whether the results obtained are due to a faulty design rather than to learners' actual abilities. As was the case in Werker's

(1986) study, individuals with some prior knowledge of non-native languages were incorrectly classified as monolinguals.

The second concern relates to the use of artificial languages in general. In reading the rule reported above, the first impression is that one is not reading the rule of a language, but rather a sequence of letters or symbols which have some kind of internal structure that must be identified. Relevance theory tells us that learners make use of what they perceive as relevant to the learning task. Without meaning to simplify the issue, a sequence of letters may not be perceived as being sufficiently relevant to learn a real language and, as a result, prior learning experience may not be put to use as the authors' may have hypothesized.

Let us now turn to examine one other important but much neglected factor for the study of multilingualism, that is whether the number of languages known to the speaker affects cognitive development and the language acquisition processes in some significant ways.

## Number of Language Known: Does it Make a Difference?

In the preceding sections we examined whether the knowledge of prior languages exerts a positive or negative influence on learning processes, finding that positive effects overwhelmingly prevail over negative ones in most domains. Since prior language knowledge has already been associated with a number of benefits, the next question is whether having knowledge of more languages can also lead to some additional benefits. In other words, does the number of languages known make a difference?

There are only a few studies which examine the effect of the number of languages known to the speaker on learning processes. One of these studies dealt with the relationship between the number of languages known and the ability to provide accurate translations.

Gibson and Hufeisen (2003) examined multilingual learners of English (n = 10) or German (n = 26) as non-native languages, with the aim to assess whether prior knowledge of non-native languages positively or negatively affects accuracy rates in translation. Learners, who were not familiar with the same number of languages, were asked to complete a translation task which involved translating a text from an unknown language (Swedish) into their respective non-native languages (English or German). The text was taken from a beginner's Swedish textbook and described the life of three children. The authors then analysed accuracy rates in translation using a chi-square test of interaction and found a significant progressive increase in accuracy rates with the increase in number of languages known. For instance, learners of German as an L2 showed an accuracy rate of 59%, those with German as an L3 of 74%, and those with German as an L4 of 81%.

Although the number of participants was small, the progressively higher accuracy rates point to a possible association between the number of languages known and the ability to provide an accurate translation in an unknown language. Clearly, an individual with knowledge of several languages has access to more information that can aid in the task of translating from an unknown to a known language, as the task given required. The authors in fact conclude that the number of languages a person is familiar with can affect the ability to 'overcome the lexical and syntactic traps in the [translation] task, as well as apply their metalinguistic strategies to figure out the correct translation (Gibson and Hufeisen, 2003: 99).

With respect to reading and listening comprehension, it is reasonable to expect similar results as prior knowledge is likely to be put to use when trying to understand the incoming written or oral message. To my knowledge, productive skills have not been examined directly; nonetheless there is some research which has found a clear association between speaking, number of languages known, and levels of communicative anxiety.

Dewaele (2002) conducted a study on the effect of several variables, including the number of languages known, on levels of communicative anxiety. He focused on oral communication as this is believed to be one of the most anxiety-provoking situations for non-native speakers. Participants to the study were 106 students of which 35 were bilinguals, 33 trilinguals and 38 quadrilinguals. These participants were asked to complete a sociodemographic questionnaire which contained questions related to age, language background, gender, and levels of communicative anxiety in each language in three different situations – when speaking with friends, to strangers and in public. A five-point Likert scale was used to measure levels of communicative anxiety. With respect to number of languages known, Dewaele (2002) found that the strongest difference in anxiety levels appears to be between the L1 and the L2. Speaking in the second language causes higher levels of anxiety than speaking in the first language, anxiety then lowers in subsequent languages. With respect to speaking in the L2, anxiety levels also lower the more languages are known to the speaker, i.e. multilinguals are less anxious when speaking the L2 than bilinguals. Dewaele explains these findings saying that multilinguals have learned to use more languages and, as a result, have become better communicators, have more self-confidence and have increased their self-perceived competence.

One other question is whether additional language knowledge and metalinguistic knowledge may also affect multilinguals' acceptability of L1 sentences. That is to say, do multilinguals become more tolerant of contentious structures in their own native language? This is what Kemp (1999) asked in a study with 30 multilinguals, all native-speakers of English. These participants were divided into three groups: speakers with knowledge of 3–5 languages, 6–7 languages, and 8+ languages. They were given 20 English sentences and were asked to (1) express a judgement of acceptability; (2) indicate, on a scale from 1 to 10, how sure they were of the judgement expressed; and (3) underline any problem found and explain what the problem was. Using a non-parametric correlation test (Spearman's *rho*) for analysis, Kemp found that acceptability rates for contentious sentences increased with the number of languages known to the speaker. She also found that those with a higher number of languages were better at explaining what was wrong with the sentences they were shown. In a later study (Kemp, 2001) additionally asked whether those with more languages are also better at learning a new language. The ability to learn Basque was tested with 30 English L1 multilingual speakers. As in the previous study, she found a positive effect, i.e. the more languages participants were familiar with, the better they were at learning Basque. She also found an association between explicit grammatical metalinguistic awareness and achievement.

In sum, even though the amount of research on the effect of the number of languages known is still limited, the few studies that are available already point to the importance of this variable for language acquisition research.

# Chapter 7
# *Conclusion*

At the beginning of this book I raised two main questions. The first was whether multilinguals should be considered as learners and speakers in their own right as opposed to L2 learners or bilinguals, and therefore whether a more explicit distinction between Second Language Acquisition and Third or Additional Language Acquisition is warranted. The second question was how proficient in a non-native language L2 learners are supposed to be before they can begin to be classified as L3 learners in empirical research.

The first question was raised because the language acquisition and the speech production literature treat multilingual phenomena according to two basic assumptions. On the one hand, we have scholars who assume there is no meaningful difference between bilinguals' and multilinguals' processes and accordingly classify all speakers of one or more non-native language as L2 learners or speakers, especially when proficiency in the previously learned non-native languages is low. On the other, we have scholars who argue that this position is not acceptable, as meaningful differences between these learners' processes exist and must be accounted for. The book then set out to examine the empirical evidence in favour of both positions.

All considered, the end balance is in favour of the view that a difference between the two types of speakers exists, as prior linguistic knowledge has been repeatedly shown to affect multilinguals' processes in a number of ways. Clearly, multilinguals have more knowledge that can be used and drawn upon during the acquisition and production process which bilinguals do not have at their disposal, and this additional knowledge seems to play more of a central role than was previously assumed. While the book has attempted to highlight why a difference between Second Language Acquisition and Third or Additional Language Acquisition is warranted, it must be noted that clear empirical evidence in support of the no-difference assumption was not found.

This takes us to the second question raised. When dividing the participants to a study into groups, how do we decide whether the subject is an L2 learner or a multilingual learner? It is still difficult to provide a truly useful answer to this question for two main reasons. On the one hand, hardly any studies have focused on this specific variable so we are not able to identify threshold levels with some accuracy. On the other, those studies that provide some information on non-native language proficiency usually indicate learners' self-rated proficiency scores, or years of formal instruction, and this type of information should ideally be supplemented with other more rigorous measures of language proficiency. Despite this limitation, some studies have shown that as little as one year of formal instruction can affect third or additional language performance to a significant extent, hence the careful distinction between L2 learners and multilingual learners remains an essential step to avoid a significant bias in research.

The fact that we cannot yet provide some clear-cut answers about possible threshold levels also raises the additional question of what criteria have been followed up to now. The decision of whether an individual is an L2 learner or a multilingual learner has usually been left to the discretion of individual researchers who have been more or less conservative in their judgements, with the result that it is not uncommon to find studies where those who have 'some' knowledge of a prior foreign language are incorrectly classified as monolinguals, or those who speak several languages are classified as bilinguals.

From the discussions in the preceding chapters, it is clear that the amount of research on multilinguals' processes is limited, especially when compared to the overwhelming amount of research available in SLA and Bilingualism. The opposite, however, is also true, i.e. what is now available is sufficiently abundant for us to be able to draw some conclusions about multilinguals and the distinctiveness of their processes.

## Major Findings and Some Suggestions for Future Research

This section provides a synthesis of the major findings presented throughout the book, aiming to show how information on multilinguals' processes can add to the current body of knowledge on second language acquisition and speech production. Some suggestions for further research are also included. Given that more thorough discussions are presented in each chapter, the summary below provides only a brief description of the conclusions reached, with an indication of the relevant chapters or paragraphs where further information can be found.

## Multilingual learners are Influenced by the L1 as well as the non-native languages

Crosslinguistic influence (CLI), although defined as a field of study concerned with native and non-native language influence, has traditionally focused on L1 influence and L2 learner behaviour. A comprehensive theory of CLI cannot, however, be based on L1 influence alone, as a wide range of phenomena would inevitably remain unexplored and unexplained. Multilinguals have knowledge of more than two languages by definition, so the possible sources of influence automatically increase with the number of languages the individual is familiar with. Empirical evidence indicates that transfer can occur from the L1 as well as the non-native languages, which means that, in the case of multilinguals, the native language does not always have a privileged status and must be looked at together with other possible sources of transfer, particularly with respect to how the competition between languages may be resolved. Moreover, non-native language influence has been found to occur in lexis, phonetics and phonology, morphology and syntax, and therefore seems to be quite pervasive. Transfer has also been found to occur from more than one language at the same time. This type of transfer, which I referred to as combined CLI, remains little explored to date (see Chapters 2 and 3).

## Language distance affects crosslinguistic influence in multilinguals

Language distance has been repeatedly discussed as one of the crucial triggers of crosslinguistic influence in relation to L2 learners as well as multilingual learners. With multilinguals, however, the role of language distance is not as straightfoward as it may be with L2 learners due to the possible combination of close and distant languages in the mind. Three different combinations were closely examined with respect to CLI: (1) when learners have knowledge of related and unrelated languages; (2) when learners have knowledge of languages that belong to the same language family, but not the same subgroup within the family; (3) when learners have knowledge of languages that belong to the same family, and to the same subgroup within the family.

When multilinguals have knowledge of related and unrelated languages, evidence suggests that they are overwhelmingly influenced by the language that is the closest to the target language, regardless of whether this is the native or a non-native language. On some occasions, learners are also influenced by the more distant languages, but instances of this kind are rare and tend to involve lexical items that are phonetically similar to the target language form. Morover, the items involved tend to belong to the same language class, and the speaker usually has some knowledge of the target expression.

When languages belong to the same language family, but not to the same subgroup within the family, two general tendencies have been identified. First, learners continue to be influenced by the languages that are more closely related to the target language, irrespective of whether this is the native or a non-native language. Second, learners may be influenced by more than one language at the same time (combined CLI). The influence from more than one language becomes even more prominent when all languages belong to the same language family and to the same subgroup within the family. In this case, the native language does not seem to have a priviledge status, and in fact the non-native languages seem to be learners' favourite sources of information in most occasions (see Chapter 2).

## Language proficiency determines amount and type of transfer in multilinguals, and affects the lexical retrieval process

The effect of language proficiency on crosslinguistic influence was examined in relation to proficiency in the target language, and proficiency in the previously learned non-native languages. With respect to proficiency in the target language, CLI seems to occur more frequently at the early stages of acquisition, even though it can also occur at later stages, as the literature on L1 influence also found. With respect to the relationship between proficiency in the non-native languages and CLI, the influence was equally found to occur from non-native languages speakers know well than from non-native languages speakers do not know well. This is perhaps the most important result of all as it offers further evidence that those learners who have some knowledge of a non-native language, for instance one or two years of formal instruction, should not be regarded as L2 learners but as third or additional language learners in empirical research. Not doing so would most likely introduce a potential bias that could lead to unreliable and inconclusive results. This said, even though some knowledge of a non-native language may influence target language production and development, it was also found that different proficiency levels in the previously known non-native language(s) can lead to different types of transfer in production. For instance, transfer of meaning was found to be mostly associated with high proficiency in the source language, while transfer of form was found to be mostly associated with low fluency in the source language (see Chapters 2 and 3).

Proficiency in the target language was also found to affect the lexical retrieval process and speakers' ability to inhibit potential competitors. Research found varying processing difficulties according to learners' proficiency levels in the target language. Multilingual speakers seem to be better able to execute control in the stronger and more fluent languages than in the less fluent languages, where instances of crosslinguistic influence are therefore more likely to arise (see Chapter 4).

## Recency of use affects crosslinguistic influence in multilinguals

Recency of use was discussed in relation to psycholinguistic perspectives which view access to linguistic information to be hindered or facilitated by the frequency of access to the item itself. The frequency effect, which is a well documented phenomenon in the psycholinguistic literature, maintains that it is easier to access a word which is used frequently than a word that is used less frequently. According to this principle, learners are more likely to be influenced by those languages that are used often, and in the recent past. The empirical evidence partly confirms this claim. Recency of use has been found to variably affect the amount of influence from a source to a target language. On the one hand, evidence indicates that learners tend to transfer from those languages that were used in the recent past and are still relatively fresh in the mind. On the other, there is also evidence that transfer occurs from languages not used for as long as thirty years, even though these instances seem to be mostly restricted to lexical influence. These results would suggest that recency of use is not a key trigger of CLI, and that its role is determined by its interaction with other dominant factors like proficiency level or language distance. More research is needed to clarify the extent of the interaction between these factors and how the competition among them may be resolved. On the whole, while it can be said that our understanding of the role of the recency factor is still partial, the little we know adds to our current body of knowledge as this factor was never examined in relation to L1 influence, with the exception of cases of attrition. Research on recency of use seems to be highly promising for areas of inquiry such as language loss and language maintenance, particularly in relation to non-native languages (see Chapter 2).

## Length of residence and exposure to a non-native language environment affects crosslinguistic influence in multilinguals

Length of residence and exposure to a non-native language environment is another factor which is mostly relevant to multilingualism. As far as we can see, length of residence and exposure to a non-native language environment seems to increase multilinguals' reliance on a particular source language in production. This said, not much is known about the effect of this factor on the amount and type of instances of CLI, particularly over an extended period of time. For instance, we can hypothesize that the effect of residence will decrease with time, or we may want to examine whether transfer is more likely to increase from languages used recently in the non-native language environment as opposed to the native language environment, for example when the non-native language is studied at school in one's home country. These are possible venues for future research, but many more angles can be easily tackled, particularly as hardly any research is currently available on this specific factor (see Chapter 2).

## Order of acquisition determines the relationship between the multilingual's languages

Order of acquisition is another factor that it makes sense to examine only in relation to multilinguals. While little research has focused on order of acquisition so far, results have shown some interesting associations with respect to the relationship that languages may establish with one another during the acquisition process. Given the same language combination, research has found that the second and the third language develop connections of different strengths with the native language, and that this connection may ease or obstruct the path of transfer in production. More specifically, the third language has been found to have a stonger connection with the second language than with the native language. On the basis of these initial findings, several questions in relation to the strength of association between languages can be raised. For instance, we may want to examine the relationship between strength of association and factors such as order of acquisition, typology and proficiency level. Moreover, if second and third languages are confirmed to be more closely connected with one other than with the first language, this type of evidence could provide further support for the separation hypothesis of the multilingual lexicon. As was the case with the previous factor, many other venues could be tackled, ranging from the relationship between the strength of interconnections and the organization of knowledge in multilingual memory to the relationship between order of acquisition and CLI (see Chapter 2).

## Multilinguals may be influenced by more than one language at the same time

A distinction was made between one-to-one and many-to-one type of associations in CLI. The first defines instances of transfer from one language to another, for example from the L1 to the L2, the L2 to the L3, the L2 to the L1 and so forth. The second refers to instances of combined CLI, a type of transfer that can occur when two or more languages interact with one another and concur in influencing the target language, or whenever one language influences another, and the already influenced language in turn influences another language in the process of being acquired. It was noted that we cannot feasibly continue to examine CLI data following the assumption that transfer can only come from one of the speakers' languages, as research has traditionally done in the past. When more sources are available, these sources have to be accounted for, whether used or unused by the learner. Several instances of combined CLI were reported in the book, with the intent to show how the source of the influence can rest with more than one language at the same time – a possibility that hypotheses about CLI do not currently account for (see Chapters 2 and 3).

## Non-native language proficiency affects lexico-semantic organization

The addition of languages to the mind raises the question of what type of relationship the new language is likely to develop with the previous languages already in the mind in terms of organizational structure. Proficiency in the non-native language is clearly an important factor in this regard. From previous research with bilinguals, we know that an additional language may develop a word association or a concept mediation type of organizational structure with the L1, depending on the proficiency level reached in the non-native language. This hypothesis was extended to multilinguals with knowledge of weak and strong non-native languages. The weak language was hypothesized to show a word-association type of structure and the strong language a concept-mediation type of structure. This hypothesis was confirmed and proficiency level in the non-native language was indeed found to affect lexico-semantic organization. Moreover, the relationship between two languages was also argued to change over time. A question which instead has remained almost completely unaddressed relates to the type of relationship that non-native languages establish with one another at a single point in time and over time, especially in view of the rapid changes in proficiency level non-native languages are subject to (see Chapter 5).

## Heavy processing loads slow down multilinguals in the execution of some tasks

Does having more knowledge in the mind slow down multilinguals' processes in some meaningful way? Some studies have found that it does, showing very modest delays in the execution of some tasks in multilinguals in comparison to monolinguals or bilinguals. These delays, however, are in the range of milliseconds, and are therefore to be regarded as a fairly negligent consequence of multilingualism (see Chapter 6). As Chapter 6 discusses, the negative consequences of multilingualism are minimal in comparison to the cognitive advantages that can be gained.

## Prior language knowledge and previous learning experience have a positive effect on third or additional language learning

Bilingualism and multilingualism have been associated with a broad range of effects in grammar, syntax, surface structures, writing skills, lexical learning and pragmatic competence. Clearly, prior knowledge does impact learning processing in many ways. One of the most important questions about these effects is whether bi/multilingualism positively or negatively affects third or additional language achievement and learners' cognitive development. Research has shown that bi/multilingualism has a positive effect on learning processes, but mostly when learning occurs in additive contexts. Moreover, research has pointed to two factors of major influence for the individual: literacy in the previous languages, and metalinguistic awareness. Both these factors have been found to be positively associated with foreign language achievement and cognitive development in multilinguals (see Chapter 6).

## A Final Comment

This book has focused on multilinguals' cognitive and psycholinguistic processes in Third or Additional Language Acqusition, but many more areas of inquiry could have been easily included. As Hufeisen (2004: 145) has noted, adding a language is not just a matter of adding knowledge to the mind and defining how this knowledge is used. Adding languages to the mind brings about an entire range of effects which can influence the individual's 'personal life and learning experience, individual learning strategies [. . .] and/or knowledge about one's own learner type'. Clearly, adding a language to the mind is bound to enrich us linguistically and culturally, and what is gained can generate effects of various kinds. Some of these effects were discussed in the book while some others remain to be identified to date.

Reflecting more broadly on the role of language and of language learning within societies, we all know that languages can be a source of struggle or a source of freedom in many parts of the world. In some countries, dominant political powers try to suppress minority languages and minority cultures, while other countries deliberately introduce measures to protect minority languages with the intent to encourage the spread of multilingualism within the social environment. Even though the sociolinguistic aspects of multilingualism were not the focus of this book, one cannot forget that language acquisition research eventually informs educational practices, and therefore touches peoples' lives. It is my hope that a better awareness of the effects of multilingualism on learning processes may ultimately reach the effect of encouraging governments to support multilingual education more systematically and promote multiculturalism where possible.

# References

Abunuwara, E. (1992) The structure of the trilingual lexicon. *European Journal of Cognitive Psychology* 4: 4, 311–322.

Abu-Rabia, S. (1998) The influence of the Israel-Arab Conflict on Israeli-Jewish Students Learning Arabic as a third language. *Language, Culture and Curriculum* 11: 2, 154–164.

Ahukanna, J. G. W., Lund, N. J. and Gentile, R. J. (1981) Inter- and intra-lingual interference effects in learning a third language. *Modern Language Journal* 65, 281–287.

Albert, M. L. and Obler, L. K. (1978) *The Bilingual Brain*. New York: Academic Press.

Alcantarini, E. (2005) *L'inglese L3*. Unpublished thesis, Università degli Studi di Bologna.

Aronin, L. and Toubkin, L. (2002) Language interference and language learning techniques transfer in L2 and L3 immersion programmes. *International Journal of Bilingual Education and Bilingualism* 5: 5, 267–278.

Au-Yeung, J., Howell, P., Davis, S., Charles, N. and Sackin, S. (2000) UCL survey of bilingualism and stuttering. Third World Congress of Fluency Disorders, Nyborg, Denmark, 7–11 August.

Baetens Beardsmore, H. and Kohls, J. (1988) Immediate pertinence in the acquisition of multilingual proficiency: the European Schools. *Canadian Modern Language Review* 44, 680–701.

Baker, C. and Prys Jones, S. (1998) *Encyclopedia of Bilingualism and Bilingual Education*. Clevedon: Multilingual Matters.

Bardel, C. and Lindqvist, C. (to appear) The role of proficiency and psychotypology in lexical cross-linguistic influence. A study of a multilingual learner of Italian L3. In M. Chini, P. Desideri, M. E. Favilla and G. Pallotti (eds) *Atti del VI Congresso di Studi dell'Associazione Italiana di Linguistica Applicata*, Napoli, 9–10 February 2006. Perugia: Guerra Editore.

Barik, H. C. and Swain, M. (1976) A longitudinal study of bilingual and cognitive development. *International Journal of Psychology* 11, 251–263.

Beauvillain, C. and Grainger, J. (1987) Accessing interlexical homographs: some limitations of a language-selective access. *Journal of Memory and Language* 26, 658–672.

Ben-Zeev, S. (1977) Mechanisms by which childhood bilingualism affects understanding of language and cognitive structures. In P. A. Hornby (ed.) *Bilingualism: Psychological, Social and Educational Implications*. New York: Academic. 29–55.

Bhatia, T. K. (2004) *The Handbook of Bilingualism*. Oxford: Blackwell Publishers.
Bialystok, E. (1987) Words as things: development of word concepts by bilingual children. *Studies in Second Language Learning* 9, 133–140.
Bialystok, E. (1988) Levels of bilingualism and levels of linguistic awareness. *Developmental Psychology* 24: 4, 560–567.
Bialystok, E. (1991) Metalinguistic dimensions of bilingual language proficiency. In E. Bialistok (ed.) *Language Processing in Bilingual Children*. Cambridge: Cambridge University Press. 113–140.
Bialystok, E. (2001a) *Bilingualism in Development, Language, Literacy and Cognition*. Cambridge: Cambridge University Press.
Bialystok, E. (2001b) Metalinguistic aspects of bilingual processing. *Annual Review of Applied Linguistics* 21, 169–181.
Bialystok, E. (2004) The impact of bilingualism on language and literacy development. In K. Bhatia and W. C. Ritchie (eds) *The Handbook of Bilingualism*. Malden, MA: Blackwell Publishing. 577–601.
Bialystok, E. and Ryan, E. B. (1985) A metacognitive framework for the development of first and second language skills. In B. L. Forrest-Pressley, G. G. MacKinnan and T. G. Waller (eds) *Metacognition, Cognition and Human Performance*. New York: Academic. 7, 207–252.
Bild, E. R. and Swain, M. (1989) Minority language students in a French immersion programme: their French proficiency. *Journal of Multilingual and Multicultural Development* 10: 3, 255–274.
Bley-Vroman, R. (1983) The comparative fallacy in interlanguage studies: the case of systematicity. *Language Learning* 33, 1–17.
Bock, K. (1995) Sentence production: from mind to mouth. In J. L. Miller and P. D. Eimas (eds) *Speech, Language, and Communication*. San Diego, CA: Academic Press. 181–216.
Bouvy, C. (2000) Towards the construction of a theory of cross-linguistic transfer. In J. Cenoz and U. Jessner (eds) *English in Europe: The Acquisition of a Third language*. Clevedon: Multilingual Matters. 143–156.
Brohy, C. (2001) Generic and/or specific advantages of bilingualism in a dynamic plurilingual situation: The case of French as official L3 in the school of Samedan (Switzerland). *International Journal of Bilingual Education and Bilingualism* 4: 1, 38–49.
Butler, Y. G. and Hakuta, K. (2004) Bilingualism and second language acquisition. In K. Bhatia and W. C. Ritchie (eds) *The Handbook of Bilingualism*. Malden, MA: Blackwell Publishing.
Cantoni, G. P. (1997) Keeping minority languages alive: the school's responsibility. In J. Reyhner (ed.) *Teaching Indigenous Languages*. Flagstaff, AZ: Northern Arizona University.
Caramazza, A. and Brones, I. (1979) Lexical access in bilinguals. *Bulletin of the Psychonomic Society*, 13, 212–214.
Caramazza, A. and Coltheart, M. (2006) Cognitive neuropsychology twenty years on. *Cognitive Neuropsychology* 23: 1, 3–12.
Carroll, S. E. (1992) On cognates. *Second Language Research* 8: 2, 93–119.
Cenoz, J. (2001) The effect of linguistic distance, L2 status and age on cross-linguistic influence in third language acquisition. In J. Cenoz, B. Hufeisen and U. Jessner (eds) *Cross-linguistic Influence in Third Language Acquisition: Psycholinguistic Perspectives*. Clevedon: Multilingual Matters. 8–20.

Cenoz, J. (2003a) The additive effect of bilingualism in third language acquisition: a review. *International Journal of Bilingualism* 7: 1, 71–87.

Cenoz, J. (2003b) The role of typology in the organization of the multilingual lexicon. In J. Cenoz, B. Hufeisen and U. Jessner (eds) *The Multilingual Lexicon*. Dordrecht: Kluwer Academic Publishers. 103–116.

Cenoz, J. and Valencia, J. F. (1994) Additive trilingualism: evidence from the Basque Country. *Applied Psycholinguistics* 15, 195–207.

Cenoz, J. and Genesee, F. (1998) Psycholinguistic perspectives on multilingualism and multilingual education. In J. Cenoz and F. Genesee (eds) *Beyond Bilingualism: Multilingualism and Multilingual Education*. Clevedon: Multilingual Matters. 16–32.

Cenoz, J. and Hoffmann, C. (2003) Acquiring a third language: what role does bilingualism play? *International Journal of Bilingualism*, 7: 1, 1–6.

Cenoz, J., Hufeisen, B. and Jessner, U. (eds) (2001) Third language acquisition in the school context. *International Journal of Bilingual Education and Bilingualism* (special issue).

Cenoz, J., Hufeisen, B. and Jessner, U. (2003) Why investigate the multilingual lexicon? In J. Cenoz, B. Hufeisen and U. Jessner (eds) *The Multilingual Lexicon*. Dordrecht: Kluwer Academic Publishers. 1–9.

Chamot, Anna Uhl. (1973) Phonological problems in learning English as a third language. *International Review of Applied Linguistics* XI: 3, 243–250.

Chandrasekhar, A. (1978) Base language. *International Review of Applied Linguistics* XVI: 1, 62–65.

Charkova, K. D. (2004) Early foreign language education and metalinguistic development: a study of monolingual, bilingual and trilingual children on noun definition tasks. In L. Santelmann, M. Verrips, F. Wijnen and C. Levelt (eds) *Annual Review of Language Acquisition* 3: 1, 51–88. Amsterdam: John Benjamins.

Chen, H. C. and Leung, Y. S. (1989) Patterns of lexical processing in a nonnative language. *Journal of Experimental Psychology: Learning, Memory and Cognition* 12, 316–325.

Chomsky, N. (1995) *The Minimalist Program*. Cambridge, MA: MIT Press.

Clyne, M. (1997) Some of the things trilinguals do. *The International Journal of Bilingualism* 1: 2, 95–116.

Clyne, M. and Cassia, P. (1999) Trilingualism, immigration and relatedness of languages. *I.T.L. Review of Applied Linguistics* 123–124, 57–74.

Clyne, M., Rossi Hunt, C. and Isaakidis, T. (2004) Learning a community language as a third language. *The International Journal of Multilingualism* 1: 1, 33–52.

Cohen, A. D. (1995) In which language do/should multilinguals think? *Language, Culture and Curriculum* 8: 2, 99–113.

Cook, V. (1991) The poverty of the stimulus argument and multicompetence. *Second Language Research* 7: 2, 103–117.

Cook, V. (1992) Evidence for multicompetence. *Language Learning* 42: 4, 557–592.

Cook, V. (1995) Multi-competence and the learning of many languages. *Language, Culture and Curriculum* 8, 93–98.

Cook, V. (1997a) Monolingual bias in second language research. *Revista de Estudios Ingleses* 34, 35–50.

Cook, V. (1997b) The consequences of bilingualism for cognitive processing. In A. M. B. de Groot and J. Kroll (eds) *Tutorials in Bilingualism. Psycholinguistic Perspectives*. Mahwah, NJ: Lawrence Erlbaum Associates. 279–299.

Cook, V. (2001) *Second Language Learning and Language Teaching*. London: Arnold.

Cook, V. (2003) (ed.) *Effects of the Second Language on the First.* Clevedon: Multilingual Matters.

Corder, S. (1971) Idiosyncratic dialects and error analysis. *International Review of Applied Linguistics* IX, 149–159.

Costa, A. (2004) Speech production in bilinguals. In T. K. Bhatia and W. C. Ritchie (eds) *The Handbook of Bilingualism.* Malden, MA: Blackwell Publishing. 201–223.

Costa, A. and Caramazza, A. (1999) Is lexical selection language specific? Further evidence from Spanish-English bilinguals. *Bilingualism: Language and Cognition* 2, 231–244.

Costa, A., Colomé, A. and Caramazza, A. (2000) Lexical access in speech production: the bilingual case. *Psicologica*, 21, 403–437.

Cristoffanini, P, Kirsner, K. and Milech, D. (1986) Bilingual lexical representation. The status of Spanish-English cognates. *Quarterly Journal of Experimental Psychology* 38A, 367–393.

Cummins, J. (1976) The influence of bilingualism on cognitive growth: A synthesis of research findings and explanatory hypotheses. *Working Papers on Bilingualism* 9, 1–43.

Cummins, J. (1979) Linguistic interdependence and the educational development of bilingual children. *Review of Educational Research* 49: 2, 222–251.

Cummins, J. (2001) Instructional conditions for trilingual development. *International Journal of Bilingual Education and Bilingualism* 4: 1, 61–75.

Dagenais, D. and Day, E. (1998) Classroom language experiences of trilingual children in French immersion. *The Canadian Modern Language Review* 54: 3, 376–393.

De Angelis, G. (1999) Interlanguage transfer and Multiple Language Acquisition: a case study. Paper presented at TESOL 1999, New York City.

De Angelis, G. (2005a) Interlanguage transfer of function words. *Language Learning* 55: 3, 379–414.

De Angelis, G. (2005b) Multilingualism and non-native lexical transfer: an identification problem. *International Journal of Multilingualism* 2: 1, 1–25.

De Angelis, G. (2005c) The acquisition of languages beyond the L2: psycholinguistic perspectives. *Rassegna Italiana di Linguistica Applicata* 2–3, 397–409.

De Angelis, G. and Selinker, L. (2001) Interlanguage transfer and competing linguistic systems in the multilingual mind. In J. Cenoz, B. Hufeisen and U. Jessner (eds) *Cross-linguistic Influence in Third Language Acquisition: Psycholinguistic Perspectives.* Clevedon: Multilingual Matters. 42–58.

de Bot, K. (1992). A bilingual production model: Levelt's 'speaking' model adapted. *Applied Linguistics* 13: 1, 1–24.

de Bot, K. (2002) Cognitive processing in bilinguals. In R. B. Kaplan (ed.) *The Oxford Handbook of Applied Linguistics.* 287–300.

de Bot, K. and Schreuder, R. (1993) Word production in the bilingual lexicon. In Schreuder, R. and Weltens, B. (eds) *The Bilingual Lexicon.* Amsterdam: John Benjamins Publishing Company. 191–214.

De Groot, A. (1993) Word-type effects in bilingual processing tasks. In R. Schreuder and B. Weltens (eds) *The Bilingual Lexicon.* Amsterdam: John Benjamins Publishing Company. 27–51.

De Groot, A. and Hoecks, J. (1995) The development of bilingual memory: evidence from word translation by trilinguals. *Language Learning* 45: 4, 683–724.

Dell, G. S. (1986) A spreading-activation theory of retrieval in sentence production. *Psychological Review* 93, 283–321.

Dell, G. S. (1995) Speaking and mispeaking. In L. R. Gleitman and M. Liberman (eds) *Language. An Invitation to Cognitive Science*. 2nd edn. Vol. 1. Cambridge, MA: MIT Press. 183–208.

Dell, G. S., Jiuliano D. and Govindjee, A. (1993) Structure and content in language production: a theory of frame constraints in phonological speech errors. *Cognitive Science* 17, 149–196.

Dewaele, J.-M. (1998) Lexical inventions: French Interlanguage as L2 versus L3. *Applied Linguistics* 19: 4, 471–490.

Dewaele, J.-M. (2001) Activation or inhibition? The interaction of L1, L2 and L3 on the language mode continuum. In J. Cenoz, B. Hufeisen and U. Jessner (eds) *Crosslinguistic Influence in Third Language Acquisition: Psycholinguistic Perspectives*. Clevedon: Multilingual Matters. 69–89.

Dewaele, J-M. (2002) The effect of multilingualism and socio-situational factors on communicative anxiety of mature language learners. In J. Ytsma and M. Hooghiemstra (eds) *Proceedings of the Second International Conference on Trilingualism*, Leeuwaarden: Fryske Akademie (CD Rom).

Diaz, R. M. (1985) Bilingual cognitive development: addressing three gaps in current research. *Child Development* 56, 1356–1378.

Diaz, R. M. and Klingler, C. (1991) Towards an explanatory model of the interaction between bilingualism and cognitive development. In E. Bialystok (ed.) *Language Processing in Bilingual Children*. Cambridge: Cambridge University Press. 167–191.

Dijkstra, T. (2003) Lexical processing in bilinguals and multilinguals: the word selection problem. In J. Cenoz, B. Hufeisen and U. Jessner (eds) *The Multilingual Lexicon*. Dordrecht: Kluwer Academic Publishers. 11–26.

Dijkstra, T. and Van Heuven, W. J. B. (1998) The BIA model and bilingual word recognition. In J. Grainger and A. Jacobs (eds) *Localist Connectionist Approaches to Human Cognition*. Hillsdale, NJ: Erlbaum. 189–225.

Dijkstra, T. and van Hell, J. V. (2003) Testing the language mode hypothesis using trilinguals. *International Journal of Bilingual Education and Bilingualism* 6, 2–16.

Dufour, R. and Kroll, J. F. (1995) Matching words to concepts in two languages: a test of the concept mediation model of bilingual representation. *Memory and Cognition* 23: 2, 166–180.

Ecke, P. (2001) Lexical retrieval in a third language: evidence from errors and tip-of-the-tongue states. In J. Cenoz, B. Hufeisen and U. Jessner (eds) *Cross-linguistic Influence in Third Language Acquisition: Psycholinguistic Perspectives*. Clevedon: Multilingual Matters. 90–114.

Ecke, P. (2003) Tip-of-the-tongue states in a polyglot: a longitudinal case study. Paper presented at the Third Conference on Third Language Acquisition and Trilingualism, Tralee, Ireland, 3–5 September.

Edwards, J. (1994) *Multilingualism*. London: Routledge.

Edwards, V. (2004) Foundations of bilingualism. In T. K. Bhatia and W. C. Ritchie (eds) *The Handbook of Bilingualism*. Oxford: Blackwell Publishing, 7–31.

Elwert, W. T. (1973) Das zweisprachige Individuum: ein Selbstzeugnis. *Studien zu den romanischen Sprachen Band* IV (1–81) Wiesbaden: Franz Steiner Verlag.

Eviatar, Z. and Ibrahim, R. (2000) Bilingual is as bilingual does: metalinguistic abilities of Arabic-speaking children. *Applied Psycholinguistics* 21, 451–471.

Fantini, A. (1985) *Language Acquisition of a Bilingual Child*. Clevedon: Multilingual Matters.

Festman, J. (2004) *Lexical Production as Evidence for Activation and Control Processes in Trilingual Lexical Retrieval*. Unpublished Ph.D. thesis, Bar-Ilan University.

Flynn, S. (1983) *A Study of the Effects of Principal Branching Direction in Second Language Acquisition: The Generalization of a Parameter of Universal Grammar from First to Second Language Acquisition*. Ph.D. dissertation, Ithaca, NY, Cornell University.

Flynn, S. (1987) *A Parameter-Setting Model of L2 Acquisition: Experimental Studies in Anaphora*. Dordrecht: Reidel.

Flynn, S. and Lust, B. (1981) Acquisition of relative clauses in English. *Cornell Working Papers in Linguistics* 1, 1. Department of Modern Languages and Linguistics, Ithaca, NY, Cornell University.

Flynn, S., Foley, C. and Vinnitskaya, I. (2004) The cumulative-enhancement model of language acquisition: comparing adults' and children's patterns of development in first, second and third language acquisition of relative clauses. *International Journal of Multilingualism* 1: 1, 3–16.

Fouser, R. J. (2001) Too close for comfort? Sociolinguistic transfer from Japanese into Korean as an L≥3. In J. Cenoz, B. Hufeisen and U. Jessner (eds) *Cross-linguistic Influence in Third Language Acquisition: Psycholinguistic Perspectives*. Clevedon: Multilingual Matters. 149–169.

French, R. M. and Jacquet, M. (2004) Understanding bilingual memory: models and data. *Trends in Cognitive Science* 8: 2, 87–93.

Fuller, J. M. (1999) Between three languages: composite structure in interlanguage. *Applied Linguistics* 20: 4, 534–561.

Galambos, J. S. and Goldin-Meadow, S. (1990) The effects of learning two languages on levels of metalinguistic awareness. *Cognition* 34, 1–56.

Garrett, M. F. (1975) The analysis of sentence production. In G. H. Bower (ed.) *The Psychology of Learning and Motivation*. San Diego, CA: Academic Press. 133–177.

Garrett, M. F. (1982) Production of speech: observations from normal and pathological language use. In A. Ellis (ed.) *Normality and Pathology in Cognitive Functions*. London: Academic Press. 19–76.

Gass, S. and Selinker, L. (eds) (1983) *Language Transfer in Language Learning*. Rowley, MA: Newbury House.

Gass, S. and Selinker, L. (2001) *Second Language Acquisition. An Introductory Course*. Hillsdale, NJ: Lawrence Erlbaum Associates.

Gibson, M. and Hufeisen, B. (2003) Investigating the role of prior foreign language knowledge: translating from an unknown language into a known foreign language. In J. Cenoz, B. Hufeisen and U. Jessner (eds) *The Multilingual Lexicon*. Dordrecht: Kluwer Academic Publishers. 87–102.

Gibson, M., Hufeisen, B. and Libben, G. (2001) Learners of German as an L3 and their production of German prepositional verbs. In J. Cenoz, B. Hufeisen and U. Jessner (eds) *Cross-linguistic Influence in Third Language Acquisition: Psycholinguistic perspectives*. Clevedon: Multilingual Matters. 138–148.

Giesbers, H. (1989) *Code-switching tussen Dialect en Standaardtaal*. Amsterdam: P. J. Meertens-Instituut.

Goodenough, F. (1926) Racial differences in the intelligence of school children. *Journal of Experimental Psychology* 9, 388–397.

Green, D. W. (1986) Control, activation and resource: a framework and a model for the control of speech in bilinguals. *Brain and Language* 27, 210–223.

Green, D. W. (1998a) Mental control of the bilingual lexico-semantic system. *Bilingualism: Language and Cognition* 1: 2, 67–81.

Green, D. W. (1998b) Schemas, tags and inhibition. *Bilingualism: Language and Cognition* 1: 2, 100–104.

Griessler, M. (2001) The effect of third language learning on second language proficiency: an Austrian example. *International Journal of Bilingual Education and Bilingualism* 4: 1, 50–60.

Grosjean, F. (1985) The bilingual as a competent but specific speaker-hearer. *Journal of Multilingual and Multicultural development* 6: 6, 467–477.

Grosjean, F. (1992) Another view of bilingualism. In R. J. Harris (ed.) *Cognitive Processing in Bilinguals*. Amsterdam: North Holland. 51–62.

Grosjean, F. (1997) Processing mixed language: issues, findings and models. In A. M. B. de Groot and J. Kroll (eds) *Tutorials in Bilingualism. Psycholinguistic Perspectives*. Mahwah, NJ: Lawrence Erlbaum Associates. 225–254.

Grosjean, F. (1998) Studying bilinguals: methodological and conceptual issues. *Bilingualism: Language and Cognition* 1: 2, 131–149.

Grosjean, F. (2001) The bilingual's language modes. In J. L. Nicol (ed.) *One Mind, Two Languages: Bilingual Language Processing*. Oxford: Blackwell. 1–22.

Grosjean, F. (2004) Studying bilinguals: methodological and conceptual issues. In T. K. Bhatia and W. C. Ritchie (eds) *The Handbook of Bilingualism*. Malden, MA: Blackwell Publishing. 32–63.

Gulutsan, M. (1976) Third language learning. *The Canadian Modern Language Review* 32, 309–315.

Haggis, B. M. (1973) Un cas de trilinguisme. *Linguistique* 9, 37–50.

Hakuta, K. (1986) *Mirror of language*. New York: Basic Books.

Hamers, J. F. and Blanc, M. H. A. (1989) *Bilinguality and Bilingualism*. Cambridge: Cambridge University Press.

Hammarberg, B. (2001) Roles of L1 and L2 in L3 production and acquisition. In J. Cenoz, B. Hufeisen and U. Jessner (eds) *Cross-linguistic Influence in Third Language Acquisition: Psycholinguistic Perspectives*. Clevedon: Multilingual Matters. 21–41.

Hammarberg, B. and Hammarberg, B. (1993) Articulatory re-setting in the acquisition of new languages. Reports from the Department of Phonetics, University of Umeå, Phonum, 2: 61–67.

Hansegård, N. E. (1968) *Tvåspråkighet eller halvspråkighet? (Bilingualism or semilingualism?)* Stockholm: Aldus/Bonniers.

Harley, T. A. (1995) *The Psychology of Language*. Erlbaum (UK) Taylor & Francis.

Hawkins, R. (2001) *Second Language Syntax*. Oxford: Blackwell Publishers.

Herdina, P. and Jessner, U. (2000) The dynamics of third language acquisition. In J. Cenoz and U. Jessner (eds) *English in Europe. The Acquisition of a Third Language*. Clevedon: Multilingual Matters. 84–98.

Herdina, P. and Jessner, U. (2002) *A Dynamic Model of Multilingualism: Perspectives of Change in Psycholinguistics*. Clevedon: Multilingual Matters.

Heredia, R. R. and Brown, J. M. (2004) Bilingual memory. In K. Bhatia and W. C. Ritchie (eds) *The Handbook of Bilingualism*. Malden, MA: Blackwell Publishing.

Herwig, A. (2001) Plurilingual lexical organisation. In J. Cenoz, B. Hufeisen and U. Jessner (eds) *Cross-linguistic Influence in Third Language Acquisition: Psycholinguistic Perspectives*. Clevedon: Multilingual Matters. 115–137.

Hoffmann, C. (2001) Towards a description of trilingual competence. *International Journal of Bilingualism* 5: 1, 1–17.

Hufeisen, B. (2000) A European perspective: tertiary languages with a focus on German as L3. In J. W. Rosenthal (ed.) *Handbook of Undergraduate Second Language Education.* Mahwah, NJ: Lawrence Erlbaum Associates. 209–229.

Hufeisen, B. (2004) Critical overview of research on third language acquisition and multilingualism published in the German language. *International Journal of Multilingualism*, 1: 2, 141–154.

Ianco-Worral, A. (1972) Bilingualism and cognitive development. *Child Development* 43, 1390–1400.

Jarvis, S. (2000) Methodological rigour in the study of transfer: identifying L1 influence in the interlanguage lexicon. *Language Learning* 50: 2, 245–309.

Jarvis, S. and Odlin, T. (2000) Morphological type, spatial reference, and language transfer. *Studies in Second Language Acquisition* 22, 535–556.

Jaspaert, K. and Lemmens, G. (1990) Linguistic evaluation of Dutch as a third language. In M. Byram and J. Leman (eds) *Bicultural Education and Trilingual Education: The Foyer Model in Brussels.* Clevedon: Multilingual Matters. 30–56.

Jessner, B. (1999) Metalinguistic awareness in multilinguals: cognitive aspects of third language learning. *Language Awareness* 8: 3 and 4, 201209.

Jessner, U. (2003) The nature of cross-linguistic interaction in the multilingual system. In J. Cenoz, B. Hufeisen and U. Jessner (eds) *The Multilingual Lexicon.* Dordrecht: Kluwer Academic Publishers. 45–55.

Jessner, U. (2005) Multilingual metalanguage, or the way multilinguals talk about their languages. *Language Awareness* 14: 1, 56–68.

Jordens, P. (1977) Rules, grammatical intuitions and strategies in foreign language learning. *Interlanguage Studies Bulletin* 2: 2, 5–7.

Kecskes, I. and Papp, T. (2000) *Foreign Language and Mother Tongue.* Hillsdale, NJ: Lawrence Erlbaum.

Kellerman, E. (1977) Towards a characterization of the strategy of transfer in second language learning. *Interlanguage Studies Bulletin* 2, 58–145.

Kellerman, E. (1978) Giving learners a break: native language intuitions as a source of prediction about transferability. *Working Papers on Bilingualism* 15, 59–92.

Kellerman, E. (1979) Transfer and non-transfer: where are we now? *Studies in Second Language Acquisition* 2, 37–57.

Kellerman, E. (1983) Now you see it, now you don't. In S. Gass and L. Selinker (eds) *Language Transfer in Language Learning.* Rowley, MA: Newbury House. 112–134.

Kellerman, E. (1984) The empirical evidence for the influence of the L1 in interlanguage. In A. Davies, C. Criper and A. P. R. Howatt (eds) *Interlanguage.* Edinburgh: Edinburgh University Press. 98–122.

Kellerman, E. (1987) *Aspects of Transferability in Second Language Acquisition.* Ph.D. Thesis, University of Nijmegen.

Kellerman, E. (2001) New uses for old language: cross-linguistic and cross-gestural influence in the narratives of non-native speakers. In J. Cenoz, B. Hufeisen and U. Jessner (eds) *Cross-linguistic Influence in Third Language Acquisition: Psycholinguistic Perspectives.* Clevedon: Multilingual Matters. 170–191.

Kemp, C. (1999) Multilinguals' performance on a grammaticality judgement task: do other languages make a difference? Paper presented at the International Conference on Third Language Acquisition and Trilingualism, 16–18 September, Innsbruck, Austria.

Kemp, C. (2001) *Metalinguistic Awareness in Multilinguals: Implicit and Explicit Grammatical Awareness and its Relationship with Language Experience and Language Attainment.* Unpublished Ph.d. Thesis, University of Edinburgh.

Keshavarz, M. H. and Astaneh, H. (2004) The impact of bilinguality on the learning of English vocabulary as a foreign language (L3). *Bilingual Education and Bilingualism*, 7: 4, 295–303.

Klein, E. C. (1995) Second versus third language acquisition: is there a difference? *Language Learning* 45: 3, 419–465.

Kramsch, C. (2006) The multilingual subject. *International Journal of Applied Linguistics* 16: 1, 97–110.

Kroll, J. F. (1993) Accessing conceptual representations for words in a second language. In R. Schreuder and B. Weltens (eds) *The Bilingual Lexicon*. Amsterdam: John Benjamin Publishing. 53–82.

Kroll, J. F. and Curley, J. (1988) Lexical memory in novice bilinguals: the role of concepts in retrieving second language words. In M. M. Gruneberg, P. E. Morris and R. N. Sykes (eds) *Practical Aspects of Memory: Current Research and Issues*. Vol. 2. London: John Wiley and Sons. 389–395.

Kroll, J. F. and Sholl, A. (1992) Lexical and conceptual memory in fluent and nonfluent bilinguals. In R. Harris (ed.) *Cognitive Processing in Bilinguals*. Amsterdam: Elsevier. 191–204.

Kroll, J. F. and Stewart, E. (1994) Category interference in translation and picture naming: evidence for asymmetric connections between bilingual memory representations. *Journal of Memory and Language* 33, 149–174.

Kroll, J. F. and Dijkstra, T. (2000) The bilingual lexicon. In R. B. Kaplan (ed.) *The Oxford Handbook of Applied Linguistics*. Oxford: Oxford University Press. 301–321.

Lambert, W. E. (1975) Culture and language as factors in learning and education. In A. Wolfgang (ed.) *Education of Immigrant Students*. Toronto: Ontario Institute for Studies in Education.

Larsen-Freeman, D. and Long, M. (1991) *An Introduction to Second Language Research*. London: Longman.

Lasagabaster, D. (2000) Language learning and the development of metalinguistic awareness. *Rassegna Italiana di Linguistica Applicata* 1/00, 103–116.

Lasagabaster, D. (2001) The effect of knowledge about the L1 on foreign language skills and grammar. *International Journal of Bilingual Education and Bilingualism* 4: 5, 310–331.

Lee, P. (1996) Cognitive development in bilingual children: a case for bilingual instruction in early childhood education. *The Bilingual Research Journal* 20: 3 and 4, 499–522.

Leman, J. (1990) Multilingualism as norm, monolingualism as exception: the Foyer Model in Brussels. In M. Byram and J. Leman (eds) *Bicultural Education and Trilingual Education: The Foyer Model in Brussels*. Clevedon: Multilingual Matters. 7–15

Leung, Y. (2005) L2 versus L3 initial state: a comparative study of the acquisition of French DPs by Vietnamese monolinguals and Cantonese-English bilinguals. *Bilingualism: Language and Cognition* 8: 1, 39–61.

Levelt, W. J. M. (1989) *Speaking: From Intention to Articulation*. Cambridge, MA: MIT Press.

Levelt, W. J. M. and Meyer, A. S. (2000) Word for word: multiple lexical access in speech production. *European Journal of Cognitive Psychology* 12: 4, 433–452.

Levelt, W. J. M., Roelofs, A. and Meyer, A. (1999) A theory of lexical access in speech production. *Behavioural and Brain Sciences* 22, 1–75.

Li, P. (1998) Mental control, language tags, and language nodes in bilingual lexical processing. *Bilingualism: Language and Cognition* 1: 2, 92–93.

Lococo, V. (1976) A cross-sectional study on L3 acquisition. *Working Papers on Bilingualism* 9, 44–75.

Mägiste, E. (1979) The competing language systems of the multilingual: a developmental study of decoding and encoding processes. *Journal of Learning and Verbal Behavior* 18, 79–89.

Mägiste, E. (1984) Learning a third language. *Journal of Multilingual and Multicultural Development* 5: 5, 415–421.

Mägiste, E. (1986) Selected issues in second and third language learning. In J. Vaid (ed.) *Language Processing in Bilinguals: Psycholinguistic and Neuropsychological Perspectives*. Hillsdale, NJ: Lawrence Erlbaum Associates. 97–122.

Malakoff, M. and Hakuta, K. (1991) Translation skill and metalinguistic awareness in bilinguals. In E. Bialystok (ed.) *Language Processing in Bilinguals*. Cambridge: Cambridge University Press. 141–166.

Matthews, P. H. (1997) *The Concise Dictionary of Linguistics*. Oxford: Oxford University Press.

Mayer, M. (1969) *Frog, Where Are You?* New York: Puffin Pied Piper.

McClelland, J. L. and Rumelhart, D. E. (1981) An interactive activation model of context effects in letter perception. Part 1: An account of basic findings. *Psychological Review*, 88, 375–405.

McLaughlin, B. and Nayak, N. (1989) Processing a new language: does knowing other languages make a difference? In W. H. Dechert and M. Raupach (eds) *Interlingual Processes*. Tübingen: Gunter Narr Verlag. 5–16.

Mitchell, R. and Myles, F. (1998) *Second Language Learning Theories*. London: Arnold.

Möhle, D. (1989) Multilingual interaction in foreign language production. In W. H. Dechert and M. Raupach (eds) *Interlingual Processes*. Tübingen: Gunter Narr Verlag. 179–194.

Muñoz, C. (2000) Bilingualism and trilingualism in school students in Catalonia. In J. Cenoz. and U. Jessner (eds) *English in Europe: The Acquisition of a Third Language*. Clevedon: Multilingual Matters. 157–178.

Myers-Scotton, C. (2002) *Contact Linguistics*. Oxford: Oxford University Press.

Nation, R. and McLaughlin, B. (1986) Experts and novices: An information-processing approach to the 'good language learner' problem. *Applied Psycholinguistics* 7, 51–56.

Navés, T., Miralpeix, I. and Celaya M. L. (2005) Who transfers more . . . and what? Crosslinguistic influence in relation to school grade and language dominance in EFL. *International Journal of Multilingualism* 2: 2, 2005.

Nayak, N., Hansen, N., Krueger, N. and McLaughlin, B. (1990) Language-learning strategies in monolingual and multilingual adults. *Language Learning* 40: 2, 221–244.

Nemser, W. (1971) Approximative systems of foreign language learners. *International Review of Applied Linguistics* IX, 115–123.

Odlin, T. (1989) *Language Transfer. Cross-linguistic Influence in Language Learning*. Cambridge: Cambridge University Press.

Odlin, T. and Jarvis, S. (2004) Same source, different outcomes: a study of Swedish influence on the acquisition of English in Finland. *International Journal of Multilingualism* 1: 2, 123–140.

Oksaar, E. (1983) Multilingualism and multiculturalism from the linguist's point of view. In T. Husen and S. Opper (eds) *Multicultural and Multilingual Education in Immigrant Countries*. Wenner Gren Symposium Series, Vol. 38, Oxford: Pergamon Press, 17–36.

Orr, G. (1987) Aspects of the second language acquisition of Chichewa noun class morphology. Unpublished Ph.D, thesis, Los Angeles: University of California.

Pandey, P. (1991) A psycholinguistic study of democratic values in relation to mono-, bi- and trilingualism. *Psycholingua* 21, 111–113.

Paradis, M. (1987) *The Assessment of Bilingual Aphasia*. Hillsdale, NJ: Erlbaum.

Paradis, M. (1997) The cognitive neuropsychology of bilingualism. In A. de Groot and J. Kroll (eds) *Tutorials in Bilingualism*. Mahwah, NJ: Lawrence Erlbaum Associates. 331–354.

Pavlenko, A. (1999) L2 influence on L1 in second language learning. Paper presented at TESOL 1999, New York.

Pavlenko, A. and Jarvis, S. ( 2001) Conceptual transfer: new perspectives on the study of cross-linguistic influence. In E. Németh (ed.) *Cognition in Language Use*. International Pragmatics Conference, Vol. 1. Antwerp: International Pragmatics Association. 288–301.

Pavlenko, A. and Jarvis, S. (2002) Bidirectional transfer. *Applied Linguistics* 23: 2, 190–214.

Peal, E. and Lambert, W. E. (1962) The relation of bilingualism to intelligence. *Psychological Monographs* 76: 27, 1–23.

Pennington, M. (1999) Equivalence classification in language transfer. Paper presented at TESOL 1999, New York.

Potter, M. C., So, K. F., von Eckardt, B. and Feldman, L. B. (1984) Lexical and conceptual representation in beginning and proficient bilinguals. *Journal of Verbal Learning and Verbal Behaviour* 23, 23–38.

Poulisse, N. (1997) Language production in bilinguals. In A. M. B. de Groot and J. Kroll (eds) *Tutorials in Bilingualism. Psycholinguistic Perspectives*. Mahwah, NJ: Lawrence Erlbaum Associates. 201–224.

Poulisse, N. (1999) *Slips of the Tongue. Speech Errors in First and Second Language Production*. Amsterdam: John Benjamins Publishing Company.

Poulisse, N. and Bongaerts, T. (1994) First language use in second language production. *Applied Linguistics* 15: 1, 36–57.

Ricciardelli, L. A. (1992a) Bilingualism and cognitive development in relation to threshold theory. *Journal of Psycholinguistic Research* 21, 301–316.

Ricciardelli, L. A. (1992b) Creativity and bilingualism. *Journal of Creative Behaviour*. 26, 242–254.

Ringbom, H. (1986) Crosslinguistic influence and the foreign language learning process. In E. Kellerman and M. Sharwood-Smith (eds) *Crosslinguistic Influence in Second Language Acquisition*. Oxford: Pergamon Press. 150–162.

Ringbom, H. (1987) *The Role of the First Language in Foreign Language Learning*. Clevedon: Multilingual Matters.

Ringbom, H. (2001) Lexical transfer in L3-production. In J. Cenoz, B. Hufeisen and U. Jessner (eds) *Cross-linguistic Influence in Third Language Acquisition: Psycholinguistic Perspectives*. Clevedon: Multilingual Matters. 59–68.

Ringbom, H. (2002) Levels of transfer from L1 and L2 in L3- acquisition. In J. Ytsma and M. Hooghiemstra (eds) *Proceedings of the Second International Conference on Trilingualism.* Leeuwaarden: Fryske Akademie (CD Rom).

Ringbom, H. (2003) If you know Finnish as L2, there will be no major problem learning Swahili. Paper presented at the Third International Conference on Trilingualism and Third Language Acquisition, Tralee, Ireland, 4–6 September.

Rivers, W. M. (1979) Learning a sixth language: an adult learner's daily diary. *The Canadian Modern Language Review* 36: 1, 67–82.

Saer, D. J. (1923) The effects of bilingualism on intelligence. *British Journal of Psychology*, 14, 25–38.

Safont Jordà, M. P. (2005) Pragmatic production of third language learners of English: a focus on request acts modifiers. *International Journal of Multilingualism* 2: 2, 84–104.

Sagasta Errasti, M. P. (2003) Acquiring writing skills in a third language: the positive effects of bilingualism. *International Journal of Bilingualism* 7: 1, 27–42.

Sanders, M. and Meijers, G. (1995) English as L3 in the elementary school. *ITL Review of Applied Linguistics* 107–8, 59–78.

Sanz, C. (2000) Bilingual education enhances third language acquisition: evidence from Catalonia. *Applied Psycholinguistics* 21, 23–44.

Scarborough, D. L., Gerard, L. and Cortese, C. (1984) Independence of lexical access in bilingual word recognition. *Journal of Verbal Learning and Verbal Behaviour* 23, 84–99.

Schachter, J. (1974) An error in error analysis. *Language Learning* 24: 2, 205–214.

Schmidt, R. W. and Frota, S. N. (1986) Developing basic conversation ability in a second language: a case study of an adult learner of Portuguese. In R. Day (ed.) *Talking to Learn: Conversation in Second Language Acquisition.* Rowley, MA: Newbury House. 237–326.

Schönpflug, U. (2000) Word fragment completions in the second and third language. In J. Cenoz and U. Jessner (eds) *English in Europe. The Acquisition of a Third Language.* Clevedon: Multilingual Matters. 121–142.

Schönpflug, U. (2003) The transfer-appropriate-processing approach and the trilingual's organization of the lexicon. In J. Cenoz, B. Hufeisen and U. Jessner (eds) *The Multilingual Lexicon.* Dordrecht: Kluwer Academic Publishers. 27–43.

Schwartz, B. D. and Eubank, L. (1996) What is the L2 initial state? Introduction. *Second Language Research* 12: 1, 1–6.

Schwartz, B. D. and Sprouse, A. (1996) L2 cognitive states and the full transfer/full access model. *Second Language Research* 12: 1, 40–72.

Selinker, L. (1969) Language Transfer. *General Linguistics* 9: 2, 67–92.

Selinker, L. (1972) Interlanguage. *International Review of Applied Linguistics* 10: 3, 209–231.

elinker, L. and Baumgartner-Cohen, B. (1995) Multiple Language Acquisition: 'Damn it, why can't I keep these two languages apart?' *Language, Culture and Curriculum* 8: 2, 115–121.

Shanon, B. (1991) Faulty language selection in polyglots. *Language and Cognitive Processes* 6, 339–350.

Sharwood-Smith, M. (1983) On first language loss in the second language acquirer: problems of transfer. In S. Gass and L. Selinker (eds) *Language Transfer in Language Learning.* Rowley, MA: Newbury House. 222–231

Sharwood-Smith, M. (1994) *Second Language Learning. Theoretical Foundations.* London: Longman.

Sharwood-Smith, M. and Kellerman, E. (1986) Crosslinguistic influence in second language acquisition: an introduction. In E. Kellerman and M. Sharwood-Smith (eds) *Crosslinguistic Influence in Second Language Acquisition.* New York: Pergamon Press, 1–9.

Shibatani, M. (1990) *The Languages of Japan.* Cambridge: Cambridge University Press.

Sholl, A., Sankaranarayanan, A. and Kroll, J. (1995) Transfer between picture naming and translation: a test of asymmetries in bilingual memory. *Psychological Science* 6: 1, 45–49.

Sikogukira, M. (1993) Influence of languages other than the L1 on a foreign language: a case of transfer from L2 to L3. *Edinburgh Working Papers in Applied Linguistics* 4, 110–132.

Singh, R. and Carroll, S. (1979) L1, L2 and L3. *Indian Journal of Applied Linguistics* 5, 51–63.

Singleton, D. (1987) Mother and other tongue influence on learner French: a case study. *Studies in Second Language Acquisition* 9, 327–346.

Singleton, D. (1999) *Exploring the Second Language Mental Lexicon.* Cambridge: Cambridge University Press.

Singleton, D. (2003) Perspectives on the multilingual lexicon: a critical synthesis. In J. Cenoz, B. Hufeisen and U. Jessner (eds) *The Multilingual Lexicon.* Dordrecht: Kluwer Academic Publishers. 167–176.

Stedje, A. (1977) *Tredjespråksinterferens i fritt tal-en jämförande studie.* In R. Palmberg and H. Ringbom (eds). Papers from the Conference on Contrastive Linguistics and Error Analysis. Stockholm and Åbo, 7–8 February. Åbo: Åbo Akademi.

Stemberg, J. P. (1984) Structural errors in normal and agrammatic speech. *Cognitive Neuropsychology* 1, 218–313.

Skutnabb-Kangas, T. and Toukomaa, P. (1976) *Teaching Migrant Children's Mother Tongue and Learning the Language of the Host Country in the Context of the Socio-cultural Situation of the Migrant Family.* Helsinki: The Finnish National Commission for UNESCO.

Swain, M., Lapkin, S., Rowen, N. and Hart, D. (1990) The role of mother tongue literacy in third language learning. *Language, Culture and Curriculum* 3: 1, 65–81.

Taylor, B. (1975) The use of overgeneralization and transfer learning strategies by elementary and intermediate students of ESL. *Language Learning* 25: 73–107.

Thomas, J. (1988) The role played by metalinguistic awareness in second and third language learning. *Journal of Multilingual and Multicultural Development* 9: 3, 235–246.

Thomas, J. (1992) Metalinguistic awareness in second- and third-language learning. In R. J. Harris (ed.) *Cognitive Processing in Bilinguals.* Amsterdam: North-Holland. 531–545.

Torrance, E. P., Gowan, J. C., Wu, J. M. and Aliotti, N. C. (1970) Creative functioning of monolingual and bilingual children in Singapore. *Journal of Educational Psychology*, 61, 72–75.

Tsushima, W. T. and Hogan, T. P. (1975) Verbal ability and school achievement of bilingual and monolingual children of different ages. *Journal of Educational Research* 68, 349–353.

Tulving, E. and Colotla, V. (1970) Free recall in trilingual lists. *Cognitive Psychology*, 1970, 1, 86–98.

Uljin J. M., Wolfe S. and Donn, A. (1981) The lexical transfer effect of French knowledge in the acquisition of English by Native Vietnamese Speakers. Report No. 6 F.L.A. Research THE, Eindhoven University of Technology.

Vainikka, A. and Young-Scholten, M. (1996) Gradual development of L2 phrase structure. *Second Language Research* 12: 1, 7–39.

Valencia, J. F. and Cenoz, J. (1992) The role of bilingualism in foreign language acquisition. *Journal of Multilingual and Multicultural Development* 13: 5, 433–449.

Van Gelderen, A., Schoonen, R., de Glopper, K., Hulstijn, J., Snellings, P., Simis, A. and Stevenson, M. (2003) Roles of linguistic knowledge, metacognitive knowledge and processing speed in L3, L2 and L1 reading comprehension: a structural equation modeling approach. *International Journal of Bilingualism* 7: 1, 7–21.

Van Hell, J. G. and de Groot, A. M. B. (1998) Conceptual representation in bilingual memory: effects of concreteness and cognate status in word association. *Bilingualism: Language and Cognition* 1: 3, 193–211.

Van Hell, J. G. and Dijkstra, T. (2002) Foreign language knowledge can influence native language performance in exclusively native contexts. *Psychonomic Bulletin and Review* 9: 4, 780–789.

Vildomec, V. (1963) *Multilingualism*. Netherlands: A. W. Sythoff-Leyden.

Voorwinde, S. (1981) A lexical and grammatical study in Dutch-English-German trilingualism. *ITL Review of Applied Linguistics* 52, 3–30.

Wei, L. (2003a) Activation of lemmas in the multilingual mental lexicon and transfer in third language learning. In J. Cenoz, B. Hufeisen and U. Jessner (eds) *The Multilingual Lexicon*. Dordrecht: Kluwer Academic Publishers. 57–70.

Wei, L. (2003b) The multilingual mental lexicon and lemma transfer in third language learning. Paper presented at the Third International Conference on Trilingualism and Third Language Acquisition, Tralee, Ireland, 4–6 September.

Weinreich, U. (1953) *Languages in Contact*. Publications of the Linguistic circle of New York. No.1.

Werker, J. F. (1986) The effect of multilingualism on phonetic perceptual flexibility. *Applied Psycholinguistics* 7, 141–156.

Williams, S. and Hammarberg, B. (1998) Language switches in L3 production: implications for a polyglot speaking model. *Applied Linguistics* 19: 3, 295–333.

Wilson, D. and Sperber, D. (2006) Relevance theory. In G. Ward and L. Horn (eds) *Handbook of Pragmatics*. Oxford: Blackwell. 607–632.

Yelland, G., Pollard, J. and Mercury, A. (1993) The metalinguistic benefits of limited contact with a second language. *Applied Psycholinguistics* 14, 423–444.

Zatorre, R. J. (1989) On the representation of multiple languages in the brain: old problems new directions. *Brain and Language* 36: 1, 127–147.

Zimmermann, R. (1992) Lexical knowledge: evidence from L1 and L2 narratives and L1-L2 translations. In C. Mair and M. Markus (eds) *New Departures in Contrastive Linguistics. Neue Ansätze in der Kontrastiven Linguistik*. Innsbruck: Verlag des Instituts fur Sprächwissenschaft.

Zobl, H. (1992) Prior linguistic knowledge and the conservatism of the learning procedure: grammaticality judgements of unilingual and multilingual learners. In Gass, S. and Selinker, L. (eds) *Language Transfer in Language Learning*. Rowley, MA: Newbury House. 176–196.

Lightning Source UK Ltd.
Milton Keynes UK
UKOW03f1412061013

218521UK00006B/12/P